## Independence and Accountability of the Indian Higher Judiciary

This book analyses the functioning of the Supreme Court of India and High Courts using the lens of judicial independence and accountability. Through extensive conceptual analysis, it posits that both concepts—independence and accountability—irrespective of jurisdiction, are not in conflict as is commonly assumed. Instead, both lead to 'an effective judiciary'.

It uses this doctrinal understanding of 'an effective judiciary' to assess four key, yet academically overlooked, facets of judicial functioning in India where judicial independence and judicial accountability have critical significance—appointment, transfer, impeachment and post-retirement employment of judges. It provides a detailed narrative of each of these facets traversing the early years of independence, the Emergency and the present era of appointment of judges by a judicial collegium. It specifically discusses the National Judicial Appointments Commission case (NJAC), where the Supreme Court struck down the constitutional amendment establishing the NJAC, a new method for appointment of judges, and argues why the judgment does not lead to 'an effective judiciary'. This narrative explains how the dominant understanding of judicial independence as insulation of the judiciary from government, and accountability as its antithesis, took hold.

Taking into account recent events—controversial collegium decisions, government–judiciary disagreements over appointments and the landmark press conference by senior justices of the Supreme Court—the book ends by suggesting certain reforms. These reforms strike an appropriate balance between judicial independence and accountability and truly promote 'an effective judiciary'. They have the potential to take India closer to the higher judiciary its Constitution envisages and its citizens deserve. Its lessons are relevant not just for India but also for judiciaries elsewhere confronting their own struggles with independence and accountability.

**Arghya Sengupta** is Research Director at Vidhi Centre for Legal Policy, a think-tank based in New Delhi. His research focuses on constitutional law, administrative law and the intersection of law and technology.

# Independence and Accountability of the Indian Higher Judiciary

ARGHYA SENGUPTA

CAMBRIDGE
UNIVERSITY PRESS

**CAMBRIDGE**
**UNIVERSITY PRESS**

University Printing House, Cambridge CB2 8BS, United Kingdom

One Liberty Plaza, 20th Floor, New York, NY 10006, USA

477 Williamstown Road, Port Melbourne, vic 3207, Australia

314 to 321, 3rd Floor, Plot No.3, Splendor Forum, Jasola District Centre, New Delhi 110025, India

79 Anson Road, #06–04/06, Singapore 079906

Cambridge University Press is part of the University of Cambridge.

It furthers the University's mission by disseminating knowledge in the pursuit of education, learning and research at the highest international levels of excellence.

www.cambridge.org
Information on this title: www.cambridge.org/9781108485654



First published 2019

Printed in India by Nutech Print Services, New Delhi 110020

*A catalogue record for this publication is available from the British Library*

ISBN 978-1-108-48565-4 HB

*To my father,*

*who would have been quietly proud.*

# Contents

# Contents

# Acknowledgements

This book may have been written by me but credit for its inspiration, conceptualisation and completion lies elsewhere. Above all else, my deepest debt of gratitude is to my parents. Had it not been for their unquestioned support, constant encouragement and quiet faith in my ability, this book would have remained unwritten. Going back a bit in time, had it not been for my mother's gut instinct, I might never have ended up as a law student in the first place!

Happily, having taken up the law, this book is the product of my doctoral work at Oxford. Anyone who has done doctoral work, particularly in law, will know how lonely and depressing such research can often be. Much credit for constantly showing me the light at the end of long, dark tunnels and guiding me ever-so-gently goes to Professor Paul Craig, my thesis supervisor.

The book benefited greatly from many conversations and feedback received over the last decade. In no particular order, heartfelt thanks to Jeff King, Bibek Debroy, Shruti Kapila, Jonathan Morgan, Faisal Devji, Fali Nariman, Abhinav Chandrachud, Anil Divan, Tehmtan Andhyarujina, Arvind Datar, Justice (Retd.) B. N. Srikrishna, Justice (Retd.) S. B. Sinha, Justice (Retd.) Ruma Pal, Justice (Retd.) Jasti Chelameswar, Justice (Retd.) J. S. Verma, Salman Khurshid, Ashok Sekhar Ganguly, Soli Sorabjee, Prashant Bhushan, Gopal Subramanium, Alok Prasanna Kumar, Maidul Islam, Debanshu Mukherjee, Ciara Kennefick, Shiv Swaminathan, Ritin Rai and Lavanya Rajamani. Special thanks particularly to Arun Jaitley, Justice (Retd.) A. P. Shah and A. K. Ganguli for their personal insights and experiences, many of which motivated me to write this book in the first place.

My gratitude to St. Catherine's College and the Rhodes Trust for their financial support; to all the staff at the Bodleian Law Library, the Indian Institute Library, Oxford, the Supreme Court Judges' Library, New Delhi, and the library of the National Law School of India, Bangalore, for help with locating research; to the editors of Public Law, Law Quarterly Review and Indian Journal of Constitutional Law, where earlier versions of sections of Chapters 2 and 5 have been published; and to all my colleagues at the Vidhi Centre for Legal Policy, returning to whom everyday is a source of much joy in my life. Particularly at

Vidhi, this book would not be complete were it not for the painstaking research assistance of Rukmini Das, Akshat Agarwal, Gargi Rohi and Pranay Modi, to whom I shall remain indebted.

Finally, it was Chhotomashi, whose strident opinions, passionate argumentation and courage of conviction made me want to do something as a young academic to build a better judiciary that can be the foundation for a better India. The reason why I wrote this book as an analytical account of judicial independence and accountability in India and not a tirade of grievances against the ills of the system, is solely a reflection of the influence of Dhvani, my wife. She keeps me real and teaches me to be a calmer, fairer and better version of myself everyday. I hope I have been able to reflect some of that in this book.

Arghya Sengupta
January 2019

# Abbreviations

| | |
|---|---|
| AIR | All India Reporter |
| Art. | Article |
| Govt. | Government |
| IBA | International Bar Association |
| MANU | Manupatra Online Legal Database |
| SC | Supreme Court |
| SCC | Supreme Court Cases |
| UN | United Nations |
| W/P | Writ Petition |

# Cases

## Indian Cases

## Other Cases

# Statutes

## Indian Statutes and Other Legislative Documents



## Other Statutes

# Introduction

# 1

No Supreme Court and no judiciary can stand in judgment over the sovereign will of Parliament representing the will of the entire community. If we go wrong here and there it can point it out, but in the ultimate analysis, where the future of the community is concerned, no judiciary can come in the way.

—Jawaharlal Nehru, 1st Prime Minister of India, 1949

The judicial system has an important role to play ultimately in ensuring better public governance.... There is no area where the judgments of the Supreme Court have not played a significant contribution in governance—good governance—whether it be environment, human rights, gender justice, education, minorities, police reforms, elections and limits on constituent powers of Parliament to amend the Constitution. This is only illustrative.

—Justice Y. K. Sabharwal, 36th Chief Justice of India, 2006

At the time of the Constitution of India coming into force, few could have imagined the public prominence the Indian higher judiciary, comprising the Supreme Court of India and 24 High Courts in the states, would achieve seven decades hence.[1] Nehru's conceptualisation of the judiciary as a hands-off guardian, pointing out governmental errors 'here and there', is today a relic that has been consigned to the entrails of history. Today, the higher judiciary, the Supreme Court in particular, as Justice Sabharwal's opinion proclaims, is an institution integral to the governance of the country. With liberalised rules of standing, wide powers and a range of remedies, the court is frequently called

1 The term 'higher judiciary' is used as shorthand in this book to refer to the Supreme Court of India and High Courts in the states.

upon to decide knotty questions, on matters affecting everyday life in India.[2] It sees itself as a court with a duty 'to ensure the rule of law'[3] wherever and whenever infractions may occur. Consequently, in public perception, it has, in the evocative words of a commentator, transformed itself into a 'Supreme Court for Indians'.[4]

For an institution as powerful and prominent in the public mind, it is curious that concomitant attention has not been paid to analysing its internal processes. Key internal processes—appointment of judges, transfer of judges between High Courts and impeachment of judges—have seldom been the subject of sustained critical attention. The last analytical account to critique the system of judicial appointments and transfers was published in 1996.[5] Disciplining of judges and their impeachment have been analysed in short journalistic opinion pieces and scholarly comments, but have never been the subject of a detailed study.[6] Two consequences have followed such a conspicuous lack of academic engagement. First, quite naturally, it has meant that appropriate scrutiny of these processes has not been carried out. Second, it has led to an implicit acceptance of a peculiar understanding of judicial independence that underlies the design of these processes.

Judicial independence has been the foremost value that has been sought to be protected in appointments, transfers and impeachment of judges. Following a history of executive interference in judicial appointments and

2 Lavanya Rajamani and Arghya Sengupta, 'The Supreme Court,' in *The Oxford Companion to Politics in India*, ed. Niraja Gopal Jayal and Pratap Bhanu Mehta (New Delhi: Oxford University Press, 2010), 80.

3 *Mohd. Hussain v. State (Govt. of NCT) Delhi, (2012)* 2 SCC 584 (Supreme Court of India).

4 Upendra Baxi, 'The Avatars of Indian Judicial Activism: Explorations in the Geography of (In)justice,' in *Fifty Years of the Supreme Court of India: Its Grasp and Reach*, ed. S. K. Verma and K. Kusum (New Delhi: Oxford University Press, 2000), 156–57.

5 H. M. Seervai, *Constitutional Law of India*, vol. 3 (New Delhi: Universal Law Publishing, 2008, rep., 4th ed.). Recently, two publications by advocate Santosh Paul have sought to fill this void; see Santosh Paul (ed.), *Choosing Hammurabi: Debates on Judicial Appointments* (Gurugram: LexisNexis, 2013); Santosh Paul, *Appointing our Judges: Forging Independence and Accountability* (Gurugram: LexisNexis, 2015).

6 For illustrative examples, see Nikhil Chakravartty, 'Reflections on Impeachment Debate,' *Mainstream* 31, no. 28 (1993): 5; M. Vijaywargiya, 'No Allocation of Judicial Work to a Judge under Impeachment: Need for Constitutional Amendment,' *Indian Bar Review* 27, no. 1 (2000): 163.

transfers,[7] a reactionary conception of judicial independence championed by the Supreme Court and institutionalised as constitutionalised doctrine, came into being. This conception saw the judiciary itself, to the exclusion of coordinate organs of government, as indispensable to the protection of its own independence.[8] This was not a sudden development—strains of this view could be seen both at the time of the drafting of the Constitution[9] and in the early years of independent India.[10] However, pursuant to executive interference in appointments and transfers manifesting itself, this view gained considerable traction. Any substantive role for the executive in processes pertaining to the judiciary was seen as anathema to judicial independence. Since the executive role in appointments was tied to an accountability rationale,[11] platitudes on the need to balance judicial independence and accountability were often repeated,[12] though unsurprisingly never leading to any significant enquiry of the meaning and import of these concepts in India's constitutional framework.

This book has two central purposes: First, to document and critically analyse the various mechanisms of appointments, transfers, impeachment and post-retirement employment in government-appointed positions, of judges of the Indian higher judiciary, from the viewpoint of constitutional doctrine. This involves a close scrutiny of the landmark judicial decisions and seminal developments in each of these four areas. Second, to analyse the justifiability of such processes and the rationales underlying them in terms of judicial independence and accountability. Where such processes are found unsatisfactory, a broad framework for reform is suggested. Through these two purposes, the book seeks to fill an extant gap in academic literature studying the internal processes of the higher judiciary. At the same time it proposes an

7 See Chapter 2, Section 2B, and Chapter 3, Section 3A.1.

8 *Supreme Court Advocates-on-Record Association* v. *Union of India*, (1993) 4 SCC 441 (Supreme Court of India) (Justice Verma) (hereinafter '*SCAORA*').

9 B. Shiva Rao et al., *The Framing of India's Constitution, Select Documents*, vol. IV (New Delhi: The Indian Institute of Public Administration, 1966), 193.

10 Law Commission of India, *Reform of Judicial Administration*, 14th Report, Ministry of Law and Justice, Government of India, 1958 (hereinafter 'Law Comm., 14th Report').

11 Text accompanying notes 18 and 19 in Chapter 2.

12 Soli Sorabjee, 'Judicial Accountability,' *Indian Express*, 8 May 2005, available at http://expressindia.indianexpress.com/news/columnists/print.php?content_id=69957 (accessed 25 September 2012); Justice J. S. Verma, 'Judicial Accountability Includes All,' *Deccan Herald*, 30 August 2009, available at http://www.deccanherald.com/content/22337/judicial-accountability-includes-all.html (accessed 25 September 2012).

analytical conception of judicial independence and accountability, which can be used to critique and reform such processes, not only in India but also elsewhere in the common law world.

This book focuses on four key facets of the internal processes pertaining to the higher judiciary in India: appointment of judges, transfer of judges between High Courts, impeachment of judges and post-retirement employment of judges in government-appointed positions. There are two reasons dictating this choice: First, these facets all have significant ramifications on judicial independence, accountability or both. This is not to suggest that other internal processes of the judiciary do not have similar ramifications—in-house disciplinary procedures, disclosure of assets of judges as well as the applicability of the Right to Information Act are some prominent aspects of judicial functioning that raise similar questions. But those are topics for another time and perhaps another book given their weighty normative significance. Second, the four issues which are discussed cover pre-tenure (appointments), in-tenure (transfers and impeachment) and post-tenure (post-retirement employment) aspects of judicial functioning. Their analysis thus combines breadth in tackling issues pertaining to different aspects of judicial functioning while facilitating the depth of analysis that these issues warrant.

The conceptual question that the book considers is the effect that these four facets of judicial functioning have on judicial independence and accountability. The choice of this conceptual question is a natural one—the significance of judicial independence to internal judicial processes is widely accepted. It was uppermost in the minds of the framers of the Indian Constitution as well as the foremost concern animating judges of the Supreme Court who have, over the years, been frequently called on to adjudicate the constitutional validity of such mechanisms. At the same time, the progressive insulation of the judiciary that has been occasioned by its dominant role in protecting judicial independence has resulted in widespread calls for greater judicial accountability. Thus far, such demands have been resisted by the judiciary because of a fear of judicial independence being threatened, albeit without a cogent explanation of why this must be so. The latest round of this confrontation has perhaps been its most feisty—with the Supreme Court declaring the Constitution (99th Amendment) Act, 2014 (hereinafter '99th Amendment') and the National Judicial Appointments Commission Act, 2014 (hereinafter 'NJAC Act'), which together established the National Judicial Appointments Commission (hereinafter 'NJAC') to appoint judges, unconstitutional in *Supreme Court Advocates-on-Record Association* v. *Union of India* (hereinafter '*NJAC Case*').[13] This judgment

[13] (2015) 11 SCALE 1 (*NJAC Case*).

marked the onset of a trying phase of executive–judiciary relations with testy and inconclusive negotiations on a memorandum of procedure to implement appointment procedures pursuant to the judgment[14] and itinerant stand-offs on appointment of particular judicial candidates.[15] In this atmosphere of contestation, internal fissures in the judiciary started to appear. The four seniormost puisne judges of the Supreme Court, Justices Chelameswar, Gogoi, Lokur and Joseph, gave an unprecedented press conference that strongly suggested executive interference in judicial functioning;[16] Justice Chelameswar spoke candidly, on multiple occasions, on the need for the judiciary to be more transparent in its functioning.[17]

This book uses the existing controversy as a starting point of a larger enquiry into judicial independence and accountability. Such an enquiry is not only of intrinsic value but also facilitates the development of an analytical tool to assess the justifiability or otherwise of measures relating to the internal processes of the judiciary in India and elsewhere.

[14] Jatin Gandhi, 'Memorandum of Procedure in Limbo as Govt, Top Judges Lock Horns,' *Hindustan Times*, 9 February 2018, available at https://www.hindustantimes.com/india-news/memorandum-of-procedure-in-limbo-as-govt-top-judges-lock-horns/story-YDgHxTqFs2aq5D7Tza1iIO.html (accessed 23 July 2018).

[15] For instance, the Centre asked the collegium to reconsider its recommendation appointing Justice K. M. Joseph to the Supreme Court. The collegium, however, decided to reiterate its recommendation. See G. Ananthakrishnan and S. Singh, 'Govt. Snubs Supreme Court,' *Indian Express*, 27 April 2018, available at https://indianexpress.com/article/india/govt-rejects-joseph-supreme-court-judge-all-eyes-on-chief-dipak-misra-5153173/ (accessed 23 July 2018); Samanwaya Rautray, 'SC Collegium Agrees to Reiterate Justice KM Joseph's Name for Elevation to Top Court,' *Economic Times*, 11 May 2018, available at https://economictimes.indiatimes.com/news/politics-and-nation/sc-collegium-agrees-to-reiterate-justice-k-m-josephs-name/articleshow/64125077.cms (accessed 23 July 2018).

[16] ABP News, Judge's Press Conference, 12 January 2018, available at https://www.youtube.com/watch?v=BcZAsRxPnJA (accessed 23 July 2018).

[17] Justice Chelameswar, in an interview with Karan Thapar, spoke about the need for a periodic audit of the collegium system to ensure that it was progressing on the right lines, 'Full Transcript of Justice Jasti Chelameswar's Interview,' *Bar & Bench*, 8 April 2018, available at https://barandbench.com/devils-advocate-v-judge-full-transcript-karan-thapar-interview-justice-jasti-chelameswar (accessed 23 July 2018); Justice Chelameswar further stressed on the need for transparency in judicial appointments at a public event, Vakasha Sachdev, 'SC Judges Appointed on Basis of "Impressions": Justice Chelameswar,' *The Quint*, 10 April 2018, available at https://www.thequint.com/news/india/justice-chelameswar-supreme-court-appointments-impressions-reform (accessed 23 July 2018).

This book has three substantive parts. Part I comprising Chapters 2, 3 and 4 describes and analyses the different mechanisms used for appointments (pre-tenure), transfers and impeachment (in-tenure) and the practice pertaining to post-retirement employment of judges in government-appointed positions (post-tenure). Each chapter in Part I follows a similar structure—analysing the conceptualisation of these mechanisms in the Constituent Assembly that was tasked with framing the Indian Constitution, providing a broad overview of the practical working of the various mechanisms and closely scrutinising a seminal event or landmark development pertaining to each facet of judicial functioning.

The analytical study of judicial appointments in Chapter 2 describes the two key appointment mechanisms followed—the executive-led process that was in practice till 1993 and subsequently the process led by a collegium of Supreme Court justices that is in operation today. It isolates for specific critique the majority judgment by Justice Verma in *Supreme Court Advocates-on-Record Association* v. *Union of India* (hereinafter '*SCAORA*')[18] which established the collegium method of judicial appointment. Through this critique, it argues that the collegium method is based on an indefensible interpretation of the Constitution. It then undertakes a case study—the proposed appointment of Justice Paul Daniel Dinakaran, the Chief Justice of Karnataka High Court, to the Supreme Court. This example is intended to demonstrate the systemic deficiencies of the collegium process of appointment in practice. It further critiques the Supreme Court's striking down of the NJAC in the *NJAC Case* as being unconscionable in constitutional law. Last, developments since then, such as the stalemate between the judiciary and the executive over the memorandum of procedure, internal dissensions within the judiciary led by Justice Chelameswar advocating for greater transparency and the continuous back and forth over the appointment of Justice K. M. Joseph, have been contextualised as pointing to the infirmities in the current system of judicial appointments. Thus, not only is the collegium method unjustifiable as a matter of constitutional law but it also suffers from grave defects in practice.

Since transfers have followed the same processes as appointments, Section 3A of Chapter 3 analyses executive and collegium-led transfers. Regarding the former, it argues that requiring consent of the judge as a precondition to transfer, as has been argued by the notable constitutional scholar Seervai,[19] renders the power to transfer nugatory. At the same time it criticises the

[18] *SCAORA*.

[19] Seervai, *Constitutional Law of India*, 2698–706, 2788–810.

practice of the collegium using transfers as disciplinary measures to enforce accountability. Neither is this the purpose of transfers nor can such transfers be considered to be in 'public interest', a fundamental criterion that, according to the Supreme Court itself, must underlie all transfers.[20] Section 3B of Chapter 3 deals with the only disciplinary measure to enforce judicial accountability expressly sanctioned by the Constitution—impeachment. It uses the only impeachment motion to have resulted in a vote in the Indian parliament—that of Justice V. Ramaswami of the Supreme Court of India (formerly Chief Justice of Punjab and Haryana High Court)—as a case study to highlight the deficiencies of this process as an accountability mechanism. On the basis of this and other examples of partial use of the impeachment provision, it argues that impeachment has not served its constitutional rationale of holding judges optimally accountable.

Rounding off Part I, Chapter 4 discusses post-retirement employment of judges in government-appointed positions. Instances of post-retirement employment have raised widespread concerns of the systemic detriment caused to judicial independence.[21] By collecting and analysing data of 50 retirees of the Supreme Court (with 1 October 2012 as the cut-off date for retirement and 1 April 2013 for post-retirement appointment), it assesses the nature of the post-retirement office, the time gap between retirement and post-retirement appointment and the post-retirement appointing authority. It thus presents a description of the pervasiveness of post-retirement employment of judges in government-appointed positions, its justifications and the possible impact it has on judicial independence.

As evident from the three paragraphs immediately above, each of these facets of judicial functioning affects the independence of judges and their accountability in disparate ways. However, to understand the precise nature of such impact, it is necessary to have a conceptual understanding of judicial independence and accountability. Part II undertakes such an analysis.

20 *SCAORA*.

21 For illustrative examples, see Madhav Shrihari Aney, Shubhankar Dam and Giovanni Ko, 'Jobs for Justice(s): Corruption in the Supreme Court of India,' *Research Collection School of Economics* (2017), available at https://ink.library.smu.edu.sg/cgi/viewcontent.cgi?article=2927&context=soe_research (accessed 23 July 2018); Hemant Kumar, 'Retirement or Re-employment of Judges?' *Lawyers' Update*, November 2012, available at http://lawyersupdate.co.in/LU/8/1031.asp (accessed 24 May 2014); Sudhanshu Ranjan, 'For Judges, Life Begins after Retirement,' *Navhind Times*, 25 October 2012, available at www.navhindtimes.in/opinion/judges-life-begins-after-retirement (accessed 7 May 2013).

Chapter 5 builds on an analytical account of public accountability advanced primarily by Mark Bovens[22] to understand judicial accountability in a fivefold conceptual framework. Given the disparate use of the term 'judicial accountability', not just in India, but also elsewhere,[23] such a framework allows for a close understanding of the various dimensions of the concept, filtering out illegitimate uses from legitimate ones. The answers to the questions—who is accountable, to whom, for what, and why, and how such accountability is enforced—provide a heuristic device that is used to analyse the interface between judicial accountability and independence.

This is achieved by using an analogous fivefold conceptual structure to understand judicial independence in Chapter 6. Like judicial accountability, judicial independence too is used in a variety of ways by scholars, judges and public commentators.[24] Its various uses need to be classified and legitimate uses identified. Specifically the rationale for why judicial independence is desirable needs to be enquired into. Such an enquiry demonstrates deep linkages with judicial accountability and separation of powers.

These linkages are articulated in Chapter 7. Though both judicial independence and accountability serve a variety of salutary purposes, the quest for 'an effective judiciary' is posited as a unifying purpose underlying both concepts. An effective judiciary encompasses the need for impartial adjudication by judges and for a judicial institution that enjoys public confidence, checking and balancing, and in turn being checked and balanced by, coordinate organs of government. Both judicial independence and judicial accountability, it is argued, are virtues that serve this ideal. This analytical conclusion provides a normative basis to reconcile judicial independence and accountability in theory and also provides a doctrinal basis for devising effective mechanisms for internal working of the higher judiciary in India.

Part III brings the book full circle by applying the results of the analytical exercise in Part II to the findings in Part I. Chapter 8 distils the analytical conclusions of Part II into a doctrinal device—whether the measure in question leads to an effective judiciary. This device consists of a five-step enquiry that can be used as an analytical tool to assess the justifiability or otherwise of actual processes in terms of their impact on judicial independence and accountability. Section 8B of Chapter

22 Mark Bovens, 'Analysing and Assessing Public Accountability: A Conceptual Framework,' *European Law Journal* 13, no. 4 (2007): 447.

23 See Chapter 5, Section 5B.

24 See Chapter 6, Section 6A.

8 applies the doctrine to mechanisms of appointments, transfers, impeachment and post-retirement employment of judges of the Indian higher judiciary. The results of the exercise are varied; the intention, however, is common—to provide a definitive and substantial method to assess the internal processes of the Indian higher judiciary in independence–accountability terms.

Wherever such measures are found to be unjustifiable, Chapter 9 proposes appropriate reform. Neither is this reform proposal holistic nor is it overly detailed. Instead, this chapter is designed to serve two purposes: First, to suggest changes to existing reform proposals pertaining to appointments, transfers and impeachment so that the mechanisms better accord with the need for judicial independence and accountability. Second, where no such reforms have been suggested, such as in post-retirement employment of judges, to provide the broad framework for reform that might be followed. The overarching motivation in suggesting such reform, and indeed this book itself, is to ensure that the internal processes of the Indian higher judiciary rest on secure normative foundations.

This book makes two key contributions to its field of study. First, it addresses a gulf in Indian legal scholarship—no analytical study has thus far been undertaken on the four facets of internal functioning of the Indian higher judiciary from the standpoint of constitutional doctrine. Appointments and transfers have been the subject of sociological analyses and case-specific critiques;[25] impeachments and post-retirement employment have not been the subject of any sustained scrutiny. By describing mechanisms pertaining to these four facets of judicial functioning and critiquing existing mechanisms, this book provides a key resource for scholars, judges, lawyers and others keen to understand the Indian higher judiciary closely.

Second, it provides a novel argument for reconciling judicial independence and accountability. Either these concepts are largely seen in opposition to each other or a need to find a balance between the two is simply asserted. Are they indeed in opposition? Why should they be balanced? And most critically, on what basis should this balance be sought? By attempting to provide an answer to these questions, the book transcends platitudes to develop a richer understanding of these concepts. I hope it is of use to students of the judiciary and its practitioners in general irrespective of which jurisdiction they are in, and to those tasked with reform of the existing mechanisms in India in particular.

25 There have been excellent sociological works on judicial appointees since which have not tackled key analytical questions. For illustrative examples, see G. H. Gadbois, Jr., *Judges of the Supreme Court of India: 1950–1989* (New Delhi: Oxford University Press, 2011); Vijay K. Gupta, *Decision Making in the Supreme Court of India* (New Delhi: Kaveri Books, 1995).

# PART I

# THE INDIAN EXPERIENCE

# Pre-Tenure Questions

## *Appointments to the Higher Judiciary*

# 2

Appointment of judges in India has been the site of the most fractious battles over the independence of the higher judiciary. To provide a coherent account of this narrative, this chapter is divided into five sections. Section 2A deals with the constitutional position on judicial appointments as determined by the Constituent Assembly. Section 2B analyses the constitutional practice in the post-independence phase of appointments led by the executive. Section 2C deals with constitutional adjudication, analysing the three seminal cases pertaining to judicial appointments—*SP Gupta* v. *Union of India* (hereinafter '*Gupta*');[1] *SCAORA*[2] and *In re: Presidential Reference* (hereinafter '*Presidential Reference*'),[3] with specific focus on critiquing the collegium method of appointment that is in use at present. The consequences of such constitutional adjudication are highlighted through a case study of the proposal to appoint Justice Dinakaran as a judge of the Supreme Court of India. The case study is not intended to serve as a generalisable example; nonetheless, it is illustrative of the grave deficiencies from which the collegium system suffers. Section 2D analyses how the Supreme Court struck down the NJAC in the *NJAC Case*,[4] thereby thwarting a parliamentary attempt to reform the process of judicial appointments. The last, Section 2E, deals with developments relating to the memorandum of procedure post the *NJAC Case* which have characterised the stalemate between the executive and the judiciary over judicial appointments. It also looks at the internal dissensions within the judiciary, led by Justice Chelameswar advocating for reform and

1 1981 Supp (1) SCC 87; MANU/SC/0080/1981 (Supreme Court of India) (hereinafter '*Gupta*').

2 *SCAORA*.

3 AIR 1999 SC 1; MANU/SC/1146/1998 (Supreme Court of India) (hereinafter '*Presidential Reference*').

4 *NJAC Case*.

greater transparency. Together, these sections analyse the legal basis of the different systems of appointment that have been used as well as identify the conceptual questions that the operation of such systems raise.

## 2A Constitutional Position: The Constituent Assembly on Judicial Appointments

Debates in the Constituent Assembly regarding appointments to the higher judiciary were brief.[5] However in the discussions that took place, there was a keen perception of the ends which had to be achieved—the independence of the judiciary and safeguarding the dignity of the institution, the interests to be accommodated—a balance between governmental oversight and judicial autonomy in administration, a sharp awareness of the constitutional position in other jurisdictions and equally a realisation of the need to institute a system that would be effective in India's political culture. The aim of the discussions was clear—reaching a consensus on a system which would best ensure the independence and dignity of the judiciary as an anti-majoritarian bulwark in India's constitutional democracy, comprising judges, who in Nehru's words would be 'of the highest integrity ... people who can stand up against the executive government and whoever may come in their way'.[6]

There were two themes that formed the fulcrum around which issues regarding appointments were debated–the independence of the judiciary and, to a lesser extent, ensuring the dignity of the judicial office. As far as the independence of the judiciary and judicial appointments is concerned, an early understanding of the concept in an Indian report, which formed the basis for discussion in the Constituent Assembly, can be found in the report of the Sapru Committee published in 1946.[7] This report, which heavily criticised the colonial system of appointment for allowing excessive executive discretion,[8] understood

5 Debates were held on 29 July 1947, 23 May 1948, 24 May 1948, 27 May 1948, 6 June 1948 and 7 June 1948. The brevity of the first debate that laid the foundation for future discussions led to considerable disappointment in the House. Sir N. Gopalaswami Ayyangar, *Constituent Assembly of India Debates (Proceedings)*, vol. IV (July 1947), 901 (hereinafter 'CAD').

6 CAD, vol. VIII (May–June 1949), 246–47.

7 Tej Bahadur Sapru (ed.), *Constitutional Proposals of the Sapru Committee* (New Delhi: Padma Publications, 1945) (hereinafter '*Sapru Committee*').

8 At that time, the governing provision was s. 200(2) of the Government of India Act, 1935, which read: 'Every judge of the Federal Court shall be appointed by His

the need for independence as a check against party politics and executive influence. In terms of legal provision it meant that appointments would have to be taken out of the unfettered discretion of the executive. Thus for the first time a consultative method of appointment was proposed—the precursor to Art. 124 and Art. 217 of the Constitution—with judges of the Supreme Court appointed by the president in consultation with the chief justice of India, and judges of the High Courts also appointed by the president, in consultation with the chief justice of the High Court, the premier (governor) of the province concerned and the chief justice of India.[9] The rationale behind the provision thus was that the inclusion of the apolitical office of the chief justice of India for Supreme Court appointments, as well as the chief justice of the High Court for High Court appointments, would ensure an appropriate counterbalance to political factors that may influence the selection by the executive. Though the final word would be with the president, it was felt that a multiplicity of high constitutional authorities, some of whom were apolitical, would ensure that judges of the highest quality would be appointed.

In discussions regarding this proposal in the Constituent Assembly after it had been affirmed by the Union Constitution Committee,[10] there was considerable unanimity amongst the members that the president was the appropriate authority to make appointments. This would necessarily imply acting according to the aid and advice of the Council of Ministers. The threat of politicisation which would flow would hence have to be offset and consultation with the chief justice of India and other judges of the Supreme Court and the High Courts, as the president may deem necessary, would be sufficient safeguards against executive abuse of power. It was clear that the provision for consultation would be entirely discretionary on the president, though given colonial practice, it was expected that the convention of speaking to the chief justice before making appointments would continue. The need to make consultation mandatory, the weight attached to the opinion of those consulted and the course of action in

---

Majesty by warrant under the Royal Sign Manual and shall hold office until he attains the age of sixty-five years.' There was a similar provision for appointments to the High Court under s. 220(2), albeit the retirement age was sixty years.

9 *Sapru Committee*, 193, para 259, Recommendation 13(3).

10 See Minutes of the Union Constitution Committee Meeting, 11 June 1947 in Shiva Rao et al., *Framing of India's Constitution*, vol. II, 559. For the final provision adopted, see Clause 18, Report of the Union Constitution Committee, 4 July 1947, in Shiva Rao et al., *Framing of India's Constitution*, vol. II, 574, 583, 584. See also CAD, vol. IV (July 1947), 887.

case of disagreements were not deliberated, since there was an implicit belief that the need for non-politicisation of the judiciary was a widely shared principle.

The Drafting Committee adopted the provision of the Union Constitution Committee with the addition of a proviso which made consultation with the chief justice of India mandatory.[11] By the time this provision was taken up for discussion on the floor of the assembly, several members, for the first time, moved beyond the simplistic and hitherto unquestioned notion of independence of the judiciary as the need to prevent politicisation to a richer discussion of what the concept entailed. According to K. T. Shah, a preliminary distinction would have to be made between separation of powers and independence of the judiciary. Whereas the former implied that executive and judicial powers did not vest in the same authority, the latter was more all-encompassing, requiring functional separation of the judiciary from the other organs of government as well.[12] Carrying this idea forward, K. M. Munshi believed that the primary ramifications of functional judicial independence would be on the need to ensure fixed salaries once an appointment is made, the process of removal and post-retirement employment of judges.[13] In expressing this view, he seemed to be echoing the understanding of judicial independence in the United States of America which did not (and does not) consider appointments *per se* to be an independence issue.[14] The need for functional independence was nuanced by T. T. Krishnamachari, who cautioned the assembly not to get carried away with the idea of independence as that would result in a judiciary that would become an '*Imperium in Imperio* ... operating as a sort of superior body to the general body politic'.[15] This view found resonance amongst the members of the assembly, who emphasised the importance of adequate checks and balances on the judiciary which would aid in effective decision-making, which in turn would secure public confidence in the institution. In particular, A. K. Ayyar believed that for the Constitution to function it was essential that the organs of government collaborate with each other towards a common end. If judicial

11 The proviso to Draft Constitution Art. 103(2) read: 'Provided that in the case of appointment of a judge, other than the Chief Justice, the Chief Justice of India shall always be consulted.' See Draft Constitution Prepared by the Drafting Committee, 21 February 1948 in Shiva Rao et al., *Framing of India's Constitution*, vol. III, 509, 554.

12 CAD, vol. VIII (May–June 1949), 218.

13 Ibid., 220.

14 Federalist Paper No. 78 in Alexander Hamilton, James Madison and John Jay, *The Federalist* (Cambridge: Belknap Press, 2009), 508 (hereinafter 'Federalist Papers').

15 CAD, vol. VIII (May–June 1949), 389.

independence was elevated to the level of dogma, he felt, the institution shorn of its restraints could assume the role of a 'super legislature or super executive',[16] roles that it would be incompetent to play. The general agreement regarding this view meant that independence of the judiciary and not its insulation was the prevailing view of the members of the Constituent Assembly.

Responding to these views and two alternative proposals relating to appointment that had been advanced,[17] B. R. Ambedkar, the Chairman of the Drafting Committee, felt that seeking the concurrence of the chief justice of India would be giving him a veto power on appointments. Such power without any checks and balances would defeat the careful inter-institutional equilibrium that had been envisaged for the appointments process. Besides, an unchecked power had large potential for abuse, given the chief justice of India, despite being a person of high integrity, could only be expected to suffer from biases as any individual would.[18] Subsequently, the amendments seeking concurrence of the chief justice of India, for both Supreme Court appointments[19] and High Court appointments,[20] were negatived.

Two aspects of Ambedkar's response are particularly crucial. First, in refusing to accord a determinative role in the matter of appointments to the chief justice of India, Ambedkar underlines the fundamental executive nature of the power to appoint judges. His inspirations were the British and the American systems, both of which, though distinct, gave the power of appointment focally to the executive. Analogously, vesting the power of judicial appointment in the executive in India was intrinsic to the checks and balances scheme, specifically as a way in which the judiciary could remain institutionally accountable and integrated with other organs of government. The incorporation of consultation with the chief justice of India in the Constitution was hence not in any way a concession of the fundamental nature of the power of appointment. It was rather a necessary check to ensure judicial independence since conventional

16 Ibid., vol. IV (July 1947), 837.

17 A proposal was made in a Memorandum submitted by the judges of the Federal Court and the provincial High Courts in March, 1948 which required the concurrence of the chief justice of India for appointments. Shiva Rao et al., *Framing of India's Constitution*, vol. IV, 193. An alternative proposal recommended parliamentary ratification for proposed appointments: per S. L. Saksena, CAD, vol. VIII (May–June 1949), 231; per K. T. Shah, CAD, vol. VIII (May–June 1949), 234.

18 CAD, vol. VIII (May–June 1949), 258.

19 Ibid., 261.

20 Ibid., 674.

checks such as those prevalent in the United Kingdom had yet to develop in India. Second, without questioning the integrity of the chief justice of India, Ambedkar shows cognizance of the possibility of operation of inherent biases, if the chief justice were to be accorded an unchecked power. The emphasis is hence not only on the need for a multiplicity of authorities, an aspect that has been elaborately discussed in subsequent judicial decisions, but also equally on preserving an inter-institutional balance in appointments, with the judiciary and executive mutually informing and checking each other. This, as I explain subsequently in this section, is an aspect of judicial appointments which has been lost sight of in contemporary debates.

In the final analysis, the Constituent Assembly believed that judicial independence was a crucial value to be safeguarded while devising a system of appointment of judges to the higher judiciary. The drafters were unanimous that independence meant preventing politicisation of the appointments process to the higher judiciary, the main threat being the executive government. But in creating a process immune from excessive executive interference, they were cautious not to insulate the judiciary, but rather preserve an inter-institutional equilibrium. This equilibrium was sought to be effectuated through the consultative system of appointment of judges—the power focally residing in the executive but exercisable only after consultation with the chief justice of India. This incorporation of the apolitical office of the chief justice of India as a key, albeit not the determinative element of the appointments process, it was hoped, would provide a safeguard for the independence and quality of judges selected for high judicial office. It was, in other words, an authority-centric approach—a provision that secured independence by vesting high constitutional authorities with significant powers in relation to judicial appointment. As succinctly stated by K. M. Munshi, in the Constituent Assembly:

> [The] safeguards are there. Largely however it will depend on how the Judiciary works, what the spirit of the Legislature is and in what spirit the Executive works.[21]

It is these aspects of the working of the constitutional provisions relating to judicial appointments that I turn to next to assess whether they lived up to the hope, faith and expectation of the drafters of the Constitution.

[21] Ibid., 220.

## 2B Constitutional Practice: Executive-Led Appointments

The early years of the Indian republic provided a litmus test for the process of judicial appointments formulated by the drafters of the Constitution. Since the constitutional provisions did not specify details of the appointment process, a practice developed by which, for Supreme Court appointments, the proposal would be initiated by the chief justice of India and sent to the president for nomination. The president would consult the Union Ministry of Law and Justice, which would seek the views of the prime minister as well. In case of any disagreement, the matter would be sent back to the chief justice of India. This back-and-forth process would continue till a consensus was reached.[22] For High Court appointments, proposals were initiated by the chief justice of the High Court and sent to the chief minister, who after consultation with the governor would forward the recommendation to the Union Home Ministry. In case of a difference in opinion, the matter would be sent back to the chief justice. The proposal(s) would then be sent to the Union Home Ministry, which would secure the approval of the chief justice of India and advise the president accordingly.[23] Disagreements were resolved on an *ad hoc* basis and no clear practice emerged in this regard.

The working history of appointments in the first two decades suggests that a convention of consensus had developed between the constitutional functionaries. Despite considerable political pressure, presidents were known not to act except with the concurrence of the chief justice of India in deciding on appointments.[24] Granville Austin, in fact, goes so far as to claim that the chief justice of India during Nehru's tenure as prime minister, owing to convention and his strength of character, virtually had 'a veto over appointment decisions'.[25] Though this was clearly not Ambedkar's intention, as evidenced from his speech in the Constituent Assembly,[26] it was widely believed that attaching maximum weight to the opinion of the chief justice would ensure apolitical appointments and thereby secure respect and independence for the judiciary.

22 Law Commission of India, *The Method of Appointment of Judges*, 80th Report, Ministry of Law and Justice, Government of India, 1979, 6 (hereinafter 'Law Comm., 80th Report').

23 Law Comm., 14th Report, 71.

24 B. P. Sinha, *Reminiscences and Reflections of a Chief Justice* (New Delhi: BK Publishing, 1985), 98.

25 Granville Austin, *Working a Democratic Constitution: The Indian Experience* (Oxford: Oxford University Press, 1999), 125.

26 CAD, vol. VIII (May–June 1949), 258.

However, the merits of this consultation process, as it operated in practice, were questioned in the Law Commission of India's seminal 14th Report titled *Reform of Judicial Administration*.[27] On the basis of interviews conducted across the country with judges and members of the Bar and responses to questionnaires circulated widely, the commission noted that communal and regional considerations had often determined judicial appointments.[28] As a result, merit had ceased to be the only criterion as the drafters had envisaged and as the Law Commission felt should be the case. One key reason identified for the existing state of affairs, especially in High Court appointments, was the dominant role played by the executive. Though the Law Commission did not allege that the consultation process was being bypassed, it suggested that despite consultation with the chief justice of the High Court and the chief justice of India, extraneous considerations continued to play a role in appointments, owing to High Court chief justices complying with the choice of the state executive.[29] The commission, however, did not state why consultation with the chief justice of India, which was envisaged as a secondary compulsory check on High Court appointments, was also inadequate to weed out appointments based on extraneous considerations. It recommended, on the basis of its findings, an amendment to Art. 217. The amendment provided that every High Court appointment would be 'on the recommendation of the Chief Justice (of the High Court)' and with the 'concurrence of the Chief Justice of India'.[30] Though it did not make an analogous recommendation with regard to Art. 124, it stated that communal and regional considerations should play no part in appointments to the Supreme Court which should be purely on merit.[31]

Two aspects of the report are significant. The first is the conspicuous absence of any analysis of judicial independence while dealing with the issue of appointments. This suggested a perpetuation of the understanding of independence of the judiciary as its non-politicisation as had been prevalent in the early stages of the drafting of the Constitution. The second relates to the suggested amendment of Art. 217, requiring appointments to be 'on the recommendation of the Chief Justice of the High Court' and with the 'concurrence of the Chief Justice of India',[32] thereby proposing a predominant role for the judiciary in

[27] Law Comm., 14th Report.

[28] Ibid., 34.

[29] A number of sources are cited by the Law Commission in coming to this conclusion, including an opinion by an unnamed former chief justice of India. See Law Comm., 14th Report, 72.

[30] Law Comm., 14th Report, 106.

[31] Ibid., 55.

[32] Ibid.

the matter of appointments.[33] Coming as it did merely eight years after the Constitution had come into force, the need to amend confirmed the drafters' worst fears of the judiciary being politicised if left to the executive. At the same time, it questioned the efficacy of consultation, envisaged as a constitutional check on the executive. It hence suggested a divergence between the intention of the drafters and the practice of appointments hitherto followed. In terms of substance, the suggested amendments were symptomatic of a growing belief that the judiciary itself was best placed to decide on its own composition and ensure appointments in a non-politicised manner. This was a belief that would ebb and flow constantly in India's political and judicial circles, before resurfacing powerfully three decades hence.

Through the next decade, appointment of judges continued according to the original constitutional provision. The Law Commission recommendations were not implemented and thus the judiciary continued to play a significant, albeit not a preponderant, role in the matter of appointments.[34] It was at this juncture, armed with a super-majority in the legislature and having made promises of social justice, that the government began to actively interfere with the composition of the higher judiciary. Its most significant step was the supersession of the three seniormost justices of the Supreme Court in appointing Justice A. N. Ray, the fourth puisne judge, as the chief justice of India, breaking the seniority convention that had been followed since the inception of the Supreme Court.[35] Justifying this move, the law minister, Mohan Kumaramangalam, proposed a radical reinterpretation to the appointments process. According to him, the political philosophy of judges should align with the spirit of social justice that is ingrained in the Constitution. This philosophy of the judge, as determined by the executive, would be relevant to appointment to the higher judiciary. For appointment of the chief justice of India, he stated that both the political views of the judge and his/her 'stability in crucial areas of law'[36] would be taken into

[33] Ibid., 106.

[34] The proposals were rejected by the Rajya Sabha on 24 November 1959 chiefly on the ground that of 211 appointments made since 1950, 210 had been with the concurrence of the chief justice of India and 196 had been with the clear concurrence of all constitutional functionaries involved. See 'Rajya Sabha Debates,' 24 November 1959 as cited in Law Comm., 80th Report, 19.

[35] For a detailed account, see Kuldip Nayar (ed.), *Supersession of Judges* (New Delhi: Indian Book Co., 1973).

[36] Mohan Kumaramangalam, *Judicial Appointments: An Analysis of the Recent Controversy over the Appointment of the Chief Justice of India* (New Delhi: Oxford & IBH Pub. Co., 1973), 83.

account. Further, appointment of the chief justice of India was at the discretion of the executive and it could not be considered bound by a convention which had led to harmful consequences.[37]

Taking this interpretation at face value, it is clear that it had the potential to significantly affect judicial independence, resulting in a committed judiciary, as has been widely argued.[38] Politically, there is little doubt that using the veneer of determining the conformity of the social philosophy of judges with the spirit of social justice embodied in the Constitution, the government was steadily attempting to reshape the composition of the judiciary.[39] Consequently, as incidents of executive interference in judicial composition and administration multiplied, the issue of judicial appointments came up for hearing in the Supreme Court.

## 2C Constitutional Adjudication: The Three Judges' Cases

### 2C.1 The First Judges' Case

In *Gupta*[40] (First Judges' Case), three specific questions were at issue before a seven-judge bench of the court: Whether a circular issued by the

37 Ibid.

38 This theory and the attempts by the government to take an active role in judicial appointment have been criticised widely for severely damaging judicial independence. Most critics proceed on the basis that the real attempt behind the supersession and the theoretical justification was not a desire to correct the deficiencies in the appointments process but rather to pack the judiciary with government loyalists. N. A. Palkhivala, *Our Constitution: Defaced and Defiled* (New Delhi: MacMillan, 1974), 93. This book analyses the impact of a committed judiciary on judicial independence in Chapter 8 after analysing judicial independence as a concept in Chapter 6.

39 Three governmental acts which severely undermined the independence of the judiciary were the supersession of Justice H. R. Khanna, the lone judge to have decided against the government in the landmark *habeas corpus* case during the Emergency, *ADM Jabalpur* v. *Shivkant Shukla*, (1976) 2 SCC 521 (Supreme Court of India) (hereinafter '*ADM Jabalpur*'); a leaked proposal to set up a judicial body superior to the Supreme Court and drastically curtail the powers of the latter (see H. M. Seervai, *The Emergency, Future Safeguards and the Habeas Corpus Case: A Criticism* [Mumbai: NM Tripathi Pvt Ltd., 1978], 125); and a mass transfer order of sixteen judges of various High Courts issued in May 1976, during the height of the Emergency (discussed in Chapter 3, Section 3A.1). For an analysis, see T. R. Andhyarujina, 'A Committed Judiciary: Indira Gandhi and Judicial Appointments', in *Appointment of Judges to the Supreme Court of India: Transparency, Accountability and Independence*, ed. Arghya Sengupta and Ritwika Sharma (New Delhi: Oxford University Press, 2018).

40 *Gupta*.

law minister seeking the consent of additional judges in High Courts and proposed appointees to be transferred was constitutionally permissible; whether short-term *ad hoc* extensions and non-renewal of appointment of additional judge Justice S. N. Kumar of the Delhi High Court were valid as per Art. 224; whether the transfer of Chief Justice K. B. N. Singh from the Patna High Court to the Madras High Court was valid as per Art. 222. Decision on these issues hinged on the foundational question as to whether the opinion of any particular constitutional functionary can be said to have primacy in the consultation process prior to appointment of a judge. In a judgment spanning 724 pages of written text, containing seven cross-cutting opinions, the Supreme Court denied specific relief to the petitioners in each of the claims.[41] In the process, it laid down the constitutional position regarding appointments and its interface with judicial independence, though not entirely authoritatively, given the ambiguity that characterised several opinions on crucial questions of law.

On the point of law regarding the requirements of the consultative process in Art. 217 for appointments to the High Court (and Art. 222 for transfers), there was broad unanimity amongst the judges. Building on the decision in *Union of India* v. *Sankalchand Sheth* (hereinafter '*Sankalchand*'),[42] it was held that consultation would have to be full and effective; in order to be full and effective, relevant and identical facts must be present before the participants in the consultation process, the decision must be on the basis of these facts, that is, it must not be taken on irrelevant grounds, there must be complete application of mind and deliberation and the willingness of the person proposed to be appointed or transferred must be taken into consideration by the chief justice of India.[43] The split in the majority vote was owing to the varying factual determinations by the respective judges regarding whether the constitutionally mandated consultation process for appointment under Art. 217 and transfer under Art. 222 had been carried out in relation to the non-renewal of the tenure

[41] For a succinct summary of the judgment and discussion of the central issues involved, see Jill Cottrell, 'The Indian Judges' Transfer Case,' *International and Comparative Law Quarterly* 33 (1984): 1032.

[42] (1977) 4 SCC 193; MANU/SC/0065/1977 (Supreme Court of India). The case is discussed in detail in Chapter 3, Section 3A.1.

[43] These points were succinctly summarised in the judgment of Justice Fazal Ali, *Gupta*, para 563. It must be noted that Justice Bhagwati in addition mandated that the consent of the judge concerned must be taken before transfer, the earlier position he had adopted in *Sankalchand*. See Justice Bhagwati, *Gupta*, para 139.

of additional judge Justice S. N. Kumar of the Delhi High Court and transfer of Chief Justice K. B. N. Singh. A similar and deeper split occurred with regard to the question of whether in case of internal disagreements between constitutional functionaries, the opinion of the chief justice of India as the *paterfamilias* of the judiciary should gain primacy, a split that shaped the future course of the debate on judicial appointments in India.

Two judges, Justices Gupta and Tulzapurkar, stated that the president should ordinarily accept the view of the chief justice of India in case there was disagreement between the chief justice of India, the chief justice of the concerned High Court and the governor of the state. While Justice Gupta simply asserted this proposition as a natural corollary of the chief justice of India's position as the 'highest dignitary of Indian Justice',[44] Justice Tulzapurkar delved into the drafting history of Art. 217 to buttress his conclusion. According to him, Art. 217 did not presume that the authorities to be consulted were coordinate. He believed that the role of the governor was to merely ascertain 'information about the antecedents, local affiliations' and was incorporated to provide a token representation to the state government in High Court appointments owing to its role in financing the institution.[45] Between the chief justice of India and the chief justice of the High Court he felt that the opinion of the former should have primacy for three reasons. First, the chief justice of India is the head of the Indian judiciary and his seniority would intuitively presuppose primacy; second, this was not beyond the intention of the drafters since provision of primacy did not tantamount to a veto being exercised by the chief justice of India, a result the drafters specifically wished to avoid; third, allowing the president, the head of the executive, to act as an umpire between two competing proposals for appointment would compromise the independence of the judiciary. These views presented a further attempt at strengthening the authority-centric approach, this time by according the greatest possible weight to the opinion of a single authority, the chief justice of India.

I believe that these reasons are flawed for failing to understand the rationale of the process of appointment envisaged by the drafters in Art. 217 and attempting to introduce a hierarchy where none naturally exists. First, suggesting that the positions of the constitutional functionaries are not coordinate since the governor of the state has a minor part to play is a proposition with dangerous

44 This phrase was originally used by Justice Krishna Iyer in *Shamsher Singh* v. *State of Punjab*, AIR 1974 SC 2192 (Supreme Court of India).

45 *Gupta*, para 626 (Justice Tulzapurkar).

ramifications. It suggests that antecedents of a judge, her affiliations and reputation, which the drafters felt the governor would be in the best place to assess, are less consequential for appointment than is her legal acumen. Integrity of a judge, ascertained primarily by her antecedents, is a primary consideration for judicial appointments and belittling its importance and consequently the role played by the governor is absurd. Second, Justice Tulzapurkar's subsequent points for advocating primacy are flawed for both principled and practical reasons. On principle, he offers no understanding of judicial independence by which a decision made by the executive in choosing between a recommendation made by the chief justice of India on the one hand and that by the chief justice of the concerned High Court on the other, both high constitutional functionaries themselves, is violative of the concept. The choice to be made by the president is highly circumscribed, having passed through numerous filters, and hence leaves little scope for arbitrariness. Suggesting that the mere act of making such a restricted choice violates judicial independence makes the concept unjustifiably brittle, a defence of which Justice Tulzapurkar does not offer. Practically too, there are serious difficulties in importing a language of primacy into the consultation process. Primacy according to the *Oxford Dictionary* means 'pre-eminence'[46] and would literally mean that the president would consider the opinion of the chief justice of India first. In a consultation process, of course, pre-eminence in terms of time is meaningless if both opinions are to be ultimately considered, which in this case they must. Hence, the understanding of primacy which remains is that of pre-eminence in terms of weight. The issue of pre-eminence in terms of weight was discussed and categorically rejected by the drafters when the amendment that sought concurrence of the chief justice of India was negatived. If primacy, as understood by Justice Tulzapurkar, need not mean concurrence or a veto (which he says it does not[47]), it has little value as it stands in terms of adding weight to the chief justice of India's opinion. Even without this requirement, the president would have to give the greatest weight to both opinions placed before him and would have to provide strong and cogent reasons for the choice he makes. Adding the primacy requirement is thus superfluous.

[46] Angus Stevenson (ed.), *The Oxford Dictionary of English* (Oxford: Oxford University Press, 2010, 3rd ed.), available at http://www.oxfordreference.com/view/10.1093/acref/9780199571123.001.0001/m_en_gb0661030 (accessed 27 September 2013) (hereinafter 'OED').

[47] *Gupta*, para 626 (Judge Tulzapurkar).

The remaining five judges,[48] in my opinion, correctly refused to infuse the language of primacy into the consultation process. Delving into the Constituent Assembly debates, they held that the authorities in Art. 217 were envisaged to be coordinate, each serving a distinct consultative function. Besides, the fact that the last word would be with the president would not *per se* be a breach of judicial independence. On the contrary, such a mode of executive-led appointments would introduce an element of accountability in the process, given the popularly elected nature of the government.[49] In effect, this amounted to perpetuating the *status quo* insofar as the consultation process was concerned. It perfectly conformed to the letter of the Constitution and the original intention of the drafters. But such conformity was scarcely a guarantee for actually securing judicial independence, contestations regarding which well outlived the decision itself. The executive still had the final word in appointment of judges, though its powers had been judicially circumscribed and the significance of the role of the chief justice of India underlined. But the larger questions on the content of judicial independence and the mechanism best designed to protect it in the appointments process remained wide open, given the ambiguity and internal dissensions which are unfortunately, though not entirely unjustifiably, the living hallmarks of this decision.

### *2C.2 The Second Judges' Case*

The refusal to accord primacy to the opinion of the chief justice of India by the majority in *Gupta* was widely interpreted as a victory for the executive. Leading members of the Bar such as Seervai saw the majority decision as an example of judicial timidity which would destroy its independence.[50] Upendra Baxi, a leading commentator on the Supreme Court, while scathingly critical of the petition itself as an attempt by the Bar to close ranks, was equally critical of the majority decision for bolstering the position of the executive in a manner which would

48 There is, however, a slight divergence in the opinion of Justice Pathak in this matter, compared to the remaining four judges. Justice Pathak says on the one hand that no opinion should have primacy, while suggesting on the other that the opinion of the chief justice of India cannot be said to enjoy 'mere parity with the opinion of the Chief Justice of the High Court before him'. This suggests that the opinion of the chief justice of India should be given greater weight. *Gupta*, para 891 (Justice Pathak). This has led commentators to suggest that Justice Pathak was in favour of according *de facto* primacy to the opinion of the chief justice of India. See Seervai, *Constitutional Law of India*, 2845.

49 *Gupta*, para 29 (Justice Bhagwati).

50 Seervai, *Constitutional Law of India*, 2854.

undoubtedly erode existing safeguards for the independence of the judiciary.[51] In journalistic writing too, executive supremacy in appointments was greeted with trepidation, still scarred by Indira Gandhi's previous attempts to interfere with the internal working of the judiciary (Mrs Gandhi was the prime minister at the time of this decision as well).[52] Non-primacy of the chief justice of India was thus equated with primacy of the executive, evidence of a judicial capitulation that paid mere lip service to, and consequently failed to secure, judicial independence.

The instability in the political arena through the end of the eighties and early nineties meant that the task of eliminating the perceived threat of executive arbitrariness and safeguarding the independence of the judiciary fell once again to the judiciary itself. In *Subhash Sharma and others* v. *Union of India*,[53] a public interest litigation was filed seeking a writ of *mandamus* against the government to fill up vacancies in judicial posts in the Supreme Court and several High Courts. The three-judge bench of the Supreme Court felt that the delay in filling up vacancies could be attributed to the non-justiciability of the fixation of strength of judges and the process of consultation prior to appointment, upheld in *Gupta*. Two specific questions decided by the majority in *Gupta* were placed for reconsideration before a larger bench: whether refusing to accord primacy to the opinion of the chief justice of India in the process of consultation was correct in law and whether the fixation of judge strength in courts should be considered justiciable.[54]

A nine-judge bench of the Supreme Court was constituted to reconsider *Gupta* on the two points referred to it. In *SCAORA*[55] (Second Judges' Case), a seven-judge majority (five judges speaking through Justice Verma) substantially overruled *Gupta* and fundamentally altered the nature of the appointments process in Art. 124 and Art.217 of the Constitution.[56] In doing so, it expounded

51 Upendra Baxi, 'The Myth and Reality of Judicial Independence: The Judges Case and All That,' in *Courage, Craft and Contention: The Indian Supreme Court in the Eighties*, ed. Upendra Baxi (Mumbai: NM Tripathi Pvt Ltd., 1985), 23, 55.

52 For an illustrative example, see Arun Shourie, *Mrs. Gandhi's Second Reign* (New Delhi: Vikas Publishing House, 1983), 266–68.

53 1991 Supp (1) SCC 574; MANU/SC/0643/1990 (Supreme Court of India) (hereinafter '*Subhash Sharma*').

54 Ibid., para 46.

55 *SCAORA*.

56 Two judges, Justices Ratnavel Pandian and Kuldip Singh, gave concurring opinions substantially agreeing with the lead opinion of Justice Verma; the slight divergences are not significant for the book.

its conception of judicial independence, traced the need for primacy of the opinion of the chief justice of India to this conception and laid down the detailed procedure to be followed to effectuate its decision in the actual working of the appointments process. Justice Ahmadi in a minority judgment advanced an understanding of judicial independence that refused to accord primacy to the opinion of the chief justice of India, while at the same time recognising the deficiencies of the appointment process.[57]

On the issue of appointments, eight points made by Justice Verma are seminal. First, in the event of disagreement between constitutional functionaries involved in the consultation process prior to a judicial appointment under Art.124 and Art. 217, the opinion of the chief justice of India would have primacy.[58] Second, this opinion would not be his personal opinion but rather the opinion of the judiciary 'symbolised by the Chief Justice of India'.[59] Third, in reaching this opinion, representative of the judiciary as a whole, the chief justice of India would have to consult two of his seniormost colleagues and any other judge who may have knowledge in this regard.[60] Fourth, a similar process would be followed by the chief justice of the High Court in presenting her opinion on potential appointees. Fifth, this requirement of primacy did not mean concurrence of the chief justice. Sixth, no appointment could be confirmed by the president if the chief justice of India had not positively opined in favour of it.[61] Seventh, in exceptional circumstances, the president, for cogent reasons that would have to be disclosed to the chief justice, could reject the opinion of the chief justice of India. Eighth, this interpretation of Art.124 and Art. 217 flowed from the concept of judicial independence, which was a fundamental constitutional purpose and would be severely affected if the executive had primacy.[62]

### *2C.2.a Flaws in Reasoning*

While Justice Verma's keen urge, reflected throughout his opinion, to protect judicial independence from the deleterious consequences that may flow from not

[57] Justice Punchhi also gave a dissenting opinion, holding that unfettered primacy of the chief justice of India should be established in the consultation process under Art. 124 and Art. 217.

[58] *SCAORA*, para 57 (Justice Verma).

[59] Ibid., paras 56 and 80.

[60] Ibid., para 68 (Justice Verma).

[61] Ibid., para 71 (Justice Verma).

[62] Ibid., paras 19–20 (Justice Verma).

according primacy to the opinion of the chief justice of India is well-intentioned, his attempt to correct this by not only according primacy but also introducing a judicial collegium for appointments proceeds on a misreading of the majority opinion in *Gupta*, is logically unsound and constitutionally impermissible in terms of interpretation. Justice Verma interprets the majority decision in *Gupta* as mandating executive primacy in the process of appointments. In my opinion, this is a misreading since the majority categorically rejected the language of primacy itself in the consultation process. It viewed consultation as a non-hierarchical process wherein the authorities were coordinate with every opinion having significant and equal weight. In the event of disagreement, the fact that the last word would be with the president is not indicative of executive primacy, but rather a natural corollary of the fact that the Constitution invests the power of appointment in the president, similar to the executive nature of the power to appoint in most common law jurisdictions. To read in the language of primacy into this opinion is deeply flawed.

Even on the merits of Justice Verma's view that the executive should not play the chief role in the appointments process, the reasons he provides are unsatisfactory. Justice Verma suggests that the historical change from the pre-constitutional position of absolute discretion of the executive in appointments to the current provision for consultation and the practice of chief justice of India's opinion being given the greatest weight points towards a lack of executive primacy. In my view, the historical change adverted to was certainly designed to constrain the executive in the matter of appointments. Unfettered discretion was considered anathema in the constitutional framework and hence an inter-institutional equilibrium was sought to be achieved by the consultation process prior to appointment. Neither does this derogate from viewing appointments as an executive function nor is it connected to a question of institutional primacy. Similarly, the practice of giving the opinion of the chief justice of India the greatest weight in the consultation process was a healthy convention that had developed, given that the chief justice was best placed to provide insights regarding the legal acumen of a particular candidate. This does not, however, mean that the judiciary has unfettered primacy in appointments, as Justice Verma's decision in effect postulates.

Next, Justice Verma assumes that the converse of executive primacy (the mechanism followed at the time of the judgment) is primacy of the opinion of the chief justice of India. This assumption is clear from the fact that his rejection of executive primacy is immediately followed by his view that the opinion of the chief justice of India, therefore, has primacy, without any reasoned justification for this positive assertion.[63] This assertion presupposes the language of primacy in Art. 124 and Art. 217, where none exists. Further, it makes the faulty logical leap from negating a contrary assertion (executive primacy) to using this negative implication as proof for a positive assertion (primacy of the chief justice of India) which is not its sole or exact converse. The latter logically does not flow from the former and evidence of this purported causality is absent in Justice Verma's judgment.

Further, as a matter of interpretation, the reading in of primacy in Art. 124 and Art. 217 is strained. The word in the constitutional text which the majority opinion uses to interpret the provisions to mean primacy being accorded to the opinion of the chief justice of India is 'consultation', which appears in relation to three constitutional functionaries in Art. 217(1) and whose verb forms 'consult' and 'consulted' appear in Art. 124(2). Apart from the criticism that the plain meaning of the word 'consult' or any of its attendant forms do not lend themselves to an interpretation that means according primacy to the opinion of the person consulted,[64] the word, if observed carefully, appears twice in Art. 124(1), first in relation to the chief justice (in the proviso) and second in relation to other judges, consulting whom the president may deem necessary (in the main article). It is fallacious to suggest that the word in its first form means primacy, whereas in its second form does not.[65] Further, by suggesting that the opinion of the chief justice symbolises the views of the entire judiciary, the interpretation renders redundant the clause in Art. 124(1) that allows the president to seek opinions from other judges. A unified opinion of the judiciary, as synthesised by the chief justice of India, cannot be a literal import of Art. 124(1) or Art.217(1).

Even if the defence is sought to be justified by the possibility of a purposive interpretation as Justice Verma[66] and a noted academic suggest,[67] I believe this justification is inadequate for two reasons. First, Justice Verma identifies the purpose of the provision on appointments to be the need to select the best

[63] Ibid., paras 45–46 (Justice Verma).

[64] The word 'consult' according to *The New Shorter Oxford English Dictionary* means 'to confer', 'deliberate', 'take into consideration ...' See Lesley Brown (ed.), *The New Shorter Oxford English Dictionary*, vol. I (Oxford: Clarendon Press, 1993, 4th ed.), 490.

[65] The same argument can be made for consultation prior to High Court appointments as well. See Seervai, *Constitutional Law of India*, 2953.

[66] *SCAORA*, paras 19–20 (Justice Verma).

[67] M. P. Singh, 'Merit in the Appointment of Judges,' *SCC Journal* 8 (1998): 1, 6–7.

available people in a manner that would secure the independence of the judiciary and preserve democracy.[68] Though this view is correct, it is incomplete, since the text of Art. 124 and Art. 217 vests the power of appointment focally in the executive, which suggests that some form of popular accountability for judicial appointments was another relevant purpose of the provision. Attributing a restricted purpose to the appointments process is hence inadequate or, at the very least, inadequately reasoned.

Second, even if it is assumed for the sake of argument that such a restricted purpose exists, it is not explained in the majority judgment as to why a literal interpretation of Art. 124 or Art. 217 defeats the said purpose. On the contrary, the dissenting judgment by Justice Ahmadi states that in the past decade out of 547 appointments, 540 had been in accordance with the opinion of the chief justice of India,[69] which suggests little reason to fear erosion of judicial independence. Further, it is interpretatively impermissible to provide a purposive construction which conflicts with the language of the text. It is well accepted that the text of a constitution has a limited 'ability to bear'[70] and 'is not clay in the hands of the interpreter, to be mo[u]lded as he or she sees fit'.[71] In other words, purposive interpretation has a vital semantic component which sets certain limits on the extent to which such interpretation is permissible. It has already been shown that the concept of primacy in the consultative process prior to appointment conflicts with the text of the Constitution. Consultation, in the text, assumed a certain coordinate role being accorded to each of the constitutional functionaries. Picking out one of the said functionaries (the chief justice of India) and according primacy to his opinion amounts to gerrymandering with these interpretative limits set by the text and is hence impermissible.

### *2C.2.b Flaws in the Result*

Apart from its suspect reading of constitutional history, logical deficiencies and implausible interpretations, a striking aspect of the majority judgment is the lack of clarity of its *ratio decidendi*. Despite the summary of conclusions at the end of Justice Verma's opinion, inconsistencies between the conclusions and

68 *SCAORA*, paras 19–20 (Justice Verma).

69 Ibid., para 370 (Justice Ahmadi).

70 Aharon Barak, *Purposive Interpretation in Law* (Princeton: Princeton University Press, 2005), 102.

71 Douglas Laycock, 'Constitutional Theory Matters,' *Texas Law Review* 56 (1987): 767.

the reasoning make understanding considerably difficult.[72] Insofar as primacy of the chief justice of India is concerned, the connotation of primacy and what it achieves is unclear. In the course of the judgment, the question of primacy, it seems, arises only when there is disagreement between the constitutional functionaries. This would imply that if there is disagreement, the opinion of the chief justice of India prevails. This would mean rewriting the Constitution, giving a veto power to the chief justice of India, an interpretation which Justice Verma recognises as impermissible.[73] Presumably to offset this conclusion, Justice Verma says that in exceptional circumstances for cogent reasons that must be communicated to the chief justice of India, the president may reject an appointment proposed by the chief justice of India. Again, regarding the question of transfers, he uses the term 'determinativeness' in contradistinction to 'primacy', by stating that in the question of transfers, the opinion of the chief justice of India does not merely enjoy primacy but is determinative.[74] This would, in effect, mean that primacy implies the greatest possible weight being attached to the opinion of the chief justice of India, short of being determinative. This ends up as a reiteration of the *status quo*, since the majority in *Gupta* too stated that the greatest weight is to be given to the opinion of the chief justice of India, short of requiring concurrence. The import of the concept of primacy is thus caught between the Scylla of superfluity and the Charybdis of constitutional impermissibility in Justice Verma's judgment.

Second, the idea of a judicially mandated collegium to approve appointments is equally unclear in terms of actual operation. According to the judgment, the chief justice of India and the chief justice of the High Court must consult two of their seniormost colleagues, respectively, before reaching an opinion regarding the suitability or otherwise of a particular candidate. In addition, the chief justice of India would have to consult the seniormost judge who would be acquainted with the particular candidate to seek her views. The suggestion that the opinion of the chief justice of India would symbolise the views of the judiciary implies that the chief justice of India would synthesise these opinions before advising the president. However, the judgment also mentions that there may be instances of disagreement between judges when the chief justice recommends a person whom the other consulted judges reject. At these times, the recommendation of the chief justice may be overridden by the president.

72 For a careful analysis of these inconsistencies and contradictions in the summary of conclusions, see Seervai, *Constitutional Law of India*, 2953.

73 *SCAORA*, para 58 (Justice Verma).

74 Ibid., para 80 (Justice Verma, Summary of Conclusions, Clause [7]).

Thus, though the president cannot appoint a person without the concurrence of the chief justice, by this postulation she can reject a candidate proposed by the chief justice on the grounds that another functionary has rejected it for cogent reasons. The reason for attaching differential weights to a confirmation or rejection of a candidate by the chief justice of India is not explained in the judgment. In addition, this elaborate modification to the consultation machinery ends up merely adding opinions of judges to be considered by the president thereby increasing the scope of discretion available to her not to appoint a person as a judge, a clearly counter-intuitive result.

In the final analysis, Justice Verma's judgment was undoubtedly a well-intentioned response to the growing popular perception of partisan judicial appointments owing to excessive executive influence. However, in attempting to cure this malady, he interpreted the Constitution in a manner which defied established canons of construction. Further, in judicially ordering an alternative method of collegium appointments without adequate reasoning, he created an institution with weak normative foundations, based on an unquestioned faith that the judiciary would be ideally placed to set its own house in order. Little did he realise then that this act of judicial arrogation of appointment power, notwithstanding its noble intentions, would itself fall prey to undue influence and interference, tarnishing the image of the judiciary as well as questioning his own wisdom in adopting such a course of action. The next section describes how this happened, belying the faith Justice Verma placed on his future brethren.

## *2C.3 The Third Judges' Case and Its Consequences*

The lack of clarity and logical inconsistencies which beset the majority opinion in *SCAORA* rendered it a dubious precedent. Though the practice of appointment subsequent to the decision is not available as a public record, sufficient evidence exists from statements given by former judges[75] and reports

[75] The autobiography of Justice S. S. Sodhi provides a telling account of the surreptitiousness with which the system of appointments functioned pursuant to the judgment that denied him formal appointment despite having been legally confirmed as a judge of the Supreme Court (see Justice S. S. Sodhi, *The Other Side of Justice* [New Delhi: Hay House India, 2007], 293); Justice Verma himself admitted certain problems in the operation of the collegium, specifically relating to a lack of accountability. See Nagendar Sharma, 'Collegium Is a Failure, Say Top Jurists,' *Hindustan Times*, 29 November 2009, available at www.hindustantimes.com/Collegium-is-a-failure-say-top-jurists/H1-Article1-481205.aspx (accessed 13 May 2010).

in the media[76] of considerable ambiguity regarding the import of the majority judgment and practical problems arising therefrom. Matters reached a head when during the chief justiceship of M. M. Punchhi, not a single proposal forwarded by the chief justice was cleared by the Law Minister Thambi Durai, seemingly owing to non-consultation with other constitutional functionaries.[77] This semi-public standoff between a chief justice who considered consultation discretionary[78] and a law minister who asked for written records of consultation having been carried out pursuant to the letter of the judgment, necessitated intervention by the president. This led to the *Presidential Reference*[79] (Third Judges' Case) born out of a constitutional provision for reference under Art. 143 which allows the president to obtain the opinion of the Supreme Court on a question of law or fact of significant public importance. Nine specific questions were referred to the court, each of these requiring a clarification of Justice Verma's opinion in *SCAORA* in order to ensure that the constitutional interpretation of Art. 124 and Art. 217 provided a practically feasible process for future judicial appointments.

Substantively, the nine questions referred to the court were subdivided into three issues relating to the consultation process prior to appointments, the role of seniority of judges as a condition for appointment and judicial review of transfers. Only the first aspect, regarding the constitutional position pertaining to consultation, is dealt with here. The decision proceeded on the assumption that primacy of the chief justice of India was the established position of law. No reasoning justifying this position or discussing the concept of independence

[76] For several allegations of illegal appointments and transfers, see *Indian Express*, 'President Refers Judges Appointment Law to SC,' 18 July 1998, available at www.indianexpress.com/res/web/pIe/ie/daily/19980728/20950754.html (accessed 13 May 2010). For practical problems of implementing the judgment, see T. R. Andhyarujina, 'Appointment of Judges by Collegium of Judges,' *The Hindu*, 18 December 2009, available at http://beta.thehindu.com/opinion/op-ed/article66672.ece (accessed 13 May 2010).

[77] Ranjit Bhushan and Purabi Patnaik, 'Whose Right Is It Anyway?' *Outlook*, 3 August 1998, available at www.outlookindia.com/article.aspx?205943 (accessed 13 May 2010); Kuldip Nayar, 'Consultation Is the Key,' *Indian Express*, 4 August 1998, available at www.indianexpress.com/ie/daily/19980804/21650954.html (accessed 13 May 2010).

[78] For a scathing criticism of chief justice Punchhi's conduct in the question of appointments by a noted scholar, see A. G. Noorani, *Constitutional Questions and Citizens' Rights* (Oxford: Oxford University Press, 2006), 84–85.

[79] *Presidential Reference*.

of the judiciary which had been used in *SCAORA* to buttress this position was provided. Instead, the court gave concrete shape to the collegium of justices which would be responsible for shaping the opinion of the chief justice of India. Contrary to *SCAORA*, which had specified that the chief justice of India would have to consult her two seniormost colleagues before reaching her opinion, the judgment preferred to extend the collegium to the chief justice and her four seniormost colleagues for Supreme Court appointments and her two seniormost colleagues for High Court appointments. In addition, the seniormost judge of the Supreme Court acquainted with the High Court from which the potential candidate hailed (for Supreme Court appointments) and the High Court to which the candidate was proposed (for High Court appointments) would have to be consulted. Further, the chief justice of the High Court too, in forming her opinion, would have to consult her two seniormost colleagues.[80] No detailed reasoning was provided for the size of the collegium except to state its rationale—to select the best available judicial talent in the country for the higher judiciary. In addition, there was a hint that the formula of chief justice of India plus four instead of two, as *SCAORA* had held, or five as had been suggested by counsel would operate as a compromise between the divergent points of view.[81]

Two further aspects of the opinion need to be considered. First, though technically this was an advisory opinion to the president, the attorney general had in open court stated that the Government of India would consider itself bound by the opinion.[82] Hence, its effect would be to shape future appointments to the higher judiciary in India till parliament thought otherwise. Second, despite its immense ramifications and the widely couched terms of reference set by the president, it is unfortunate that the court did not deem it necessary or expedient to provide a reasoned justification for its own conclusion and buttress or even modify the reasoning adopted in *SCAORA*. The very fact of the reference being sought and the acrimony between the executive and the judiciary that preceded it were testimony to the lack of clarity and consequently the perceived ambiguity of the decisions and reasons in the majority opinion in *SCAORA*. However, in choosing to merely extend the logic of the preceding case and establishing a collegium

80 This process has been seen as leading to the 'independence of the Judiciary … (being) institutionalised'. See Fali S. Nariman, 'Judicial Independence in India,' in *Democracy, Human Rights and the Rule of Law: Essays in Honour of Nani Palkhivala*, ed. Venkat Iyer (New Delhi: Butterworths, 2000), 13, 32.

81 *Presidential Reference*, para 20 (Justice Bharucha).

82 Ibid., para 14 (Justice Bharucha).

for all future judicial appointments without revisiting the reasons that had prompted the court to take its first steps in this direction, Justice Bharucha and the unanimous court institutionalised a system of appointments which was textually unjustified, inadequately supported by reason and, with the benefit of hindsight, detrimental to the reputation of the Indian higher judiciary.

Two primary lines of criticism will be advanced against *Presidential Reference* and the collegium system of appointments as it has operated in the recent past. As a matter of interpretation, it will be argued briefly that the judicial collegium for appointments has no textual basis in the Constitution. As a matter of practice, it will be argued on the basis of a case study of the proposed appointment of Justice Dinakaran to the Supreme Court of India that the collegium system replaces the inter-institutional equilibrium envisaged in Art. 124 and Art. 217 with *de facto* judicial supremacy. By doing so, it ignores the need for checks and balances, key to the appointments process, and fails to incorporate necessary process-related safeguards to secure judicial independence.

On the question of principle, the opinion in *Presidential Reference* did not provide reasons, textual or normative, regarding the basis for institution of the judicial collegium for appointments. This would, by implication, mean that the collegium system was a consequence of primacy being accorded to the opinion of the chief justice of India. Having already established this understanding of primacy as based on an impermissible interpretation of the Constitution, it logically follows that the consequence of primacy would be without basis as well. Second the modification of the size of the collegium and the differential sizes contingent on whether the appointments in question are to the Supreme Court or to the High Court are equally without legal basis. The word 'consultation' in Art. 124 and Art. 217 certainly connotes multiplicity but not specificity in size. Further, the court makes no attempt to justify the number of persons in the collegium, either in terms of specific functions that each performs or how having a particular minimum number would be sufficient to safeguard judicial independence or ensure non-arbitrariness.[83] This lack of judicial reasoning brings into question the issue of whether creation of such a collegium can be considered a judicial function and consequently whether

83 This has led a commentator to remark that the judgment is 'one of the most remarkable rulings ever issued by a supreme national appellate court in the common law world'. Lord Cooke of Thorndon, 'Where Angels Fear to Tread,' in *Supreme But Not Infallible: Essays in Honour of the Supreme Court of India*, ed. B. N. Kirpal et al. (New Delhi: Oxford University Press, 2000), 97, 105.

the court was institutionally legitimate in ordering its creation. This is a much larger question and requires a deeper discussion regarding the scope and nature of judicial power in India's constitutional framework. For the purpose of this book, it would suffice to say that the absence of principled reasoning justifying such a move suggests *prima facie* that the court clearly acted beyond the scope of its institutional legitimacy creating an institution which had no basis in the Constitution. It is significant to note that earlier proposals which had suggested a similar collegium system or even a greater role for the judiciary had recommended the change in the form of a gap-filling convention[84] or, alternatively, through a specific constitutional amendment,[85] not through judicial interpretation.

In practice, there is a seeming consensus amongst academics, lawyers, political commentators and a large section of the judiciary that the collegium system has proved counterproductive.[86] To demonstrate why this is so and, in addition, highlight the deficiencies of the collegium procedure, the proposal for appointment of Justice Dinakaran to the Supreme Court of India will be analysed in detail.[87]

Justice Dinakaran was appointed as a judge of the Madras High Court in December 1996. In August 2008, he was appointed as chief justice of the Karnataka High Court. While functioning as chief justice, in August 2009, the Supreme Court collegium recommended his name along with four other High

[84] Law Comm., 80th Report 22; It however recommended a constitutional amendment only for implementing the provision for a consultative panel owing to its permanent institutional nature, ibid., 35.

[85] Law Comm., 14th Report.

[86] Fali Nariman, who was the winning counsel in the Second Judges Case publicly regretted his arguments saying that the collegium system had failed. See J. Venkatesan, 'Collegium System Not Working Properly: Jurists,' *The Hindu*, 13 December 2009, available at www.thehindu.com/2009/12/13/stories/2009121360091000.htm (accessed 20 May 2010). See also V. R. Krishna Iyer, 'For a National Judicial Commission—I,' *The Hindu*, 30 October 2002, available at www.hinduonnet.com/2002/10/30/stories/2002103000121000.htm (accessed 20 May 2010); Harish Khare, 'Rule of Law versus Rule of Judges,' *The Hindu*, 26 October 2006, available at www.thehindu.com/2006/10/26/stories/2006102603841000.htm (accessed 20 May 2010).

[87] A limitation of this case study is that it is based entirely on secondary materials—newspaper archives, scholarly articles and interviews with lawyers and judges acquainted with the facts. Despite the best efforts of the author, no primary material, that is communications in the collegium, between the collegium and the government and other relevant communication, could be collected.

Court chief justices for appointment to the Supreme Court.[88] At this time, four representations were addressed to the Supreme Court collegium headed by Chief Justice K. G. Balakrishnan by the Chennai-based Forum for Judicial Accountability, comprising members of the Madras Bar.[89] These representations contained detailed allegations of wrongdoing by Justice Dinakaran. The allegations pointed to egregious violations of law by him and his family members, amassing land above the limit allowed by the relevant land ceiling legislation and acquiring *benami*[90] property, his questionable integrity—owning property entirely disproportionate to known sources of income—and doubts about his judicial probity, passing orders in cases where he had a conflict of interest and effecting several curious changes in the roster of matters posted before each judge in order to serve narrow sectional interests.[91] The first representation was handed over to the chief justice of India by Fali Nariman and Shanti Bhushan, two of the seniormost members of the Supreme Court Bar, thereby lending the allegations considerable credibility.[92] Later, acting under the aegis of the Bar Association of India, Nariman was instrumental in passing a formal resolution appealing to the collegium to desist from proceeding with their recommendation of Justice Dinakaran being appointed a judge of the Supreme Court, which further strengthened the case against appointing him.[93]

88 J. Venkatesan, 'Supreme Court to Get Five New Judges,' *The Hindu*, 27 August 2009, available at www.thehindu.com/news/supreme-court-to-get-five-new-judges/article10301.ece (accessed 17 June 2013).

89 The old name of the city 'Madras' as opposed to the new, official name 'Chennai' to describe the Bar is in light of the fact that the official name of the High Court still remains the Madras High Court.

90 According to s. 2(a) of the Benami Property Transactions Act, 1988, a *benami* transaction means '(a) … any transaction in which property is transferred to one person for a consideration paid or provided by another person'. It is made a criminal offence under s. 3(3) of the Act.

91 The text of the representations along with the motion for impeachment introduced in the Rajya Sabha against Justice Dinakaran may be found at Campaign for Judicial Accountability and Judicial Reforms, 'Judge Watch: Justice Dinakaran,' available at www.judicialreforms.org/judge-watch/609-justice-dinakaran.html (accessed 17 June 2013).

92 For a succinct overview, see V. Venkatesan, 'Controversial Choice,' *Frontline* 26, no. 22 (October–November 2009), available at www.frontline.in/static/html/fl2622/stories/20091106262212200.htm (accessed 17 June 2013).

93 *The Hindu*, 'Do Not Elevate Dinakaran,' 28 November 2009, available at www.thehindu.com/news/national/do-not-elevate-dinakaran/article56522.ece (accessed 17 June 2013).

Both the scale and the nature of these allegations contained in the representations, combined with the stature of the lawyers who were their chief advocates, resulted in a public uproar.[94] Forced to respond, the collegium, however, did not decide on the matter either way, ordering a probe by the collector of the district where Justice Dinakaran was alleged to have amassed properties beyond the legally permissible limit.[95] The collector submitted a report largely validating the allegations made in the representations to the collegium.[96] Justice Dinakaran and sections of the Madras Bar denied these findings and deemed the report motivated.[97] The National Commission of Scheduled Castes as well as one of the most powerful Dalit leaders, Mayawati, stepped into the controversy, in support of Justice Dinakaran (a Dalit Christian), saying that he was being victimised on account of his Dalit status.[98] Little evidentiary support buttressed either claim.

Faced with an escalating political controversy regarding its diversity in composition, the collegium decided to institute an 'independent probe' into the matter by the Survey of India.[99] This amounted to taking a *prima facie* view that

[94] Forum for Judicial Accountability, 'Issues of Deep Concern,' *Outlook*, 16 September 2009, available at www.outlookindia.com/article.aspx?261852 (accessed 17 June 201); V. R. Krishna Iyer, 'Issues Raised by L'affaire Dinakaran,' *The Hindu*, 17 September 2009, available at www.thehindu.com/opinion/op-ed/issues-raised-by-laffaire-dinakaran/article21767.ece (accessed 17 June 2013); Sugata Srinivasaraju and Chandrani Banerjee, 'His Feudal Lordship,' *Outlook*, 5 October 2009, available at www.outlookindia.com/article.aspx?262025 (accessed 17 June 2013).

[95] J. Venkatesan, 'Collegium Defers Decision on Dinakaran,' *The Hindu*, 18 September 2009, available at www.thehindu.com/news/national/collegium-defers-decision-on-justice-dinakaran/article22096.ece (accessed 17 June 2013).

[96] V. Venkatesan, 'Controversial Choice'; Dhananjay Mahapatra, 'Dinakaran Out of SC List,' *Times of India*, 3 October 2009, available at http://articles.timesofindia.indiatimes.com/2009-10-03/india/28094901_1_justice-dinakaran-collegium-recommendation-supreme-court-collegium (accessed 17 June 2013).

[97] J. Venkatesan, 'Collegium Defers Decision on Dinakaran.'

[98] 'Govt "Silent" on Campaign Against SC in Judiciary: NCSC,' *Mint*, 24 September 2009, available at www.livemint.com/Politics/T0mozhi9F7rZ1OfiuntpHL/Govt-silent-on-campaign-against-SC-in-judiciary-NCSC.html (accessed 17 June 2013); 'Mayawati Writes to PM on Dinakaran Issue,' *Daily News and Analysis,* 19 December 2009, available at www.dnaindia.com/india/1325456/report-mayawati-writes-to-pm-on-dinakaran-issue (accessed 17 June 2013).

[99] B. Kolappan, 'Survey Work Begins in Kaverirajapuram,' *The Hindu*, 8 January 2010, available at www.hindu.com/2010/01/08/stories/2010010854680400.htm (accessed 17 June 2013).

the representations made by Justice Dinakaran against the collector's report, specifically that its motivations were questionable, were valid, thereby requiring a differently constituted probe committee. In the meantime, the collegium delinked his appointment from that of four other High Court chief justices who were sought to be elevated to the Supreme Court.[100]

Despite this controversy over his appointment to the Supreme Court, Justice Dinakaran continued normal functioning as the chief justice of the Karnataka High Court. A section of the Karnataka Bar went on strike, refusing to plead if Justice Dinakaran still presided over the High Court.[101] In December 2009, a month after the strike, after an impeachment motion had been admitted in the Rajya Sabha against him, Justice Dinakaran, seemingly voluntarily, ceased judicial work as chief justice pending completion of the enquiry against him.[102] It was only at this time that the collegium, after a communication to this effect from the Law Ministry, decided to officially 'put on hold' their recommendation to the president to appoint Justice Dinakaran to the Supreme Court. It is significant to note that despite the admittance of an impeachment motion, the collegium did not officially 'withdraw' their nomination of Justice Dinakaran.[103]

In spite of being the subject of impeachment proceedings, Justice Dinakaran continued exercising the administrative functions of the chief justice of Karnataka High Court while desisting from judicial functions. The collegium, with its legitimacy sourced from the decisions in *SCAORA* and *Presidential Reference*, had no power to order him to stop exercising such functions. The anomaly of this situation was pointed out in a public letter by his brother judge, Justice D. V. Shylendra Kumar, who requested him to cease exercising such

[100] They took oath on 17 November 2009: Jatin Gandhi, 'Cloak and Stagger,' *Open*, 12 December 2009, available at www.openthemagazine.com/article/nation/cloak-and-stagger (accessed 17 June 2013).

[101] Prashant Bhushan, 'The Dinakaran Imbroglio: Appointments and Complaints Against Judges,' *Economic and Political Weekly* 44, nos 41–42 (2009): 10–12.

[102] J. Venkatesan, 'Dinakaran Will Continue in His Post, Says CJI,' *The Hindu*, 18 December 2009, available at www.thehindu.com/news/dinakaran-will-continue-in-his-post-says-cji/article66979.ece (accessed 17 June 2013).

[103] The term used in all news reports to describe this is that the appointment has been put 'on hold'. See J. Venkatesan, 'Dinakaran's Elevation Put on Hold,' *The Hindu*, 10 October 2009, available at www.thehindu.com/news/national/dinakarans-elevation-put-on-hold/article32105.ece (accessed 17 June 2013); Dhananjay Mahapatra, 'CJI Initiates "Discreet" Probe Against Dinakaran,' *Times of India*, 3 October 2009, available at http://articles.timesofindia.indiatimes.com/2009-10-03/india/28094901_1_justice-dinakaran-collegium-recommendation-supreme-court-collegium (accessed 17 June 2013).

functions.[104] However, Justice Dinakaran refused, citing the lack of any provision that required him to do so.[105] The collegium, alarmed by the prospect of a long-drawn-out impeachment proceeding during which time the Karnataka High Court would be hamstrung without a fully functioning chief justice, asked Justice Dinakaran to proceed on leave.[106] He, however, refused, correctly stating that the collegium did not have the legal power to make such a request.[107] With the procedural vacuum in which the collegium was operating having been exposed, first by the lack of provision enabling any disciplinary measures pending an impeachment proceeding and second by Justice Dinakaran's refusal to accede to the collegium's request of going on leave, the collegium took the curious step of recommending his transfer as chief justice of the Sikkim High Court.[108]

The unstated, albeit evident, rationale for such a decision was to shift him to the smallest High Court in the country with a comparatively minor case load and limited administrative functions. The grave principled objections to such a move raised by the Sikkim Bar which threatened a boycott of (and did boycott) Justice Dinakaran's oath-taking ceremony (if the transfer materialised) were ignored by the collegium.[109] Justice Dinakaran took oath as the chief justice

[104] Justice D. V. Shylendra Kumar, 'Extraordinary Situations Call for Extraordinary Measures,' 17 December 2009, available at http://sites.google.com/site/justdvskumar/extraordinary-measures (accessed 18 June 2013).

[105] Evidence of this can be found in a subsequent letter to Justice Dinakaran from Justice Kumar. See Justice D. V. Shylendra Kumar, 'Open Letter/Appeal to the Chief Justice, High Court of Karnataka, Bangalore,' 8 March 2010, on file with the author.

[106] J. Venkatesan, 'Justice Dinakaran Asked to Go on Leave,' *The Hindu*, 3 April 2010, available at www.hindu.com/2010/04/03/stories/2010040363460100.htm (accessed 18 June 2013).

[107] Press Trust of India, 'Defiant Karnataka CJ Refuses to Go on Leave,' *Times of India*, 6 April 2010, available at http://articles.timesofindia.indiatimes.com/2010-04-06/india/28135084_1_justice-dinakaran-chief-justice-abuse-of-judicial-office (accessed 18 June 2013).

[108] V. Venkatesan, 'Question of Propriety,' *Frontline* 27, no. 9 (April–May 2010), available at www.frontline.in/static/html/fl2709/stories/20100507270903300.htm (accessed 18 June 2013). The transfer was confirmed in July 2010 and orders were issued. See *Times of India*, 'Controversial Chief Justice Dinakaran Shifted to Sikkim High Court,' 30 July 2010, available at http://articles.timesofindia.indiatimes.com/2010-07-30/india/28290732_1_sikkim-hc-karnataka-high-court-uttarakhand (accessed 18 June 2013).

[109] J. Venkatesan, 'Supreme Court Collegium Sticks to Shifting Justice Dinakaran to Sikkim,' *The Hindu*, 30 April 2010, www.thehindu.com/news/national/supreme-court-collegium-sticks-to-shifting-justice-dinakaran-to-sikkim/article418119.ece (accessed 18 June 2013).

of the Sikkim High Court on 9 August 2010[110] and acted in both his judicial and administrative capacity till his resignation in 2011 while impeachment proceedings were ongoing.

The Justice Dinakaran episode holds a number of crucial lessons regarding the operation of the processes of judicial appointments, transfers, in-house disciplining and impeachment. Focusing specifically on the collegium-led method of judicial appointment, this series of incidents exposes three significant drawbacks of this process. First, the elevation of Justice Dinakaran to the Supreme Court despite a history of purported irregularities capable of being revealed by a simple enquiry points strongly to the institutional incapacity of the judicial collegium in performing the task of being the focal decision-maker in appointing judges. Appointing a judge would require a thorough verification of antecedents, financial records and a close perusal of past judicial decisions. The task hence has both an objective and a subjective element: the objective element involves enquiring into the judge's personal particulars, financial details, reports of judgments delivered, and so on, and the subjective element involves an assessment of the suitability of the person as a judge on the basis of the objective material collected.

The collegium, while well placed to take a subjective view on the suitability of a candidate, is institutionally incapable of performing this task without a secretariat and a permanent staff to collect the objective data that is a necessary precondition. Even if such data collection facilities are not available within the collegium, there must be an established process by which the collegium can call on specific bodies that are mandated by law to assist it. While an argument may be made that the Union government would be responsible for verifying aspects of the judge's record, namely those relating to his character and financial antecedents, the memorandum of procedure for appointment of Supreme Court Judges that was in operation at the time casts considerable doubt over this possibility. Paragraph 3.5 of the procedure reads:

> After receipt of the final recommendation of the Chief Justice of India, the Union Minister of Law, Justice and Company Affairs will put up the recommendations to the Prime Minister who will advise the President in the matter of appointment.[111]

[110] *The Hindu*, 'Dinakaran Sworn in as Chief Justice,' 9 August 2010, available at www.thehindu.com/news/national/other-states/dinakaran-sworn-in-sikkim-chief-justice/article560720.ece (accessed 18 June 2013).

[111] Department of Justice, Ministry of Law and Justice, Government of India, 'Memorandum Showing the Procedure for Appointment of the Chief Justice of

This gives rise to an impression, confirmed by subsequent practice, of the government not performing any substantive verification function once the recommendation for appointment is made by the collegium. This makes the absence of information collecting capacity, either internally in the collegium or a mandated process prior to recommending a name for appointment, imperative. The lack of such capacity and consequently the lack of information about Justice Dinakaran arguably allowed the ill-conceived decision to recommend him to be taken in the first place. The alternative conclusion to institutional incapacity is to infer the prevalence of extraneous considerations within the judicial collegium despite knowledge of such irregularities. Though unproven, these are allegations that have only grown shriller as questionable judicial appointments have continued to rise.[112]

Second, the series of incidents starting with his recommendation up to his transfer to the Sikkim High Court demonstrates a gaping procedural vacuum in the functioning of the collegium. Needless to say, the memorandum of procedure cited earlier is conspicuously silent on every procedural aspect that became a cause for concern in the Justice Dinakaran appointment—the lack of an established process for raising objections to recommendations, the *ad hoc* nature in which the objections were dealt with, the lack of provisions regarding the status and functioning of a judge against whose elevation objections have been raised and the ambiguity surrounding the legal basis for placing a recommendation 'on hold'. Even the disclosure of the fact that the collegium had recommended five judges including Justice Dinakaran for appointment was not through an official press statement but rather through a news article whose source is unclear.[113] It is only subsequent to this article that the representations against Justice Dinakaran were made by the Forum for Judicial Accountability. Further, it has been acknowledged that it was the intervention of Fali Nariman, Shanti Bhushan and other stalwarts of the Supreme Court Bar that forced the collegium to take cognizance of the allegations of irregularity against Justice Dinakaran.[114] No procedure existed to take into account objections as a matter

India and Judges of the Supreme Court of India', available at http://doj.gov.in/sites/default/files/memosc.pdf (accessed 18 June 2013).

112 Soli Sorabjee, 'It's Time Judges Stopped Appointing Themselves and Shed Nepotism,' *New Indian Express*, 26 May 2013, available at http://newindianexpress.com/opinion/Its-time-judges-stopped-appointing-themselves-and-shed-nepotism/2013/05/26/article1605918.ece (accessed 18 January 2013).

113 J. Venkatesan, 'Supreme Court to Get Five New Judges.'

114 Bhushan, 'Dinakaran Imbroglio.'

of course, the grounds on which they would be permitted, the requirements of standing for a person to file such objections and the range of actions open to the collegium were such objections received. An equally key legal void was the status and functioning of a judge when the collegium is acting upon such objections. Justice Dinakaran's anomalous position—exercising administrative functions and not judicial ones—can be attributed largely to the lack of legally established consequences were a collegium to find *prima facie* merit in objections that required further investigation. The lack of such provisions not only led to such an anomalous situation but also created considerable discord and disharmony amongst the judges and advocates in Karnataka High Court.[115]

To a considerable extent, such lack of procedure in the functioning of the collegium method of appointment alongside the ambiguity surrounding substantive powers the collegium has can be attributed to the *SCAORA* and *Presidential Reference* decisions, which established the judicial collegium and reworked the constitutional method for appointing judges. Neither did the judicial collegium, vested with focal power to appoint by these two judgments, have any textual basis in the Constitution nor could its establishment be linked in any meaningful way to constitutional doctrine. In establishing it, the court was acting quasi-legislatively, setting up a mode of appointment that it felt would best ensure independence of the judiciary. The procedural gaps in this mode of appointment, demonstrated by the Justice Dinakaran episode, underline the fact of the establishment of the collegium as a quasi-legislative exercise as well as highlight the imperfections salient within it. The concretisation of a long-standing practice of wide consultation through the creation of the collegium in *SCAORA*, followed up by giving it firm institutional status and form in *Presidential Reference*, meant that it was incumbent upon the court to specifically chart out a procedure for the institution's own functioning as well as its dealings with other powers and authorities. The court did partially embark on this exercise in *Presidential Reference*, giving the exact size of the collegium, the other judges who would have to be consulted before making specific appointments and stipulating that all communications would have to be in writing. However, the functioning of the in-house procedure within the collegium, how the proceedings ought to be made optimally transparent, the power of the collegium to invite and investigate

[115] Specifically, Justice D. V. Shylendra Kumar, whose letter to Chief Justice Dinakaran has been adverted to above, engaged in a visible, public denouncement of Justice Dinakaran. Two letters were written by him on 8 March 2010 to Chief Justice Dinakaran and his colleagues on the Karnataka High Court respectively and a third letter was written on 9 March 2010 to the general public (on file with the author).

objections to proposed appointments, as well as withdrawal or rejection of a proposed appointee, all in issue in the appointment of Justice Dinakaran (as well as several other procedural aspects), were not considered at all. Much of this oversight can be attributed to the fact that in creating a new mechanism for appointments and vesting it with wide powers, the court was not acting within the zone of its core competence. While exercising such functions, a large number of interests have to be taken into account, a range of possible fact situations considered and diverging factors balanced. From the judgments in these cases, it is clear that the court accounted for few of these, laying down a new mechanism for appointments pursuant simply to representations made by the parties before it and what it felt would be in the best interests of the independence of the judiciary. This, the court believed, would be achieved if the power to appoint was vested in itself, since it had an unshakeable faith in its successors acting in good faith and after due deliberation in selecting their future brethren. Not only was such a view speculative when used as an argument to override the need for procedural checks and substantive delineation of powers that the collegium would possess in the appointments process, but it was also pernicious. Especially so when despite evidence during the Justice Dinakaran episode that pointed to the need for laying down such procedures, the collegium failed to do so, sanguine in the faith that the judges in *SCAORA* and *Presidential Reference* vested in them.

Finally, the proposed appointment of Justice Dinakaran and the collegium's handling of the issue led to severe damage to the credibility of the judiciary. It is axiomatic that the fact that a person against whom such serious charges were levelled could even be a serving judge of the Madras High Court or the chief justice of Karnataka High Court, let alone be proposed as an appointee to the Supreme Court, gravely affects judicial credibility. This point is evidenced by the large number of newspaper editorials, interviews and opinions of judges, lawyers as well as lay commentators.[116] Further, the fact that the collegium, despite being apprised of such allegations, failed to take any definitive steps to defuse the

[116] See, for example, J. Venkatesan, 'Collegium System Not Working Properly'; V. Venkatesan, Question of Propriety. See also Bhushan, 'Dinakaran Imbroglio'; Krishna Iyer, 'Issues Raised by L'affaire Dinakaran'; Ashish Tripathi, 'Has Collegium System of Judges' Appointment Outlived Its Utility,' *Deccan Herald*, 20 April 2011, available at http://www.deccanherald.com/content/155018/has-collegium-system-judges-appointment.html (accessed 1 March 2017); Satya Prakash, 'A Matter of Transparency,' *Hindustan Times*, 31 August 2013, available at http://www.hindustantimes.com/delhi/a-matter-of-transparency/story-YHfexnKKNqah7YODZcFSmI.html (accessed 1 March 2017).

situation, refusing first to take a decision and belatedly ordering an independent enquiry with a view to ascertaining the allegations, led to a full-blown crisis. Specifically its refusal to withdraw its nomination of Justice Dinakaran sharply and publicly exposed the flaws of the collegium method that had earlier been the subject of criticism largely within the legal community. The unseemly caste angle to this row espoused by those close to Justice Dinakaran himself[117] mired the appointments process, and by implication the judiciary, in a larger political dispute. The opacity of the process, which meant that such allegations could neither be confirmed nor refuted, led to large amounts of speculation, which further affected the credibility of the judiciary itself in the public eye.

Today the collegium method of appointment continues despite public confidence having eroded substantially. It is doctrinally indefensible, practically unwieldy and pervaded by deep procedural and substantive flaws. Further, as the Justice Dinakaran episode demonstrates, failing to reform the system as it exists and operates currently has led to enormous damage to the credibility of the judiciary and its institutional accountability. These were recognised by the Supreme Court even as it struck down the Constitution (99th Amendment) Act, 2014, and the NJAC Act enacted to replace the ill-functioning collegium. Unfortunately, both the judgment and the aftermath had the undeniable effect of making the discourse around the Indian higher judiciary overtly political. Why this became so is explained in the next section.

## 2D. Constitution Confrontation: The *NJAC Case*[118]

### 2D.1 Analysis of the Judgment

In the *NJAC Case*,[119] the Supreme Court of India by majority (Justices Khehar, Lokur, Joseph and Goel) struck down the NJAC as unconstitutional. The 99th Amendment to the Constitution enacted by parliament to create the NJAC was

[117] Dhananjay Mahapatra, 'Finally Justice Dinakaran Resigns,' *Times of India*, 30 July 2011, available at http://articles.timesofindia.indiatimes.com/2011-07-30/india/29832583_1_justice-dinakaran-sikkim-high-court-thiruvallur-collector (accessed 18 June 2013).

[118] Parts of this section have been extracted from Arghya Sengupta, 'Appointment of Judges and the Basic Structure Doctrine in India,' *Law Quarterly Review* 132 (2016): 201, where it was originally published.

[119] *NJAC Case*.

held to violate judicial independence, which is part of the basic structure of the Constitution that cannot be amended. Justice Chelameswar wrote a dissenting opinion. According to him, while judicial independence is part of the basic structure, there was nothing in the 99th Amendment to offend it.

As a result of the judgment, the method of appointment reverted to the pre-amendment position, that is, the determinative view would be that of a collegium of senior justices of the Supreme Court headed by the chief justice of India. It was precisely to alter such judicial supremacy in appointment of judges that the NJAC was established. It was to consist of six members—the chief justice of India, two seniormost puisne judges of the Supreme Court, the union minister for law and justice and two eminent persons to be selected by a committee comprising the chief justice of India, the prime minister and the leader of the opposition in the Lok Sabha (lower house of parliament).[120] An appointment could only be made if a special majority of five members voted affirmatively (as provided for in the NJAC Act).[121]

The majority of the judges considered the composition of the NJAC to suffer from two defects that rendered it unconstitutional—first, the presence of the law minister was held to affect judicial independence; second, the vesting of the effective power to veto a nomination in any two members (who might be the non-judicial members) was considered offensive to the predominant judicial role in appointment, which was held to be part of the basic structure of the Constitution. Two of the judges (Justices Khehar and Goel) found the inclusion of two eminent persons without any necessary knowledge of law or the qualities necessary to assess the potential worth of a candidate itself vague and consequently unconstitutional. One judge (Justice Lokur) held the role of the chief justice of India in appointment of judges to have been unconstitutionally diminished from what was originally intended by the framers of the Constitution and what had been the consistent practice in independent India. Taken together, the NJAC was declared unconstitutional even before it could start functioning.

Justice Chelameswar in dissent held that nothing in precedent or conceptual argument suggested that judicial primacy in appointment of judges is a necessary component of judicial independence or the basic structure of the Constitution.

[120] S. 3 of the Constitution (99th Amendment) Act, 2014, introduced Article 124A to the Constitution of India.

[121] Proviso to s. 5(2), The National Judicial Appointments Commission Act, 2014 (Supreme Court); s. 6(6), The National Judicial Appointments Commission Act, 2014 (High Court).

Further, the basic structure includes many fundamental features such as separation of powers, democracy, and checks and balances, of which judicial independence is one. Merely impinging on one aspect of this structure would not, by itself, make a constitutional amendment unconstitutional. It could only be after a holistic assessment of the amendment on all facets of the basic structure that such a conclusion could be reached. Since the only significant impact of the amendment was on judicial primacy, understood as the determinative view in appointment being that of the judiciary, which is not a *sine qua non* for judicial independence, no question of violation of the basic structure arose in this case.

The primary reason provided by the majority for striking down the presence of the union minister for law and justice on the NJAC was one of conflict of interest.[122] Given that the Union of India is the largest litigant in the country, having the union law minister as a member of the NJAC would affect the perception of impartiality, necessary for an independent judiciary. While it is indeed correct to say as a matter of fact that in India, the central government is the largest litigant, to infer that the government consequently will have no role in a commission to appoint judges is, with respect, too quick. Were such a conflict of interest rule valid, then in countries where the ruling government has a significant role in appointment while being a significant litigating party at the same time (say, the United Kingdom, Australia or the United States of America), or in India prior to 1993, that is before the introduction of judicial collegium-led appointment when appointments were primarily by the executive, the logical inference would be that the said judiciaries lack independence. This would be a rather simplistic claim. Nonetheless, even if such a conflict of interest rule were to be applied, the only valid inference from such a rule can be that the government must not have a determinative role in appointing judges. Needless to say, having one member out of a commission of six, as in the case of the NJAC, hardly provides such a determinative role.

Insofar as striking down the inclusion of two eminent persons on the NJAC is concerned, the reasoning of the majority is curious. While it is entirely correct to state that no substantive qualifications, except the requirement of eminence, are prescribed for these two persons, it is essential to note that a committee of three high functionaries, the chief justice of India, the prime minister and the leader of the opposition in the Lok Sabha (lower house of parliament), is prescribed for selection of such persons. Even if vesting of the power to appoint eminent persons in such high functionaries was found to be

[122] *NJAC Case*, para 167 (Justice Khehar).

inadequate without laying down clear guidelines on what constitutes eminence, as Justice Chelameswar points out in dissent, to strike down a constitutional amendment for vagueness amounts to 'judicially mandating inflexible standards for constitutional drafting'.[123]

Further, the majority held that allowing any two members on the NJAC the power to veto a nomination affects judicial primacy.[124] This view is normatively as well as legally indefensible. Normatively, judicial independence as a concept aims to insulate the judiciary from pressures that will be perceived to impede an impartial and effective discharge of the judicial function. There is no particular normative reason as to why a role for non-judges in confirming appointments, that is, even before a judge has assumed office to adjudicate matters, necessitates such a conclusion. On the contrary, one might imagine that it is precisely their inclusion that can prevent the judiciary from being, or becoming, a self-perpetuating old boys' club.

In this context, it is critical to recollect that the framers of the Constitution expressly envisaged that the power of appointing judges would be an executive function. Any appointment would be by the president after consultation with the chief justice of India for the Supreme Court (Art. 124) and the chief justice of India, chief justice of the High Court and governor of the concerned state for the High Courts (Art. 217). This makes both the reading in of judicial primacy and any suggestion of incorporating it as part of the basic structure deeply suspect.[125]

At the same time, it is undoubtedly true that *SCAORA* held that there ought to be primacy of judges, symbolised by the view of the chief justice of India, in appointment. Its interpretation was based on its understanding of Art. 124 and Art. 217 that the view of the chief justice of India, as an apolitical authority, ought to be given the greatest weight. It was also reacting to the executive's attempts to browbeat the judiciary into submission as described above. [126]

However, given that Art. 124 and Art. 217 were themselves amended by parliament by the 99th Amendment to establish the NJAC, there is no basis in law to conclude that judicial primacy, as held in *SCAORA*, is inviolable for all times to come. This is why Justice Lokur's view in the *NJAC Case* that the

[123] Ibid., para 111 (Justice Chelameswar).

[124] Ibid., para 239 (Justice Khehar).

[125] See Section 2A on CAD and appointments.

[126] See Section 2C.2.

99th Amendment by whittling down the role envisaged for the chief justice of India has violated the basic structure is, with respect, incorrect. If it is simply an established practice that appointments previously were largely in accordance with the views of the chief justice, there is no proposition in law that the same cannot now be changed by parliament. On the contrary, if consistent practice can constitute basic structure of a written constitution, then that structure ceases to remain very basic.

Justice Chelameswar, in dissent, provides a coherent approach to discovering what constitutes the basic structure. From an analysis of precedent, he draws a distinction between the basic structure of the Constitution and its constituent features, known as basic features.[127] He then proposes what is in essence a two-step test: Does the amendment affect a basic feature of the Constitution? If yes, does it affect it in a manner that destroys its basic structure? This provides the flexibility to balance different elements of the basic structure such as rule of law, separation of powers and judicial independence which might be affected in different ways by a single amendment. To simply draw a conclusion that affecting one feature would *ipso facto* make an amendment unconstitutional, as the majority has done, is, with respect, too hasty.

This is also because a constitutional amendment is the highest expression of parliamentary sovereignty. While it is established in Indian constitutional law that the courts have the power to strike down an amendment, judicial deference has meant that courts have taken every effort to read down provisions of any amendments which might be challenged, rather than strike them down.[128] By reversing this well-established trend by striking down the entire 99th Amendment and the NJAC Act without any serious effort to read it down, the court has recalibrated the constitutional relationship between the judiciary and parliament.

Its principled merits notwithstanding, functioning effectively as an appointments commission is equally a matter of attention to detail and learning from past mistakes. The key limitation of the NJAC was that it represented

[127] For an analysis, see Sengupta, 'Justice Chelameswar's Dissent'.

[128] Until the *NJAC Case*, the Supreme Court of India either read down or struck down constitutional amendments only in parts. This happened on six previous occasions in 65 years, in *Kesavananda Bharati* v. *State of Kerala*, (1973) 4 SCC 225; *Indira Gandhi* v. *Raj Narain*, (1975) Supp SCC 1; *Minerva Mills* v. *Union of India*, (1980) 3 SCC 625; *P. Sambamurthy* v. *State of Andhra Pradesh*, (1987) 1 SCC 362; *L. Chandra Kumar* v. *Union of India*, (1997) 3 SCC 261; and *Kihoto Hollohan* v. *Zachillhu*, (1992) Supp 2 SCC 651.

an extension of the authority-centric approach towards ensuring a method of appointing judges that secures judicial independence while selecting the best candidates for judicial office. Process-related considerations, albeit present, were inadequate. In terms of criteria for selection, the NJAC Act parrots the generic need for 'ability, merit and any other criteria of suitability as may be specified by regulations'.[129] It also requires seniority to be considered when appointing sitting High Court judges to the Supreme Court or appointing a chief justice of a High Court.[130] Critically, however, it does not mention how seniority is to be considered alongside merit and ability. At the same time, it does not provide adequate details of the shortlisting process prior to selection.

Regarding High Court appointments, it leaves the power to nominate judges to the chief justice of the High Court in consultation with his two seniormost colleagues; for Supreme Court appointments no nomination process is prescribed. As a result, it fails to provide a clearly delineated, criteria-based process of nomination of persons to fill judicial vacancies. No search committees or secretariat for preparing records of possible candidates is envisaged. It would not be a surprise were such a system to be implemented that it would, like the collegium before it, not be primed for selecting the best candidates for judicial office.

This approach, seen earlier in the Constituent Assembly and then again with the establishment of the collegium by the Supreme Court in its *SCAORA* judgment, espouses the view that if the power to appoint resides in high authorities, the values that the appointment process seeks to embody will automatically ensue. Unfortunately, authority-centric approaches, whether executive-led or collegium-led, have not optimally secured such values. However, there remains a considerable gulf between possible inefficacy of an appointments mechanism, which can be corrected by subsequent process-related developments, and its unconstitutionality. The *NJAC Case* has set the clock back on reform, affirming, much like the Supreme Court had done earlier in 1993, the court's self-belief in setting its own house in order. While the merits of such a belief are a matter of subjective opinion, two decades of experience with the collegium have belied any expectations of judge-led appointments as the panacea for procedural and substantive concerns surrounding judicial appointments. Moreover, the manner in which such a belief was converted into constitutional law was clearly illegitimate. Particularly, as a result of the Supreme Court holding that a method of appointment of judges which is not led

129 S. 5(2), NJAC Act (for Supreme Court); S. 6(3) NJAC Act (for High Courts).

130 Proviso to s. 5(2), NJAC Act (for Supreme Court); S. 6(1) NJAC Act (for chief justice of High Court).

by the chief justice of India and which does not hold some semblance of judicial primacy is violative of the basic structure of the Constitution, any meaningful reform is made seemingly insurmountable. To do so will require the Supreme Court reversing itself, a prospect that is theoretically possible, though currently remote. This is especially so in the light of the stalemate between the government and the judiciary pertaining to judicial appointments that has emerged consequent to the *NJAC Case*.

## 2D.2 The Aftermath

The aftermath of the *NJAC Case* has seen an internecine conflict between the executive and the judiciary over judicial appointments. Fuelled by mutual mistrust and characterised by increasingly public bickering over interstitial disagreements, both the judiciary and the executive appear to have taken hardened positions, which holds out little hope of a détente. This has primarily centred around the memorandum of procedure, a reworked version of which containing improvements to the collegium system was recommended by the court in a consequent order in the *NJAC Case*.[131]

Considerable internal dissension has also emerged within the judiciary in this period. A section of judges have openly advocated reform of internal processes. This has been led by Justice Chelameswar who called for transparency in judicial appointments and refused to attend collegium meetings, preferring instead to record his views in writing. Other members of the legal fraternity have advised caution, arguing that any internal dissension within the judiciary would provide leeway to the executive and hurt the independence of the judiciary.[132] It would be useful to consider both these developments in turn in order to understand the *status quo* pertaining to judicial appointments.

[131] Order dated 16 December 2015 in *Supreme Court Advocates-on-Record Association v. Union of India*, Writ Petition (Civil) No. 13 of 2015, available at https://www.supremecourtofindia.nic.in/jonew/judis/43188.pdf (accessed 5 August 2018) (hereinafter '*NJAC Consequential Order*').

[132] For an illustrative example, see Fali Nariman, 'My Unsolicited Suggestion,' *Indian Express*, 7 September 2016, available at https://indianexpress.com/article/opinion/columns/supreme-court-judges-appointment-transparency-collegium-working-system-3017291/ (accessed 23 July 2018); see also response to Nariman's article, Arghya Sengupta, 'An Unsolicited Response,' *Indian Express*, 12 September 2016, available at https://indianexpress.com/article/opinion/columns/fali-s-nariman-article-my-unsolicited-suggestion-justice-chelameswar-lack-of-transparency-collegium-judge-appointments-3026362/ (accessed 23 July 2018).

### 2D.2.a The Inconclusive Memorandum of Procedure

Scarcely has a document originally envisaged as laying down matters of relatively minor procedural detail become such an article of faith between warring organs of state. The term 'memorandum of procedure' appears to have been used for the first time, not as a term of art. Instead, it simply described a document that would concretise certain procedural details pertaining to file movements between the collegium and the executive and time limits in the process of judicial appointments, which were laid down by the Supreme Court itself in *SCAORA*.[133] Consequently, two such documents were formulated—one for appointments to the Supreme Court, including the appointment of the chief justice of India and the second for appointment to High Courts, including of chief justices, and transfer between High Courts.[134] Since they only contained matters of procedure—relating to initiation of a proposal for appointment, requirements of medical certification and coordination between different constitutional authorities—no controversy regarding their clauses arose.

However, when the court, in the *NJAC Case*, after declaring the NJAC to be unconstitutional, suggested that it would hold a consequential hearing to improve the collegium system, the memorandum of procedure provided a convenient medium for effectuating such improvements. For this purpose, the court invited public submissions on four categories—eligibility criteria, creation of a secretariat, complaints mechanism and transparency measures. '11500 pages of views'[135] were submitted, which were summarised and presented for the court's consideration. However, when it came to actually ordering such improvement, the Government of India contended that the task of preparing a memorandum of procedure, as per *SCAORA*, should be vested in the executive in consultation with the chief justice of India.[136] The court acquiesced to this procedure being adopted and laid down certain 'broad suggestions for consideration'.[137] These included fixing a minimum age for eligibility, need

[133] *SCAORA*, para 478, point (13).

[134] Memorandum of procedure of appointment of Supreme Court Judges, available at http://doj.gov.in/appointment-of-judges/memorandum-procedure-appointment-supreme-court-judges (accessed 24 July 2018); Memorandum of Procedure of appointment of High Court Judges, available at http://doj.gov.in/appointment-of-judges/memorandum-procedure-appointment-high-court-judges (accessed 24 July 2018).

[135] *NJAC Consequential Order*, para 5.

[136] Ibid., para 6.

[137] Ibid., para 11.

for a separate secretariat in each High Court and the Supreme Court for appointments, making provision for minuting all collegium discussions while keeping them confidential, publishing the eligibility criteria and procedures online, setting up an appropriate mechanism for complaints against a prospective candidate and provision for interaction of such candidates with the Supreme Court collegium.[138]

Much like *SCAORA* wherein the court created the collegium for appointing judges and *Presidential Reference* wherein the court embarked on a legislative exercise to lay down the size of the collegium and the procedures it would follow, the consequential order of the court was a similarly speculative foray into the legislative domain. The fact of a court inviting public suggestions and then seeking to incorporate them through judicial diktat dispensed with any pretence of the exercise not being a judicial one. This is why its ultimate suggestions on improvements to the collegium are shorn of any reasoning, except for its belief that the changes would result in a better functioning collegium that would command greater public confidence.

The court in such a legislative avatar is not, as this chapter has demonstrated, a novel development. It is a legacy of a belief that the court itself is best placed to ensure its own independence and smooth functioning. Such a belief may cut both ways—the history of Indira Gandhi's attempts to browbeat the judiciary provides a good cause to insulate the courts from the executive. However, such insulation cannot sacrifice the Constitution itself, which explicitly makes the power to appoint judges an executive act. Even more so, when the collegium system, a manifestation of such a belief, was widely acknowledged to have faced unanticipated difficulties[139] and was overhauled by parliament—to persist with such a belief and recommend improvements is stubbornness at best, and perhaps turf protection at worst.

In either event, the court's attempts appear to have been viewed by the government as a political act that warranted a political response. With the tenures of three chief justices having elapsed since the order of the court accepting the attorney-general's submission that the government would

[138] Ibid., para 10.

[139] V. Venkatesan, 'Honesty Matters: Interview with Justice J. S. Verma, Former Chief Justice of India,' *Frontline*, 10 October 2008, available at https://www.frontline.in/static/html/fl2520/stories/20081010252003500.htm (accessed 24 July 2018); Fali S. Nariman, 'A Case I Won—But Which I Would Prefer to Have Lost,' in *Before Memory Fades: An Autobiography*, ed. Fali S. Nariman (Carlsbad: Hay House, 2010).

formulate a memorandum of procedure in consultation with the chief justice of India, a finalised memorandum is nowhere in sight. Newspaper reports reveal two sticking points—a clause that allows the executive to veto a candidate on national security grounds and another clause that keeps the secretariat for screening candidates under the administrative control of the Ministry of Law and Justice, Government of India.[140] It was subsequently reported that the Supreme Court collegium, led by the chief justice of India, had unanimously rejected the national security clause and sent its comments to the government. It appears that the government has been silent since receiving such a communication.[141]

The continued obduracy of the government and the uncompromising stance adopted by the court imply that this innocuous procedural document has now become a site for a political contest on a matter of constitutional law. As a result, appointments have suffered. From January 2016 to July 2017, at the peak of the conflict, there have only been 10 appointments to the Supreme Court with eight vacancies.[142] The position in the High Courts is

[140] Sheela Bhatt, 'Memorandum of Procedure: Behind the Scenes, Govt and SC in Tug of War Over Appointments and Turf,' *Indian Express*, 15 July 2016, available at https://indianexpress.com/article/india/india-news-india/supreme-court-high-court-judge-appointment-procedure-criteria-collegium-government-judiciary-2914823/ (accessed 24 July 2018); Maneesh Chhibber, 'MoP on appointments: SC Puts Its Foot Down, Rejects Govt Plan to Veto Postings on National Security Grounds,' *Indian Express*, 24 March 2017, available at https://indianexpress.com/article/india/mop-on-appointments-sc-puts-its-foot-down-rejects-govt-plan-to-veto-postings-on-national-security-grounds-collegium-4582978/ (accessed 24 July 2018).

[141] '#JudgesConference: Read the Letter Written by Four Senior Most Judges to CJI Misra,' *Bar & Bench*, 12 January 2018, available at https://barandbench.com/judges-conference-read-letter/ (accessed 24 July 2018).

[142] Justice A. M. Khanwilkar appointed on 13 May 2016, Justice D. Y. Chandrachud appointed on 13 May 2016, Justice Ashok Bhushan appointed on 13 May 2016, Justice L. Nageswara Rao appointed on 13 May 2016, Justice Sanjay Kishan Kaul appointed on 17 February 2017, Justice Mohan S. Shantangoudar appointed on 17 February 2017, Justice S. Abdul Nazeer appointed on 17 February 2017, Justice Navin Sinha appointed on 17 February 2017, Justice Deepak Gupta appointed on 17 February 2017 and Justice Indu Malhotra appointed on 27 April 2018. The total strength of the Supreme Court is 31, including the chief justice. See Supreme Court (Number of Judges) Act, 1956, as amended in 2009. At the time of writing this chapter (July 2018), there were 23 judges. On 16 July 2018 the collegium reiterated its recommendation to appoint Justice K.M. Joseph and also recommended the names of Justice Vineet Saran and Justice Indira Banerjee for appointment. See 'Collegium Resolution Reiterating Recommendation to Appoint Justice K. M. Joseph', available at https://www.supremecourtofindia.nic.in/pdf/collegium/16072018_reconsideration_KMJoseph.pdf (accessed 25 July 2018) and Collegium Resolution Appointing Justice Vineet

even more disturbing.[143] The sticking points appear to be fig leaves masking a power struggle over the reins of the determinative power to appoint judges. With both sides having taken entrenched positions, short of a degree of statesmanship being displayed by all stakeholders to find a way out of the impasse, no resolution appears in sight.

### *2D.2.b Chelameswar and the Crusade for Transparency*[144]

The grim outlook for appointments to the higher judiciary described above is exacerbated by the sharp division within the judiciary, and the legal fraternity on the whole, on the principled stand for transparency adopted by Justice Chelameswar as a member of the judicial collegium. Subsequent to the *NJAC Case*, with negotiations with the government on the memorandum of procedure seemingly stalled, Justice Chelameswar decided to not attend collegium meetings, communicating his views in writing. According to news reports, the reason for his non-participation was the 'opaque' and 'non-transparent' method of functioning of the collegium.[145] He reiterated these grievances in a letter to Chief Justice Khehar stating that no established procedure governs collegium meetings, an agenda is often not circulated and sometimes 'discussions across the coffee table' are treated as collegium meetings.[146] Further, puisne judges are treated by chief justices as 'supplicants'.[147] The import of his charges was clear—

Saran and Justice Indira Banerjee, available at, https://www.supremecourtofindia.nic.in/pdf/collegium/16072018_SC_Apptt_fresh_2.pdf (accessed 25 July 2018).

143 Data released by the Ministry of Law and Justice indicates large vacancies in High Courts such as Allahabad (67), Calcutta (35) and Karnataka (32), available at http://doj.gov.in/appointment-of-judges/vacancy-positions2018 (accessed 24 July 2018) (hereinafter 'Judicial Vacancies [2018]').

144 Portions of this section have been extracted from Sengupta, 'Unsolicited Response.'

145 *Times of India*, 'CJI Hopes to "Sort Out" Issues Raised by SC Judge on Collegium's Functioning,' 3 September 2016, available at https://timesofindia.indiatimes.com/india/CJI-hopes-to-sort-out-issues-raised-by-SC-judge-on-collegiums-functioning/articleshow/53995340.cms (accessed 24 July 2018); Bhadra Sinha, 'Revolt in SC Collegium: Senior Judge Boycotts Meet Over Lack of Transparency,' *Hindustan Times*, 3 September 2016, available at https://www.hindustantimes.com/india-news/revolt-in-sc-collegium-senior-judge-boycotts-meet-over-lack-of-transparency/story-g9MofXzIxCuHeRv1Q72VHI.html (accessed 24 July 2018).

146 Dhananjay Mahapatra, 'Collegium Meetings Follow No Principles of Law, Says SC Judge,' *Times of India*, 28 August 2017, available at https://timesofindia.indiatimes.com/india/collegium-meetings-follow-no-principles-of-law-says-sc-judge/articleshow/60250720.cms (accessed 24 July 2018).

147 Ibid.

the collegium functioned as an old boys' club with favourite candidates being chosen sans procedure, criteria or semblance of the rule of law being followed. Scarcely has there been such a damning indictment of the functioning of the collegium since Justice Pal's description of the collegium as 'possibly the best kept secret in the country'.[148]

Despite the gravity of the charges, noted members of the legal fraternity questioned Justice Chelameswar's actions.[149] Particularly, Fali Nariman, the grand doyen of the Bar, was trenchant in his criticism that any public expression of dissent by a judge would erode independence of the judiciary as 'governments would simply rejoice and even attempt to step in'. [150] He advised Justice Chelameswar to 'quit and then complain about why he quit'.[151] The citadel, in his view, 'never falls, except from within'.[152]

This criticism, by focusing entirely on the form of the action taken by Justice Chelameswar, while remaining silent on its substance, misses the wood for the trees. On the question of form, to argue that any dissent within the ranks of the judiciary, notwithstanding its content, would affect the independence of the judiciary is a simplistic conclusion. It is a platitude that governments in power rejoice when there is dissension amongst members of the higher judiciary. This can be extended further—governments in power may always be on the lookout for opportunities to weaken the judiciary, be it creating internal dissensions, magnifying instances of judicial impropriety, or dangling the carrot of post-retirement appointments or the stick of impeachment. If fear of governmental interference is the bellwether for determining the rightness of actions relating to the judiciary, then the righteous battle fought by Nariman and senior members

[148] Justice Ruma Pal, 'An Independent Judiciary,' 5th V.M. Tarkunde Memorial Lecture (New Delhi), 2011, available at https://docslide.us/documents/5th-vm-tarkunde-memorial-lecture-2011.html (accessed 24 July 2018).

[149] Soli Sorabjee, 'Clear Collegium Mess to Maintain Public Image of the Judiciary,' *New Indian Express*, 25 September 2016, available at http://www.newindianexpress.com/opinions/columns/soli-j-sorabjee/2016/sep/25/Clear-collegium-mess-to-maintain-public-image-of-the-judiciary-1522741.html (accessed 24 July 2018). Several other questions regarding the personal motivations of Justice Chelameswar have also been raised as a matter of speculation; Dhananjay Mahapatra, 'Justice Chelameswar Lit the Fire and Burnt His Fingers,' *Times of India*, 23 June 2018, available at https://timesofindia.indiatimes.com/india/justice-chelameswar-lit-the-fire-and-burnt-his-fingers/articleshow/64705278.cms (accessed 24 July 2018).

[150] Nariman, 'My Unsolicited Suggestion.'

[151] Ibid.

[152] Ibid.

of the Bar in petitioning the collegium to reconsider its decision to appoint Justice P. D. Dinakaran to the Supreme Court despite a severely blemished record must rank very high on the list of actions that have played right into the hands of the government.

One might even argue that an unhealthy fixation with norms of judicial rectitude to the exclusion of substantive norms of propriety and legality has facilitated the functioning of the collegium in a rule-free environment. The revelations made by Justice Chelameswar, and earlier by Justice Pal, buttressed by publicly available information pertaining to the proposed appointment of Justice Dinakaran, suggest that many skeletons have remained in the collegium's closet, protected by the need to preserve judicial rectitude. Unfortunately, the continued silence of members of the judicial and legal fraternity has had the side effect of stultifying meaningful reform of a poorly functioning system. The citadel, to use Nariman's words, appears to have already crumbled from within—the choice is whether to remain oblivious to this reality or accept it in order to reform it.

As a matter of substance, even the most dogmatic defender of judicial independence may not be in a position to make a decent argument that the concerns raised by Justice Chelameswar do not require to be addressed urgently. Judges of the Supreme Court and High Courts wield massive powers over the lives of ordinary Indians. The least that citizens deserve is to know how such judges are selected—that there are clearly established criteria, that records are maintained with views of those who participated at selection meetings and that names were not selected on a whim. Transparency is the first step towards demonstrating that decisions are based on reason and not caprice.

It appears to be a consequence of Justice Chelameswar's principled stance that the collegium today publishes the names of the persons recommended for judgeship together with their brief comments on whether the candidate was found suitable. [153] Further, no candidate for judgeship to a High Court is confirmed without an interaction with the collegium of the Supreme Court. These are improvements for which the Supreme Court collegium led by the chief justice of India should be commended. Though necessary, they are, however, not sufficient in introducing the requisite degree of transparency into the functioning of the collegium.

[153] Justice Chelameswar also returned to collegium meetings, possibly once these changes were agreed to; Krishnadas Rajagopal, 'Now, SC Collegium to Make Judge's Appointments Transparent,' *The Hindu*, 6 October 2017, https://www.thehindu.com/news/national/sc-collegium-to-make-its-recommendations-public/article19807802.ece (accessed 24 July 2018).

### 2D.2.c The Long-Winded Appointment Saga of Justice K. M. Joseph

Despite reforms such as those described above, there are still no published qualitative criteria for appointment of judges to the Supreme Court and High Courts. This lacuna is responsible for the unseemly recent controversy that has erupted between the government and the judiciary (particularly Justice Chelameswar) regarding the proposed appointment of Justice K. M. Joseph to the Supreme Court. Justice Joseph, the chief justice of Uttarakhand High Court, was recommended by the Supreme Court collegium for elevation to the Supreme Court on 10 January 2018 along with Indu Malhotra, a senior advocate. The resolution recommending his appointment stated that seniority, merit and integrity were taken into account, and despite the fact that he was the 45th most senior High Court judge (including chief justices), he was found to be 'more deserving and suitable in all respects than other chief justices and senior puisne judges of High Courts.'[154] The Government of India, after three months, notified the appointment of Indu Malhotra alone.[155] Simultaneously, it wrote back to the collegium asking it to reconsider the recommendation of Justice Joseph.[156] The reasons advanced by the government supporting such reconsideration were (*a*) seniority: there were eleven High Court chief justices senior to him who ought to have been considered first, (*b*) regional over-representation: Kerala High Court, to which Justice Joseph belonged, already had representation in the Supreme Court whereas nine other High Courts had no representation and (*c*) diversity: no Scheduled Caste/ Scheduled Tribe judge was part of the Supreme Court, a factor that ought to be taken into account by the collegium.

The Government of India's decision to ask the collegium to reconsider the recommendation of Justice Joseph was a course of action that was envisaged by the *SCAORA*. Pertinently, the judgment allowed the government to put forward

[154] Resolution appointing Justice K. M. Joseph and Indu Malhotra to the Supreme Court of India, 10 January 2018, available at https://www.supremecourtofindia.nic.in/pdf/collegium/j_apptt_supreme_court.pdf (accessed 24 July 2018).

[155] Notification appointing Indu Malhotra, available at http://doj.gov.in/sites/default/files/Orders%20of%20appointment%20of%20Ms.%20Indu%20Malhotra%20to%20be%20Judge%20of%20the%20SCI%20%2826.04.2018%29.pdf (accessed 24 July 2018).

[156] Ananthakrishnan G. and Sushant Singh, 'Govt Snubs Supreme Court: All Eyes on chief justice Dipak Misra as Centre Asks Collegium to Reconsider Justice KM Joseph's Name,' *Indian Express*, 27 April 2018, available at https://indianexpress.com/article/india/govt-rejects-joseph-supreme-court-judge-all-eyes-on-chief-dipak-misra-5153173/ (accessed 24 July 2018).

'good reasons' suggesting unsuitability of the recommended candidate, which would allow the collegium to reconsider their earlier view if satisfied, or reiterate it, if not.[157] Examples of such reasons provided in the *SCAORA* include reasons of unsuitability recorded by judges other than the chief justice of India in the collegium or the chief justice of the High Court relating to character, conduct, health or fitness to hold office.[158]

The possibility of the collegium reconsidering an appointment when good reasons are supplied by the government is based on the premise that there is a normative consensus on relevant reasons for appointment and non-appointment of a candidate. This is, however, not true, as a matter of fact. While certain reasons are unarguably relevant, such as verifiable claims of lack of integrity and poor health preventing due fulfilment of office, others such as particular understandings of diversity, a specific conception of regional representation and a strict adherence to seniority are norms on which there is no clearly articulated consensus. Diversity of caste and region (and religion) have often been suggested as unwritten criteria for appointment.[159] While an extensive analysis of the socio-economic backgrounds of judges cannot be delved into here, it would suffice to say for our purpose that their use has often been strategic rather than principled.[160]

The reasons supplied by the government in asking the collegium to reconsider Justice Joseph's appointment, in the absence of any principle except past practice as a barometer, appear similarly strategic. Seniority has never been a strict criterion for appointment of judges to the Supreme Court—several judges on the Supreme Court today were appointed after ignoring their senior brethren;[161] the lack of Scheduled Caste and Scheduled Tribe representation is equally true of all appointments made since 2010 when the last judge belonging to the Scheduled

[157] *SCAORA*, para 7, Conclusions (Justice Verma).

[158] *SCAORA*, para 8, Conclusions (Justice Verma).

[159] Abhinav Chandrachud, *The Informal Constitution* (New Delhi: Oxford University Press, 2011), 263–64.

[160] Gadbois, *Judges of the Supreme Court of India*, 8–9.

[161] For an illustrative example, sitting Justices Shantanagoudar and Nazeer were appointed to the Supreme Court despite Justices Chellur and Ramesh being senior to both of them and Justice Chellur alone senior to the former. See Krishnaprasad, 'In Elevation to SC, Two HC Judges "Supersede" Seniors,' *The Hindu*, 16 February 2017, available at https://www.thehindu.com/news/national/karnataka/In-elevation-to-SC-two-HC-judges-%E2%80%98supersede%E2%80%99-seniors/article17314177.ece (accessed 25 July 2017). Several similar instances exist.

Castes demitted office; and regional representation is a fig leaf since there never has been any consensus on which High Court is entitled to how many places on the Supreme Court, if at all such quotas can be said to exist. Kerala High Court itself, from which Justice Joseph hails, has for long periods in the last decade had two representatives, one of the disqualifying factors advanced to support reconsideration in the present case.[162]

Unsurprisingly, the collegium did not find weight in these reasons and decided to reiterate its recommendation 'in-principle'. However, it did not actually reiterate it but deferred its decision till other suitable candidates were found, which would allow a combined recommendation to be made. This curious response of the collegium appeared to confirm the fact that the collegium was internally divided and the delay in reiteration might have been occasioned by Justice Chelameswar's impending retirement (he retired on 22 June 2018 and was replaced by Justice Sikri on the collegium).[163] Justice Joseph's name was finally reiterated by the new collegium on 16 July 2018 and he was appointed as a judge of the Supreme Court on 7 August 2018.[164]

## 2E Conclusion

In conclusion, debates around appointments to the higher judiciary in India have chiefly focused on devising and subsequently moulding a system that would best safeguard judicial independence. Understanding judicial independence to mean non-politicisation, the drafters formulated a system of appointment

[162] For instance, Justices Cyriac Joseph and K. G. Balakrishnan, both from the High Court of Kerala, served on the Supreme Court from 7 July 2008 to 27 January 2012 and 6 August 2000 to 12 May 2010 respectively, thus serving together for almost two years.

[163] Justice Chelameswar on his retirement described Justice Joseph as 'an outstanding judge' and that he had 'repeatedly ask(ed) for it (his appointment).' *Times of India*, 'Chelameswar Laments Non-elevations of Justice Joseph as SC Judge,' 22 June 2018, available at https://timesofindia.indiatimes.com/india/chelameswar-laments-non-elevation-of-justice-joseph-as-sc-judge/articleshow/64701991.cms (accessed 25 July 2018).

[164] Collegium Resolution Reiterating the Recommendation to Appoint Justice K. M. Joseph to the Supreme Court, 16 July 2018, available at https://www.supremecourtofindia.nic.in/pdf/collegium/16072018_reconsideration_KMJoseph.pdf (accessed 25 July 2018). For appointment, see notification dated 3 August 2018, available at http://doj.gov.in/sites/default/files/Orders%20of%20appointment%20of%20Justice%20K.M.%20Joseph%20as%20Judge%20of%20SCI%20%2803.08.2018%29.pdf (accessed 7 August 2018).

wherein a multiplicity of authorities and a coordinated balance between the political executive and the apolitical judiciary would perform this task. Excessive dominance of the executive, culminating in the proposal for a committed judiciary advanced during Mrs Gandhi's tenure as prime minister, necessitated a reconsideration of the original formulation. For two decades, the judges of the Supreme Court sought to fortify the existing provisions with additional safeguards to ensure that independence of the judiciary and consequently its public stature was maintained, resisting any creative reinterpretation of the Constitution. Ultimately, however, in 1993 (clarified in 1998), the court, stressing the need for multiplicity, to the exclusion of the inter-institutional aspect, arrogated the power of appointments to itself, believing that unelected and apolitical judges would best ensure the independence of the judiciary. Not only were these decisions textually unjustified and in breach of the constitutional design but also 25 years of practice had upset the faith that Justice Verma in penning the majority opinion had placed on his future brethren. The operation of the collegium system of appointments has brought forth a seeming emasculation of any effective form of judicial accountability and fostered a culture of opacity. As the Justice Dinakaran episode demonstrated, the collegium has little capacity to perform the focal task of selection of judicial personnel, a disability that is aggravated by its entirely opaque functioning closed to public consultation of any kind. The damage to the credibility of the higher judiciary that has been caused as a consequence has been immense.

These principled and practical deficiencies of the collegium system made the reform of the process of appointments a matter for urgent action. However, the reform undertaken by the union government in 2014—creating the NJAC to replace the collegium—was struck down by the Supreme Court as violating judicial independence and hence unconstitutional. The collegium system was restored with certain indicative suggestions for its reform. The judgment, as a matter of constitutional law, was deeply flawed. As a matter of providing a workable method for appointing judges, the judgment spawned an internecine conflict between the judiciary and government that has politicised the entire discourse around judicial appointments. Further, the continuing resistance to Justice Chelameswar and his vocal demands for transparency, both within the judiciary and outside, only buttress the salient and unfortunate truth that chances of genuine reform of the judicial appointments process to restore the exalted status of the judiciary in the public mind, particularly its independence, appear extremely remote at present. The warnings of the framers of the Constitution to keep the judiciary independent and preserve its innate dignity appear particularly prescient today.

# In-Tenure Questions

## *Mechanisms for Judicial Discipline*

# 3

Disciplining judges of the higher judiciary in India, the guardians of the country's Constitution, has always been an inconvenient exercise. As occupants of high judicial offices, charged with upholding the majesty of the law and the ends of justice, judges benefit from a public perception of infallibility, an other-worldly sense of virtue. Contributing significantly to this perception are the personnel who have held high judicial offices in India—men and women of supreme learning and erudition who have brought dignity to their offices by virtue of occupying them.[1] But as is inevitable with any human institution, cut through the wondrous accoutrements and over time its bare mortality begins to show. Judges, like other fallible human beings, require disciplining, for personal misconduct, corruption, bias and poor quality of work, among other things. At the same time, such disciplinary measures must be taken carefully, neither seeking to influence the decision-making independence of the judge or the judicial institution nor affecting the dignity and high status of the judicial office in public perception. Achieving such a balance is a difficult task, one that has caused much inconvenience to both the government of the day and the chief justices at the time, who have been vested with this responsibility.

When action is taken against an allegedly errant judge, generally it assumes one of three forms or a combination of them: first, an in-house punitive procedure conducted internally under the supervision of the chief justice of India usually on the receipt of a complaint; second, a transfer of a High Court judge from one High Court to another for actual or purported misconduct; third, if the matter is deemed serious enough to warrant removal of a judge, impeachment by parliament in accordance with Art. 124(4) for judges of the Supreme Court

[1] For an insightful biographical account of 83 judges of the Supreme Court from its inception in 1950 to 1989, see Gadbois, *Judges of the Supreme Court of India*; for a follow-up till the present day, see Chandrachud, *Informal Constitution*.

of India and Art. 124(4) read with Art. 218 for judges of the High Courts. This chapter will analyse the second and third of the aforesaid mechanisms for disciplinary action to assess whether on an overall analysis they are efficient and practically workable.[2] Such an analysis will highlight the questionable legal basis for the operation of judicial transfers[3] and the insufficiency of impeachment as a disciplinary mechanism besides demonstrating other strengths and weaknesses of extant mechanisms. In doing so it will point out the impact that transfers and impeachment have on judicial independence and accountability, thereby setting the foundation for a detailed enquiry into possible avenues for reform in Part III of the book.

## 3A Transfers

The power to transfer a judge from one High Court to another is, according to Art. 222 of the Constitution, vested in the president of India, who has to act in consultation with the chief justice of India in exercising such power.[4] In the Constituent Assembly, the power to transfer High Court judges was initially deemed insufficiently significant to find place in the Draft Constitution. A proposed amendment to Art. 193 of the Draft Constitution seeking to expressly

[2] The first method, in-house disciplining, is excluded from this analysis because of insufficient information. Apart from the existence of such a procedure, which is disclosed in a public document, its processes and instances of use are not available publicly. Discussions with retired judges expected to be familiar with its working also yielded little to base an analysis on.

[3] Transfer of High Court chief justices has not been dealt with in this Chapter. This is because such transfers are ordinarily pursuant to a policy of having a judge who does not belong to that High Court as its Chief Justice, and rarely for disciplinary purposes. Certain instances of its use as a disciplinary mechanism have, however, been included where relevant.

[4] Art. 222 of the Constitution of India reads:

> 222. Transfer of a Judge from one High Court to another
>
> (1) The President may, after consultation with the Chief Justice of India, transfer a Judge from one High Court to any other High Court
>
> (2) When a Judge has been or is so transferred, he shall, during the period he serves, after the commencement of the Constitution (Fifteenth Amendment) Act, 1963, as a Judge of the other High Court, be entitled to receive in addition to his salary such compensatory allowance as may be determined by Parliament by law and, until so determined, such compensatory allowance as the President may by order fix.

include a provision for the transfer of High Court judges was summarily rejected by the constitutional adviser.[5] This was the only known reference to the power to transfer before the revised version of the Draft Constitution was circulated to the members on 3 November 1949, which contained the new Art. 222.[6] Defending this inclusion, Ambedkar said in the assembly that such a provision was necessary to underline the fact that transfer of High Court judges was permissible and that they would be eligible for a compensatory allowance in the event of a transfer being ordered.[7] The transfer of judges was viewed as a device to promote convenience of the general administration, ostensibly similar to transfers of other government employees. No reported debate ensued subsequent to this provision being justified by Ambedkar on the floor of the assembly. This was possibly owing to its predominant conception as an internal administrative measure.

Two developments have, however, questioned the understanding of the drafters in this regard. First, in 1976, during the Emergency, the Indira Gandhi government ordered the mass transfer of 16 High Court judges, seemingly those who had handed down judgments unfavourable to the government. Second, in 1993, the focal power to transfer judges was itself transferred to a collegium of the chief justice of India and four seniormost judges of the Supreme Court by *SCAORA*. Whereas the former raises significant questions concerning decisional independence of judges from the executive government, the latter calls for both an allied analysis of the extent of safeguards necessary to protect decisional independence and scrutiny of the efficacy of transfers as possible internal accountability measures. It is these two points that this section enquires into,[8] through an analysis of the seminal judicial decisions and accompanying political

5 Shiva Rao et al., *Framing of India's Constitution*, vol. IV, 165.

6 Ibid., 826; see also the justification as proposed by the Drafting Committee in the Letter by the Drafting Committee to the President of the Constituent Assembly accompanying this draft on 3 November 1949; Shiva Rao et al., *Framing of India's Constitution*, vol. IV, 748.

7 Per B. R. Ambedkar, CAD, vol. XI (November 1949), 580.

8 This does not mean that these are the only significant questions concerning the power to transfer judges. Transfers, *per se*, involve several questions of policy, especially concerning the wisdom of having transferred chief justices in all High Courts on various policy grounds and the policy of having one-third judges in each High Court from outside the state. For more, see V. D. Tulzapurkar, 'Our Judicial System' in *Selection and Appointment of Supreme Court Judges: A Case Study*, ed. Rajeev Dhavan and Alice Jacob (Mumbai: NM Tripathi Pvt Ltd., 1978), 93.

developments that have made transfers a central feature of any discussion on judicial independence and accountability in India today, contrary to the understanding prevalent in the Constituent Assembly.

### *3A.1 Sankalchand, Seervai and Executive-Led Transfers*

Until the tenure of Indira Gandhi's Emergency government, the connection between transfers and judicial independence was remote. This was because over 25 years, there were only 25 times that this power had actually been exercised.[9] In addition, these transfers were invariably initiated by the chief justice of India, to ensure the smooth administration of justice.[10] Though at the time, some of these transfers were controversial as the concerned judges felt that the orders were punitive,[11] there were never any reported grievances that the transfers affected their independence or that of the judiciary on the whole. The fact that the chief justice of India, rather than the executive government, was focally responsible for exercising the power of transfer contributed significantly to this impression.

In 1976, however, the Indira Gandhi government in an unprecedented move ordered the mass transfer of 16 High Court judges.[12] The judges were chosen, from informed opinions at the time, on account of them having rendered decisions unfavourable to the government.[13] One of the judges, Justice Sankalchand Sheth of the Gujarat High Court, challenged his order of transfer to the Andhra Pradesh High Court as unconstitutional, impleading both the Union of India and the chief justice of India, Justice A. N. Ray, as respondents. The Gujarat High Court invalidated the transfer on the ground that 'consultation' as envisaged by Art. 222 had not been carried out with the

9 Exhibit No. 1 annexed to the affidavit filed by the Union of India in *Sankalchand*; see *Sankalchand*, para 115 (Justice Bhagwati); Seervai, *Constitutional Law of India*, 2701.

10 P. B. Gajendragadkar, *To the Best of My Memory* (Mumbai: Bharatiya Vidya Bhavan, 1983), 166–72.

11 For an illustrative example, see transfer of Justice P. C. Reddy from Hyderabad to Madras High Court; Gajendragadkar, *To the Best of My Memory*, 165–69.

12 According to accounts, a list of 56 judges had been prepared for transfer, and the transfer of 16 judges was its first tranche; Seervai, *Constitutional Law of India*, 2698.

13 Evidence of this can be seen in the judgment of Justice Untwalia in *Sankalchand*, para 134 where he writes:

> [T]he orders of transfers were made by and large in cases of Judges who had shown exemplary courage and independence even during the period of emergency in delivering judgments which were not to the liking of the men in authority, including the judgments in many MISA cases.

chief justice of India.[14] The matter was appealed to the Supreme Court, which gave a lengthy reasoned judgment in this case, despite the parties having arrived at an amicable settlement, according to the terms of which Justice Sheth would be re-transferred to the Gujarat High Court.

In *Sankalchand*,[15] the Supreme Court unanimously held that transfers under Art. 222 could only be ordered if they were in 'public interest'. Though 'public interest' was not defined expressly, certain characteristics are implicit in the judgment. Key amongst them, according to Justices Chandrachud, Bhagwati and Untwalia, was that transfers could not be punitive in nature.[16] To punish a judge, the constitutionally envisaged procedure was impeachment under Art. 218 read with Art. 124.[17] A transfer could not be used as a substitute or an *ad hoc* shortcut in case of judicial misbehaviour.

According to the judges, a key feature that ought to be protected while transferring judges was judicial independence, which was a 'cardinal feature' of India's constitutional scheme. Interpreting the scope and meaning of 'consultation' with the chief justice of India, the key judicial independence safeguard, the judges unanimously held that such consultation was mandatory; it would have to be full and effective, that is, based on full and identical facts which must constitute the basis for the final decision.[18] Further, the advice provided by the chief justice, which would take into account the views of the judge proposed to be transferred, would ordinarily be accepted; if rejected, it would have to be accompanied by a reasoned justification. All the judges were careful, however, to stress that consultation did not mean concurrence. Reflecting this, Justice Krishna Iyer in a nuanced understanding stated that the court must be careful in remaining independent of executive interference but at the same time accountable to the public at large.[19] Leaving the executive with the last word would, presumably in his opinion, achieve such a balance.

14 *Sankalchand* v. *Union of India*, (1976) 17 GLR 1017 (High Court of Gujarat, India).

15 *Sankalchand*.

16 *Sankalchand*, para 15 (Justice Chandrachud), para 48 (Justice Bhagwati), para 133 (Justice Untwalia).

17 *Sankalchand*, paras 15–16 (Justice Chandrachud).

18 In elucidating the meaning of the word 'consultation' they quoted with approval the view expressed by Justice Subba Rao in the case of *Pushpam* v. *State of Madras*, MANU/TN/0194/1953 (Madras High Court, India), wherein it was held: 'The word "consult" implies a conference of two or more persons or an impact of two or more minds in respect of a topic in order to enable them to evolve a correct, or at least, a satisfactory solution.'

19 *Sankalchand*, para 67 (Justice Krishna Iyer).

For three of the five judges, protection of judicial independence to this extent was sufficient. However, Justices Bhagwati and Untwalia dissented and read down transfers to further require prior consent of the concerned judges, thereby excluding compulsory transfers. This, they believed, was justified as only such an interpretation could protect judicial independence, a '[h]igh and noble purpose of the Constitution'.[20] Further, seeking consent of the judge sought to be transferred was, according to them, a convention that had been followed since the Constitution came into force up to the present transfer order,[21] and transforming this conventional safeguard into a judicially read-down constitutional safeguard would bolster judicial independence significantly.

The reading in of substantive safeguards while interpreting the word 'consultation' to protect judicial independence was a view unanimously held by the court and requires little further comment or analysis. Two other key points in the judgment, however, holding certain transfers to be impermissible owing to their characterisation as punitive and the issue of whether consent of the judge concerned ought to be a precondition to his/her transfer, merit deeper scrutiny. Justice Chandrachud's view that transfers cannot be used as a substitute for impeachment when there has been judicial misbehaviour is valid. This is because the drafters clearly envisaged a carefully constructed impeachment procedure as the only constitutional check on the functioning of judges, given their concern for judicial independence. Allowing transfers to act as a supplementary or alternative check is clearly antithetical to this constitutional scheme. Especially if such transfers are at the behest of the executive, they may directly impinge on judicial independence, held to be a cardinal feature of the Constitution. Even otherwise, the transfer of misbehaving judges from one High Court to another is bad in law since such a transfer cannot be in general public interest, a precondition laid down by the court in this case. This is because any definition of public interest must include the interest of the litigants in the transferee High Court.[22] No argument can plausibly be made that their interest will be served by having their disputes adjudicated by an allegedly misbehaving judge.

20 ibid., para 59 (Justice Bhagwati).

21 ibid., para 115 (Justice Bhagwati).

22 This argument was made by eminent senior advocate Fali S. Nariman in the context of the transfer of a judge who had allegedly misbehaved from the Gujarat High Court to the Sikkim High Court; see Fali S. Nariman, 'Unfair, a Slur on Sikkim if Judge Unfit for Gujarat is Sent There,' *Indian Express*, 9 February 2007, available at www.indianexpress.com/news/unfair-a-slur-on-sikkim-if-judge-unfit-for-gujarat-is-sent-there-says-nariman/22856/0 (accessed 8 January 2013).

However, characterising such impermissible transfers as 'punitive', while not inaccurate, is unhelpful. Though the mass transfer order was most certainly generally intended to punish the 16 judges, the mere description of such transfers as 'punitive' is silent on two key additional characteristics: Who is responsible for meting out such punishment? What is the specific intention behind such an order? In this case, the order was passed at the behest of the government against judges deciding matters against it. Crucial to its impermissibility is thus not just its punitive nature, which is retrospective in its conceptualisation, but equally its prospective potential in affecting decisional independence of the judiciary by the executive. Had the order been at the initiative of the chief justice of India and intended specifically to punish a judge for misbehaviour short of the degree that would attract impeachment, it may not be impermissible, as subsequent cases demonstrate.[23] Thus, introducing a test of whether a transfer is 'punitive' in order to determine its permissibility is unhelpful, an issue that we shall return to in greater length in the discussion on consensual transfers below.

Second, the reading down of transfers as 'consensual' by Justices Bhagwati and Untwalia in this case, and reiterated by Justice Bhagwati in *Gupta* and argued persuasively by Seervai[24] and Baxi,[25] besides others in their commentaries, was a worthy attempt at securing the end of judicial independence, albeit through questionable interpretative means. Since several commentators have advanced such arguments, for the sake of convenience, this section uses Seervai's arguments as a shorthand for referring to the entire gamut, given its comprehensiveness as well as the fact that such a view was originally advanced by Seervai as counsel for Justice Sheth in the Gujarat High Court.

Seervai's main justification for reading the power to transfer under Art. 222 as exercisable only with the consent of the judge concerned is that this interpretation best protects the independence of the judiciary. Though Seervai admits that the word 'transfer' connotes both consensual and non-consensual transfers, when two interpretations are possible, then that interpretation which best accords with the constitutional scheme should be adopted. If this means that in certain genuine cases the power to transfer will be rendered nugatory, then that will be the lesser of the two evils and consequently not as significant as the need to protect judicial independence, which according to him 'is the highest

23 *SCAORA*.

24 Seervai, *Constitutional Law of India*, 2698–706, 2788–810.

25 Upendra Baxi, *The Indian Supreme Court and Politics* (Lucknow: Eastern Book Co., 1980), 198–208.

public interest in the administration of justice'.[26] Seervai also points to consent of the judge being taken as a convention that had been established since the coming into force of the Constitution. Given the Indira Gandhi government's wanton breach of the established convention, he argues that consent should be recognised in law as implied by Art. 222 of the Constitution.

Requiring the consent of judges to their proposed transfer is a significant safeguard for judicial independence, based on the presumption that a judge would not consent to a punitive order, or one that sought to stifle his/her decisional independence or that of the judiciary on the whole. However, incorporating such a requirement as a matter of constitutional law is arguably contrary to the intention of the drafters, is based on a convention of questionable veracity, renders the power to transfer for genuine administrative reasons completely nugatory and wrongly conflates the notion of a punitive transfer and a non-consensual one.

In the Constituent Assembly, two statements by Ambedkar, representing the views of the Drafting Committee, demonstrate that the drafters had envisaged transfers to be compulsory and did not view consent of the judge as a precondition. First, Ambedkar affirmatively answered a question he put to himself as to whether an order transferring a High Court judge ought to be:

> [A]ccompanied by some kind of pecuniary allowance which would compensate him for the monetary loss that he might have to sustain by reason of the transfer?[27]

It is important to note that the additional allowance was not offered as an *incentive* to accept a transfer, which would have been the case had consent been a precondition. On the contrary, it was *compensatory*, which suggests that it was offered as a palliative to tide over the difficulty caused by a transfer that the judge may have been voluntarily unwilling to accept.

Second, the Drafting Committee felt that

> It was desirable to treat all the judges of the High Courts throughout India as forming one single cadre like the I.C.S. and that they should be liable to be transferred from one High Court to another.[28]

It is instructive that the Drafting Committee considered transfers of High Court judges as a liability of their office, analogous to those of Indian Civil Service (ICS)

26 Seervai, *Constitutional Law of India*, 2705.

27 Per B. R. Ambedkar, CAD, vol. XI (1949), 580.

28 Ibid.

officers. ICS officers were freely transferable throughout India and the question of their consent was irrelevant. Ambedkar envisaged judges to be treated similarly, though of course with the safeguards of consultation with the chief justice of India and convenience to the general administration as the only legitimate grounds for transfer. Thus, getting transferred was viewed as a liability attached to judicial office in the High Court. On this basis, it is clear that the Constituent Assembly, whose intent is significant for interpreting the Constitution,[29] did not consider consent of the judge as a precondition to him/her being transferred.[30]

Second, the existence of a convention requiring such consent that had existed up to the mass transfer of 16 judges impugned in *Sankalchand* is debatable. That over the last 25 years, 25 judges had been transferred with their consent was submitted by way of affidavit by the Union of India in the *Sankalchand* case.[31] Further, an assurance of the fact that up to 1963, for the transfers that took place, consent of the transferred judge was taken was given by Law Minister A. K. Sen on the floor of parliament.[32] However, subsequently, discerning the continuance of such a practice is difficult. Chief Justice Gajendragadkar, in his autobiography, describes two instances of seemingly non-consensual transfers recommended by him. In the case of the chief justice of the Andhra Pradesh High Court (not named, inferred that it is Justice Palagani Chandra Reddy), Gajendragadkar received complaints of a demonstrable lack of independence, including questionable administrative orders concerning transfer of subordinate judges being passed. After an informal enquiry verifying such allegations, Gajendragadkar proposed to transfer him as chief justice of the Madras High Court. Gajendragadkar writes:

> But the Chief Justice of Hyderabad was not willing to be transferred though constitutionally the Union Government could transfer him.[33]

Justice Reddy was indeed transferred to Madras and served the rest of his tenure as chief justice there.

Again, in relation to the seniormost puisne judge of the Patna High Court who was being considered for chief justice-ship (not named, inferred that it is Justice

29 *Fagu Shaw* v. *State of West Bengal*, AIR 1974 SC 613 (Supreme Court of India); Special Reference No. 1 of 2002, (2002) 8 SCC 237 (Supreme Court of India).

30 For additional arguments supporting this position, see *Gupta*, paras 902–06 (Justice Pathak).

31 *Sankalchand*, para 61 (Justice Bhagwati).

32 A. G. Noorani, 'Transfer of High Court Judges,' *Economic and Political Weekly* 15, no. 38 (1980): 1578.

33 Gajendragadkar, *To the Best of My Memory*, 165–69.

Khaleel Ahmed), Gajendragadkar found serious allegations of groupism against him and that most other judges were not on talking terms with him.[34] Consequently, he recommended his transfer as chief justice of Orissa High Court. Again, like in the previous case, he suggests that the judge in question was unwilling but after the constitutional process was complete, the transfer was ordered.[35]

Two points become salient from this account. First, Gajendragadkar as chief justice with the power to recommend transfers neither considered the constitutional position to require consent of the judge concerned nor did he recognise the existence of a convention in this regard. Second, though in neither of these cases is it available from the record whether the judges actually consented to the transfer prior to the order being issued, it is highly unlikely that they did so. This is the most plausible conclusion given their initial disinclination to the transfer, the conspicuous absence of any reference to their opinion having changed and Gajendragadkar's constitutional view of a transfer being a compulsory order. In light of this, existence of an unbroken convention requiring consent of the judge proposed to be transferred, on the basis of which it was sought to be incorporated into Art. 222, is questionable.

Further, Seervai's argument requiring consent as a precondition to transfer renders nugatory the power of transfer vested in the president of India. As Justice Desai points out in his opinion in *Gupta*, requiring consent of the judge transforms the power to transfer vested in the president under Art. 222 into a power to request the concerned judge for a transfer. This is of a fundamentally different nature and upholding such a construction would be tantamount to rewriting the Constitution.[36] Seervai's main argument in response to this is that the power of the president in this regard must be harmoniously construed with the right of a judge to resign under Art.217(1) proviso (a).[37] The only possible harmonious construction is to require the judge's consent prior to transfer since otherwise a judge by exercising his right to resign can extinguish the 'public interest' requirement essential for every transfer to be ordered by the president, based on the presumption that it would not be in the public interest for the judge, being upright and capable,

34 Ibid., 170.

35 A similar view, that transfers without consent are permissible under Article 222, has been expressed by Gajendragadkar's predecessor as chief justice of India, Justice B. P. Sinha; see Sinha, *Reminiscences and Reflections*, 91.

36 *Gupta*, paras 805–806 (Justice Desai).

37 Seervai, *Constitutional Law of India*, 2799–801.

to resign office. While this argument is layered, it would suffice to deal with it through the following counter-proposition: The right of the concerned judge to resign does not affect the power of the president to recommend his/her transfer *per se*. At the time the president orders the transfer, in Seervai's argument, the judge has not actually resigned (which would have made the order void *ab initio*) but has merely indicated his desire to do so. To suggest that the expression of such desire takes away the power of the president to transfer is flawed. Further, even if the judge does resign, he/she may make the operation of the transfer order meaningless but does not take the power to transfer away. This is because such resignation is not necessarily against the public interest. Just because a transfer must be in public interest does not mean that the fact that the transfer fails to happen, or that the judge sought to be transferred demits office, is against the public interest. It is merely an incident of the legitimate exercise of a constitutional power. While sufficient safeguards exist that would prevent such a situation from coming to pass, its principled (and hypothetical) possibility of occurrence does not mean that the power to transfer itself should be circumscribed.

Second, such a scenario is unlikely to unfold with regularity since the majority judgments in both *Sankalchand* and *Gupta* state that the judge sought to be transferred must be informed prior to the decision and his/her opinion sought. His/her opinion and the hardships that he/she would face are one of the factors that must be taken into account by the chief justice of India while being consulted by the president in this matter. Thus, in the plane of theory, which is where Seervai makes his argument, the possibility of an unwilling judge actually being transferred despite his/her views and resigning pursuant to the same is unlikely.

On this basis, Justice Desai's view that requiring prior consent renders the power of transfer nugatory remains valid. Further, it must be observed that while not reading in consent would not necessarily lead to judicial independence being impinged upon, owing to the safeguard of consultation that has been laid down, reading it in, as Seervai argues, would necessarily render the power to transfer nugatory *in every instance*. If a balance is to be achieved as Seervai argues, it must be primarily on the basis of probability of the interests sought to be protected being thwarted. In the former case, when consent is not read in, the possibility of judicial independence being affected is not a necessary consequence whereas in the latter case, where prior consent is mandatory, the power of transfer being rendered nugatory will necessarily happen in every case. On such a balance too, Seervai's argument is unpersuasive.

Finally, on the basis of the fact that the transfer of Justice Sheth caused him pain, damage and loss[38] and was intended to do so,[39] Seervai argues that a transfer of a judge without his/her consent is punitive. There is a key logical fallacy with this argument, pointing which out is without prejudice to my earlier argument that introducing the idea of a 'punitive transfer' is unhelpful. First, all non-consensual transfers are plainly not punitive. Gajendragadkar's example of the transfer of the chief justice of Andhra Pradesh High Court shows as to how a non-consensual transfer was certainly not intended to cause damage, pain or loss and was instead taken to ensure convenience of the general administration of the High Court. For not satisfying the intention limb of Seervai's test, such a non-consensual transfer ought not to be considered punitive. At the same time, were Seervai to argue, as he does elsewhere[40] that a non-consensual transfer is *per se* punitive because it causes damage, loss or pain to the concerned judge, then such damage, loss or pain was specifically sought to be nullified by the compensation to be provided under Art. 222(2). As a result, in the eyes of the law, such non-consensual transfers would not be punitive, even under Seervai's modified definition. Thus, while Seervai is right in identifying the intention to cause damage, loss or pain to the judges as the key rationale for the transfer order of the 16 judges (and the 40 others who had been identified), his move to conflate such intention with the lack of consent to the transfer is flawed.

In the final analysis, the majority in both *Sankalchand* and *Gupta*, while sticking closely to the text of the Constitution, created two doctrinal categories of 'punitive transfers' which were impermissible and the safeguard of 'public interest' which would have to be the ground for every transfer. The latter was nebulous in its content, whereas the former was unhelpful, apart from being nebulous as well. The minority, in accepting an argument that transfers would have to be based on the consent of judges, interpreted the Constitution in an indefensible manner. Overall, while the judgments may have been well-meaning in their intention to secure judicial independence, they were unsound in principle, as demonstrated, and resulted in a muddled jurisprudence in practice, as the subsequent section shows.

38 Ibid., 2801.
39 Ibid., 2803.
40 Ibid., 2805.

### 3A.2 *The Second and Third Judges' Cases and Collegium-Led Transfers*

The scope of safeguards to prevent abuse of the power to transfer judges under Art. 222 was the subject of renewed litigation in the Supreme Court in *SCAORA*, discussed earlier in the context of appointments. The decision in this case laying down the scope and meaning of Art. 222 was an extension of one of the key questions in this case, which involved a determination of whether the chief justice of India would have primacy in the matter of appointment of judges. Since both the provision on appointments and transfers were analogous insofar as the requirement of 'consultation with the Chief Justice of India' is concerned, several counsel and the majority of judges extended the ambit of the referred question to encompass the constitutional position regarding Art. 222 as well. From the judgments it is evident that the need to protect the independence of the judiciary in in-tenure matters and ensure consistency in the constitutional interpretation of Art. 217(1) and Art. 222(1) prompted such an interpretive exercise. Grave doubts, however, remain about the validity of such an exercise.[41]

The majority of the court speaking through Justice Verma held that in the matter of transfers, the opinion of the chief justice of India would be determinative.[42] This opinion would not be his/her personal opinion but that of a collegium of the chief justice and the four seniormost judges of the Supreme Court. In addition, any senior chief justice of a High Court, a Supreme Court judge whose opinion may be significant or any other person considered relevant by the chief justice and, in the case of judges other than the chief justices of a High Court, the chief justice of the High Court from which the transfer is taking place must be consulted. It would be deemed, since the recommendation to transfer has emanated from the high office of the chief justice of India, to not be punitive. Finally, the opinion of the judiciary being determinative in transfers 'eliminates' the need for further judicial review—accordingly, transfers would be entirely non-justiciable except regarding the sole question of whether the chief justice of India has been consulted or not.

41 Ibid., 2927–964.

42 Space precludes a discussion of the concurring judgments (Justice Kuldip Singh and Justice Ratnavel Pandian) and dissenting judgments (Justice Ahmadi and Justice Punchhi). For more, see Seervai, *Constitutional Law of India*, 2927–964.

These determinations were clarified in the cases of *Ashok Reddy* v. *Union of India*[43] (hereinafter '*Reddy*') and *Presidential Reference.*[44] In *Reddy*, the court held that *SCAORA* had not eliminated judicial review but merely circumscribed it to a narrow ambit on account of the prevalence of the judicial element in the decision to transfer in the first place. In *Presidential Reference*, the court held that in case of transfers, the collegium of the Supreme Court, comprising the chief justice of India and four seniormost judges, would have to consult the chief justices of the transferor and transferee High Courts apart from any Supreme Court judges who are in a position to provide relevant material before recommending a transfer to the president. All opinions would have to be expressed in writing and the response of the judge sought to be transferred must also be considered before the final decision is taken by the collegium. In addition, it clarified that no substantive ground concerning the reason for transfer could be the subject of review.

Analysing *SCAORA*, as supplemented by *Reddy* and *Presidential Reference*, it is evident that arrogation of the power of transfer by the Supreme Court, analogous to the power of appointment, was based on an impermissible reading of the Constitution. Reasons for this assertion are the same as the reasons provided in relation to Art. 124 in Chapter 2 and are not restated here.[45] However, in relation to transfers, the judgment in *SCAORA* not only underlines the primacy of the opinion of the chief justice and the collegium but also makes it determinative. The use of the term 'determinative' in contradistinction to 'primacy' suggests a sense of irrevocable finality that makes the decision completely immune to questioning, either by the executive or subsequently by way of judicial review. It is submitted that there is no warrant in the constitutional text to justify such a reading. Further, since the rationale for laying down the law in relation to the power to transfer judges lay in its analogy with the power to appoint judges, both requiring consultation with the chief justice of India, it is entirely flawed to suggest that 'consultation' in case of Art. 124 and Art. 217 has one meaning and in relation to Art. 222 has another, without added justification.

At the same time, not only is the decision of the chief justice of India to be considered determinative but it is also to be deemed non-punitive. Justifying this, the majority holds that there is no reason for any judge to consider his/

43 AIR 1994 SC 1207; MANU/SC/0400/1994 (Supreme Court of India) (hereinafter '*Ashok Reddy*').

44 *Presidential Reference.*

45 See Chapter 2, Section 2C.2.a.

her transfer 'punitive' when it is made pursuant to the determinative opinion of the chief justice of India.[46] Such a view bolsters the argument made in the previous sub-section of the usage of 'punitive' being unhelpful. What Justice Verma focally has in mind in both these cases is not a punitive transfer *per se* but a particular type of punitive transfer wherein the transfer is at the behest of the executive and is intended to affect the decisional independence of the judge. It does not consider other types of punitive transfers, especially transfers in lieu of impeachment. The greater concern is that in deeming such transfers to be non-punitive and consequently non-justiciable, the court is deeming black to be white.[47] While the court's belief that transfers made by the chief justice of India will be non-punitive may have been wishful and proved in due course to be incorrect, deeming such provision non-punitive is plainly illegitimate. The court, unlike the legislature, as Seervai argues, does not have the power to create a legal fiction.[48] This is because creation of such a fiction can never be justified by reasoned argument, something a judicial decision must always do. If this deeming is illegitimate, consequently the premise for considering the decision non-justiciable disappears. In any event, considering such a decision non-justiciable owing to the administrative decision to transfer being taken internally within the judiciary in the first place wrongly conflates the judiciary acting in an administrative capacity taking the decision to transfer and in a judicial capacity while exercising judicial review. There is a fundamental principled difference between the two situations, one that the court failed to grasp.

In the final analysis, the court justifies its decision in *SCAORA* on the basis of the need to protect the independence of the judiciary. There is no discussion on how the power to transfer was misused in order to affect judicial independence subsequent to the decision in *Gupta*, necessitating such an intervention. Even if such misuse is assumed, the court in taking away the power of the executive to transfer judges and arrogating it to itself, while circumscribing the possibility of checks and balances at the same time, crosses the line between seeking an independent judiciary and an insulated one. In insulating itself not only from executive interference but also eviscerating judicial review, it comes close to becoming the *imperium in imperio* that the drafters cautioned against.[49] At

46 *SCAORA*, para 62 (Justice Verma). This view is buttressed in *Ashok Reddy*, para 9 (Justice Verma).

47 Seervai, *Constitutional Law of India*, 2958.

48 Ibid.

49 CAD, vol. VIII (May–June 1949), 389.

the same time, it opens up the possibility of secretive transfers for unknown reasons, as some that took place subsequently, leading to the distinct impression of transfers being an internal disciplinary device meant to foster individual behavioural accountability, often rightly but sometimes otherwise.

## 3A.3 *Transfer as a Disciplinary Mechanism*

Pursuant to *SCAORA*, a new transfer policy was instituted by Chief Justice Venkatachaliah in consultation with the government.[50] According to this policy, there was a move to transfer judges, popularly termed 'uncle judges', who had kith and kin practising in the same court to other High Courts.[51] This was part of a move to ensure that one-third of the judges in every High Court hailed from other High Courts.[52] Over 60 transfers were made in the first year and several transfers purportedly continue to be made on this ground till date.[53] In all the transfers that are made, very brief reasons for the order are provided subsequent to a collegium resolution to this effect.[54]

The combination of a large number of transfers coupled with the lack of substantive reasons has meant that speculation concerning their rationale has been rife. In several instances, judges were transferred owing to alleged misconduct. The transfer of Justice Dinakaran as chief justice of the Karnataka

50 The original text of the policy could not be found by the author. In a discussion with Justice Venkatachaliah, it was suggested to the author that there was no official policy but a set of commonly agreed norms. For more, see Law Comm., 14th Report, 100.

51 Manoj Mitta, 'M.N. Venakatachaliah Takes Important Step to Restore Judicial Credibility,' *India Today*, 15 October 1993, available at https://www.indiatoday.in/magazine/nation/story/19931015-m-n-venkatachaliah-takes-important-step-to-restore-judicial-credibility-811668-1993-10-15 (accessed 25 July 2018).

52 Law Commission of India, *Reforms in the Judiciary—Some Suggestions*, 230th Report, Ministry of Law and Justice, Government of India, 2009, 9 (hereinafter 'Law Comm., 230th Report'); Maneesh Chibber, 'CJI Wants Future Judges to Clarify if Kin Practising in Court,' *Indian Express*, New Delhi, 11 November 2008, available at www.indianexpress.com/news/cji-wants-future-judges-to-clarify-if-kin-practising-in-court/383993/0 (accessed 8 January 2013).

53 Sodhi, *Other Side of Justice*, 86–87; Kiran Tare, 'Matter of Honour,' *India Today*, 12 November 2011, available at www.indiatoday.intoday.in/story/bombay-hc-nishita-mhatre-dileep-bhosale-transfer-of-judges/1/159602.html (accessed 8 January 2013).

54 Collegium Resolution, dated 3 October 2017, available at https://www.supremecourtofindia.nic.in/pdf/collegium/2017.10.03-Minutes-Transparency.pdf (accessed 25 July 2018). The reasons provided are in summary form, usually suggesting that the transfer is for 'the better administration of justice.'

High Court to Sikkim High Court, pursuant to allegations of impropriety and large-scale corruption in land holdings,[55] the transfer of Justice C. S. Karnan from Madras High Court to Calcutta High Court owing to conduct unbecoming of a judge in the Madras High Court[56] and the transfer of Justice B. K. Roy as the chief justice of the Punjab and Haryana High Court to the Gauhati High Court and subsequently to Sikkim High Court after a mass strike by judges of Punjab and Haryana owing to the chief justice's alleged factionalism and casteism and strong expressions of disaffection by judges in Gauhati[57] are examples. In other cases, transfer is to facilitate fair investigation into misconduct by allegedly tainted judges.[58] Since such cases of transfers are widely publicised, there is a general impression in the Bar that transfers commonly are a punitive device for misbehaving judges. So prevalent is this view that several judges subscribe to it as well, irrespective of the actual reasons that may underlie a transfer.[59]

There are three key concerns with transfers as they operate currently. First, the transfers in the last two decades that have been ordered in response to alleged improprieties by sitting judges, though they cannot be challenged, are in violation of the fundamental principles laid down by the Supreme Court. As was held in *Sankalchand*, transfers must be in 'public interest'. Such 'public interest' includes not only the interest of the public in the High Court from which the transfer is taking place but also the High Court to which the tainted judge is being transferred. It cannot be argued that the transfer of such a judge is in the public interest of the latter. This is especially so in cases such as that of

[55] See Chapter 2, Section 2C.

[56] Smita Chakraburtty, 'The Curious Case of Jusice Karnan,' *Economic and Political Weekly* 52, no. 18 (2017); D. Suresh Kumar, 'Justice Karnan's Judicial Journey,' *The Hindu*, 16 February 2016, available at https://www.thehindu.com/news/national/justice-karnan-vs-supreme-court-the-saga-of-a-defiant-judge/article18414667.ece#spl-article-14077424 (accessed 25 July 2016).

[57] J. Venkatesan, 'BK Roy Is Gauhati High Court Chief Justice,' *The Hindu*, 5 February 2005, available at www.hindu.com/2005/02/05/stories/2005020505881100.htm (accessed 8 January 2013)

[58] UNI, 'SC: Collegium Recommends Transfer of Judges Involved in GPF Scam,' *Indlaw*, 22 December 2008, available at www.indlaw.com/guest/DisplayNews.aspx?10A6D9D5-DEDA-4932-A5D6-8687E44E2AC1 (accessed 8 January 2013).

[59] See views of Justice Palshikar, former Judge of the Bombay High Court sought to be transferred to the Rajasthan High Court; Tare, 'Matter of Honour'; V. G. Palshikar, 'Transfer of Judges', All India Seminar on Judicial Reforms, New Delhi, 5 December 1998.

Justice Dinakaran, where the allegation was not one limited to his functioning as the chief justice in Karnataka but involved severe indictments to his moral character and respect for the law. Further, the inevitable transfer of such judges to the High Courts of Gauhati or Sikkim has led to these courts being considered 'dumping grounds' of the Indian higher judiciary.[60] Such an impression can never lead to securing the public confidence of the judiciary in the seven states of the Northeast (over which the writ of the Gauhati High Court extended till early 2013[61]) and Sikkim.

Second, the fact that substantive reasons for the transfer are not provided has meant that there is no scope for knowing, and consequently questioning, the justifiability of such transfers. A reasoned order is a fundamental principle of administrative law. Its non-application, by a collegium of judges themselves, in the case of transfer of their colleagues is gravely unsound. Further, the lack of reasons has meant that they have been substituted with wanton speculation and rumours, whose veracity is inherently questionable and severely damaging to the public reputation of the judiciary.[62] Responsibility for such an undesirable practice having developed must lie with the Supreme Court itself. Its decision in *SCAORA* rendering the grounds of transfer immune from judicial review provided future collegiums the warrant to dispense with the disclosure of reasons altogether. Though the resolution by the collegium on 3 October 2017 to provide reasons for transfer of judges is welcome, in practice thus far, there has only been one instance of transfer (of Justice Hrishikesh Roy from Gauhati

60 Kamaroopi, 'Punishment Postings: Centres and Peripheries,' *Economic and Political Weekly* 37, no. 49 (2002): 4877; *The Sentinel*, 'Junkyard for Judges,' Editorial, 3 December 2002, available at http://www.mail-archive.com/assam@pikespeak.uccs.edu/msg02480.html (accessed 8 January 2013).

61 Three new High Courts were announced by the Government of India in January 2013 pursuant to the passing of The North-Eastern Areas (Reorganisation) and Other Related Laws (Amendment) Act, 2012. They were established in the states of Meghalaya, Manipur and Tripura; J. Venkatesan, '3 New High Courts for NE,' *The Hindu*, 26 January 2013, available at www.thehindu.com/news/national/3-new-high-courts-for-ne/article4345372.ece (accessed 23 September 2013). Whether these new High Courts will also become 'dumping grounds' is an enquiry that is currently ahead of its time.

62 For an illustrative example, see the uncharacteristic outburst pertaining to his transfer from Delhi High Court to Madhya Pradesh High Court by a sitting judge Justice S. N. Aggarwal at his farewell speech. Ajmer Singh, 'MP HC Judge Says SC Judge Got Him Moved out of Delhi,' *Indian Express*, 25 August 2012, available at www.indianexpress.com/news/mp-hc-judge-says-sc-judge-got-him-moved-out-of-delhi/992931 (accessed 8 January 2013).

High Court to Kerala High Court) where the reason proffered has been 'in the interest of better administration of justice'.[63] It remains to be seen whether more detailed reasons will be provided in more complex cases of transfer.

## 3A.4 *Conclusion*

In the final analysis, as a consequence of vesting the focal power to transfer High Court judges in the collegium headed by the chief justice of India, the Supreme Court foreclosed further development of the law relating to substantive safeguards of grounds on the basis of which transfers could be carried out. While the safeguards laid down until the decision in *SCAORA*—namely the consultative process that would have to be followed and that transfers would have to be non-punitive and in public interest—were insufficient to guard against threats to judicial independence, dispensing with them altogether without a careful analysis of their shortcomings was unwise. Such an analysis would have revealed that the key threats to judicial independence came from transfers at the behest of the executive designed to interfere in the decision-making process. A doctrinal response to this would have been to build on the foundational understanding of 'public interest' and allow transfers only on certain explicated tenets of such an understanding, taking into account both the transferor and transferee High Courts. Concomitant with this ought to have been the requirement that substantive reasons for such transfer orders pursuant to the consultative process in Art. 222 be made public. The details of such an understanding together with the broad avenues for reform of the transfer system to incorporate the requirements of judicial independence and accountability will be dealt with subsequently towards the end of the book.

Aside from its positive impact on judicial independence and accountability, such an approach towards assessing the validity of transfers would have been an improvement over the system of closed, judiciary-led transfers laid down by the court in two ways. First, it would proceed on a defensible interpretation of the Constitution. Second, it would reiterate the fundamental proposition that transfers on account of judicial misbehaviour would not be permitted. This is because the transfer of any judge alleged to have misbehaved can never lead to bolstering public interest in the transferee High Court, even if it may be

[63] The collegium resolution reads: 'The Collegium Resolves to Recommend that Mr. Justice Hrishikesh Roy, Judge, Gauhati High Court, Be Transferred, in the Interest of Better Administration of Justice, to Kerala High Court.' Collegium Resolution, dated 10 January 2018, available at https://www.supremecourtofindia.nic.in/pdf/collegium/cj_apptt_gauhati.pdf (accessed 25 July 2018).

useful for the transferor court. Since the doctrine underscores the need for an assessment of both High Courts, transfers intended to punish for misbehaviour would be unconstitutional. Under the present law, such transfers are deemed non-punitive and hence valid. By limiting transfers to exclude its use against purportedly misbehaving judges, they can be restored as a mechanism for administrative convenience that is consonant with judicial independence, rather than a mechanism for judicial accountability that continually threatens it and is widely perceived as doing so.

## 3B Impeachment

Tackling judicial indiscipline through impeachment of the concerned judge, thereby removing him/her from office, did not form a significant subject for debate in the Constituent Assembly. There were two brief discussions—while debating the provisions of the report of the Union Constitution Committee and at the time when the final draft of the Constitution was approved.[64] In these discussions, two matters were essentially contested: first, the phraseology of the grounds on which impeachment would be justified; second, the procedure by which a judge would be removed. In both cases, the key determinant was to devise a framework that would best secure the independence of the judiciary and befit the high status of judicial office.

In the countries whose practices the Constituent Assembly surveyed, removal of a judge could only be on the grounds of misbehaviour/misconduct or incapacity/infirmity of body or mind.[65] Deriving from this, the Constituent Assembly, in its final formulation, posited that a judge of the Supreme Court or the High Court could be removed only on the ground of 'proved misbehaviour or incapacity'. The incorporation of the adjective 'proved' to qualify misbehaviour was a response to the comments in the assembly that the allegations against a judge should be enquired into judicially.[66] Though some members like M. Ananthasayanam Ayyangar vociferously advocated that this be done by a tribunal of judges or a similar independent body,[67] the majority deemed it appropriate to allow parliament to lay down the procedure by a statutory

64 The discussions took place on 29 July 1947 and 24 May 1949. See CAD, vol. IV (July 1947), 895 and CAD, vol. VIII (May–June 1949), 229, respectively.

65 CAD, vol. IV (July 1947), 895.

66 A. K. Ayyar, CAD, vol. IV (July 1947), 12, 889.

67 M. A. Ayyangar, CAD, vol. IV (July 1947), 895.

law.[68] This position, while underlining the political nature of the impeachment process, fettered the discretion of parliament to remove judges at will, requiring a procedure to be laid down for proving allegations against a judge, that is, an impeachment trial.[69]

With regard to the authority for removal, following the practice in England, the United States and large sections of the Commonwealth, the Constituent Assembly vested such power in parliament, which would recommend removal to the president through the presentation of an address. The possibility of extraneous political influences in parliament, which were pointed out as potential impediments to an appropriate removal procedure, was sought to be offset by the Drafting Committee introducing a further amendment requiring not just two-thirds of the members of each house, present and voting, to support the address for removal of the judge but also half the total membership of the house.[70] This made it clear that the address would have to be separately made and passed in both houses of parliament by a simple majority of the total members and a two-thirds majority amongst those present and voting.

In adopting such a provision, the Constituent Assembly placed a significant responsibility on the shoulders of future parliaments. This involved not just the responsibility to pass an appropriate law to regulate the impeachment trial, that is, the procedure for investigation of misbehaviour or incapacity, but also the faith that in acting as the constitutional authority with the power to recommend removal to the president, it would act in a fair, just and responsible manner. Regarding the former, parliament responded, after a significant time gap, in 1968 with the Judges (Inquiry) Act (hereinafter 'JIA').[71] The JIA provides for a three-

68 CAD, vol. IV (July 1947), 904.

69 Art. 124(4) of the Constitution uses a hybrid of removal methods, incorporating both address and impeachment. Address refers to the method used *inter alia* in Great Britain where a judge can be removed pursuant to resolutions with the requisite majorities in both Houses of parliament. Technically, the grounds on which such an address could be moved were untrammelled. Impeachment, on the other hand, requires a trial, and was adopted *inter alia* in the US Constitution, as an alternative to address since it would require proof that 'high crimes and misdemeanors' had indeed been committed. This book uses the term 'impeachment' for the procedure in India, as is the established practice in Indian secondary literature in this context. For the historical difference between the two terms, see Raoul Berger, *Impeachment: The Constitutional Problems* (Cambridge: Harvard University Press, 1974), 122–65.

70 CAD, vol. VIII (May–June 1949), 262.

71 For a brief summary of the procedure under the Act, see Law Commission of India, *The Judges (Inquiry) Bill, 2005,* 195th Report, Ministry of Law and Justice, Government of India, 2006, 3–4, 24–25 (hereinafter 'Law Comm., 195th Report').

member independent committee to be set up by the speaker of the Lok Sabha or chairman of the Rajya Sabha to investigate allegations, frame charges, hear the affected judge and set out its findings in its report. If it finds the judge guilty of misbehaviour or incapacitated, then the presiding officer of the concerned house has to pursue the motion leading to the presentation of an address, or else it lapses. Space precludes a discussion of the intricacies of the JIA.[72]

Regarding the latter, as is presently demonstrated, parliament has so far proved itself largely unworthy of the faith reposed in it by the Constituent Assembly. The subsequent sub-sections of this section, through an analysis of the only instance when an impeachment motion was actually voted on by parliament, as well as the instances where an impeachment motion could not be brought because of a lack of numbers in parliament, a rejection by the presiding officer or owing to resignation of the judge during the pendency of the proceeding, will demonstrate the wisdom, or otherwise, in setting up such a mechanism. Specifically, it will look at whether the process of impeachment has given teeth to the need for judicial accountability, while maintaining judicial independence at the same time.

### *3B.1 Impeachment Proceedings against Justice V. Ramaswami: A Case Study*

From the time the Constitution came into force, the impeachment proceeding against Justice V. Ramaswami remains the only instance when such a measure under Art. 124(4) of the Constitution was taken to its constitutionally mandated conclusion, having been put to vote on the floor of both houses of parliament. The abstention by the Congress Party on a whip being issued by its leadership that led to the motion being defeated in the Lok Sabha has been widely seen as highlighting the political machinations associated with an impeachment proceeding, thereby severely delegitimising its viability as an effective mechanism for judicial accountability.[73] While this inference warrants further scrutiny, to do so would require a holistic assessment of the impeachment proceeding itself. This must necessarily begin with the public demands for Justice Ramaswami's removal owing to his alleged financial improprieties coming to light, through the investigation and findings of the committee constituted under section 3(2) of the JIA and the judicial decisions handed down by the Supreme Court in this

72 Ibid.

73 Madhav Godbole, *The Judiciary and Governance in India* (New Delhi: Rupa & Co., 2009), 557; Chakravartty, 'Reflections on Impeachment Debate.'

context, culminating finally in the parliamentary debate and the impeachment motion being put to vote.

### 3B.1.a The First Phase

The allegations forming the core of the motion for impeaching Justice Ramaswami concerned his activities during his tenure as the chief justice of the Punjab and Haryana High Court between November 1987 and October 1989. In a report by the accountant general of Punjab and Haryana, several instances of financial irregularities in the purchase of carpets, furniture and other items, handpicking of suppliers for official High Court supplies without following due process and rampant misuse of official perks for personal benefit were found, which were carried out by, or at the behest of, Justice Ramaswami. In the face of mounting public pressure calling for impeachment,[74] the chief justice of India, Sabyasachi Mukharji, advised Justice Ramaswami to proceed on leave during the pendency of the investigation (Justice Ramaswami had, on 6 October 1989, been elevated to the Supreme Court).[75] Though he had no specific legal authority to order such action, the chief justice invoked his general duty to maintain judicial propriety as a justificatory rationale. Further, since impeachment proceedings had not commenced and the continuance of Justice Ramaswami in office would, in the opinion of the chief justice, lower public confidence in the judiciary, he set up an informal committee of three of his Supreme Court colleagues to enquire into these allegations and whether they 'rendered it embarrassing for him to function as a judge'.[76] This marked the first phase of the impeachment episode, taking place even prior to the notice for the impeachment having been tabled in parliament.

From the perspective of taking cognisance of judicial misconduct, Chief Justice Mukharji's intervention was commendable. Instead of waiting for parliament to make up its mind regarding the possibility of an impeachment motion allowing the reputation of the judiciary to be tarnished by the continuance of a tainted judge in the interim, the decisive action by him to publicly advise Justice Ramaswami to go

[74] S. Sahay, *Gone at Last? The Story of V Ramaswami's Impeachment* (New Delhi: Har Anand Publications, 1993).

[75] 'Chief Justice of India's Statement to the Bar of the Supreme Court,' 20 July 1990, available at www.indiancorruptjudges.com/Plot4Plot/008_00.htm#sawant (accessed 19 December 2012). This fact is also mentioned in the decision of the Supreme Court in *Sub-Committee on Judicial Accountability* v. *Union of India*, (1991), 4 SCC 699 (Supreme Court of India) (hereinafter '*SCOJA*').

[76] Sahay, *Gone at Last?* 114–17.

on leave and set up an in-house committee to ascertain the gravity of allegations provided a major fillip for the possibility of a speedy and effective mechanism for judicial accountability for misconduct. In doing so, the chief justice introduced an element of internal accountability for misconduct, distinct from the constitutionally mandated impeachment process that viewed judges as accountable to the political organs of state. This held great potential especially in situations when impeachment could not be resorted to owing to diverse parliamentary delays.[77]

However, the informal nature of the enquiry, an unavoidable necessity given the paucity of time, the lack of express statutory authorisation, and its nebulous objectives meant that the effectiveness of such an accountability device was severely questionable. Faced with an uncertain question, on a delicate matter, involving a recalcitrant colleague who refused to cooperate, the internal committee equivocated in its replies. It suggested that a decision to ask the judge to go on leave would be justified only if the 'appropriate authorities established facts from which an inference of moral turpitude became inescapable' and refused to recommend such an action itself.[78] As a result, Justice Ramaswami returned to work shortly thereafter and doubts continued to linger about effective interim measures to hold purportedly misbehaving judges accountable. While this view does not suggest that a mechanism would be effective only if it led to the final finding of guilt, the fact that the enquiry was not *ex ante* geared towards any such determination, without the mandate or the powers to enforce sanctions, severely affected its effectiveness. This primarily pointed to the need for legally mandated and internally enforced disciplinary measures short of impeachment for serious allegations of judicial misconduct being authorised, either prior to or during the pendency of an impeachment proceeding.

### *3B.1.b The Second Phase*

The dissatisfaction generated by the internal report spurred the Supreme Court Bar Association and senior lawyers into action. The association proposed a resolution to impeach Justice Ramaswami and threatened to boycott his court.[79] Shanti Bhushan, senior advocate and former union law minister, recounts in his memoirs how he took a draft impeachment motion to the Left parties and the

[77] For an insightful critical analysis of the procedure followed by Chief Justice Mukharji, see Rajeev Dhavan, 'Removing Judges: The Quest for Fair Solutions,' *The Indian Advocate* XXIII (1991): 42, 45–47.

[78] Vijaywargiya, 'No Allocation of Judicial Work,' 166.

[79] Ibid.

Bharatiya Janata Party.[80] One hundred and eight Lok Sabha members signed the motion and a committee comprising Justice Sawant (judge, Supreme Court of India), Justice Desai (chief justice, Bombay High Court) and Justice Chinnappa Reddy (retired judge, Supreme Court of India, as a distinguished jurist) was set up by the speaker.[81] This marked the beginning of the second phase of the impeachment episode.

The striking feature of this second phase of the impeachment proceeding was the hostile attitude taken by Justice Ramaswami to the proceedings against him with the seeming support of the government at the time. The judge refused to participate in the proceedings himself and questioned its jurisdiction on several occasions.[82] At the same time, at the stage when the enquiry committee was constituted, during its pendency and when its report was ready for submission to the speaker, supporters of the judge as well as the government attempted to drop proceedings, failing which they tried to protract it by taking frequent recourse to the Supreme Court. While it was entirely legitimate to seek judicial review since this was the first impeachment under the Constitution and grounds for review were thus an open question, the regularity with which such recourse was taken and the stance adopted by the judge himself, petitioning the court seemingly by proxy, brought into question both the efficiency and effectiveness of the impeachment process.

Immediately after the Enquiry Committee was constituted by the speaker, the Lok Sabha was dissolved. The government took the view that the motion for impeachment lapsed as a result of the dissolution of the house. Hence, in principle, it refused to facilitate Justice Sawant and Justice Desai's functioning as committee members, while continuing to be sitting judges. The matter was brought to court by the Supreme Court Bar Association as well as a group of advocates.[83] In this case, in which Justice Ramaswami himself was impleaded as a respondent, the court was called upon to decide not only whether the impeachment motion lapsed on dissolution of the Lok Sabha but

80 Shanti Bhushan, *Courting Destiny: A Memoir* (New Delhi: Penguin, 2008), 213.

81 *Lok Sabha Debates*, 12 March 1991, Col. 115–118 (Parliament Secretariat).

82 Report of the Committee appointed under the Judges (Inquiry) Act, 1968 (Presided by Justice P. B. Sawant, Judge, Supreme Court of India) *vide* three letters from Justice Ramaswami, dated 21 January 1992, 24 January 1992, 2 February 1992: 'Supreme Court Judge Mr. Justice V. Ramaswamys Impeachment (removal) Story,' available at www.indiancorruptjudges.com/Plot4Plot/008_00.htm#sawant (accessed 19 December 2012) (hereinafter 'Sawant Committee').

83 *SCOJA*.

also more crucially on three fundamental questions concerning the nature of the impeachment process: First, whether and to what extent impeachment was a parliamentary process where judicial intervention was constitutionally barred; second, whether the purportedly offending judge had the right to be heard before the enquiry committee was constituted by the speaker; and third, whether the JIA, which had set up an extra parliamentary enquiry committee, was constitutional.[84]

The Supreme Court, by majority, held that impeachment was an amalgam of a political and judicial process.[85] While the focal power to impeach a judge belonged to parliament, the Constitution required allegations concerning judicial misbehaviour to be proved, before the address for removal was presented before the house. Accordingly, the JIA provided that the speaker of the Lok Sabha or the chairman of the Rajya Sabha could, when a motion is moved by 100 members in the Lok Sabha or 50 members in the Rajya Sabha, respectively, set up an enquiry committee to investigate the charges against the concerned judge with a view to determining whether the misbehaviour was indeed proved or not. The majority of the court held this phase of the proceedings to be statutory in character, therefore subject to judicial review. Once, however, the motion together with the report of the committee finding proof of such misbehaviour is tabled in the house, the process becomes an internal proceeding of parliament, not subject to judicial oversight according to Art. 122 of the Constitution.[86] This, however, does not imply that the judge has a right to be heard prior to the enquiry committee being constituted. Though rules of natural justice would apply during the enquiry, since the constitution of the enquiry committee was prior to the enquiry *per se* and was an action that did not prejudice the judge in any way, she would not have a right to be heard at this stage.

[84] For a case analysis, see Seervai, *Constitutional Law of India*, 2909–27.

[85] The minority view (Justice Sharma) considered the process to be parliamentary from the outset thereby ousting court jurisdiction.

[86] Art. 122 of the Constitution of India reads:

(1) The validity of any proceedings in Parliament shall not be called in question on the ground of any alleged irregularity of procedure

(2) No officer or member of Parliament in whom powers are vested by or under this Constitution for regulating procedure or the conduct of business, or for maintaining order, in Parliament shall be subject to the jurisdiction of any court in respect of the exercise by him of those powers.

At the same time, the investigative mechanism established by the JIA, involving two sitting judges, a Supreme Court judge or chief justice and a chief justice of one of the High Courts, and a distinguished jurist, to be selected by the speaker of the Lok Sabha or the chairman of the Rajya Sabha, was held to be entirely constitutional. Nowhere in the Constitution did the court find a mandate that the entire impeachment proceeding would have to be solely parliamentary. In fact, in the Constituent Assembly debates, matters of proof of misbehaviour were left by parliament to decide by appropriate law.[87] To suggest that by vesting parliament with such power, the intention was to fetter parliament's law-making power by not allowing the appointment of independent judges and jurists, whose judicial training would be instrumental in establishing proof of misbehaviour, was, according to the court, a misreading of the constitutional provision.

The decision of the court in allowing judicial review till the point the report of the Enquiry Committee together with the motion was placed in parliament, upholding the constitutionality of the JIA, attempted to achieve a fine balance between respecting the fundamentally political nature of the impeachment process in the Constitution and the need to ensure that the accused judge was not left without remedy against a blatant illegality. With the aid of a legal fiction that the speaker of the Lok Sabha/chairman of the Rajya Sabha, when first admitting the motion for impeachment and setting up a committee, acts in a statutory character and not in a parliamentary one, the court provided a sound legal underpinning for its decision vesting itself with the jurisdiction to exercise oversight. For the court to assume such jurisdiction was entirely justifiable, as without it, a purportedly errant judge would be left without any recourse, even if the provisions of the JIA were not complied with.

However, a key consequence of such a decision was to allow Justice Ramaswami and his supporters to take frequent recourse to the court during the pendency of the committee's work, thereby judicialising the process. Two more judicial review applications were filed before the Supreme Court in a short span of time by Krishna Swami, a long-time acquaintance of Justice Ramaswami, and Sarojini Ramaswami, his wife.[88] In *Krishna Swami* v. *Union of India*,[89] the

87 M. A. Ayyangar, CAD, vol. IV (July 1947), 899.

88 Another petition in public interest was filed by Lily Thomas after the vote on the impeachment motion in the Lok Sabha, calling for judicial intervention; see *Ms. Lily Thomas* v. *The Speaker*, Lok Sabha, (1993) 4 SCC 434 (Supreme Court of India).

89 1992 (4) SCC 605 (Supreme Court of India) (hereinafter '*Krishna Swami*').

petitioner prayed for a reconsideration of the judgment in *SCOJA*[90] insofar as its decision not to quash the order of the speaker in setting up the Enquiry Committee was concerned. It was claimed that the speaker had not applied his mind in making the decision. Further, it was also claimed that the proceedings of the enquiry committee were vitiated by irregularities. The Supreme Court dismissed the petition on the ground that the petitioners (Raj Kanwar, an advocate from Haryana, was another petitioner) did not have the *locus standi* to ask for reconsideration since they were not parties to the earlier decision. Further, despite several opportunities, they refused to implead Justice Ramaswami, who would be a necessary party should such reconsideration take place. On these preliminary grounds, the petition was found to not be maintainable.

In *Sarojini Ramasawmi* v. *Union of India*[91] (hereinafter '*Sarojini Ramaswami*'), the question before the court was whether the petitioner, the wife of Justice Ramaswami, who was acting on his behalf, would be able to get a copy of the report of the Enquiry Committee before it was sent to the speaker in order to file a judicial review application before the proceeding became internal to parliament, as per the decision in *SCOJA*. By majority, the court held that the petitioner would indeed receive a copy, but not for the purpose of filing a judicial review application but for putting up an effective defence in parliament. Judicial review would not be available at this stage because the committee was not a tribunal whose decisions are necessarily final. If the finding is one of guilty, then the said finding is recommendatory and inchoate, given the parliament has to take a final decision on that basis. If the finding on the other hand is not guilty, then the proceeding comes to an end, and no question of the judge filing a judicial review petition against it arises. However, judicial review would be available to the judge if the parliament, acting on the report of the committee, did present and pass an address in each house, pursuant to which the president passed an order removing her. In such a judicial review application, illegalities if any during the functioning of the Enquiry Committee could be raised as well.

This decision presents a legal conundrum. If the committee functions during the statutory stage of the impeachment process, then according to the decision in *SCOJA*, in principle, its report should be subject to judicial review. However, the court bars the possibility of judicial review at that stage on the ground that the decision of the committee is not final. This reasoning is suspect for two

[90] *SCOJA*.

[91] (1992) 4 SCC 506 (Supreme Court of India).

reasons. Insofar as the decision of the committee is to find the judge not guilty of misbehaviour or not suffering from incapacity, the decision is final according to section 6(1) of the JIA. This should make the decision reviewable. Again, the decision of the committee insofar as finding the judge guilty of misbehaviour is not recommendatory, as the judgment suggests. As the report of the Enquiry Committee in this instance and the report of the Enquiry Committee established to investigate charges of misbehaviour against Justice Soumitra Sen of the Calcutta High Court demonstrate,[92] the committee itself makes a final determination of guilt.[93] The decision is inchoate only in relation to the final decision by parliament to impeach or not. In and of itself, it is a final decision of a committee established by statute.

Instead of basing its decision on the finality of legal proceedings, which leads to a logical tangle, the court ought to have refused judicial review on the ground that once the report is ready and presented to the house by the presiding officer after receiving it from the committee, it is part of parliamentary proceedings and hence non-reviewable. Since a combined reading of sections 4 and 6 of the JIA suggests that the report is to be submitted to the presiding officer by the committee at the conclusion of its investigation in order to be dealt with according to section 6(1) or section 6(2) depending on its findings, there is no occasion when the aggrieved judge can receive it before parliamentary proceedings commence. This would have provided a sound, alternative ground for denying judicial review at this stage. Such a conclusion would also be practical, warranted by considerations of avoiding delay and protracting proceedings.

Further, the fact that the court hastened to add the availability of judicial review challenging the presidential order of removal at the conclusion of the impeachment proceeding is a platitude. Technically, given that the order of the president is after the parliamentary process is complete, there is no bar to

92 Rajya Sabha Secretariat, 'Motion for Removal of Mr. Justice Soumitra Sen, Judge, Calcutta High Court,' New Delhi, 2011, available at http://rajyasabha.nic.in/rsnew/Soumitra_Sen_Judge.pdf, 55 (accessed 9 September 2013) (hereinafter 'RS Secretariat Motion'); Report of the Inquiry Committee constituted under sub-section (2) of section 3 of the Judges Inquiry Act, 1968 (Presided by Justice B. Sudershan Reddy, Judge, Supreme Court of India).

93 The report of the Inquiry Committee (ibid) concluded:

> In view of the findings on Charge I and Charge II above, the Inquiry Committee is of the opinion that Justice Soumitra Sen of the Calcutta High Court is guilty of 'misbehaviour' under Article 124(4), read with proviso (b) to Article 217(1) of the Constitution of India.

judicially reviewing it. At the same time, the purpose of expressly reiterating the existence of such review is unclear. Given that the statutory part of the impeachment process is already reviewable and the parliamentary process is non-reviewable *per se* because parliament is not obliged to disclose its exact reasons for removing the judge, the remit of such review is arguably restricted to the report of the enquiry committee and any gross illegality therein. While this may be a theoretical possibility, if parliament has applied its mind to this question and notwithstanding decided to impeach the judge, the court should resist entertaining such applications. This is especially so in the light of the fact that impeachment, in genesis and operation, is fundamentally a political process. The rationale for such power being vested in the elected organs of state is to ensure that the highest judicial officers, accused of misbehaviour, are removed, if at all, in an open, transparent and publicly accountable fashion. Such openness and public accountability could be best ensured by vesting such power in parliament, a politically accountable and entirely transparent institution. Though the court's concern for maintaining the rule of law by preventing illegality is justifiable, an equal recognition of the special nature of the impeachment process and its political underpinnings would have been appropriate. To suggest that only the court can provide the final imprimatur on an impeachment proceeding when the Constitution suggests otherwise is unduly presumptuous.

An additional concern stemming from repeated judicial applications is the inefficiency it creates in the impeachment process. While in this case, such applications may be partially attributable to the fact that this was the first impeachment under the Constitution, it does at the same time make the proceedings excessively unwieldy and protracted. After all, from the time the initial notice for the constitution of the enquiry committee was issued in March 1991, to the final decision of the court in *Sarojini Ramaswamy* and *Krishna Swami*, both of which were handed down on the same day in August 1992, more than 17 months had elapsed. At the same time, Justice Ramaswami's conduct in seemingly pursuing these litigations by proxy during these months, not cooperating with the enquiry and threatening to divulge confidential judicial information, while still a serving judge of the Supreme Court, brought considerable disrepute to the judiciary.[94] While a purportedly errant judicial officer, no matter how uncooperative, must certainly enjoy due process, a system that allows her to repeatedly delay proceedings and take up a slew

94 Gobind Das, *The Supreme Court in Quest of Identity* ( Lucknow: Eastern Book Co., 2000, 2nd ed.), 284–99; Noorani, *Constitutional Questions and Citizens' Rights*, 21.

of specious defences shows both the judge and the process of impeachment in poor light. It also sets an unhealthy precedent. Following this case, the opportunities for judicial review were utilised by Justice Dinakaran, who faced impeachment proceedings subsequently, and approached the court on several occasions challenging diverse aspects of the constitution of the inquiry committee as well as its jurisdiction.[95] The overall result has been to render the impeachment process inefficient, giving rise to the inevitable impression that a clever constitutional judge could work a pliable system to her advantage without effective countervailing checks.

### *3B.1.c The Third Phase*

In the third phase of the impeachment episode, the Sawant Committee's report was tabled in parliament. The committee found Justice Ramaswami guilty of 11 of the 14 charges, including wilful and gross misuse of office, negligence in the discharge of duties and habitual extravagance at the cost of the public exchequer, all of which 'brought disrepute to the high judicial office'. A discussion of the exact nature of findings is unnecessary; it would suffice to say that the conclusion of misbehaviour being proved was straightforward.[96]

Following this, parliament was witness to a fiercely contested debate on the motion. When the motion was put to vote, despite overwhelming evidence pointing towards the guilt of Justice Ramaswami, members of the Congress Party abstained, pursuant to a whip issued by the party leadership. In great part due to such abstention, the motion was defeated. Justice Ramaswami was absolved of his misconduct and the first constitutional impeachment of a Supreme Court judge failed owing to extraneous considerations affecting the vote (or non-vote) of the members of parliament.[97]

Though the reasons for the abstention of the members of parliament belonging to the Congress Party may have been numerous, it is a fact that a whip was issued by the party leadership advising its members, several of whom wished to vote in favour of impeachment, to abstain.[98] The rationale for the whip

95 *Justice PD Dinakaran* v. *Hon'ble Judges Inquiry Committee*, W/P (Civil) No. 217 of 2011 (5 July 2011) (Supreme Court of India); *Justice PD Dinakaran* v. *Judges Inquiry Committee*, W/P (Civil) No. 218 of 2011 (26 August 2011) (Supreme Court of India).

96 Sawant Committee.

97 For a detailed account, see Chakravartty, 'Reflections on Impeachment Debate.'

98 *Times of India*, 'On a Suicidal Path,' 13 May 1993; Bhushan, *Courting Destiny*, 217.

has been the subject of much speculation with suggestions of caste, region and personal equations of Justice Ramaswami with individual politicians having been cited as relevant factors.[99] Irrespective of the actual reason(s), the conclusion that considerations extraneous to the determination of misbehaviour influenced the decision is inescapable. Such an eventuality is a plausible incident of any form of political accountability, since a range of factors, strictly not relevant for the determination of the narrow question of misbehaviour, may become relevant on account of political considerations. Though plausible in theory, the Constituent Assembly, in drafting this provision, could scarcely have imagined that such an eventuality would actually occur. So great was their belief in the integrity of judges and the uprightness of parliamentarians that thoughts of its misuse or wrongful use were never considered. But the uniformly unimpeachable integrity of its judges and the moral uprightness of its parliamentarians had dissipated substantially since the time of independence, a change that the legal position on impeachment had clearly failed to keep pace with.

In the USA, the first constitutional impeachment proceeding of Justice Chase had resulted in a defeated motion that epitomised the salutary principle that no judge would be impeached because of the substance of a decision that was rendered, no matter how biased they may have been. That was a result engineered by a shrewd political compromise between the Federalists and a section of anti-Jeffersonian Republicans in the Senate.[100] In India, the politics that led to the defeat of the motion to impeach Justice Ramaswami was perverse—it became a symbol of brazen immunity of judges from punishment, a precedent that the impeachment procedure could be wrecked by deft politicking.

### *3B.2 Lessons and Conclusion*

The overwhelmingly political nature of the impeachment process manifested itself again in relation to allegations of corruption against Justice Punchhi, at a time when he was the seniormost puisne judge in the Supreme Court. Despite several allegations of biased judgments and repeated abuse of official position,[101] the requisite number of signatures to move an impeachment motion could not be garnered. Though the reasons for this may be numerous, a key reason was

[99] *Times of India*, '70 Cong. MPs Were in Favour of Motion,' 13 May 1993.

[100] William H. Rehnquist, *Grand Inquests: The Historic Impeachments of Justice Samuel Chase and President Andrew Johnson* (New York: William Morrow, 1992).

[101] V. Venkatesan, 'Judging the Judges,' *Frontline* 14, no. 20 (October 1997), available at www.frontlineonnet.com/fl1420/14200180.htm (accessed 19 December 2012).

the lack of political support from across party lines supporting such a motion, based arguably on considerations other than the purported allegations of misbehaviour.[102] Again, the lack of political support in favour of a judge led to the resignation of Justice Dinakaran, the chief justice of the Sikkim High Court, and Justice Soumitra Sen, judge of the Calcutta High Court. In the case of Justice Sen, the Enquiry Committee found him guilty of financial misappropriation at the time he was appointed receiver by the High Court and making false statements in this regard to the High Court.[103] Justice Sen, however, refused to resign and instead made an impassioned speech in parliament, claiming, much like Justice Ramaswami, that he was innocent of the charges and he was being made a scapegoat as several judges accused of significantly more egregious charges of corruption were not being investigated.[104] Despite this, and owing in part to an effective speech by Arun Jaitley, then leader of the opposition in the Rajya Sabha,[105] the house voted to impeach him. However, before the Lok Sabha could confirm such impeachment as required constitutionally, Justice Sen resigned, having failed to stitch together a political majority necessary to prevent such an eventuality. In the case of Justice Dinakaran, which was considered more fully in Chapter 2, the resignation came pursuant to the enquiry committee constituted under the JIA deciding to commence its enquiry, owing to strong public pressure.

Recently, an impeachment motion was moved against the chief justice of India, Dipak Misra, by 64 members of parliament in the Rajya Sabha. The charges related to alleged misbehaviour in a case relating to corruption in medical college admissions, a conflict of interest in continuing to deal with the same matter as chief justice on both the administrative and judicial sides, antedating a letter regarding mentioning of urgent matters before the chief justice of India, misusing his authority as master of the roster in sending sensitive matters to particular

[102] Bhushan, *Courting Destiny*, 218–24. A contrary view saw vested interests in the Supreme Court, specifically the Committee of Judicial Accountability, as responsible for the effort to prevent Justice Punchhi from becoming chief justice of India. For both points of view, see Janak Raj Jai (ed.), *Assault on Judiciary and the Role of Parliament* (New Delhi: Associated Legal Advisers, 1995).

[103] RS Secretariat Motion.

[104] Ashok Bagriya, 'Justice Sen Defends Himself in Parliament,' *IBN Live*, 17 August 2011, available at http://ibnlive.in.com/news/justice-sen-defends-himself-in-parliament/176427-37.html (accessed 4 June 2014).

[105] Ibid.

benches and acquiring land as an advocate on the basis of a false affidavit.[106] This was the first impeachment motion to be moved against a chief justice of India.

These charges were levelled in a particular political as well as judicial context. The immediate trigger for the impeachment motion appeared to be a judgment by a bench comprising the chief justice of India rejecting a petition demanding an independent investigation by the Central Bureau of Investigation (CBI) into the death of Judge Loya, a subordinate judge in Maharashtra, who died while hearing a politically sensitive criminal matter in which the party president of the Bharatiya Janata Party, Amit Shah, was an accused.[107] Despite several doubts being expressed about the manner of death and the request for an independent probe, the Supreme Court, in its judgment, found no reason to institute a fresh enquiry.[108] Though the merits of this judgment cannot be gone into here, it read like a trial court judgment without a trial having been conducted.

The judicial context was the shroud that hung over cases pertaining to the Prasad Education Trust and its petition for permission to admit students.[109] At a time when the cases were being heard by a bench headed by Chief Justice of India (CJI) Misra, the CBI arrested several persons, including a former judge of the Allahabad and Odisha High Courts, Justice Quddusi, for corruption. Certain taped conversations were also recovered.[110] A petition asking for an independent probe into the matter was moved before Justice Chelameswar, the seniormost puisne judge, since the matter appeared to implicate CJI Misra. The order by Justice Chelameswar's bench to list the matter before the five seniormost judges of the Supreme Court was quashed by a bench led by the CJI. In quashing

106 'Explanatory Note on the Motion for Impeachment of Mr. Justice Dipak Misra, Chief Justice of India,' available at https://barandbench.com/read-impeachment-motion-chief-justice-india-dipak-misra/ (accessed 25 July 2018).

107 *Tehseen Poonawalla* v. *Union of India*, (2018) 6 SCC 72 (Supreme Court of India) (hereinafter '*Poonawalla*').

108 Ibid., para 102.

109 Order dated 4 September 2017 in *Prasad Education Trust* v. *Union of India*, Writ Petition (Civil) No. 797/2017 (Supreme Court of India), available at https://www.supremecourtofindia.nic.in/supremecourt/2017/27428/27428_2017_Order_04-Sep-2017.pdf (accessed 23 July 2018) (hereinafter '*Prasad Education Trust*').

110 The High Court of Delhi, however, ordered the withdrawal of all reporting on the tapes and restrained the media from further reporting since the allegations in the tapes were yet to be proven. See Order dated 21 April 2018 in *Ishrat Masroor Qudussi* v. *Foundation for Independent Journalism*, CS No. 184/18 (High Court of Delhi), available at https://drive.google.com/file/d/1LG4bUII_cQU3bPK-KLL9L_jIDXg9WMf2/view (accessed 25 July 2018).

the order, the bench reiterated the principle that the CJI was the master of the roster and no matter (even if it pertained to himself plausibly) could be listed by any other judge of the court.[111] The fundamental legal principle of not being a judge in one's own cause appeared to be secondary to the pragmatic interest of smooth listing of cases.

In this context, initiation of an impeachment motion, from the perspective of ensuring judicial independence and accountability, was a double-edged sword. Its initiation, the day after the decision of the bench headed by the chief justice to reject an independent probe into the death of Judge Loya, irrespective of the merits of the decision, adversely affected the decisional independence of judges. If decisions in political matters entail the Damocles' sword of impeachment hanging over a judge's head, judicial independence is indubitably compromised and the court becomes a plaything for political manoeuvring.[112]

On the other hand, impeachment appeared to be the only recourse left for an independent investigation into allegations concerning the actions of CJI Misra, in relation to the medical college case, purported impropriety in allocation of benches in the Supreme Court, antedating an order and filing a false affidavit as a lawyer. A petition seeking an independent probe into the medical college case was dismissed in controversial circumstances as discussed earlier.[113] As a result, the court itself appeared openly hostile to any effort to ensure accountability of the CJI through judicial means.

On balance, the vice president, in his capacity as the presiding officer of the Rajya Sabha, where the motion was initiated, rejected it. The power to admit or

[111] Order dated 10 November 2017 in *Campaign for Judicial Accountability and Reform* v. *Union of India*, Writ Petition (Criminal) No. 169 of 2017, available at https://www.supremecourtofindia.nic.in/supremecourt/2017/34846/34846_2017_Order_10-Nov-2017.pdf (accessed 23 July 2018) (hereinafter '*CJAR [November 2017]*').

[112] Arghya Sengupta, 'Court Is Now a Plaything of Politicians for Political Gains,' *Hindustan Times*, 21 April 2018, available at https://www.hindustantimes.com/opinion/court-is-now-a-plaything-of-politicians-for-electoral-gains/story-xP1vjHQ9GNFPsSrCPyRF9O.html (accessed 25 July 2018).

[113] Order dated 1 December 2017 in *Campaign for Judicial Accountability and Reforms* v. *Union of India*, Writ Petition (Criminal) No. 169 of 2017 (Supreme Court of India), available at https://www.supremecourtofindia.nic.in/supremecourt/2017/34846/34846_2017_Judgement_01-Dec-2017.pdf (accessed 25 July 2018). The order was the culmination of a judicial process that appeared more concerned with the role of the CJI as the master of the roster than the nature of the allegations into judicial corruption relating to the Prasad Medical Trust.

reject the motion is vested in him by section 3 of the JIA. However, such power had never been exercised in the past and as a matter of convention, the initiation of an impeachment motion had led to the constitution of a committee to enquire into the charges. In this case too, there was certainly material that raised the possibility of misconduct. But so mired were such charges in appearing to seek political gains that the presiding officer, in his wisdom, and after consultation, rejected it.[114] A petition was subsequently filed in the Supreme Court challenging his decision but was, after an inconclusive hearing, withdrawn.[115]

The case study and other examples alluded to demonstrate that impeachment of judges in the Constitution today suffers from a mismatch between its foundational rationale and the levels of probity extant in the Indian higher judiciary. At the time the Constitution was drafted, judges were viewed as exemplars of virtue, persons of the highest integrity. A provision vesting parliament with the power to impeach them was only introduced as a last resort measure, the drafters confident that the occasion to use it would rarely arise. Thus, it was made a procedurally difficult exercise, requiring heightened majorities and proof of misbehaviour to be established, so that it would not be misused by parliament thereby jeopardising judicial independence.

Given the declining levels of probity in the higher judiciary and the partisan nature of politics, impeachment has not been effective in promoting judicial accountability. Though judges are still held in high esteem, numerous examples of judicial misconduct publicly abound.[116] The long and procedurally onerous process of impeachment is thus unsuited to deal with more regular occurrences

114 Chairman, Rajya Sabha's order rejecting the motion of impeachment against Mr. Justice Dipak Misra, Chief Justice of India, available at https://drive.google.com/file/d/1Nsipason7GYq66pkDQ1bC56A-qy9ACqQ/view (accessed 25 July 2018).

115 The petition filed by certain persons in the Supreme Court of India was withdrawn after the bench constituted to hear the petition refused to divulge details regarding the administrative order constituting the bench. See 'Congress Withdraws Petition on CJI's Impeachment,' *Outlook*, 8 May 2018, available at https://www.outlookindia.com/website/story/five-judge-sc-bench-to-hear-cong-mps-plea-on-cjis-impeachment-today/311775 (accessed 25 July 2018). This incident cast further doubts about the method of allocation of benches by the chief justice.

116 T. R. Andhyarujina, 'Disciplining the Judges,' *The Hindu*, 19 February 2010, available at www.thehindu.com/opinion/lead/disciplining-the-judges/article109167.ece (accessed 19 December 2012); V. R. Reddy, 'Judges and Medals,' *The Indian Advocate* 31 (2000): 27; Anil Divan, 'Judging the Judges,' *Indian Express*, 5 December 2002, available at www.indianexpress.com/storyOld.php?storyId=14190 (accessed 19 December 2012).

of judicial misconduct. Further, any possibility of doing so was dealt a severe setback with the Ramaswami episode, exacerbated by the failed impeachment of Chief Justice Misra, both of which appeared to suggest that holders of public office could not always be counted on to act without political compulsions, even on a matter such as impeachment, belying the faith of the drafters of the Constitution in this regard. Despite judicial efforts to streamline the process and incorporate elements of legal accountability, its fundamentally political nature has meant that reforming it from within has proved a difficult exercise. The Constitution envisaged statesmen deciding on questions of impeachment; instead its working has largely thrown up partisan politicians.

This points to the need to both closely scrutinise precisely how impeachment as a measure fails to promote judicial accountability, and explore other disciplinary measures which can be resorted to, in order to serve such purpose. The need for alternative disciplinary measures has been recognised for a considerable period and recommended strongly by the 195th Law Commission Report.[117] However, concerns over judicial independence have meant that they have yet to become law. At the same time, the ineffectiveness of the impeachment process demonstrated by the Justice Ramaswami episode brought to light the irresponsible nature of large sections of the parliament and the indecorous behaviour of the judge himself, bringing great disrepute to the judiciary. By reducing an exalted constitutional responsibility into a matter for petty political bargain, parliament proved unworthy of the faith that the drafters of the Constitution placed in it. At the same time, both by committing large-scale financial improprieties as established by the enquiry committee and by lacking the grace to repent and resign in its aftermath, Justice Ramaswami shattered the unimpeachable integrity that judges had hitherto exemplified. As a result, public confidence in the judiciary suffered severely, as impeachment hereinafter began to be seen as pliable to political manipulation. This is an impression that has persisted till today, to change which requires urgent and radical reform of the impeachment process and complementary disciplinary mechanisms. This is dealt with in Part III of this book along with similar reforms relating to judicial appointments, transfers and post-retirement employment.

[117] Law Comm., 195th Report, 500–02.

# 4 Post-Tenure Questions

## *Post-Retirement Appointments of Judges by Government*

During the career of Judges, many carrots are held out to deflect judicial performance from the path of rectitude. Judicial afternoons and evenings are sensitive phases, the incumbent being bothered about post-retiral prospects. The Executive plays upon this weakness to bend the integrity or buy the partiality of the elderly brethren.

—Justice V. R. Krishna Iyer, former judge, Supreme Court of India[1]

The employment of retired Supreme Court and High Court judges in government-appointed positions following their retirement is an increasingly common phenomenon in India today. Retired judges are called upon to preside over tribunals, chair statutory commissions and conduct commissions of enquiry, besides fulfilling a number of other key governance roles. The government justifies such post-retirement employment on the grounds that these positions require judicial personnel of the highest integrity and nothing in the Constitution prohibits employing retired Supreme Court and High Court judges who are considered suitable for the purpose. At the same time, from the point of view of retired judges, such employment gives them an opportunity to contribute to the public good at an age when their mental faculties are still sharp and provides them with a standard of living comparable to their previous entitlements as a Supreme Court or High Court judge.

Though mutually beneficial for retired judges and the government, from the point of view of public interest, the matter is much more serious and subtle than such a simplistic summary might suggest. Most crucially, as Justice Krishna Iyer's trenchant observation demonstrates, the prospect of post-retirement employment can severely damage judicial independence. Justice Krishna Iyer is not alone in identifying these insidious effects of post-retirement remunerative

1 V. R. Krishna Iyer, *Justice at Crossroads* (New Delhi: Deep and Deep, 1992), 60–61.

employment of judges by government. P. K. Sen, K. T. Shah, H. V. Kamath, K. Santhanam, M. A. Ayyangar, Naziruddin Ahmad and Jaspat Roy Kapoor spoke in the Constituent Assembly of the specific need for the Constitution to prohibit such employment;[2] the seminal 14th Report of the Law Commission of India came down heavily on the practice, arguing that it not only affected judicial independence but also eroded the dignity and high status of the judicial office;[3] Seervai too advocated a complete prohibition, conditional on an increase in judicial salaries and pensions, reasoning that the independence of the judiciary was more significant than the need to have judicial members presiding over tribunals and commissions.[4]

Despite wise counsel from several constitutional stalwarts, not only has post-retirement employment continued but it has also flourished over time. This is primarily a consequence of three intertwined factors. First, tribunals and commissions, several of which require retired judges to preside or act as members, have proliferated in the past few decades. This has meant that post-retirement employment of judges is now required in several circumstances by law. Second, there has been no consensus on increasing the retirement age of judges. After the 15th Constitution Amendment Act, 1963, by which the retirement age of High Court judges was increased to 62, no further upward revision of retirement ages of High Court and Supreme Court judges has been effected. This has resulted in judges and governments believing, arguably with justification, that retired judges, at 62 in the High Court and 65 in the Supreme Court, are still in a position to use their wide experience in public interest. Third, pensions and post-retirement benefits of judges are widely considered to be altogether insufficient.[5] Despite several increases over the years, retirement benefits are inadequate substitutes to the trappings of power and its concomitant perks that commission or tribunal chairpersons enjoy.[6]

2 CAD, vol. VIII (May–June 1949).

3 Law Comm., 14th Report, 45–46.

4 Seervai, *Emergency, Future Safeguards and the Habeas Corpus Case*, 128.

5 This view was most persuasively advanced by the 1st Law Commission in 1958 which believed that pensions of judges ought to be increased to two-thirds of the last drawn salary to ensure that judgeship is sufficiently incentivised and retired judges remain financially secure. Law Comm., 14th Report, 44. Despite several increases, the pension drawn by judges is today only equal to half of the last drawn salary. See The High Court and Supreme Court Judges (Salaries and Conditions of Service) Amendment Act, 2009.

6 This is evidenced by comparing the pensions payable to retired judges and chief justices of the High Courts and the Supreme Court as per the Schedule to the

This chapter provides a detailed analysis of the law and practice relating to post-retirement remunerative employment of judges by government. To this end, it first analyses the constitutional position relating to post-retirement employment of judges in Art. 124(7) for Supreme Court retirees and Art. 220 for High Court retirees. It points out the curious history of these two provisions and allied amendments which were proposed in the Constituent Assembly. On this basis it argues that its explicit non-extension to post-retirement employment in government-appointed positions was the product of constitutional oversight. Second, on the basis of data regarding the post-retirement employment of 50 retirees of the Supreme Court,[7] it provides the empirical basis as to why such employment ought to be regulated, given its widespread prevalence. This provides the foundation for an argument in Chapter 8 of the book as to why normatively such pervasive post-retirement employment adversely affects judicial independence and, therefore, requires reform. This takes into account allied concerns about the retirement age of judges and statutory requirements for retired judges to preside over tribunals and commissions.

In addressing post-tenure factors affecting the independence of the judiciary, this chapter restricts itself to post-retirement employment of judges in government-appointed positions alone as such employment, in principle, raises considerable concern regarding the possibility of judges adjudicating impartially. It excludes non-remunerative employment and employment in non-government-appointed roles, such as acting as arbitrators or chamber practitioners. Though these may also impact judicial independence, such impact is non-systemic and contingent on the facts and circumstances of each particular case. It cannot be validly claimed that in principle such post-retirement employment gives rise to the perception of judicial independence being impacted. Though there may be instances where this indeed may happen in practice, establishing such a causal factor as a general matter is difficult, especially since data on non-government employment such as arbitrator appointments and legal opinions being provided

Supreme Court Judges (Salaries and Conditions of Service) Act, 1958, and the First Schedule to the High Court Judges (Conditions of Service) Act, 1954, with the provisions for remuneration in the parent statutes setting up various commissions and tribunals to which retired judges are appointed. For an illustrative example, see section 3 of the Telecom Disputes Settlement and Appellate Tribunal (Salaries, Allowances and other Conditions of Service of Chairperson and Members) Rules, 2000, which provides that the chairperson of the tribunal shall get the salary, allowances and benefits that a serving Supreme Court judge receives.

7 The data collected uses 1 October 2012 as the cut-off date for retirements from the Supreme Court and traces 50 retirees from that date backwards. Post-retirement appointments till 1 April 2013 are considered. Since this is point-in-time data, its conclusions are insightful, though not determinative of overall trends.

are not publicly available. On these grounds, the scope of this chapter is limited to post-retirement employment in government-appointed positions.

## 4A The Constitutional Position

In the Constitution, Art. 124(7) and Art. 220 deal with the regulation of post-retirement employment of Supreme Court and High Court judges respectively. Whereas Art. 124(7) prohibits a retired Supreme Court judge from 'plead(ing) or act(ing) in any court or before any authority within the territory of India',[8] Art. 220 adds both a qualification and an exception to this provision for retired High Court judges. First, it limits the restriction only to permanent judges of the High Court, thereby expressly excluding additional and acting judges appointed under Art. 224 from the remit of such prohibition. Second, it allows permanent judges to whom this prohibition extends to practise in the Supreme Court and High Courts other than the High Court(s) where they have held office as a permanent judge.[9] These distinctions were not present in the original Constitution but were instead brought in by the Constitution (7th Amendment) Act, 1956.[10]

The Constituent Assembly discussions regarding this proposal are significant insofar as the extent of the restriction is concerned. Barring sitting judges themselves, who in a memorandum suggested that they should be allowed to revert to the Bar on retirement unless pensions were increased substantially,[11]

8 Art. 124(7) of the Constitution of India reads: '(7) No person who has held office as a Judge of the Supreme Court shall plead or act in any court or before any authority within the territory of India.'

9 Art. 220 of the Constitution of India reads:

> Restriction on practice after being a permanent Judge—No person who, after the commencement of this Constitution, has held office as a permanent Judge of a High Court shall plead or act in any court or before any authority in India except the Supreme Court and the other High Courts.

10 The Statement of Objects and Reasons to the Constitution (7th Amendment) Act, 1956, suggests that the rationale for this amendment was to undo the total bar on post-retirement practice that operated previously that was a deterrent for members of the Bar accepting judgeship. See The Constitution (7th Amendment) Act, 1956 (India).

11 Memorandum representing the views of the Federal Court and of the chief justice representing all the Provincial High Courts of the Union of India (March 1948) in Shiva Rao et al., *Framing of India's Constitution*, vol. IV, 195, 197–199. The memorandum also suggested that the prohibition should not apply to temporary and additional judges.

there was a principled consensus that post-retirement employment of judges ought to be curtailed. Wide differences, however, existed regarding the extent of such curtailment. In their comments and suggestions to the Draft Constitution, Sapru[12] and Ayyar[13] espoused the position that all post-retirement practice of judges who had been appointed, whether permanent or additional, ought to be prohibited. Sapru was particularly forceful in his view that the reversion of a judge to the Bar was a pernicious practice, as was demonstrated by the convention in England to prohibit it. Its key impact was on judicial independence, as a retired judge could use her influence with her former colleagues to garner decisions in her favour.[14] On the contrary, sitting judges,[15] the Home Ministry,[16] Chief Justice Ram Lal of the East Punjab High Court[17] and Justice Meredith of the Patna High Court[18] specifically argued that such a prohibition should not extend to additional or temporary judges. Were such a provision introduced, the possibility of filling up vacancies from the Bar would become exceedingly difficult, thereby reducing the quality of judges.

After considering these suggestions, the Drafting Committee placed an amended provision before the assembly. The provision prohibited all post-retirement practice of all High Court and Supreme Court judges. Such an omnibus provision was passed on the basis that elsewhere the committee had recommended deletion of the provision allowing for the appointment of additional judges entirely. This was fiercely opposed in the assembly by Hukam Singh, B. M. Gupte and H. V. Kamath, all of whom feared that stringent restrictions on post-retirement practice coupled with low pensions and a low retirement age of 60 would result in an erosion of the quality of judges. Hukam Singh specifically suggested that restriction on practice of High Court judges should be limited to the High Court in question and courts subordinate to it. Though his amendment was rejected at the time, it was reintroduced as part of the Constitution (7th Amendment) Act, 1956, as shown earlier.[19]

Equally relevant was a proposal by P. K. Sen for a new provision, Draft Art. 103A (and an analogous Art. 196A for the High Court) specifically prohibiting sitting

12 Shiva Rao et al., *Framing of India's Constitution*, vol. IV, 172.

13 Ibid., 207.

14 *Sapru Committee*, 173.

15 Shiva Rao et al., *Framing of India's Constitution*, vol. IV, 195, 197–99.

16 Ibid., vol. IV, 204–05.

17 Ibid., vol. IV, 171.

18 Ibid., vol. IV, 171–72.

19 Constitution (7th Amendment) Act, 1956.

or retired judges of the Supreme Court or High Courts from holding an office of emolument under the Government of India or that of a state.[20] An exception clause in relation to sitting judges when nominated by the president with the consent of the chief justice of India to a temporary office and in situations when an Emergency is in force was also provided for. The primary rationale underlying such a prohibition was the need to uphold the independence of the judiciary such that 'there should be no temptation before any Supreme Court Judge of the possibility of his being offered any office of profit after retirement'.[21] Such a provision was approved by the Constituent Assembly in case of the auditor-general[22] as well as the chairman and members of the Union and State Public Service Commissions.[23] The history of high-placed officials in government and some judges had, according to the members who sponsored and supported the amendment, necessitated the inclusion of such a provision for sitting and retired Supreme Court and High Court judges as well.

The rejection of the underlying principle of these amendments was based on Ambedkar's view that whereas the Public Service Commissions (and presumably the auditor-general) were engaged in deciding matters in which the government is directly interested, the same would not be true for the judiciary. In his view, the judiciary would be primarily concerned in deciding 'the issue between citizens and very rarely between citizens and the Government'.[24] Consequently, the possibility of the executive influencing the judiciary would be remote and thus no real threat to the independence of the judges would exist. On the contrary, Ambedkar believed that the expertise of judges could be put to good use when such specific expertise was necessary. He cited the example of Justice

20 CAD, vol. VIII (May–June 1949), 263.

21 Ibid.

22 Art. 148(4) of the Constitution of India reads: 'The Comptroller and Auditor-General shall not be eligible for further office either under the Government of India or under the Government of any State after he has ceased to hold his office.'

23 Art. 319 of the Constitution of India reads:

> Prohibition as to the holding of offices by members of Commission on ceasing to be such members—On ceasing to hold office—
>
> (a) The Chairman of the Union Public Service Commission shall be ineligible for further employment either under the Government of India or under the Government of a State…
>
> Similar restrictions apply to the chairman and members of the State Public Service Commission and members of the Union Public Service Commission.

24 CAD, vol. VIII (May–June 1949), 259.

Varadachariar, who was then a member of a commission investigating certain income tax questions, as such an instance.[25]

Ambedkar's view is curious for the time at which it was expressed, and plainly antiquated in today's context. In colonial times, the higher judiciary may have been primarily a forum for settlement of private disputes between citizens *inter se*, distinctly inferior to the legislature and executive in terms of its power. With the onset of the Constitution, however, Ambedkar could hardly have claimed to believe that this position would continue unchanged. Part III of the Constitution contained fundamental rights enforceable by citizens against the state; Part XI contained relations between the Union and the states outlining the legislative competence of each. In several instances of cases involving legislative competence as well as in alleging a fundamental rights violation, the higher judiciary would deal entirely with citizen–state disputes. As the key drafter of the Constitution, Ambedkar's failure to recognise this issue as significant for determining the character of the higher judiciary is somewhat surprising. Needless to say, such a view has even lesser currency today. The very fact that the governments and their instrumentalities are the predominant litigants in India's higher judiciary[26] bears testimony to this fact.

Thus, the rejection of P. K. Sen's amendment (and analogous amendments) completely barring post-retirement employment in government was based on a fundamental misconception of the judicial role in independent India. Again an amendment that would have a similar effect, proposed by Member of Parliament N. C. Chatterjee during the passage of the Constitution (7th Amendment) Act, 1956, was also partially rejected, seemingly on analogous grounds. Chatterjee recommended that Art. 220 be amended to allow additional judges to practise post-retirement in the High Court where they served, as well as permanent judges to practise in other High Courts and the Supreme Court. At the same time, he sought to expressly prohibit retired permanent judges from holding any office 'other than a judicial or quasi-judicial appointment'.[27] Whereas the former suggestions were accepted and became part of Art. 220, the latter was

25 Ibid., 260.

26 A recognition of this may be found in the National Litigation Policy announced by the Minister for Law and Justice, Government of India, on 23 June 2010. See National Litigation Policy 2010 (India), available at http://pib.nic.in/newsite/erelease.aspx?relid=62745 (accessed 24 April 2013).

27 *Lok Sabha Debates*, 5 September 1956, vol. 1, col. 324–26 (Parliament Secretariat) (on the Constitution (9th Amendment) Bill, 1956).

rejected.[28] The key restriction, however, remained the prohibition on a retired judge pleading or practising in a court where he/she served as judge or any court hierarchically inferior to it.

Decisions of the Supreme Court and High Courts interpreting the scope and extent of the prohibition enumerated in Art. 124(7) and Art. 220 have, unsurprisingly, reflected this narrow understanding of the drafters and parliamentarians. The overwhelming trend has been to constrict the scope of the restriction, thereby allowing retired judges to both plead and act before a wide range of authorities besides taking up post-employment government work and political positions.[29] As a result, post-retirement employment of judges has become an established feature of quasi-judicial governance in India, despite several judicial independence concerns being forcefully articulated in the Constituent Assembly and parliament.

In *Ananga Udaya Singh Deo* v. *Ranganath Misra*,[30] the issue before the Orissa High Court was whether the respondent, a former chief justice of India, could become a member of parliament (Rajya Sabha) in light of the restriction in Art. 124(7). Repelling the contention that parliament was an 'authority' and becoming a member of parliament would constitute 'acting' for purposes of the said article, the court held that in interpreting Art. 124(7), attention must be paid to Art. 220, the analogous provision for High Court judges, specifically to its marginal note which read: 'Restriction on practice after being a permanent judge.' Accordingly, the restriction in Art. 124(7) should be limited to post-retirement practice. Since acting as a legislator did not constitute such practice, the bar would not apply.[31]

[28] The 72nd Report of the Law Commission persuasively extended this line of thinking by allowing retired judges, subject to certain safeguards, to practice in their own High Court as well. However, its suggestions have not been accepted till date. See Law Commission of India, *Restriction on Practice After being a Permanent Judge—Article 220 of the Constitution*, 72nd Report, Ministry of Law and Justice, Government of India, 1978.

[29] Several decisions have reiterated the narrowness in interpretation by refusing to prohibit chamber practice of retired judges—*Manubhai Paragji Vashi* v. *The Bar Council of India*, 1990 (92) Bom LR 470 (Bombay High Court, India); a public interest litigation has also been filed by the non-governmental organization (NGO) Common Cause, seeking to prohibit judges from engaging in chamber practice and taking up arbitration work post-retirement. See *Common Cause* v. *Union of India*, W/P (Civil) No. 866 of 2010 (Supreme Court of India). However, no reported orders have been passed in this case.

[30] AIR 2000 Ori 24 (Orissa High Court, India).

[31] This was affirmed in the Supreme Court in *Ananga Udaya Singh Deo* v. *Ranganath Misra* (2002) 1 SCC 499 (Supreme Court of India).

For similar reasons, the Kerala High Court in *Robinson* v. *State of Kerala*[32] (hereinafter '*Robinson*') held that a retired High Court judge could preside over a commission of enquiry appointed by the state government. Though the court was cognisant of the damage to judicial credibility which might be caused by post-retirement employment of judges in government-appointed positions, two countervailing reasons prevailed. First, presiding over a commission of enquiry could not be considered 'pleading or acting in any court or before any authority'. Second, the public interest in requiring a judge-led enquiry commission in a matter of grave public significance would trump any credibility concerns.

In both the aforesaid cases, the respective High Courts upheld a literal reading of the relevant articles, in conformity with the intention of the drafters. From a perusal of the counsels' arguments as reproduced in the judgment, in neither case was a purposive interpretation of Art. 124(7) and Art. 220 based on the principled need to preserve judicial independence argued. Such an argument was, however, made before the Bombay High Court in the case of *Nitin Shankar Deshpande* v. *The President of India.*[33] In this case, the issue before the Bombay High Court was whether the prohibition on post-retirement practice in Art.220 ought to be extended beyond permanent judges, as the article provided, to additional judges as well. This argument was based on the understanding that an additional judge reverting to the Bar would result in the independence of the judiciary being seriously impacted. In a nuanced judgment, the court rejected this contention on the grounds that such an interpretation was unwarranted, both textually and purposively. Textually, Art. 220, as amended by the Constitution (7th Amendment) Act, provided for the bar on post-retirement practice to apply to permanent judges only. This was the constitutionally mandated compromise between the need to protect judicial independence and at the same time not unduly curbing post-retirement opportunities and by extension the freedom of occupation guaranteed to all citizens under Art.19(1)(g). Extending this prohibition to additional judges in the face of a clear constitutional mandate to the contrary would be akin to constitutional rewriting and consequently indefensible. Purposively too, the court felt that the petitioner's fear of judicial independence being seriously impacted was overstated. Judges, the court held, could be trusted to be impartial when a former colleague reverted to the Bar. Even if such a perception was widespread, it would be illegitimate for the courts to respond to it through an interpretive exercise when the Constitution expressly stated otherwise.

32 MANU/KE/0467/2003 (High Court of Kerala, India).

33 MANU/MH/0896/2012 (Bombay High Court, India).

However, courts have not, in principle, been entirely closed to purposively interpreting provisions concerning post-retirement employment in order to protect the independence of the judiciary and the credibility of the judicial office in necessary cases. In *N Kannadasan* v. *Ajoy Khose*,[34] the appointment of an additional judge of the Madras High Court, who had, on completion of his term, not been made permanent or given an extension as an additional judge owing to adverse reports against him, as the president of the State Consumer Disputes Redressal Commission, was quashed by the Supreme Court. Though the relevant statutory provisions concerning appointment provided that any person who 'is or has been a High Court Judge' could be appointed, the Supreme Court read this provision purposively to mean a judge who serves or has retired without blemish, which would serve as a minimum eligibility criterion. Thus, though such post-retirement employment was not constitutionally prohibited, the same result was achieved through a purposive interpretation of the statutory provision in question.

On analysis though, courts have not sought to bar post-retirement remunerative government employment of judges through an indefensibly wide interpretation of the constitutional provisions requiring them to accord with judicial independence. *Per se* this is justifiable since the Constitution expressly prohibits such an interpretation, as is clear from the words used in Art. 124(7) and Art. 220 (including its marginal note), fortified by Ambedkar's views on the floor of the Constituent Assembly in this regard. At the same time, it must be noted that textual constraints and the intention of the drafters have not analogously hindered the court in adopting a squarely purposive interpretation of the provisions concerning appointment or transfer of judges. What then could be plausible causes for this differential interpretive approach?

First, it might be claimed that a fact situation which would make it necessary for courts to adopt such an interpretation of the articles regulating post-retirement employment has not arisen. While there is a kernel of truth to this view, it can hardly be said that *SCAORA* and *Presidential Reference* by which the Supreme Court radically altered the practice of appointing and transferring judges were themselves products of fact situations that necessitated such decisions. Second, the courts have broadly taken a sceptical view of the impact post-retirement employment of judges may have on judicial independence, thereby adhering to a literary interpretation. In fact, in the *Robinson* case, they have considered the public interest in having retired judges as tribunal chairpersons and presiding

[34] (2009) 7 SCC 104 (Supreme Court of India).

over commissions of enquiry to be comparatively more substantial. This is unlike the courts' views in case of judicial appointments where the impact of executive-led appointments on judicial independence was held to be substantial without any weighty redeeming features. The tenuous premises of this view have already been highlighted in Chapter 2. Regarding the balancing exercise in post-retirement employment of judges, while the conclusion the courts have reached is plausible, arriving at it intuitively rather than through a reasoned balancing exercise is too quick. The court, if and when confronted with a test case, ought to take into account the pervasiveness of the practice, the public perception in response to such appointments and the public interest in having retired judges being appointed to such positions before reaching an optimal balance. Without taking such factors into account, the otherwise divergent judicial treatment of provisions pertaining to appointment and post-retirement employment of judges may be seen as tied by a common thread—an expansion of the power and influence of judges, at the cost of the executive.

## *4B Recent Practice*

The overall doctrinal refusal by the courts in extending the ambit of Art. 124(7) to prohibit post-retirement employment by judges may have been justified on a literal reading of the constitutional text. However, the underlying bases for the judicial decisions, that is, the public interest in having retired judges perform certain post-retirement functions and the minimal impact on judicial independence, cannot be assessed without a preliminary study of both the extent of the practice and the nature of the tasks assigned to judges post-retirement. Such a study is necessary to provide the data essential to arrive at a reasoned assessment of the balancing exercise, and whether on an overall analysis, the *status quo* of the government appointing judges to several post-retirement positions ought to continue.

For this purpose, this section analyses the post-retirement employment record of a cross-section of 50 retirees of the Supreme Court, going backwards from 1 October 2012 and considering post-retirement appointments till 1 April 2013, when this study was conducted.[35] Three analytical trends are highlighted: first, to which post has the retired judge been appointed, if at all (nature of post-retirement employment); second, how long after retirement has this appointment been made (time gap between retirement and post-retirement employment); third, by whom has the appointment been made (post-retirement employment appointing authority). On the basis of this

[35] See note 7.

study, the extent of the practice of post-retirement employment of judges (or otherwise) will be demonstrated, its impact on judicial independence assessed as well as the claim of public interest in justifying retired judges taking up these posts closely scrutinised.[36]

Of the 50 retirees listed in the Appendix, 37 judges have had post-retirement employment in 46 government-appointed positions. The remaining 13 judges, according to publicly available records, have not held any post-retirement government employment[37] though 2 have been employed by the Supreme Court in a commission to delineate the border between Assam, Arunachal Pradesh and Nagaland.[38] Of the 37 who have held such employment, 24 retired judges have been appointed a total of 33 times (several judges have had more than one appointment), either as chairpersons or as members of statutory commissions or statutory tribunal positions. Eighteen of these appointments have been to 14 commissioner positions [39] and the remaining 15 appointments to 10 statutory tribunal positions.[40] All 15 appointments as chairpersons of statutory tribunals and 13 out of 14 commissioner positions have required a judge of the Supreme Court or (in certain circumstances) chief justice of High Court (sitting or retired) by law.[41] This accounts for the majority of all post-retirement employments.

Four retirees have been appointed, at least once, to eight non-statutory government-appointed committees and commissions. These are in the nature of bodies which have been set up by executive fiat and none of them require sitting or retired judges of the higher judiciary to be appointed. Four retired judges have been appointed as commissioners of enquiry on five occasions under the

36 The table can be found in the Appendix. Please note an inherent limitation of the study. For all retirements from 2 October 2007 to 1 October 2012 who have not been employed post-retirement, the assessment assumes this *status quo* to continue and cannot factor in subsequent changes after 1 October 2012, even though they may be within the time gap categories considered by this study.

37 Justices G. B. Pattanaik, V. N. Khare, R. C. Lahoti, Ruma Pal, S. N. Variava, Y. K. Sabharwal, B. P. Singh, C. K. Thakker, Tarun Chatterjee, R. V. Raveendran, Cyriac Joseph, Deepak Verma and S. H. Kapadia.

38 Justices Variava and Tarun Chatterjee.

39 Multiple judges have been appointed as Chairperson of the National Human Rights Commission and the Law Commission of India.

40 Multiple judges have been appointed as Chairperson of the Vansadhara Water Disputes Tribunal, Competition Appellate Tribunal, Telecom Disputes Settlement Appellate Authority and the Authority on Advance Rulings under the Income Tax Act.

41 There are minor variations in the exact qualifications. These are not relevant for the point being made.

Commissions of Inquiry Act, 1952. This represents a distinct type of statutory commission which is appointed to enquire into matters of public importance on an *ad hoc* basis. The commissioner is not required by law to be a judge of the higher judiciary. The difference in number between retired judges and post-retirement employment positions in all these instances is explained by the fact that five judges have been appointed to a combination of one or more of such types of employment—four judges have held statutory as well as non-statutory posts appointed by the government and one has been a commissioner of enquiry in addition to holding a non-statutory government post.

If the time gap between retirement and post-retirement employment is assessed,[42] 1 judge was recommended for appointment prior to his retirement, 19 were employed within one year of their retirement, 6 between one and three years, 4 between three and five years and 3 after more than five years.[43] Of the 19 who were employed within one year of their retirement, 4 were appointed between six months and one year of their retirement, whereas 15 were appointed within six months. Of these 15, 13 were appointed within three months of their retirement with the minimum period being 10 days in a single instance.

Finally, as far as the appointing authorities are concerned, of the 46 posts to which 37 judges were appointed post-retirement, 14 appointments were solely by the executive government at the time, 5 by the government after an appropriate resolution to this effect had been passed by the parliament or state legislature, 6 by the government after consultations with the opposition pursuant to such a statutory requirement, 16 by the government in consultation with the chief justice of India or his nominee or a representative of the judiciary (in addition to the members of the political opposition or a special committee or neither), 4 on the nomination of the chief justice of India and 1 by a special political committee. The 14 executive appointments were to a range of non-statutory commissions as well as to certain tribunals where consultation with the chief justice of India is not a legal requirement such as the Authority on Advance Rulings under the Income Tax Act and the Railway Rates Tribunal under the Railways Act. The 5 appointments which were ratified by parliament were all

42 For those who have had more than one post-retirement employment, their first employment is considered for the purpose of this assessment.

43 Data for the date on which four judges were employed in a government position, post-retirement was not available. These are Justices S. S. M. Quadri (Authority on Advance Rulings [Income Tax]), M. B. Shah (Commission of Inquiry), D. M. Dharmadhikari (Madhya Pradesh Human Rights Commission) and P. K. Balasubramanyan (Authority on Advance Rulings [Income Tax]).

commissioners of enquiry appointed pursuant to section 3 of the Commissions of Inquiry Act, 1952, which mandates such a procedure. The 6 appointed by the government in consultation with the opposition were chairpersons of either the National or State Human Rights Commissions appointed pursuant to the Human Rights Act, 1993. The 16 appointments pursuant to consultation with the judiciary were to a range of statutory posts—state Lokayukta; chairman, Telecom Disputes Settlement Appellate Tribunal and Competition Appellate Tribunal; president, Consumer Disputes Redressal Commission; and member, National Human Rights Commission (which requires consultation with the chief justice of India in case a sitting judge's name is proposed). The 4 appointments on the nomination of the chief justice of India were of judges to head river water disputes tribunals under section 4 of the Interstate River Water Disputes Act. The appointment pursuant to a special political committee was to the post of chairman of the Press Council of India, pursuant to the procedure under section 5(2) of the Press Council Act, 1978, which requires the government to notify the recommendation of a committee consisting of the deputy chairman, Rajya Sabha (upper house of parliament), speaker, Lok Sabha (lower house of parliament) and a member of the council elected for this purpose.

Four formative inferences are discernible from these facts. First, post-retirement employment of judges from the higher judiciary in government-appointed positions is a commonly observed phenomenon with 37 out of the last 50 retirees holding such a position. Given that a majority of these appointees have held positions in statutory tribunals and commissions, it is self-evident that the pervasiveness of the phenomenon can be attributed in large part to the large number of such commissions and tribunals operating in the country.[44] Second, as the data demonstrate, for an overwhelming number of institutions where judges are employed post-retirement, judicial members are required by law (28 positions). For those where there is no such requirement (such as commissions of enquiry), it is likely that the experience, expertise and respect that retired judges command are *prima facie* considered as key reasons for their selection to such posts. Third, given that a majority of post-retirement appointments were made within one year of the concerned judge's retirement, it is likely (though by no means conclusively proven) that several proposals for post-retirement

[44] This is not a new development but can be seen in post-retirement employment of Supreme Court judges between 1950 and 1989 as well where it has been pointed out that nearly three-quarters of them had such post-retirement employment in government appointed positions. See Gadbois, *Judges of the Supreme Court of India*, 370–75.

employment are mooted while the concerned judge is still in office. The 232nd Report of the Law Commission not only affirms this fact but also states that judges themselves 'seek consideration for such appointments either on the eve of their retirement or after their retirement'.[45] Finally, wide consultation before post-retirement employment, including requiring the approval of the chief justice of India, is a growing trend with 16 such appointments having followed such a procedure. Four other appointments have been made on the nomination of the chief justice of India, suggesting that his opinion in these matters is *prima facie* determinative. Such consultation or nomination, it is presumed, is designed to safeguard judicial independence, obviating charges of executive favouritism to judges post-retirement, as well as ascertain the suitability of particular judges for particular positions given their areas of legal expertise. It is, however, curious that the device of consultation with the chief justice of India, thoroughly discredited as a mechanism to protect judicial independence in case of appointment of judges, is the chosen method for protecting judicial independence in case of post-retirement employment. As the next section demonstrates, it has also largely failed to stem public criticism of the post-retirement employments and the 'jobs for the boys' culture that it has spawned.

## 4C Lessons and Conclusion

Several former members of the Bar and judges of the Supreme Court have espoused the view that the current practice of pervasive post-retirement employment in government-appointed positions raises significant doubts about the perception of impartiality of judges and consequently their independence while in office.[46] A former law minister, Arun Jaitley, even went so far as to publicly state that certain judicial verdicts are prompted by the possibility of a post-retirement job.[47] Irrespective of the veracity of this statement, impartial adjudication, one of the key purposes of judicial independence as will be demonstrated subsequently in Chapter 6, appears to be gravely threatened by such post-retirement appointments.

This perceived threat to judicial independence is reflected in the increasing public clamour over such post-retirement appointments. The recommendation

[45] Law Commission of India, *Retirement Age for Chairpersons and Members of Tribunals—Need for Uniformity*, 232nd Report, Ministry of Law and Justice, Government of India, 2009, 10–11.

[46] As an illustrative example, see Gajendragadkar, *To the Best of My Memory*, 184.

[47] Kumar, 'Retirement or Re-employment of Judges?'

of Justice Swatanter Kumar as chairperson of the National Green Tribunal raised several eyebrows given that it was made at a time when three months of Justice Kumar's tenure on the Supreme Court remained.[48] In fact, an order by Justice Kumar to transfer environment-related cases in the High Court to the National Green Tribunal,[49] though arguably legally sound, coming as it did a few months prior to his appointment as chairman of the same tribunal, added fuel to the controversy. Again, Justice H. K. Sema's appointment to the Uttar Pradesh Human Rights Commission within days of his retirement similarly raised grave public concerns about the effect on judicial impartiality that the prospect of a post-retirement job has.[50] This is not in the nature of wayward banter as can be demonstrated by the admission by an unnamed former judge to George Gadbois that 'less well-off judges like him have an "inevitable tendency" towards the end of their tenure to be more "executive minded"'.[51]

Several similar examples abound. The import of these examples is a suggestion of the possibility of a *quid pro quo* with judges moulding their judgments in order to be in a favourable position for a post-retirement employment position. This, if proven in any given instance, would be a severe breach of norms of individual behavioural independence contained in the Restatement of the Values of Judicial Life[52] and perhaps even amount to misconduct warranting impeachment. Whether indeed such breaches have taken place is a matter for evidence that is beyond my ability to either collect or verify. Hence the argument in this book criticising the present practice of post-retirement employment of judges in government-appointed positions is limited to the doubts that the widespread prevalence of such instances raises insofar as the perception of impartiality of judges and consequently their decisional independence is concerned. On this basis, it is advocated that regulation of such post-retirement employment is imperative.

48 Dhananjay Mahapatra, 'CJI SH Kapadia Recommends Justice Swatanter Kumar as Green Tribunal Chief,' *Times of India*, 18 September 2012, available at http://articles.timesofindia.indiatimes.com/2012-09-18/india/33925050_1_sc-judge-cji-kapadia-justice-kapadia (accessed 7 May 2013).

49 *Bhopal Gas Peedith Mahila Udyog Sangathan* v. *Union of India*, (2012) 8 SCC 326 (Supreme Court of India).

50 Ranjan, 'Life Begins after Retirement.'

51 Gadbois, *Judges of the Supreme Court of India*.

52 The Restatement of Values of Judicial Life was a set of norms adopted by the Full Bench of the Supreme Court on 7 May 1997: 'Restatement of the Values of Judicial Life' (as adopted by Full Bench of Supreme Court of India on 7 May 1997), available at http://www.judicialreforms.org/files/restatement_of_values_jud_life.pdf (accessed 31 July 2012) (hereinafter 'Restatement').

However, before the mechanisms of such regulation can be dealt with, it is important to consider two key justifications for the *status quo*. First, it is contended that the age of retirement for judges—65 for the Supreme Court and 62 for the High Courts—is low, thereby allowing judges to effectively function in a suitable post-retirement office beyond the said age. Second, retired judges have considerable legal and judicial expertise, which are key desiderata for any appointment to a quasi-judicial commission or tribunal. Both are advanced as public interest justifications to ensure that the long years of experience of judges are not wasted upon their retirement.[53] A closer scrutiny of the specific impact post-retirement employment has on judicial independence and how such impact is weighed against the two aforementioned countervailing factors will be dealt with in Part III of the book.

In the final analysis, the employment of judges by the government in post-retirement positions is an established practice in India today. Three inferences can be drawn with regard to such practice. As a matter of law, such practice is consonant with the Constitution, which only restricts post-retirement litigation practice of judges. This, as this chapter demonstrates, can be attributed to Ambedkar's understanding of the courts primarily being adjudicators of disputes between private parties, not having to deal with the executive government in its capacity as a litigant, a belief that became antiquated almost as soon as it was first expressed. As a matter of principle, it has been widely felt to have the potential to affect the independence of the judiciary. The widespread prevalence of such appointments, as demonstrated by the empirical data collected and analysed, makes this principled objection a real threat rather than an imagined possibility. Finally, as a matter of prudence, such principled objection must be harmonised with the practical necessities for such appointment—the need to staff an ever-increasing number of tribunals and commissions with scarce judicial talent and expertise. How such factors are considered and harmonised with the critical need to maintain judicial independence will be the focus of the final chapter of this book after a conceptual understanding of judicial independence and accountability is developed.

[53] This does not mean that there are no other arguments in favour of or against the *status quo*. In fact, the highly remunerative nature of arbitration work as well as the low pensions that judges get is often cited as reasons for barring and allowing post-retirement employment in government appointed positions, respectively. Identifying the aforesaid two public interest justifications supporting the *status quo* is without prejudice to these (and any other) arguments that may be made in this regard.

# PART II

# A CONCEPTUAL ANALYSIS

# Judicial Accountability*

# 5

## 5A Accountability: A Very Brief Conceptual Overview

The advent of judicial accountability as a widespread phenomenon is a relatively modern development. It grew as an institutional response to the growing power of courts in adjudicating matters that were hitherto not considered within the ambit of judicial resolution. Its intellectual progenitor, from which it derived both its terminology and its conceptual moorings, is the concept of public accountability, which itself underwent a new wave in the latter half of the twentieth century.[1] Previously, public accountability was an under-theorised and seldom discussed concept. In democratic theory, it had a settled meaning, applicable to elected representatives, who had to be accountable to their constituents;[2] in public administration, it denoted a traditional book-keeping function, true to its etymological roots.[3] However, caught at the confluence of the twin developments of the multiplication of

* This chapter is a revised version of my article originally published in *Public Law*: Arghya Sengupta, 'Judicial Accountability: A Taxonomy', *Public Law*, April (2014): 245–266.

1 The term 'public accountability' is used in this chapter to denote accountability of institutions which exercise public power. This includes the legislature, executive and the judiciary, as well as accountability of public agencies such as police, health and educational services.

2 In early Athenian society, accountability was enforced by public officials having to report on their conduct to the Assembly of citizens: see Jennifer T. Roberts, *Accountability in Athenian Government* (Madison: University of Wisconsin Press, 1982); in modern representative democracy, this has been adapted to mean elected representatives being accountable to citizens through regular elections: see Patricia Day and Rudolf Klein, *Accountabilities: Five Public Services* (London: Tavistock Publishers, 1987), 6.

3 The word 'accountability' derives from giving an 'account' which itself derives from the Latin *accomptare*, itself a cognate of *computare*, meaning to calculate or count. C. T. Onions (ed.), *The Oxford Dictionary of English Etymology* (Oxford: Clarendon Press, 1966), 8.

power centres within the state requiring multiple sites of accountability and theories of New Public Management redefining traditional public administration understandings, the concept of public accountability exploded, suddenly being used in a variety of ways, with multiple meanings and diverse objectives.

To document and analyse each of these meanings and objectives is the task of an accountability historian and beyond the scope of this chapter. I am concerned with the limited task of sifting through these multiple understandings in order to delineate a plausible conceptual core of judicial accountability. This conceptual account is bolstered by jurisdiction-specific examples that demonstrate the various ways in which judicial accountability is used in practice. Such an account will provide a matrix to understand the particular dimensions of judicial accountability which are, much to our intellectual detriment, significantly under-theorised today.

Two parallel developments in governance and public administration are responsible for the profusion of the uses of public accountability in the latter half of the twentieth century. In governance, there was an increasing realisation that the traditional conception of public accountability of elected representatives, that is, ministerial responsibility to parliament in the Westminster tradition, was inadequate for a number of reasons.[4] Thus, direct bureaucratic accountability to parliament, administrative accountability to courts and accountability of various governmental authorities directly to the people were offered as necessary supplements. On the other hand, in public administration, New Public Management theories viewed public sector entities as service providers who needed to be held directly responsible for their actions to their clientele, that is, the citizens. As a result, new forms of professional, performance, managerial and market-driven accountability and control mechanisms applicable to service providers developed, chiefly in the sectors of health, education, social services and policing.[5]

Most of these meanings were derivatives of the traditional meaning of accountability, that is, holding to account or answerability.[6] However, the purposes for which such answers were sought, the mechanisms to facilitate such answerability and the authorities who were accountable and to whom such accountability was owed varied considerably. At the same time, these new understandings of accountability which were proffered were themselves

4 Peter Barberis, 'The New Public Management and a New Accountability,' *Public Administration* 76 (1998): 451, 452.

5 Day and Klein, *Accountabilities*.

6 Onions, *Oxford Dictionary*.

constantly in flux—new forms of accountability once implemented led to concomitant institutional changes, which in turn required the development of newer forms of accountability to account for the changed circumstances.[7] Both the varying motivations for the usage of accountability and its constantly changing nature owing to its reciprocal relationship with changing institutional designs meant that public accountability was largely a concept without fixed content, notoriously difficult to theorise.

In the last few years however, a concerted effort has been made to understand the core features of the concept of accountability. Most notably, Bovens[8] and Mulgan[9] have attempted to develop a coherent framework within which to understand, assess and identify limits of varying accountability regimes. This chapter derives from their work, particularly Bovens', and adopts a fivefold structure for understanding judicial accountability—who is accountable (subjects), the authorities to whom such accountability is owed (addressees), the specific actions for which the actor is accountable (subject matter), the purpose for such accountability (rationale) and the mechanisms for implementing such accountability (methods). An analysis of judicial accountability in this fivefold structure, it is believed, will shed necessary light on its conceptual core, thereby facilitating an analysis on its interface with judicial independence, dealt with in the next two chapters.

## 5B Judicial Accountability: Answering the Five Questions

Like public accountability in general, the idea that judges must be held specifically accountable for their actions has gained particular traction in the last two decades.[10] Previously, invocations of judicial accountability were mostly

7 The best example of the dynamic nature of accountability mechanisms and their application is provided by Barbara Romzek and Melvin Dubnick in relation to accountability mechanisms in NASA leading up to and following the Challenger disaster. See Barbara Romzek and Melvin Dubnick, 'Accountability in the Public Sector: Lessons from the Challenger Tragedy,' *Public Administration Review* 47, no. 3 (1987): 227.

8 Bovens, *Analysing and Assessing Public Accountability.*

9 Richard Mulgan, *Holding Power to Account: Accountability in Modern Democracies* (London; Basingstoke: Palgrave Macmillan, 2003); Richard Mulgan, 'Accountability: An Ever-Expanding Concept,' *Public Administration* 78, no. 3 (2000): 555.

10 See Guy Canivet, Mads Andenas and Duncan Fairgrieve (eds), *Independence, Accountability and the Judiciary* (London: British Institute of International and Comparative Law, 2006); Kate Malleson, *The New Judiciary: The Effects of Expansion*

platitudes of the nature that every exercise of power, including judicial power, must be accompanied by some degree of accountability. In the context of state judges in the United States of America, however, a different notion of judicial accountability prevailed, which was that judges must be directly elected by the people, which would allow them to be directly accountable, and by implication, removable by the people. Though this view of accountability had some support within the United States,[11] it had little applicability elsewhere, given the primary importance attached to judicial independence, which electing judges was squarely in conflict with. Thus, for a long time, the dominant conception of judicial accountability was a philosophically self-evident proposition that judges, being wielders of state power, must be accountable for their actions. The implications of this proposition, however, were scarcely grappled with.

With the expansion of judicial power in several countries, the implications of holding judges to account for exercise of their power became a live question. However, the notion of what judicial accountability entailed and how it would affect the prevailing understanding of judicial independence that was considered a *sine qua non* for the functioning of the judiciary varied, depending on the context of a country's particular constitutional and political culture. For example, in South Africa, accountability was the key value sought to be protected in the establishment of a Judicial Service Commission that would be responsible for appointment as well as supervising several aspects of judicial functioning.[12] Canada experimented with a system of televised confirmation

*and Activism* (Ashgate/Dartmouth, 1999); T. David Marshall, *Judicial Conduct and Accountability* (Scarborough: Carswell, 1995); Kate Malleson and Peter H. Russell (eds), *Appointing Judges in an Age of Judicial Power: Critical Perspectives from Around the World* (Toronto; Buffalo: University of Toronto Press, 2007); Edwin Cameron, 'Judicial Accountability in South Africa,' *South African Journal on Human Rights* 6 (1990): 251; Andrew Le Sueur, 'Developing Mechanisms for Judicial Accountability in the UK,' *Legal Studies* 24, no. 1 (2004):73; Nihal Jayawickrama, 'Developing a Concept of Judicial Accountability: The Judicial Integrity Group and the Bangalore Principles of Judicial Conduct,' *Commonwealth Law Bulletin* 28, no. 2 (2002): 1091; S. P. Sathe, 'Accountability of the Supreme Court,' *Economic and Political Weekly* 37, no. 15 (2002): 1383.

11 For an excellent account of the arguments both for and against elective judges, see Dorman Bridgeman Eaton, *Should Judges Be Elected? Or, the Experiment of an Elective Judiciary in New York* (New York: JW Amerman, 1873).

12 For an excellent account of the changes in judicial administration in the post-apartheid era in South Africa, see Penelope Andrews, 'The South African Judicial Appointments Process,' *Osgoode Hall Law Journal* 44 (2006): 565.

hearings of Supreme Court nominees and reformed its appointment process to ensure that it was not shrouded in secrecy.[13] In the United Kingdom, the Constitutional Reform Act was passed and the traditional roles of the Lord Chancellor abolished to ensure accountability in judicial functioning, while providing a firm institutional basis for judicial independence.[14] In the United States, a recognition that judicial accountability was not a pejorative term that would make judges less independent, but a requirement for an optimally functioning judiciary, slowly but surely emerged.[15]

Differing uses of the term in different political and constitutional contexts meant that no unifying conceptual account of judicial accountability developed. Much like public accountability, accountability of the judiciary too witnessed a conflation of diverse subjects of accountability, its subject matter, addressees, the reasons for seeking it and the range of methods that could be used to enforce it. While several such uses of accountability may have been ruses by governments attempting to hinder the functioning of a strident judiciary, the essence of the concept, whether used legitimately or not, was to seek ways and means to hold judges to account for their actions: a device to manage diverse expectations of the judicial institution and individual judges.[16]

Given these developments, it would be useful to fit the prevalent understandings of judicial accountability in the fivefold structure outlined earlier. Distinguishing between the subjects of accountability (individual and institutional), subject matter (decisional, behavioural and administrative), addressees (horizontal,

[13] Lori Hausegger, Matthew Hennigar and Troy Riddell, *Canadian Courts: Law, Politics and Process* (Don Mills: Oxford University Press, 2009), 141–211; Kate Malleson, 'Parliamentary Scrutiny of Supreme Court Nominees: A View from the United Kingdom,' *Osgoode Hall Law Journal* 44 (2006): 557.

[14] Department for Constitutional Affairs, *Constitutional Reform: Reforming the Office of the Lord Chancellor*, CP 13/03 (London: Department for Constitutional Affairs, 2003); Johan Steyn, 'The Case for a Supreme Court,' *Law Quarterly Review* 118 (2002): 382.

[15] At the forefront of this debate, campaigning aggressively against elected judges has been Justice (Retired) Sandra Day O'Connor. For an illustrative example of her views on this topic, see Sandra Day O' Connor, 'Keynote Address: Symposium on State Judicial Independence—A National Concern,' *Seattle University Law Review* 33 (2010): 559.

[16] This is derived from Romzek and Dubnick who use this understanding for accountability in the public sector: Romzek and Dubnick, 'Accountability in the Public Sector.' This is the working definition of judicial accountability that is used, where necessary, in this book.

vertical and internal), methods (legal, political, public, internal/ hard and soft) and the rationale for seeking accountability (responsible decision-making) will mean that the foundations of the concept of judicial accountability can be understood more precisely and the differences in enumeration between its various uses highlighted. Though the answers to the five questions raised above will neither be singular nor straightforward, such is the extent to which judicial accountability as a concept is under-theorised today that developing such a taxonomy for judicial accountability may have value *per se.*

## *5B.1 Individual and Institutional Accountability*

A preliminary distinction needs to be drawn between the accountability of individual judges ('individual accountability') and accountability of the judiciary as a whole ('institutional accountability'), that is, regarding the subject of accountability.[17] Individual accountability concerns the validity or otherwise of particular decisions made by judges, aspects of their out-of-court personal behaviour that may have an impact on their decision-making such as the disclosure of their financial assets or articulation of an ideology in a public lecture, and any action of an individual judge that may amount to misconduct and require disciplinary action. The source of such accountability derives from the oath taken by judges on appointment, and its rationale is to ensure answerability for the exercise of judicial power, thereby managing expectations that may be held regarding the judiciary. A classic early example of the working of individual accountability can be seen in the impeachment proceedings against Justice Samuel Chase, judge of the Supreme Court of the United States, in 1803.[18] Chase was sought to be impeached on the grounds of being partial in the trials of two anti-federalist sympathisers who had been brought before him, whom he had sentenced to be hanged and imprisoned for nine months respectively, and for making anti-Republican comments to a Baltimore Grand Jury. Considering these instances as seditious attacks against the Constitution and conduct unbecoming of a judge, the House of Representatives impeached him. However, in the Senate, the requisite two-thirds majority to confirm the

[17] This distinction has been made previously in the existing literature. For more, see United Nations Office on Drugs and Crime, *The Bangalore Principles of Judicial Conduct* (The Hague: United Nations Office on Drugs and Crime, 2002), available at http://www.unodc.org/pdf/crime/corruption/judicial_group/Bangalore_principles.pdf (accessed 12 December 2011) (hereinafter 'Bangalore Principles'); Le Sueur, 'Developing Mechanisms for Judicial Accountability.'

[18] For more, see Rehnquist, *Grand Inquests*, 1–134.

impeachment could not be garnered and thus the impeachment proceeding failed. Notwithstanding the failed impeachment, this example shows both plausible reasons and mechanisms used for enforcing individual accountability of a judge for his actions within and outside the court.

At the same time, accountability of the judiciary as an institution must be seen as a cognate yet independent category. Institutional accountability directly concerns the administrative functioning of courts, that is, the number of cases filed, the number disposed and backlogs, the spending of its allocated budget, and the exercise of its decision-making function in cases where they are perceived to have overstepped their boundaries or have erred leading to governmental intervention or appellate remedies. Recently, with the growth of institutional accountability in general, as adverted to earlier in this chapter, mission statements, annual reports and answers in response to Freedom of Information/Right to Information petitions have regularly been issued by courts relating to various aspects of their administrative functioning.[19] The extent of such accountability lies in the particular role of the judicial institution in a country's constitutional and political context and its rationale is to require courts to be answerable for diverse aspects of their functioning by virtue of being public institutions. These are thus the newest forms of enforcement of judicial accountability, mirroring the development of institutional accountability in general public accountability literature.[20]

At the same time, the exercise of the power of appointment of judges has a crucial role in ensuring institutional accountability of the judiciary. In fact, the issue of appointments and the extent to which its accountability function infringes the need for judicial independence has been one of the most complex questions confronting judiciaries and public law academics in recent times. Part of the complexity is owing to the fact that the exercise of appointment power is prior to the decision-making function being exercised by judges. Consequently, it is antecedent to the applicability of behavioural and

19 For an analysis of such forms, see Francesco Contini and Richard Mohr, 'Reconciling Independence and Accountability in Judicial Systems,' *Utrecht Law Review* 3, no. 2 (2007): 26; for a list of such forms, see Website of the UK Judiciary, 'Other forms of accountability,' available at www.judiciary.gov.uk/about-the-judiciary/the-judiciary-in-detail/jud-acc-ind/other-forms-of-accountability (accessed 12 December 2011).

20 Bruce Stone, 'Administrative Accountability in the "Westminster" Democracies: Towards a New Conceptual Framework,' *Governance* 8, no. 4 (1995): 505, 508.

administrative accountability of judges as well. This casts doubt on whether the power to appoint has any impact on judicial accountability at all.[21]

The distinction between individual and institutional accountability addresses this complexity. Thus, while the appointment power has no accountability function in relation to an individual judge given that the appointment authority is *functus officio* as far as she is concerned and incapable of exercising any check on her functioning, it continues to perform a crucial institutional accountability function. This is best exemplified by President Franklin Roosevelt's 'court-packing' plan. The plan was designed to use the power of appointment to rein in the Supreme Court that had threatened to overturn crucial New Deal legislation, which was the centrepiece of his economic recovery plan for the United States.[22] Whether the use of the said power in a given instance is justified or not, and the impact it has on judicial independence, is a conceptually distinct question that will be addressed in Chapter 7. For the purposes of this chapter, it is sufficient to note that the power of appointment can be used to shape the judiciary in the image of the power wielder, which has the effect of ensuring that the judicial institution, as it exists currently, is held accountable for its actions.

## *5B.2 Decisional, Behavioural and Administrative Accountability*

A second axis along which a taxonomy for judicial accountability can be developed concerns the aspects of judicial functioning for which accountability is sought, that is, the subject matter of accountability. On this basis, there are three broad objects: the decision-making function of judges ('decisional accountability'), the behaviour of judges both in court and specific matters out of court ('behavioural accountability') and administration and management of judicial matters

[21] It is on the basis of this understanding that judicial independence and accountability as conceptualised by the authors of the Federalist Papers did not squarely discuss the issue of appointing power, since it was assumed that such concepts would have applicability only once a judge was appointed. See Federalist Papers. Over time such a view has persisted. A speech by Satish Chandra Mishra, Member of Parliament, Rajya Sabha (upper house), India, in the context of the Judicial Appointments Commission Bill, 2013, provides an example. See *Rajya Sabha Debates*, 5 September 2013, available at http://164.100.47.5/newdebate/229/05092013/15.00pmTo16.00pm.pdf (accessed 25 September 2013).

[22] For an informative account of Roosevelt's court-packing plan and the executive–judicial relations at the time, see William Leuchtenburg, *Franklin D. Roosevelt and the New Deal* (New York: Harper and Row, 1963), 236.

('administrative accountability').[23] Applying the twofold distinction based on the subject of accountability described above, individual accountability has dimensions of all three objects of accountability, whereas institutional accountability is limited primarily to administrative accountability, though aspects of decisional accountability may also have an institutional dimension.

Decisional accountability, as is evident from its description, requires judges to be held accountable for judicial decisions made. However, as will be adverted to in the next chapter, judicial decisions are also the most significant *situs* for judicial independence to be secured. Thus, accountability for judicial decisions must be the minimum necessary to ensure fulfilment of its intended rationale in a manner not affecting judicial independence in any significant way. Ordinarily this involves ensuring that the substantive reasons used by individual judges in their decisions are defensible in law, precedent has been adhered to and that the process of adjudication has been impartial and fair.

Institutional decisional accountability, on the other hand, means the possibility of holding a judiciary, which by a consistent string of decisions has espoused a particular ideological or legal view that the other branches of government feel is inconsonant with the Constitution or beyond the jurisdiction of the courts, to account for their collective decision-making. Jurisdiction stripping of courts by governments because of an unfavourable decision being made is the most extreme example of such accountability being enforced in practice.[24] An egregious instance of this was seen with three amendments to the Constitution of India in 1975, by which the government sought to bar judicial review of proclamations of emergency (38th Amendment), insulate elections relating to the prime minister of India and the speaker of the House of the People (Lok Sabha) from judicial review (39th Amendment) and bar any criminal proceedings against the president, prime minister or governor for acts done in office or before entering office, and also bar civil proceedings against

[23] Charles Gardner Geyh uses this criterion alone for classification of accountability, and adopts a similar threefold classification, though 'administrative accountability' is termed 'institutional accountability'. See Charles Gardner Geyh, 'Rescuing Judicial Accountability from the Realm of Political Rhetoric,' *Case Western Reserve Law Review* 56 (2006): 911.

[24] In the United States, this power is derived both from Art. III and Art. I of the Constitution. The possibility of a jurisdiction-stripping law for federal courts inferior to the Supreme Court is less controversial than stripping the appellate jurisdiction of the Supreme Court itself. See Tara Leigh Grove, 'The Structural Safeguards of Federal Jurisdiction,' *Harvard Law Review* 124 (2011): 869.

the same authorities, before, after or while in office (41st Amendment). These amendments were passed at a time when the Allahabad High Court had decided an election dispute pertaining to Prime Minister Indira Gandhi against her and the matter was to come up for hearing before the Supreme Court.[25] Because the enforcement of such accountability is usually controversial, perceived to be a violation of judicial independence, it is generally couched in more acceptable terms that may be akin to holding individual judges behaviourally accountable. For example, a legislatively prescribed code of conduct for judges in the Judicial Standards and Accountability Bill, 2010, in India has been viewed by many as an effort to undermine judicial independence, though its overt objective is to check the behaviour of individual judges.[26] It has of course been defended as necessary to ensure the transparency of the judiciary and the public confidence in the institution.[27]

The second category, behavioural accountability, seeks to hold individual judges accountable for their behaviour within and outside court. The former primarily relates to statements made in the course of court proceedings. Thus, for example, clause 6 of the Code of Judicial Conduct for Judges in South Africa tabled before the Ad-hoc Joint Committee of Judicial Conduct & Disclosure of Interests, adopted under the Judicial Service Commission Act 1994, provides:

> In conducting judicial proceedings the judges personally avoid or dissociate themselves from comments or conduct by persons subject to their control that are racist, sexist or otherwise manifest discrimination in violation of the equality guaranteed by the Constitution.[28]

25 For a detailed account of the political machinations regarding barring of judicial review by the government of Indira Gandhi, see Austin, *Working a Democratic Constitution*, 314–27.

26 Ajit Prakash Shah, 'Judicial Standards and Accountability Bill,' *The Hindu*, 29 March 2011, available at www.thehindu.com/opinion/lead/article1582573.ece?homepage=true (accessed 13 December 2011); Pre-Legislative Briefing Service (PLBS), 'The Judicial Standards and Accountability Bill, 2010: A Briefing Document,' available at www.vidhilegalpolicy.in/pdf/PLBS_Briefing_Document_JSA_Bill.pdf (accessed 13 April 2014).

27 The Judicial Standards and Accountability Bill, 2010 (India), Statement of Objects and Reasons. See also Department-Related Parliamentary Standing Committee on Personnel, Public Grievances, Law and Justice, The Judicial Standards and Accountability Bill, 2010 (47th Report, Rajya Sabha Secretariat, Parliament of India, 2011).

28 Parliamentary Monitoring Group, 'Code of Judicial Conduct for Judges' (South Africa), available at http://www.pmg.org.za/files/docs/110119code_0.pdf (accessed 13 December 2011).

The latter entails accountability for any out-of-court actions by judges that may adversely affect their fitness for judicial office. This includes statements by the judge in public fora, either oral or written, record of financial assets of judges, acceptance of gifts, affiliation to a political party and a range of analogous actions that may imperil the judge acting as a fair and impartial arbiter. In most countries, this aspect of behavioural accountability is closely regulated by a code of conduct. For example, the Code of Conduct for United States Judges applicable to several categories of judges prescribes detailed canons regarding the types of permissible and impermissible extra-judicial activity.[29] Similarly clauses 3, 4 and 5 of the Guide to Judicial Conduct (2009) issued by the UK Supreme Court stress on the extra-judicial activities that a judge should refrain from being part of, since participation would lead to a reasonable apprehension of bias or a possible conflict of interest in a current or prospective case.[30] The enforcement of such accountability can be through internal disciplinary procedures or, if deemed serious enough, through an independent commission or, in the most extreme case, through impeachment by the political organs of government.

Administrative accountability on the other hand seeks to hold judges to account for administrative aspects relating to their judicial work. Such accountability is ordinarily expected to be addressed by the institution as a whole, though in certain instances, especially in judiciaries that do not hear cases *en banc*, individual administrative accountability may be necessary. Such instances of individual administrative accountability relate to the time taken by a judge to dispose of cases, the number of cases disposed of, the filing of administrative reports and other aspects relating to internal administration. An enumeration of such aspects is most often found in jurisdictions that have institutionalised performance evaluation indicators for individual judicial performance, which are primarily directed at ensuring that the administration of justice is expeditious and efficient.[31]

[29] United States Courts, 'Code of Conduct for United States Judges,' 2000, available at http://www.uscourts.gov/RulesAndPolicies/CodesOfConduct/CodeConductUnitedStatesJudges.aspx (accessed 13 December 2011).

[30] Supreme Court of the United Kingdom, 'Guide to Judicial Conduct,' 2009, available at http://www.supremecourt.uk/docs/guide-to-judicial_conduct.pdf (accessed 13 December 2013) (hereinafter 'UK Judicial Guide').

[31] For details of the history and operation of judicial performance indicators in the United States of America, where they have been widely used, see Rebecca Love Kourlis and Jordan M. Singer, 'A Performance Evaluation Program for the Federal Judiciary,' *Denver University Law Review* 86 (2008): 7.

Institutional administrative accountability can be of two types: the sum of the administrative accountability of individual judges and accountability for administrative decisions concerning the entire judiciary, usually made by the chief justice of the apex court in a country. The former is best exemplified in a court's annual report, as described earlier,[32] which presents a summary of the administrative performance of the court in the last year. The latter refers to administrative decisions such as allocation of cases to judges in courts that do not sit *en banc*, disciplining of individual judges, judicial transfers and even judicial appointments, when these actions are taken internally within the judiciary. An example of this is the system of transfers of judges between various High Courts in India, a decision *de facto* to be taken by the chief justice of India, an issue discussed in Chapter 3. These aspects of internal judicial administration, albeit not traditional judicial functions, are today so integral to the functioning of the judiciary as a state institution responsible for dispute resolution that an appropriate degree of accountability is widely considered essential.

## *5B.3 Addressees of Accountability and Methods of Enforcement*

Key to the implementation of judicial accountability, and often the source of tension with the competing value of judicial independence, are the methods of enforcement of such accountability. In order to coherently understand the vast plethora of such methods, a twofold classification based on the criteria of the addressee of accountability and the consequences of the particular enforcement method may be useful. The former leads to a fourfold sub-classification into political, legal, public and internal methods of enforcement, whereas the latter leads to a twofold sub-classification into hard and soft methods.

### ***5B.3.a Accountability Addressees: The Law or the People***

To whom judicial accountability is owed is an age-old and complex question. The historical debate, which often resurfaces in the context of reining in exceedingly powerful judiciaries, centres around the question of whether judicial accountability, in the ultimate analysis, is owed to the law itself or to the people, as the authors of the law. Divergent answers to this question result in strikingly different mechanisms for enforcement of accountability. Accountability to the law, the idea that it is the duty of the judges to remain faithful to the law, has

32 Supreme Court of Singapore, 'Justice Within Reach' (Supreme Court Annual Report 2014–15), available at http://www.supremecourt.gov.sg/data/AnnualReport/AnnualRpt2014/ (accessed 16 November 2016).

its best intellectual expositions in the writings and judgments of Chief Justice John Marshall in the United States.[33] His view in this regard is epitomised in his statement:

> This court must not yield to feelings which might seduce it from the path of duty … [it] must obey the mandate of the law.[34]

Following from this, Marshall conceptualised the idea of judicial accountability not as accountability *to* any authority, but rather responsibility *for* carrying out certain objectives that the law espouses. When applied to the judiciary, it proceeds on the presumption that the objectives of the law can be decisively ascertained by judges and all that accountability would require is the strict adherence to such objectives. This presumption is far from unproblematic, and indeed a variant of two questions at the heart of legal philosophy relating to the nature of law itself and the role of a judge in adjudication[35] and beyond the remit of this book. For our purposes, it would suffice to note that such a conception of accountability is enforced primarily by the self-restraint exercised by judges, their constitutional role of exercising judgment backed by reasons in an open and public setting.

On the contrary, the idea of judicial accountability being owed to the people is based on the fundamental premise that judicial power is an exercise of state power, which in modern constitutional democracies must derive its legitimacy from the people.[36] If this viewpoint is adopted, the mechanisms of enforcement that follow are vastly different. A pure conception of such accountability, untrammelled by, or at any rate trumping contravening considerations of judicial independence, results in the mechanism of judicial elections as a way of appointing and renewing tenures of judges.[37] A more nuanced mechanism,

33 Sotirios A. Barber, *The Constitution of Judicial Power* (London: Johns Hopkins University Press, 1993), 30.

34 *The Antelope*, 23 US 66 (1825) (US Supreme Court).

35 H. L. A. Hart, *The Concept of Law* (Oxford: Clarendon Press, 1963); Ronald Dworkin, *Law's Empire* (Cambridge: Belknap Press, 1986).

36 This was a fundamental tenet in the republican tradition of considering the people as an undifferentiated mass who entrusted different modes of state power to different representatives. Thus, judicial power was a particular mode of exercise of sovereign power suitable for legal questions that arose. See J. G. A. Pocock, *The Machiavellian Moment: Florentine Political Thought and the Atlantic Republican Tradition* (Princeton: Princeton University Press, 1975), 517–21.

37 Pamela S. Karlan, 'Two Concepts of Judicial Independence,' *Southern California Law Review* 72 (1998–99): 535.

which has recently received particular traction, is the idea of direct public accountability for judges, as will be described below.[38]

Space precludes a full account of this conceptually weighty debate concerning the ultimate addressees of judicial accountability. Instead, the primary focus of this sub-section will be on the intermediate addressees of accountability, that is, those who seek to enforce such accountability—who they are and in what way individual judges and the judicial institution are accountable to them. Linked to such intermediate addressees are the methods of enforcement of judicial accountability by them. The two enquires are thus taken up together.

### *5B.3.b Methods of Enforcement I: Legal, Political, Public and Internal*

As far as intermediate addressees of accountability are concerned, a clear threefold distinction between horizontal, vertical and internal addressees can be identified. Horizontal accountability, that is, accountability addressed to the politically elected representatives in coordinate organs of government, is enforced by methods that are, by their very nature, political. Key examples of such political methods for accountability enforcement are impeachment of judges by elected representatives, which is the standard system for removal of judges followed in many countries, the role of the coordinate wings of government in disciplining judges by imposing punishment short of impeachment, monitoring performance of judges through statutorily prescribed performance evaluation standards and tabling of reports by the judiciary before the political organs for either approval or information.[39]

Vertical accountability, on the other hand, is enforced by a range of legal and directly public methods of enforcement. The legal method, applicable to all courts, except the apex court in the country, is the right to appeal a decision by any court to a designated higher court. The presence of such legal methods for enforcing accountability ensures that decisions are reasoned and in accordance with law and precedent. In fact, these requirements of a reasoned

[38] See Section 5B.3.b.

[39] In addition, there have been several instances of political intervention in judicial functioning that have been justified on the basis of an accountability rationale. See Kim Lane Schepple, 'Declarations of Independence: Judicial Reactions to Political Pressure,' in *Judicial Independence at the Crossroads: An Interdisciplinary Approach*, ed. Stephen B. Burbank and Barry Friedman (Thousand Oaks: Sage Publications, 2002), 227.

judgment taking into account applicable laws and precedent are not only a *sine qua non* for the exercise of legal accountability but are also equally the basis for the exercise of methods of direct public accountability. The giving of reasons performs a crucial justificatory function, inasmuch as it communicates, both to the litigants and to the public, the grounds on which a decision has been made, thereby affording them the opportunity to hold judges to account by scrutinising and, if necessary, questioning the decision should the grounds be found inadequate, insufficiently reasoned or plainly wrong.[40] This public accountability function of scrutiny and criticism of judicial decisions is most commonly carried out by academics, subject area specialists and, for decisions of wide public importance, by the media. In this regard, a recent modification, brought about by several courts, is greater engagement with the popular media. Thus, the Supreme Court of the United Kingdom televises its hearings live, thereby facilitating greater transparency.[41] The Constitutional Court of South Africa, apart from publishing its decision, releases an official media summary, thereby facilitating public understanding of its decisions and allowing itself to be held accountable for them.[42]

Administrative and behavioural accountability of the judiciary and individual judges too are often enforced through direct accountability mechanisms. The most controversial form of such accountability for individual judges is the holding of popular elections for appointment, and retention elections for reappointment of judges, which is prevalent, most prominently, in several state higher judiciaries in the United States. Direct elections provide scope for maximum accountability to the public, since judges have to factor in public opinion in every aspect of their functioning. While obviously the impact of such elections on their decision-making and consequently on judicial independence is significant, as a result of which they have been roundly criticised, the behavioural accountability function they perform has long been advocated as a significant

40 For the justificatory function played by reasons, see Thomas Nagel, 'Moral Conflict and Political Legitimacy,' *Philosophy & Public Affairs* 16, no. 3 (1987): 215.

41 For the rationale for televised hearings, see Supreme Court of the UK, *Press Notice*, 16 May 2011, available at http://www.supremecourt.uk/docs/pr_1106.pdf (accessed 13 December 2013).

42 For an illustrative example, see the media summary in *Leon Joseph and others* v. *City of Johannesburg and others*, CASE CCT 43/09 (South African Constitutional Court), available at http://41.208.61.234/uhtbin/cgisirsi/20111213120031/SIRSI/0/520/S-CCT43-09 (accessed 13 December 2011).

rationale justifying their continuance.[43] Less egregious are the publication of annual reports, disclosure of financial assets and other like reporting functions, which provide information regarding the judiciary and individual judges to the public, thereby facilitating accountability.

In addition to accountability addressees outside the institution of the judiciary, several methods of accountability enforcement are internal, operationalised through checks and balances imposed by higher administrative authorities within the judiciary itself. Such mechanisms are largely directed at the enforcement of individual administrative and behavioural accountability of judges. Thus, judges in India are administratively responsible to the chief justices of their respective courts and the latter can take several minor measures such as suspending the former from work for a period of time, or a verbal censure, if evidence of conduct unbecoming of a judge not amounting to impeachment has been found.[44] At the same time, individual judges are also accountable to the chief justice for more routine functions such as ensuring timely and effective disposal of cases. Similar such measures, necessary to secure the effective institutional functioning of the judiciary without providing scope for external intervention, can be found across jurisdictions.[45]

### *5B.3.c Methods of Enforcement II: Hard and Soft*

Kate Malleson has introduced a helpful distinction within judicial accountability literature by providing for two distinct modes of enforcement of accountability based primarily on the consequences occasioned, which she describes as 'hard' and 'soft'.[46] Malleson understands hard accountability for judges as the power of political authorities to remove judges from their position when specified enumerated circumstances arise. Thus, it is an *ex post*, politically enforceable accountability with extreme consequences, as a result of which Malleson feels it to be generally inappropriate for judges. On the contrary, soft accountability refers to

43 For both these perspectives, see Karlan, 'Two Concepts of Judicial Independence'; see also Lee Epstein, Jack Knight and Olga Shvetsova, 'Selecting Selection Systems,' in *Judicial Independence at the Crossroads: An Interdisciplinary Approach*, ed. Stephen B. Burbank and Barry Friedman (Thousand Oaks: Sage Publications, 2002), 191.

44 These minor measures currently do not operate on a formal basis. For an argument for their formalisation, see Law Comm., 195th Report.

45 Michael Kirby, 'Judicial Accountability in Australia,' *Legal Ethics* 6, no. 1 (2003): 41, 49.

46 Malleson, *New Judiciary*, 37.

*ex ante* measures such as fostering of openness and representativeness in judicial functioning. These are neither enforced politically nor set up as mechanisms enforcing consequences for judicial misconduct, but rather create prior conditions that mitigate the possibility of such misconduct in the first place.[47] Thus, the distinction between these two types of accountability is based on both consequences that ensue from their enforcement and the addressee of such accountability.

Though the distinction is helpful, it has two limitations. First, as Malleson herself admits, it can function as a classificatory tool only in relation to different methods of individual accountability.[48] Measures for institutional accountability cannot easily be fitted into the binary distinction between hard and soft methods. To do this, there needs to be fresh thinking of what consequences would count as extreme enough for the judicial institution to be considered 'hard' and likewise 'soft'. It would suffice to say that such criteria cannot be the same as the criteria for individual accountability specified by Malleson, given the differing objectives, emphases and mechanisms for institutional accountability.

Second, Malleson's equation of hard accountability with political accountability is excessively restrictive. There are several mechanisms of accountability, such as publication of annual reports, mandatory responses to Right to Information/ Freedom of Information petitions and prior disclosure of judicial assets, which are *ex ante* measures that would constitute soft accountability in her categorisation. However, the same measures may have certain ensuing consequences that may not warrant impeachment, thereby not being classified as hard accountability, but be nonetheless more significant than soft accountability outcomes. For example, an internal suspension of a judge from judicial work for a period of time owing to a failure to disclose financial assets is a stringent penalty, enforced non-politically, flowing from a soft accountability mechanism. Either the definition of soft accountability or hard accountability needs to widen to incorporate such hybrid mechanisms of enforcement (and there are many more such) or, alternatively, instead of a binary distinction, hardness and softness of accountability need to be measured on a scale as a spectral value.

In my opinion, the latter option would be more appropriate. Mechanisms of accountability are already considerably diverse, and as judicial power increases, and judiciaries adapt to the particular requirements in every country's constitutional and political culture, these mechanisms will only diversify further.

47 Ibid., 41.

48 Ibid.

To account for a profusion of these methods within a binary distinction would be both difficult and also devoid of meaning since these characterisations may become excessively portmanteau. Thus, accountability mechanisms can be usefully thought of on a scale of consequential hardness, where a mechanism's position on the scale will depend solely on the intensity of the consequences of the mechanism and not the addressee of such accountability. Thus, impeachment will be seen as a harder measure than an internal suspension, only because it warrants removal as opposed to temporary suspension, and not because it is politically, as opposed to internally, enforced. At the same time, the scale will incorporate appropriately analogous understandings of hardness for institutional accountability measures. In this manner, the four types of accountability mechanisms described above—legal, political, directly public and internal—with regard to decisions, behaviour or administration, concerning a particular judge or the institution of the judiciary itself, can be classified on a scale of hardness. This provides a coherent matrix within which the interplay between different methods of accountability, both individual and institutional, can be viewed.

## *5B.4 Rationales*

The quest for greater accountability for the judiciary is of relatively recent origin. In early separation of powers literature, judicial accountability was seen as inherent in the contingent nature of the composition and functioning of the judicial institution and thus did not require express provision. The emphasis instead was on how best to secure judicial independence given the relatively weaker position of the judiciary vis-à-vis the legislature and the executive.[49] However, as judicial power increased dramatically in the last few decades in several jurisdictions and the political significance of judicial decisions rose sharply,[50] there was a concomitant increase in measures to hold the judiciary accountable. These measures have largely taken the form of greater transparency in judicial appointments[51] and judicial administration,[52] checks on behaviour

49 Federalist Papers, 510; Frederic S. Burin, 'The Theory of the Rule of Law and the Structure of the Constitutional State,' *The American University Law Review* 5, no. 3 (1966): 313.

50 An excellent account of the expansion of judicial power may be found in *The Global Expansion of Judicial Power*, ed. C. Neal Tate and Torbjörn Vallinder (New York; London: New York University Press, 1995).

51 For changes in appointments systems around the world in the last two decades in light of growing judicial power, see Malleson and Russell, *Appointing Judges in an Age of Judicial Power.*

52 Le Sueur, 'Developing Mechanisms for Judicial Accountability.'

and performance of individual judges[53] as well as attempts to make judicial decisions more accessible to the general public.[54]

The underpinning provided for such accountability measures is the justification that accountability is a necessary incident of the exercise of any power—the more the power that is exercised, the more is the accountability that ought to exist. In addition to this, in case of the judiciary, added justification for increased accountability has been sourced from the fact that judicial power represents an exercise of sovereign power. This has been advanced as a strong democratic justification to ensure that the said power is exercised accountably and could be checked by the people, from whom it was ultimately sourced.[55] Though the judiciary is unlike the legislature and the executive which in Westminster government source their legitimacy directly from the people, yet the fact that judicial power did not arise *sui generis* but was an exercise of sovereign power provided sufficient justification for such a democratic checking function. Space precludes further scrutiny of this account for judicial accountability.

At the same time, the growing incidence of the need for judicial accountability has an additional justification: the greater the political significance of judicial decisions, the greater is the need for ensuring that such decisions are made responsibly.[56] This is best exemplified by measures seeking to enforce decisional and behavioural accountability. Insofar as individual decisional accountability is concerned, at its minimum, legal measures such as the right of appeal and conventional measures such as the obligation to give reasons and follow precedent ensure the lawfulness as well as the substantive correctness of decisions. Likewise, public accountability measures such as academic criticism and media analysis of judgments seek to promote responsible decision-making by judges, by scrutinising judgments closely and making them subject to public criticism should such criticism be warranted.

53 A comprehensive account of performance evaluation measures and how they promote judicial independence can be found in J. J. Spigelman, 'Judicial Accountability and Performance Indicators,' *Civil Justice Quarterly* 21 (2002): 18.

54 See notes 41 and 42.

55 For examples of such checks being imposed across the world, see Mauro Cappelletti, 'Who Watches the Watchmen? A Comparative Study on Judicial Responsibility,' *The American Journal of Comparative Law* 31, no. 1 (1983): 1, 8–14.

56 Responsible decision-making understands responsibility as 'responsibility-as-virtue', that is, whether in the course of decision-making, the virtues considered necessary for the judiciary to uphold, are upheld. This is both substantive and procedural. See Nicolas Haines, 'Responsibility and Accountability,' *Philosophy* 30 (1955): 141, 143.

Measures seeking behavioural accountability of judges, such as the public disclosure of annual incomes, internal disciplining and, in extreme cases, impeachment for misconduct, while being ends in themselves and serving several independent purposes[57] also bear a close connection to the need for responsible decision-making. By verifying the financial position of judges and deterring possibilities of behaviour unbecoming of a judge, these measures act as preventive checks, seeking to create the conditions conducive for a responsible decision to be reached in the first place. For example, the practice requiring judges to disclose their income sources in various countries was prompted by a need to introduce transparency, which in turn would bring to light any factors that may derogate from the requirement of impartiality of a judge hearing a particular case, such as a potential conflict of interest.[58] Thus, unlike decisional accountability measures, which are directed at the decision itself, behavioural accountability measures are directed at securing the prerequisites necessary for such a decision to be made responsibly. Both, however, are similar insofar as their justifications are instrumental, leading, in different ways, to more responsible decision-making.

However, the boundaries of responsible decision-making, as an end sought by judicial accountability, are not clearly defined. Though both the substantive correctness of a decision, addressed by decisional accountability, and procedural propriety in terms of impartiality of a judge hearing a case, addressed by behavioural accountability, fall squarely within its ambit, several measures may be more problematic. This is particularly true with regard to institutional accountability measures such as jurisdiction-stripping legislations that seek to check judicial decisions for appropriateness rather than their procedural or substantive validity. Though the need to ensure responsible decision-making is cited as an ostensible justification for such measures, it is more often a smokescreen to instead ensure that particular substantive decisions favourable to the government are reached. The constitutional amendments in India seeking to limit judicial review before a crucial election dispute was heard by the Supreme Court provide a clear example of such a measure, which can scarcely be argued to be legitimately directed at responsible decision-making.[59] Even if such an argument can be made, such measures arguably achieve responsible decision-making in a manner that is antithetical to judicial independence, which has been widely considered fundamental for a

[57] Geyh, 'Rescuing Judicial Accountability,' 916.

[58] Keith E. Henderson, 'Asset and Income Disclosure for Judges: A Summary Overview and Checklist,' available at http://siteresources.worldbank.org/INTLAWJUSTINST/Resources/IncomeAssetDisclosure.pdf (accessed 31 July 2012).

[59] Austin, *Working a Democratic Constitution*.

well-functioning judiciary.[60] Similar conflicts arise with regard to institutional accountability measures such as various mechanisms for judicial appointment. The validity of such measures and whether, all things considered, they can be justified as promoting the end of responsible decision-making will be dealt with doctrinally in Part III of the book. For the purposes of this chapter, it would suffice to note that responsible decision-making is a contested concept, whose boundaries are fluid. At the same time, implicit in this understanding is the possibility of responsible decision-making serving as a bridge between judicial independence and accountability, a possibility that will be fully explored in Chapter 7.

## 5C Conclusion

Section 5A of this chapter highlighted the development of the concept of public accountability and the fivefold structure which has been used in accountability literature to classify its diverse usages. Such a structure serves as the foundation for developing a taxonomy for judicial accountability, one of public accountability's prime offshoots. Seeing judicial accountability in terms of its subjects, addressees, subject matters, rationales and methods of enforcement, as Section 5B of this chapter does, brings a degree of analytical clarity to a concept that has largely been used rhetorically, to exert a degree of popular control over increasingly powerful judiciaries. At the same time, it demonstrates that judicial accountability, despite its wide-ranging usage, is not a monolithic concept—on the contrary, people have different conceptions in mind when using judicial accountability in specific contexts. Neither are all these conceptions pejorative, attempting to illegitimately restrain judiciaries, nor are all justified in requiring judiciaries to remain responsive to popular or political considerations. Instead, as this chapter suggests, a determination of the justifiability or otherwise of the various forms and uses of judicial accountability is contingent on understanding its precise inter-relation with judicial independence, a concept it is commonly conceived of as being in competition with. To condemn judicial accountability outright or celebrate it without an analogous analysis of judicial independence would be premature. Accordingly, the next chapter follows this lead and looks at the concept of judicial independence with the intention of questioning the commonly held assumption of it being the antithesis of judicial accountability and attempting to develop more meaningful connections between them.

[60] John Ferejohn and Larry Kramer, 'Independent Judges, Dependent Judiciary: Institutionalizing Judicial Restraint,' *New York University Law Review* 77 (2002): 962.

# Judicial Independence

# 6

## 6A Judicial Independence: A Protean Concept

Judicial independence, like rule of law or accountability, is a slogan of our times. The Constitutional Reform Act, 2005, fundamentally altered the judicial apparatus in the United Kingdom with the intention of providing a firm statutory basis for judicial independence;[1] the Indian Supreme Court regularly cites the need for judicial independence in response to questions regarding accountability for its internal working;[2] it is even provided express constitutional recognition in section 165 of the Constitution of South Africa.[3] In addition, it has been considered by the International Bar Association,[4] numerous inter-governmental fora[5] and, on several occasions, by the United Nations.[6]

1 Specifically see sections 3(1), 26 and 61 and Schedules 8 and 12 to the Constitutional Reform Act, 2005 (UK).

2 The chief examples of this are *SCAORA* and *Presidential Reference*.

3 Section 165 of the Constitution of South Africa reads: 'The courts are independent and subject only to the Constitution and the law, which they must apply impartially and without fear, favour or prejudice.'

4 International Bar Association, 'IBA Minimum Standards of Judicial Independence,' 1982, available at http://www.ibanet.org/Document/Default.aspx?DocumentUid=bb019013-52b1-427c-ad25-a6409b49fe29 (accessed 31 July 2012).

5 Universal Declaration on the Independence of Justice (Montreal Declaration), 10 June 1983, available at http://www.mpil.de/ww/en/pub/research/details/projects/minerva_jud_indep/intdocs.htm (accessed 31 July 2012); Beijing Statement of Principles of the Independence of the Judiciary in the LAWASIA Region, 19 August 1995, available at http://lawasia.asn.au/beijing-statement.htm (accessed 31 July 2012).

6 United Nations Basic Principles on the Independence of the Judiciary, 1985, available at http://www2.ohchr.org/english/law/indjudiciary.htm (accessed 31 July 2012) (hereinafter 'UN Basic Principles'); endorsed by UN General Assembly, Resolution 40/32 (29 November 1985) UN Doc A/RES/40/32 and UN General Assembly, Resolution 40/146 (13 December 1985) UN Doc A/RES/40/146.

Concern for judicial independence is near-universal, extending to developed and developing countries, old legal systems and new. However, the interest in judicial independence, despite appearances, is not a modern phenomenon. Historically, in the common law world, judicial independence has been seen as a necessary prerequisite both for maintaining the rule of law and for ensuring adherence to a scheme of separated powers. During the reign of the Stuart kings in seventeenth century England, early signs of judicial independence could be seen with the growth of an independent legal profession removed from politics and the consequent functional specialisation that became the hallmark of the courts.[7] Subsequently, the Act of Settlement of 1701 represented the first institutional incorporation of judicial independence in the late middle ages, abolishing the pleasure doctrine which had made judges subservient to the Crown, and replacing it with the doctrine of good behaviour which ensured security of tenure.[8] Blackstone developed this conception of judicial independence further, as the foundation on which separation of powers and consequently public liberty rested.[9] The culmination of these developments was the Federalist Papers, key documents in the drafting of the Constitution of the United States, which established the judiciary as a co-equal and independent branch of government whose independence was constitutionally secured.[10]

Unsurprisingly, elucidations of judicial independence by different authors in different countries have led to distinct understandings of the term. Furthermore, owing to its conflation with ideas of checks and balances, separation of powers and rule of law, all of which have been used as justifications for judicial independence, its conceptual core is nebulous. Today, the term is used in an astonishingly diverse number of ways, directed at serving numerous objectives considered generally desirable for the judiciary. Thus, judicial independence is defined in a manner that justifies the politicised process of appointment of Supreme Court justices in the United States; it is the rationale that is cited for preventing the executive from setting the budget for the judiciary in Germany and it is used as the basis for the Supreme Court self-appointing future members of the court in India. As Tom Ginsburg has recently noted, 'Judicial

7 Scott Shapiro, 'Judicial Independence: The English Experience,' *North Carolina Law Review* 55 (1977): 577, 614.

8 See text accompanying note 17.

9 Herbert Broom and Edward Hadley (eds), *Blackstone's Commentaries on the Laws of England* (London: Maxwell, 1869), 322.

10 Federalist Papers, 508.

independence has become like freedom; everyone wants it but no one knows quite what it looks like.'[11]

This chapter develops a conceptual account of judicial independence to provide an idea of what 'it looks like', which in turn will be used to analyse its relation with judicial accountability. It does this by using the fivefold model laid out in Chapter 5 for judicial accountability to provide the broad conceptual contours of judicial independence. Given that both accountability and independence are relational terms, the model is useful in delineating and thereby breaking down the diverse usages of judicial independence into a coherently formed taxonomy. Development of such a taxonomy (Sections 6B.1–4) is useful as an end in itself to classify different uses of the term 'judicial independence' (without dismissing any offhand as illegitimate, though on further enquiry and dependent on context, they well might be), while at the same time recognising the conceptual and practical convergences and conflicts with judicial accountability. Key to understanding this relation lies in answering the question as to why judicial independence is necessary in the first place (Section 6B.5). On the basis of this answer, certain types of independence that are desirable for the judiciary can be understood, and a more searching enquiry into the effect that these types of independence have on judicial accountability undertaken. Such an enquiry provides the foundation for a new, conceptual approach to thinking about judicial independence and accountability developed in Chapter 7.

## 6B Answering the Five Questions

At a conceptual level, independence and accountability are both relational concepts. Like accountability, independence connotes the existence of a particular relation between two or more persons or entities. Unlike accountability though, the nature of the relation is distinct—independence connoting the absence of the relation of dependence between them.[12] Despite the obvious substantive difference, the baseline conceptual similarity in terms of being relational concepts makes the fivefold model used in the context of judicial accountability relevant for the purpose of classifying the various meanings of judicial independence with appropriate variations. A cursory

[11] Tom Ginsburg, 'Judicial Independence in East Asia: Lessons for China,' in *Judicial Independence in China: Lessons for Global Rule of Law Promotion*, ed. Randall Peerenboom (Cambridge: Cambridge University Press, 2010), 247, 248.

[12] Warner Fite, 'The Theory of Independence—Once More,' *Journal of Philosophy, Psychology and Scientific Methods* 10, no. 20 (1913): 546.

glance at the ways in which judicial independence is used demonstrates various subjects of independence (individual judges, the judiciary on the whole), persons to be independent of (litigating parties, the government), subject matters (decisions, behaviour, administration), rationales (impartiality, effectiveness in adjudication) and arrangements to secure it (constitutional, statutory, political, self-enforced). This process will not only highlight the fundamental conceptual similarity between judicial independence and judicial accountability but also precisely locate the sites where conflicts between the two may arise.

## *6B.1 Whose Independence?*

The subject of judicial independence, that is, whose independence is in question, has a long and complex history. In this regard, the development of two parallel strands can be seen: first, a conscious move towards ensuring that individual judges were not subject to pressure from government in taking particular substantive decisions; second, the continuing evolution of an independent judicial institution, functionally specialised and structurally distinct from the legislature and executive. These were the developments that underpinned the formulation of the twin categories of individual independence of judges and the institutional independence of the judiciary, commonly found in contemporary literature today.[13]

The independence of individual judges is an obvious necessity and largely uncontested today as a prerequisite of a fair judiciary. However, in medieval England, where judges had a key adjudicative function in resolving disputes and laying down the common law, judicial independence was not viewed as a fundamental and non-negotiable desideratum. The emergence of individual judicial independence as a prerequisite in practice can be significantly seen for the first time only in 1610 in Lord Coke's opinion in *Dr. Bonham's case.*[14] Coke held that the College of Physicians, which had imprisoned the applicant for practising medicine without a license, was acting as minister (in issuing summons), judge (in hearing the matters) and party (in receiving the fines), and the fusion of the three functions was unlawful.[15] For Coke, the genesis of judicial independence lay in the fundamental maxim of fairness that no person shall be a judge in her

[13] Ferejohn and Kramer, 'Independent Judges, Dependent Judiciary'; John Ferejohn, 'Independent Judges, Dependent Judiciary: Explaining Judicial Independence,' *Southern California Law Review* 72 (1998–99): 353.

[14] (1610) Hil. 7 Jac. 1, 8 Co. Rep. 114 (Court of Common Pleas, England).

[15] For an enumeration of this principle in the common law subsequently, see *City of London* v. *Wood*, (1706) 88 ER 1592 (Mayor's Court, England).

own cause. To ensure that judges exercised their power independently, they would have to be structurally insulated in some manner from the king.[16]

It was only in 1701 with the Act of Settlement, which substituted the doctrine of good behaviour for the pleasure doctrine as the guiding principle for judicial tenure, that Coke's view of individual judicial independence in *Dr. Bonham's case* secured a firm basis. The Act, which came about as a compromise between the king and parliament, mandated that judicial tenure would be granted *quam diu se bene gesserint* (during good behaviour), judges could only be removed upon address by both houses of parliament and judicial salaries would be ascertained and established.[17] Judges would no longer be answerable to the king and removable at pleasure but would rather continue to serve for life or until there was a breach of the good behaviour condition. While critics have suggested correctly that the Act of Settlement may not have been primarily intended to fulfil the lofty motive of judicial independence, but was rather a parliamentary ploy to circumscribe prerogative powers of the monarch, key amongst which was the control over the judiciary,[18] its unequivocal effect was to ensure that individual judges enjoyed the structural independence necessary for impartial decision-making in matters involving the state for the first time.

It is a testament to the significance of the Act of Settlement that the specific independence protections envisaged by it, namely establishment of financial security, security of tenure along with a procedurally onerous form of removal, continue to be seen as the fundamental tenets for individual independence of judges even today. For example, Art. III section 1 of the Constitution of the United States of America lays down the requirement of tenure during good behaviour as well as the guarantee of non-reduction of salary of all federal judges, whereas Art. II section 4 prescribes impeachment as the only method for removal of such judges.[19] Again, in the more recent drafting process of the Constitution of South Africa, the fundamental structural protections sought for the judiciary

[16] C. J. S. Knight, 'Bipolar Sovereignty Restated,' *The Cambridge Law Journal* 68 (2009): 361, 375.

[17] Act of Settlement, 1701, 12 & 13 Will III, c. 2 (UK). For an analysis of the meaning of the term 'good behaviour' as used in the Act, see Saikrishna Prakash and Steven D. Smith, 'How to Remove a Federal Judge,' *The Yale Law Journal* 116 (2006): 72.

[18] Robert Stevens, 'The Act of Settlement and the Questionable History of Judicial Independence,' *Oxford University Commonwealth Law Journal* 1 (2001): 253; Shapiro, 'Judicial Independence,' 626, 627.

[19] In relevant part, Art. III section 1 of the Constitution of the United States of America (hereinafter 'US Constitution') provides:

despite its anti-populist leanings were security of tenure and financial security.[20] Its continuing importance is best captured by the opinion of Justice Le Dain in the Canadian case *Valente* v. *The Queen*,[21] where he stated that though the concept of judicial independence 'has been an evolving one'[22] security of tenure, financial security of individual judges as well as the institutional independence of the adjudicating authority were its 'essential conditions'.[23]

As Justice Le Dain's opinion illustrates, the institution of the judiciary on the whole is a distinct subject of judicial independence. Unlike independence of individual judges, the requirement of institutional independence focuses on the appropriate degree of separation of the judiciary from its coordinate wings of government. Montesquieu's conception recognised the importance of such institutional separation—his proposal was to not have permanent judges, but rather to draw jurors directly from the people on an ongoing basis with their tenure limited to the particular disputes at hand.[24] The judiciary, as composed of rotating jurors, would thus be independent of the king, who would otherwise have exercised complete control, had judges been permanent. While such a solution achieved a modicum of institutional independence, it did so by making the judiciary a lay, semi-permanent and inherently weak institution with little specialisation, thereby leading to its unsuitability in adjudicating complex legal disputes.

Rendering the institution of the judiciary independent while according it coordinate status at par with the legislature and the executive was a key issue

---

> The Judges, both of the supreme and inferior Courts, shall hold their Offices during good Behavior, and shall, at stated Times, receive for their Services a Compensation, which shall not be diminished during their Continuance in Office.
>
> Art. II section 4 of the US Constitution provides: 'The President, Vice President and all civil Officers of the United States, shall be removed from Office on Impeachment for, and Conviction of, Treason, Bribery, or other high Crimes and Misdemeanors.'

20 For an understanding and analysis of judicial independence protections in the Constitution of South Africa, see Patrick Mtshaulana and Melanie Thomas, 'The Constitutional Court of South Africa: An Introduction,' *Review of Constitutional Studies* 3 (1996): 98.

21 *Valente* v. *The Queen*, (1985) 2 SCR 673 (Supreme Court of Canada) (hereinafter '*Valente*').

22 Ibid., 691.

23 Ibid., 685.

24 Anne Cohler, Basia Miller and Harold Stone (eds), *Montesquieu's The Spirit of Laws* (Cambridge: Cambridge University Press, 1989), 158.

confronting the framers of the Constitution of the United States of America. Though the authors of the Federalist Papers envisaged the federal judiciary as a coordinate organ, central to the overall scheme of checks and balances, they did not render it institutionally independent of the legislature and the executive.[25] In fact, the judiciary was specifically made dependent on its coordinate wings through the legitimacy accorded to political checks on it such as the Congress' power to exercise budgetary and jurisdictional control, lay down judicial procedure and case management rules as well as the executive's power to not enforce judicial decisions and significantly the power of appointment of federal judges.[26] Thus, key to securing the institutional status of the judiciary was to enmesh it within the checks and balances scheme of government thereby specifically denying any institutional independence.

However, over time and especially in the contemporary context of the emergence of powerful constitutional judiciaries in several jurisdictions, institutional independence has emerged as a distinct type of protection to be accorded to the judiciary. Specifically, the focus is on ensuring an appointments process that upholds institutional independence, administrative independence of the court, in terms of autonomy in setting its own budget, devising case management and procedural rules and disciplining of judges for misbehaviour short of impeachment.[27] A key example of such institutional independence can be seen in the German Federal Constitutional Court's quest for budgetary autonomy shortly after its formation.[28] Despite considerable governmental opposition, the court was successful in asserting its budgetary autonomy. This was a product of a sustained belief amongst judges that such administrative independence of the court was indeed a *sine qua non* for their functioning as an autonomous institution of state, coupled with intense pressure from both the opposition and the parliament, who saw greater independence of the judiciary as a key instrument

25 Federalist Papers, 510; For an analysis of Federalist Paper No. 78 which contains Hamilton's views on judicial independence, see Martin Redish, 'Good Behavior, Judicial Independence and the Foundations of American Constitutionalism,' *The Yale Law Journal* 116 (2006): 139.

26 Ferejohn and Kramer, 'Independent Judges, Dependent Judiciary.'

27 Anthony Mason, 'Judicial Independence and Separation of Powers, Some Problems Old and New,' *University of British Columbia Law Review* 24 (1990): 345; Ian Greene, 'The Doctrine of Judicial Independence Developed by the Supreme Court of Canada,' *Osgoode Hall Law Journal* 26 (1988): 177.

28 George Vanberg, 'Establishing Judicial Independence in West Germany: The Impact of Opinion Leadership and the Separation of Powers,' *Comparative Politics* 32, no. 3 (2000): 333.

in setting up the court as an effective counterweight to an otherwise powerful government. Institutional independence of the judiciary has now emerged as a distinct yet cognate category of independence that requires specific protection *per se* and to protect individual judges from systemic pressures.

These categories of individual and institutional independence are, as is evident, analogous to the like classification of subjects of judicial accountability. Thus, individual judges and the institution of the judiciary must be both independent and accountable. *Per se* this dual requirement does not itself suggest whether the concepts of judicial independence and accountability themselves are conflicting or congruent. Persons could be independent in some respects and accountable in others, or even when they are independent of someone, there could be a degree of accountability that they owe to others. In order to assess this relation more fully, it will be necessary to look at the individuals and institutions, independence from whom is considered desirable and how such independence is secured, which is the subject matter of the next sub-sections.

### *6B.2 From Whom?*

Implicit in the aforesaid discussion of the subject of judicial independence is the notion that a major threat to the independence of the judiciary emanates from the government.[29] The close links between the legislature and executive on the one hand, and with the judiciary on the other, seen in their role in the appointments process and administrative functioning of the judiciary, the government's presence before the court as a litigant, as well as a history of unwarranted interference by governments in the functioning of courts across jurisdictions, make such threats real. Defenders of judicial independence have thus vigorously sought effective insulation of both individual judges and the judicial institution on the whole from the government. Such measures are crucial, both to secure the independence of the judiciary *per se* and to ensure that such independence translates into impartiality of the judiciary as an arbiter of disputes involving the state, especially significant, given the dramatic growth in public law litigation.[30]

The latter rationale, it is apparent, is not limited to independence from the government alone. On the contrary, courts are required to be independent of

[29] The terms 'government', 'political organs of state' and 'coordinate organs of state' in this section are used to refer to the legislature and the executive or either of the two, as appropriate in the context.

[30] For a seminal understanding of public law litigation, see Abram Chayes, 'The Role of the Judge in Public Law Litigation,' *Harvard Law Review* 89 (1976): 1281.

any party to a case that may be in a position to threaten its impartiality. The impartiality of a court of law in resolving disputes, secured by its independence, is thus a more general constitutive factor of the judiciary itself, irrespective of the presence of the state as a litigant before it in a given case.[31] This idea is expressed most simply in the form of a triad—the court is an impartial arbiter between two antagonistic parties who require a conflict to be resolved.[32] Individual judges must thus be independent of all the parties to the case, not just the government alone, in all relevant ways. This implies that they must be protected from any threats to their independent status through sources of influence, temptations or actual threats. While space precludes a discussion of each of these threats, an example of a device to secure such individual independence aimed ultimately at ensuring impartiality in decision-making can be found in norms of recusal followed by judges. Across jurisdictions, specific guidelines require judges to recuse themselves in cases where their impartiality may be reasonably questioned.[33] While the exact nature of each of these formulations may differ, norms of recusal are designed to provide baseline protection in ensuring that adjudicators remain independent of parties before them and thereby impartial.[34]

In adjudication involving private parties only, such general protection against threats to individual independence of judges may be sufficient. However, in matters where the state is a litigant, the idea of the triad comes under intense strain, given the fact that the executive, an organ of state, is a litigant before the judiciary, which is another state organ. Independence of the judiciary from the government, through a number of mechanisms and arrangements that will be discussed presently, is thus structurally essential to maintaining the legitimacy of the triad and the impartiality of courts in a specific type of case, that is, one where the government is a litigant.

In addition, there is a prior, non-instrumental sense in which independence from the government has been deemed necessary. So pervasive has been the

[31] John Chipman Gray, *The Nature and Sources of Law* (New York: Columbia University Press, 1909), 109, 110. In a sophisticated understanding, impartiality has been considered necessary given the nature of the judicial forum as one which hears reasoned proofs and argument. See Lon L. Fuller and Kenneth I. Winston, 'The Forms and Limits of Adjudication,' *Harvard Law Review* 92, no. 2 (1978): 353.

[32] Shapiro, 'Judicial Independence.'

[33] As an illustrative example, see rules against appearance of bias and conflict of interest for judges of the Supreme Court of the United Kingdom. See UK Judicial Guide, paras 3.7–3.16.

[34] For more, see Grant Hammond, *Judicial Recusal: Principles, Process and Problems* (Oxford: Hart Publishing, 2009).

incidence of attempted political interference in both the composition and functioning of the judiciary that independence from the political organs of state has become desirable *per se* to retain the appearance of independence, irrespective of any case-specific impartiality considerations. Thus, historically, protections accorded to individual judges, that is, security of tenure, financial security and removal by impeachment, as demonstrated earlier, were primarily directed at insulating the judiciary from the political organs of state. Likewise, more contemporary institutional independence measures relating to administrative autonomy, self-disciplining of judges as well as appointment mechanisms, all developed with a key objective of insulating the judiciary from political interference *per se*. Such a justification for independence from political organs of state was prompted both by principle—independence of the judiciary is a *sine qua non* for maintaining the distinct institutional role of the judiciary as a coordinate organ of state—and by the experience of repeated attempts to coerce the judiciary into adopting the governmental standpoint on issues. The working of the King's Courts in England in the medieval ages,[35] the early colonial courts in America[36] and, more recently, courts in apartheid South Africa[37] and the Supreme Court of India during a short period of Emergency[38] are all testament to the need for independence of the judiciary from the government *per se* with a view to specifically retaining the appearance of independence in the public eye.

It is unsurprising that such a requirement of independence of the judiciary from its coordinate organs of state has been inevitably seen as flowing from a requirement of separation of powers. Though the exact nature of such a connection between separation of powers and judicial independence will be analysed in Chapter 7, the existence of such a linkage points to a key salient fact: the independence of the judiciary from the government cannot ever be absolute. This flows from the universally acknowledged view that separation of powers between organs of state, despite varying enumerations, is never absolute and each organ is separate in some respects and aligned in others.[39] Given the

35 G. E. Aylmer, *The King's Servants* (London: Routledge and Kegan Paul, 1974), 44.

36 Joseph H. Smith, 'An Independent Judiciary: The Colonial Background,' *University Of Pennsylvania Law Review* 124 (1976): 1104.

37 David Dyzenhaus, *Judging the Judges, Judging Ourselves: Truth, Reconciliation and the Apartheid Legal Order* (Oxford: Hart Publishing, 2003).

38 Seervai, *Emergency, Future Safeguards and the Habeas Corpus Case*, 1–59.

39 M. J. C. Vile, *Constitutionalism and the Separation of Powers* (Indianapolis: Liberty Fund, 1998, 2nd ed.), 14.

connections that exist between the judiciary and government, the key question to ask is not whether the judiciary is independent of government or not, but rather how independent the judiciary is. Thus, judicial independence from the government must be fundamentally constructed, not as a binary value, but rather a spectral one, focusing on whether it is independent of the government in ways that are relevant and to a degree that is optimal.

### *6B.3 How Is It Safeguarded?*

Judicial independence, both from litigants before the court generally and from the coordinate organs of state specifically is secured by a conspectus of rules, conventions and practices. Arrangements to secure judicial independence are distinct, geared to protect the judiciary from diverse threats, directed either at the level of the individual judge or at the institutional level. Accordingly, they can be classified into four categories: constitutional, statutory, political and self-enforced arrangements for protection.

Constitutional methods for protection of judicial independence definitionally vary depending on the constitution in question. However, in the common law world, financial security, security of tenure combined with a procedurally onerous mechanism for removal of judges are safeguards that though subject to particular variations are entrenched widely. Financial security, that is, the guarantee of a permanent, non-diminishing judicial salary during tenure, is an instrumental mechanism to protect judicial independence. Its rationale, captured succinctly by Alexander Hamilton, is based on the commonsensical view that '[i]n the general course of human nature, a power over a man's subsistence amounts to a power over his will'.[40] Thus, constitutional clauses that provide protection against salary reduction are fairly well-established. They seek to divest the legislature and the executive of the power to reduce judicial salaries, thereby ensuring that the judiciary is not dependent on its coordinate organs on this account and consequently not beholden to them in its decision-making.[41] Examples of the insidious effect control over judicial salaries can have can be seen in the courts of the British colonies in the United States prior to its independence. As an example, in Massachusetts Bay, judicial

[40] Federalist Paper No. 79 in Federalist Papers, 518.

[41] A more recent debate with regard to judicial salaries has focused on the power of government to not increase judicial salaries rather than the power to reduce salaries, the traditional concern. See Christopher E. Smith, 'Federal Judicial Salaries: A Critical Appraisal,' *Temple Law Review* 62 (1989): 849.

salaries were paid directly by the Crown from taxation revenue as specified in the Townshend Revenue Act. As a result, judges were entirely beholden to the Crown, and the possibility of impartial justice rendered negligible. Protesting against this, the House of Representatives passed a resolution that rendering judges dependent on the Crown for their salary was unconstitutional as it led to the establishment of arbitrary government in the province.[42]

Given similar experiences in other colonies,[43] the Declaration of Independence in 1776, in specifying the improprieties of the monarch, noted that '[h]e has made Judges dependent on his Will alone, for the tenure of their offices, and the amount and payment of their salaries'.[44] Rectifying this position, most state constitutions drafted in pursuance of the declaration provided for permanent salaries determined by law, epitomised by the Compensation Clause of the United States Constitution which provides:

> The Judges… shall, at stated times, receive for their services, a compensation, which shall not be diminished during their continuance in office.[45]

Security of tenure, equally significant in protecting judicial independence, guarantees tenure for as long as the constitution allows it (including for life if so allowed) protecting judges from arbitrary removal within this period.[46] It was firmly established through the incorporation of the good behaviour requirement in the Act of Settlement 1701, which responded to the most egregious threat to the independence of judges that existed hitherto, that is, the king's power to remove judges at pleasure.[47]

[42] Smith, 'Independent Judiciary,' 1120.

[43] Irving R. Kaufman, 'The Essence of Judicial Independence,' *Columbia Law Review* 80 (1980): 671, 679–87.

[44] The Declaration of Independence (1776) (USA), available at http://www.archives.gov/exhibits/charters/declaration.html (accessed 31 July 2012); for an analysis, see Carl L. Becker, *The Declaration of Independence: A Study in the History of Political Ideas* (New York: Vintage Books, 1958), 3–23.

[45] US Constitution, Art. III section 1.

[46] An authoritative understanding of security of tenure can be found in the UN Basic Principles: 'Judges, whether appointed or elected, shall have guaranteed tenure until a mandatory retirement age or the expiry of their term of office, where such exists.'

[47] C. H. McIlwain, *Constitutionalism and the Changing World: Collected Papers* (Cambridge: Cambridge University Press, 1939), 294, 302. For pre-Act of Settlement security of tenure discussions, see James C. Corson, 'Judges and Statutory Tenure in England in the Seventeenth Century,' *Juridical Review* 42 (1930): 136.

The extent of protection the judiciary had from parliament, however, remained an open question. This was especially so since good behaviour tenure in the Act of Settlement was accompanied by the vesting of power in parliament to remove judges, albeit through the device of an address being presented in both houses. On the other hand, in the United States, impeachment proceedings in the House of Representatives combined with trial in the Senate was the constitutionally mandated method for removal of federal judges. Impeachment in the United States Constitution or removal by address in the United Kingdom, by virtue of its procedure, was certainly more difficult than removal owing to displeasure of the monarch. In this sense, it provided an important fillip for judicial independence. But fear of parliamentary misuse of the power of removal was widely expressed through the course of the eighteenth century.[48]

But since then, till today, the power to impeach has not been viewed as a threat to judicial independence, being seen paradoxically as 'the only provision … which is consistent with the necessary independence of the judicial character'.[49] This understanding is revealing for a number of reasons. First, it reaffirms the view advanced in the previous section, that judicial independence is not meant to be absolute. If such absolute independence was required, vesting the power of removal in the legislature could hardly have been acceptable, let alone commended. Giving the legislature the absolute power to impeach, as Art. II section 1 of the United States Constitution does, suggests that an underlying rationale, distinct from complete insulation of the judiciary, must be found to conceptualise judicial independence. Equally, it suggests that the conceptualisation of judicial independence and how it is to be protected cannot purely be a determination based on constitutional provisions; if that were so, vesting the power of removal in a popularly elected legislature, which could use it to remove judges for flimsy and unwarranted reasons, would be anathema. Instead, protecting judicial independence equally involves looking at actual political practice, how coordinate organs of state interact and the political arrangements that make the preservation of judicial independence possible.

Political arrangements to secure judicial independence are products of the historical development of inter-institutional relations in particular

[48] Broom and Hadley, *Blackstone's Commentaries*, 150–51; this view was especially prevalent in British Colonies in America where the power of removal by address was considered untrammelled; for an analysis, see Robert Stevens, *The English Judges: Their Role in the Changing Constitution* (Oxford: Hart Publishing, 2002), 10.

[49] Federalist Paper No. 79, in Federalist Papers, 519.

constitutional contexts in countries. They are thus contingent on the terms of the separation of powers envisaged constitutionally and consequently the checks and balances considered to be legitimate.[50] Evidence of such political arrangements can be seen in most jurisdictions—the failed impeachment trial of Justice Chase of the Supreme Court of the United States, adverted to in Chapter 5, giving rise to the practice of not impeaching a judge on the basis of substantive decisions made;[51] the acceptance by the Indian parliament of the basic structure doctrine, allowing courts to strike down constitutional amendments for being unconstitutional, after a prolonged struggle with the Supreme Court that imperilled the independence of the judiciary[52] and the traditional role of the Lord Chancellor in England as the protector of judicial independence by serving as a bridge between the judiciary and the government and upholding judicial independence, by convention, in his decision-making.[53] Common to these political arrangements is the respect that, by virtue of long-established practice, is accorded to the judiciary by its coordinate wings of government, without which the protection of judicial independence, despite the most carefully constructed constitutional provisions, would remain illusory.

While by virtue of long-established practice several such political protections have become conventions, key statutory protections have also developed for securing judicial independence. The most notable statutory development in the common law has been the passage of the Constitutional Reform Act, 2005, in the United Kingdom. The Act provides a firm statutory basis for judicial independence, making its protection a statutory obligation on the Lord Chancellor. It also provides for an independent Judicial Appointments Commission to make appointments and sets up the new Supreme Court, abolishing the Appellate Committee of the House of Lords, which exercised judicial functions, and could by convention exercise legislative functions as well. Undoing the historical anomaly of the highest appellate court being a committee of parliament and replacing the conventional methods for protecting judicial independence with statutory provisions and a publicly accountable Judicial Appointments Commission for

50 Gerald N. Rosenberg, 'Judicial Independence and the Reality of Political Power,' *The Review of Politics* 55, no. 3 (1992): 369.

51 William H. Rehnquist, 'Judicial Independence: Symposium Remarks,' *The University of Richmond Law Review* 38 (2004): 579, 582–89.

52 Austin, *Working a Democratic Constitution*, 171–390.

53 Diana Woodhouse, *The Office of the Lord Chancellor* (Oxford: Hart Publishing, 2001).

appointments based on clear criteria was thus an unequivocal statement that for the courts to be independent, they had to be seen to be so.[54]

Equally, in several other jurisdictions, standards of judicial behaviour and complaints mechanisms short of impeachable offences have been provided statutory basis.[55] Several aspects of these statutes, some of which shall be dealt with presently, seek to protect the independence of judges by regulating their interactions with the general public. By making these protections statutory and thereby actionable, greater certainty has thus been attached to their protection thereby demonstrating the growing significance of judicial independence.

Apart from constitutional, political and statutory arrangements to protect judicial independence, the judiciary itself has a key role in perpetuating its own independence. This takes two forms: First, an institutionalised self-restraint exemplified in its refusal to adjudicate on political questions, matters of policy and any other matter deemed to be outside its legitimacy. Space precludes a discussion of whether and how judiciaries have exhibited such restraint; it would suffice to say that the nature of judicial decision-making is instrumental in maintaining the delicate political arrangements to secure judicial independence.[56] Second, internal codes of conduct operate as autonomous devices to protect judicial independence. The Restatement of Values of Judicial Life (1997), adopted by the full bench of the Supreme Court of India, voluntarily commits judges to recuse themselves from matters where there may be a perceived conflict of interest, not publicly express opinions of matters that are pending or likely to arise for adjudication and other analogous principles, deemed necessary to protect the independence of the judiciary.[57] Similar, albeit more detailed prescriptions, can be found in the Guide to Judicial Conduct adopted by the UK Supreme Court.[58]

The methods for protection of judicial independence are thus diverse in their scope. This suggests that threats to the judiciary are from diverse sources, while pointing out the diverse facets of the functioning of the judiciary for which

[54] For more, see Diana Woodhouse, 'United Kingdom: The Constitutional Reform Act, 2005—Defending Judicial Independence the English Way,' *International Journal of Constitutional Law* 5 (2007): 153; Steyn, 'Case for a Supreme Court.'

[55] Judicial Councils Reform and Judicial Conduct and Disability Act, 1980 (USA), 28 USC §§ 351–64.

[56] For more, see Ferejohn and Kramer, 'Independent Judges, Dependent Judiciary.'

[57] Restatement.

[58] UK Judicial Guide.

independence is a prerequisite. Having addressed the former in the previous section, it is the specific facets of judicial functioning that merit protection that are discussed in the next section.

## *5B.4 Regarding What?*

The aspects of judicial functioning for which independence is sought are contingent on the role of the judiciary in the constitutional architecture of the country in question. Proactive constitutional judiciaries exercising judicial review tend to demand independence for a range of activities fearing interference from reactionary political organs of state, whereas for restrained judiciaries the ambit is considerably more limited.[59] Irrespective of the power wielded by the judiciary, however, is the need for decisional independence, that is, independence in decision-making, which is central to the legitimate functioning of any judiciary. It has thus been widely described as the '*sine qua non* of judicial independence'.[60] Decisional independence involves safeguarding judges from threats, temptations, reprisals and other extraneous pressures, which can affect judicial decision-making.[61] It is core to judicial functioning and needs little additional explanation.

These ends served by decisional independence measures are equally the rationale for administrative independence measures, which constitute a second aspect of judicial functioning regarding which independence is sought. Calls for administrative independence have grown as an institutional response to an increasing recognition of diverse and subtle means of political interference ultimately directed at making the judiciary subservient to the government in terms of the substantive decisions made. Such interference has been seen to be directly proportionate to the growing power wielded by constitutional judiciaries.[62] At the institutional level, budgetary autonomy of the judiciary, independence in laying down case management rules and, most recently, divesting the political organs of their hitherto significant role in appointment of judges are key to securing administrative independence. The preferred

[59] This connection has been widely made. For a link between judicial power and independence, see Malleson and Russell, *Age of Judicial Power*, 3–10.

[60] Gordon Bermant and Russell R. Wheeler, 'Federal Judges and the Judicial Branch: Their Independence and Accountability,' *The Mercer Law Review* 46 (1995): 835, 838.

[61] Ferejohn and Kramer, 'Independent Judges, Dependent Judiciary,' 965.

[62] For the connection between growing power of the judiciary and threats to its independence, see Tate and Vallinder, *Global Expansion of Judicial Power.*

method to achieve this end, commonly prevalent in several countries, is the existence of a judicial commission responsible both for appointment and for several aspects of internal court administration. One of the early examples of such commissions was the South African Judicial Service Commission, which was set up as a constitutional authority under section 178 of the Constitution of South Africa, 1995. The Constitution, read with the relevant legislation, vested the commission with a key role in appointment of judges, investigation into misconduct and hearing of complaints as well as recommending removal to the president.[63]

Unlike institutional administrative functions, the scope of administrative functions of individual judges is negligible and thus no specific independence-related protection has been deemed necessary. However, for the chief justice, in whom several administrative functions vest, such individual independence becomes significant. For example, the chief justice of India is responsible for setting up panels in the Supreme Court and assigning cases to each panel. A revealing study of administrative decisions of four chief justices between 1973 and 1981 in panel selection and case assignments reveals wide divergences in the size of panel formations, the composition of judges in each panel and participation of each judge in Constitution bench decisions (five judges or more) depending on the chief justice in question.[64] At the same time, another study shows that the chief justice of India is 6.5 times less likely to be in dissent than other judges on a constitution bench.[65] This demonstrates how the administrative power of constituting benches can be used by the chief justice to affect substantive decisions of the court, especially in important cases that are heard by larger benches. Independence from the government and other sectional interests is thus crucial to ensure that these administrative tasks are performed in a fair and efficient manner.

Another aspect of judicial functioning where the judiciary has asserted its independence has been with regard to disciplining individual judges for misbehaviour short of the threshold necessary for an impeachment proceeding. While impeachment for serious misconduct is constitutionally the prerogative of the legislature subject to onerous procedural safeguards in most jurisdictions, misbehaviour short of impeachment was a grey area where increasing demands

[63] For an analysis of the Judicial Service Commission, see Hugh Corder, 'Judicial Authority in a Changing South Africa,' *Legal Studies* 24 (2004): 253, 262–65.

[64] Gupta, *Decision Making*, 95–121.

[65] Nick Robinson, 'Structure Matters: The Impact of Court Structure on the Indian and US Supreme Courts,' *The American Journal of Comparative Law* 61, no. 1 (2013): 173.

for accountability were being raised.[66] To address such concerns while respecting the independence of the judiciary which could potentially be threatened if such disciplining could be carried out at the instance of the legislature or executive, several judiciary-led disciplining methods have been devised in various jurisdictions. For example, in the United States, subsequent to the Judicial Councils Reform and Judicial Conduct and Disability Act of 1980, the federal judiciary has the power to devise its own framework for disciplining judges short of impeaching them. In India currently, the Judicial Standards and Accountability Bill, 2012, though not enforceable, envisaged the setting up of a bipartisan National Judicial Commission, which will oversee any investigation of judicial misconduct.

Decisions, behaviour and administration are thus aspects of judicial functioning regarding which independence is necessary. A key fact that emerges from the analysis in this section is that judicial independence is not a monolithic concept applicable to the judiciary on the whole but rather to specific aspects of judicial functioning. For example, a judge choosing to ignore conventional modes of dressing in a courtroom is also expressing her independence, literally interpreted. However, our analysis of the types of independence deemed necessary, as well as the persons and institutions to be independent of, demonstrates that neither absolute independence in terms of degree nor independence regarding all aspects of judicial functioning is desirable. The rejection of the monolithic conception of judicial independence in favour of decisional, behavioural and administrative independence leads us to the obvious question as to why certain kinds of independence are desirable and thereby deemed necessary, whereas others are not. It is this question of the rationale for judicial independence that is discussed next.

## *6B.5 Why?*

Most legal systems in democratic countries take the existence of judicial independence for granted. On the other hand, in non-democratic states or fledgling democracies where judiciaries are subservient to the ruling dispensation, the lack of judicial independence is lamented and the securing of such independence is seen as the bellwether of democratic change. A statement such as 'Independence of the judiciary is a basic feature of the justice system under the Constitution'[67] and 'Judicial independence and public access to justice

66 Law Comm., 195th Report.

67 K. Veeraswami, *The Perils to Justice: A Judge Thinks Aloud* (Kolkata: Eastern Law House, 1996), 118.

are important requirements for the rule of law in the human dimension'[68] are commonplace and testimony to the importance attached to judicial independence in democratic and non-democratic states alike. But they say little as to why such independence is deemed necessary. In fact, being unsupported by further argument, as they often are, they give rise to the impression that judicial independence is necessary *per se* for any judicial system to function. While this may indeed partly be the case, it is far from providing a comprehensive explanation. On the contrary, as evidenced by history and modern practice, the reasons for wanting judicial independence are complex, intertwined with knotty conceptual questions concerning impartiality, separation of powers and the rule of law.

Historically in England, as adverted to earlier, judges were never considered independent functionaries. Instead they were officers of the Crown, much like others in administration. The lack of independence was *per se* not considered to be a hindrance to adjudication for several centuries.[69] It was only when it became evident that impartial justice, specifically in matters involving the monarch, was impossible with a dependent judiciary that the demand for its independence was raised by parliament. At the same time, for parliament, it was politically imperative to prevent excessive concentration of powers in the king. Separating the judiciary from the king thus became a key demand that would secure the independence of the judiciary, thereby diminishing the power of the king.[70] Judicial independence was thus sought not for its own sake but to promote impartial justice and effectuate separation of powers in the context of the bitter struggle for political supremacy between king and parliament.

Equally, in the colonies in America and subsequently in the drafting process of the Constitution of the United States of America, judicial independence was a key device to ensure impartial adjudication. The demand for independence of judges in the colonies came from the popular legislatures who viewed judges as agents of the colonial government, incapable of rendering impartial justice.[71]

[68] Organisation for Democratic Institutions and Human Rights, *Strengthening Judicial Independence and Public Access to Justice* (OSCE Human Dimension Seminar Consolidated Summary, Warsaw, 17–19 May 2010), 2.

[69] For a history of the role of judges in England in the 17th Century up to which time this view was largely prevalent, see Aylmer, *King's Servants*, 44–57.

[70] For a view which stresses the power struggle between the king and parliament being responsible for a limited idea of judicial independence being developed, see Stevens, 'Act of Settlement.'

[71] Smith, 'Independent Judiciary.'

Evocatively, a Letter of Correspondence drafted by the inhabitants of Boston noted that the dependence of the judiciary on the Crown would

> Deprive us of every thing valuable as Men, as Christians and as Subjects, entitled, by the Royal Charter, to all the Rights, liberties and privileges of native Britons.[72]

Building on this, the authors of the Federalist Papers realised that independence of the judiciary from the colonial governor should not lead to its dependence on the popular legislature. Thus, they sought to make the judiciary a constitutional organ, optimally independent of both the Congress and the president, with the power of judicial review to check and balance them, thereby effectuating the constitutionally envisaged separation of powers scheme. Independence of the judiciary was a key element in this scheme, 'to secure a steady, upright and impartial administration of laws'[73] without which the limitations on the legislature and the executive 'would amount to nothing'.[74]

Even in the current day, demands for judicial independence where it does not exist, or exists inadequately, are made primarily with the underlying goal of seeking impartiality in adjudication or effectuation of a more workable separation of powers scheme. Criticisms of elections to appoint judges, the prevalent system for appointment in several states in the United States of America, are founded on the view that elected judges are inadequately independent of the parties in a case and thereby incapable of rendering impartial justice.[75] Again, in the United Kingdom, where no serious concerns regarding judicial independence existed, the Constitutional Reform Act, 2005, was mooted by the Labour government to 'redraw the relationship between the judiciary, the government and Parliament to preserve and increase [our] judges' independence'.[76] Specifically, the abolition of the traditional functions of the Lord Chancellor, stripping him of his right

[72] 18 Boston Records Commissioners (1887) 106 *as cited in* Smith, 'Independent Judiciary,' 1146.

[73] Federalist Papers, 511.

[74] Ibid.

[75] Roy A. Schotland, 'Six Fatal Flaws: A Comment on Bopp and Neeley,' *Denver University Law Review* 86 (2008): 233. Even Bopp and Neeley, who do not object to personal solicitation of campaign funds by candidates in judicial elections, admit that impartiality is a key value which needs to be protected: see James Bopp Jr. and Josiah Neeley, 'How not to Reform Judicial Elections: Davis, White, and the Future of Judicial Campaign Financing,' *Denver University Law Review* 86 (2008): 195.

[76] Department for Constitutional Affairs, *A Supreme Court for the United Kingdom*, CP 11/03 (Oxford: Department for Constitutional Affairs, 2003), para 7.

to sit as a judge while continuing as a member of the prime minister's cabinet, and vesting the power of judicial appointments instead in a proposed Judicial Appointments Commission were envisaged as key steps towards securing the institutional independence of the judiciary, thereby leading to a more structured separation of powers scheme.[77] Thus judicial independence, if scrutinised closely, despite its self-evidently virtuous qualities, has been widely sought for ensuring impartial adjudication and an effective separation of powers scheme. This requires a close analysis of the key linkages that exist between judicial independence on the one hand and impartial adjudication and separation of powers on the other. Let us consider each of these linkages in turn.

Independence of the judiciary and its impartiality are terms that are often used interchangeably in common parlance. Both signify a certain degree of detachment of the judiciary, and both are concerned with the relation that the judiciary has with others, institutions or individual litigants, as the case may be. But does that entail synonymy? The Bangalore Principles of Judicial Conduct, 2002, drafted and agreed upon by chief justices and judges from apex courts of several jurisdictions and the International Court of Justice, recognise each, that is, independence and impartiality, as separate values to be secured. Though the principles point to a degree of congruence between the two concepts inasmuch as both judicial independence and impartiality are seen as key elements of the rule of law, two conceptual distinctions emerge from their separate treatment in the principles. First, impartiality primarily makes sense at the level of the individual judge and his/her decision-making. The idea of the judiciary as an institution having to be impartial is either a platitude, if the word 'impartiality' is used loosely, or has the limited meaning of suggesting that the judiciary institutionally should not be biased in its decision-making.[78] Second, judicial independence is a wider concept than is judicial impartiality. While both terms are relational, independence entails the lack of dependence, of either an individual judge or the judicial institution, from the political organs of state or the parties to the case regarding decision-making, administration or factors affecting the general behavioural integrity of judges. Impartiality, on the other hand, focuses on the specific relation between the individual judge and the parties to the case in the context of a judicial decision-making process. While this may certainly

[77] Roger Masterman, *Separation of Powers in the Contemporary Constitution: Judicial Competence and Independence in the United Kingdom* (Cambridge: Cambridge University Press, 2011), 220–24.

[78] This is relevant primarily for courts which sit *en banc*, rather than courts which sit in benches where discerning institutional bias is difficult.

require independence of the judge, besides other objective factors to be met, to assess her impartiality or the lack thereof requires relating back such factors to the decision-making process undertaken by the judge and the effects thereupon. It is thus a narrower enquiry.

The latter difference suggests theoretically what the history of the quest for judicial independence suggested in practice, that judicial impartiality, widely considered integral to any decision-making process, is a key reason why judicial independence is sought in the first place. Specifically, decisional independence of individual judges from the parties to the case as well as from the government (when it is a litigating party) is prompted by concerns of impartiality. This type of impartiality, known as party impartiality, is central to judicial independence.[79] Apart from such party impartiality, issue impartiality, that is, impartiality regarding issues before court, is significant only to the extent that an individual judge does not have a committed opinion regarding her stance on particular issues that arise before her,[80] or the judiciary does not formulate a pre-fixed ideological policy in this regard.[81]

It is crucial to note that, in all cases where impartiality is in question, it is the perception of impartiality that is the key test.[82] A good example is provided by the case of *R* v. *Bow Street Metropolitan Stipendiary Magistrate and others (Ex Parte Pinochet Ugarte No. 2)*.[83] The question before the House of Lords in this case was whether its previous decision to reject an immunity plea by Pinochet, the former president of Chile, should be quashed on the ground that Lord Hoffman, one of the judges to the said decision, was a director of the Amnesty International Charity, a wholly owned subsidiary of Amnesty International, which was an intervener in the case. Pinochet's counsel did not impute any actual bias on the part of Lord Hoffman but suggested that there was an

79 In India, party impartiality is ensured through the convention of judges recusing themselves in case of a conflict of interest. This question was raised and discussed in detail in the recusal order of Justice Chelameswar in the *NJAC Case* rejecting the request that Justice Khehar recuse himself from the case.

80 UK Judicial Guide, para 3.14.

81 This is a complex concern especially in the United States, where the political views of several judges are known and many judges might be elected: Laura E. Little, 'Loyalty, Gratitude and the Federal Judiciary,' *American University Law Review* 44 (1995): 699.

82 Torstein Eckhoff, 'Impartiality, Separation of Powers and Judicial Independence,' *Scandinavian Studies* 9 (1965): 9, 12.

83 [2000] 1 AC 119 (House of Lords, UK).

appearance of such bias, which ought to be sufficient to quash the proceedings. The House of Lords upheld this argument on the ground that Lord Hoffman's association with Amnesty International Charity gave him relevant interest in the subject matter of the case, thereby making him a judge in his own cause and consequently not impartial. Likewise, impartiality requirements in codes of judicial conduct require judges to act in a manner that does not give rise to any 'perception of partiality towards [an] organisation, group or cause'[84] rather than requiring actual impartiality. The perception of impartiality in the decision-making process, impartial adjudication for short, is thus a key rationale for the independence of individual judges from the parties to the case regarding their decision-making.

The institutional independence of the judiciary from the government, especially regarding judicial administration and disciplining of individual judges, is supported by another, arguably distinct rationale, based on the concept of separation of powers. Judicial independence has been widely considered to be necessary to secure separation of powers between the three organs of government.[85] While this is often asserted dogmatically, the underlying reasons for such a linkage lie in the twin objectives of instituting a separation of powers scheme in the first place, that is, securing the functional competence of distinct institutions of government[86] and ensuring that by an efficient exercise of functions, they can uphold the rule of law.[87] The independence of the judiciary is considered necessary in order to vest the judiciary with the functional competence it requires to adjudicate, as well as to prevent transgressions by the government through such adjudication. Let us consider each of these in turn.

[84] UK Judicial Guide, para 3.5.

[85] Kaufman, 'Essence of Judicial Independence,' 688; Eckhoff, 'Impartiality, Separation of Powers,' 11.

[86] Jeremy Waldron, 'Separation of Powers in Thought and Practice,' *Boston College Law Review* 54, no. 2 (2013): 433; Nick Barber, 'Prelude to the Separation of Powers,' *The Cambridge Law Journal* 60 (2001): 59.

[87] The connection between separation of powers and rule of law is best illustrated in John Adams' drafting of Art. XXX of the Massachusetts Constitution 1780 (USA), where he writes:

> In the government of this commonwealth, the legislative department shall never exercise the executive and judicial powers, or either of them: the executive shall never exercise the legislative and judicial powers, or either of them: the judicial shall never exercise the legislative and executive powers, or either of them; to the end it may be a government of laws and not of men.

Functional competence of state institutions involves structuring the form of an institution according to the function it performs. In early separation of powers literature, the exercise of judicial functions, that is, adjudication of disputes, was not considered sufficiently distinct from the functions of the executive to warrant distinct treatment, or be vested in a separate institution. Separation of powers was, at the time, envisaged as twofold: legislative and executive.[88] However, stray references can be found in early literature pointing to the existence of certain judicial functions such as adjudicating cases of treason, which the king ought not to judge, given that he would be both judge and party to the case.[89] Over time, as more and more functions of the executive began to be recognised as judicial, the different competencies required for the exercise of judicial power became prominent.[90]

Montesquieu, the most celebrated proponent of the idea of separation of powers, challenged the consolidation of judicial power with executive power on the grounds of unfairness and impracticability. In Book VI of *The Spirit of Laws*, he advanced a limited separation of judicial power from the executive, based on the view that if the power of the prince (executive) was seen as consolidated, including the power to both execute and judge, it would be a travesty, since 'he would be both judge and party'.[91] Besides, if the prince judged, it would render superfluous his power to pardon, which was 'the finest attribute of his sovereignty'.[92]

The context and rationale of Montesquieu's limited separation are significant. At the time of writing, Montesquieu's chief concern, as is apparent in Book XI of *The Spirit of Laws*, was a joining of the three powers of legislation, execution and judging in the same person or body of persons.[93] This, according to him, would lead to a loss of liberty, as in the Italian republics, with degeneration into despotism a distinct possibility, as in Turkey.[94] Specifically, if the judge and executor were the same, 'the judge could have the force of an oppressor …

88 John Locke, 'An Essay Concerning the True Original, Extent, and End of Civil Government,' in *Two Treatises of Government*, ed. Peter Laslett (Cambridge: Cambridge University Press, 1988), 265, 364–66.

89 Vile, *Constitutionalism and the Separation of Powers*, 34–35.

90 Charles Dallison, *The Royalists Defence* (1648), available at http://gateway.proquest.com/openurl?ctx_ver=Z39.88-2003&res_id=xri:eebo&rft_id=xri:eebo:image:54815:2 (accessed 14 July 2012).

91 Cohler, Miller and Stone, *Montesquieu's The Spirit of Law*, 78.

92 Ibid.

93 Ibid., 157.

94 Ibid.

and it [*sic*] can destroy each citizen by using its particular wills.'[95] Hence, he envisaged a limited separation, which would ensure that judicial functions were not exercised by the same body of persons as those who were responsible for their execution. This was achieved by drawing jurors directly from the people, to whom they owed their direct allegiance, and limiting their tenure to particular disputes at hand. Though judicial power was thus separated from executive and legislative power, because it was seen as distinctly inferior in nature to them, it did not warrant a permanent judicial institution.

The rationale for articulating a distinct judicial power, without a separate judicial institution, was to ensure that judges were independent of the parties to the case, which very often, and most commonly in criminal law matters, was the king himself, while not having a chance to acquire power, given their temporary status. Functional competence for the judges thereby implied their ability to adjudicate impartially in matters where the king was a party. No additional qualifications were felt necessary, as evident in the lay nature of the semi-permanent judiciary. This understanding of separation of powers leading to functional competence, which in the case of the Montesquieuan judiciary required it to be independent of the king, is reminiscent of the notion of impartial adjudication being the rationale for judicial independence. Separation of powers, thus expounded, seems to require independence of individual judges from the other organs of government so that they can be impartial when such organs regularly appear before them in their capacity as litigants, despite their concomitant ability to interfere in their independent functioning. Thus, the argument from functional competence appears to essentially rest on the ability of the judiciary to adjudicate impartially.

A second rationale for judicial independence, flowing from separation of powers, concerns the rule of law. This is achieved through two means: first, by the very conceptualisation of the judiciary as an institution independent of the legislature and the executive, responsible for the exercise of judicial power, thereby preventing the excessive concentration of political power in a single organ which is antithetical to the rule of law;[96] second, by creating an institutional structure amenable to the judiciary passing judgments quashing decisions taken by the political organs of the state 'to the end it may be a government of laws and not of men.'[97]

[95] Ibid.

[96] For the connection between separation of powers and the rule of law, see Waldron, 'Separation of Powers.'

[97] Massachusetts Constitution 1780 (USA), Art. XXX; for a discussion of the phrase, see Burin, 'Theory of the Rule of Law,' 318.

One of the fundamental underpinnings of separation of powers as a means to achieve the rule of law is the need to prevent excessive powers being vested in a single institution. One of the finest expressions of this is Madison's words in Federalist No. 47 where he writes:

> The accumulation of all powers, legislative, executive, and judiciary, in the same hands, whether of one, a few, or many, and whether hereditary, self-appointed or elective, may justly be pronounced the very definition of tyranny.[98]

Integral to the scheme of separation envisaged by Madison was a bicameral legislature, a unified presidency and an independent judiciary. Though the judiciary was given constitutional status as a distinct organ, thereby making it independent of the legislature and executive insofar as the source of its authority is concerned, it was inherently weak, having no control over either the finances of the state or the army. Such infirmities were sought to be offset by a fortified conception of judicial independence. Judicial independence would thus be crucial in securing the institutional status of the judiciary, thereby reducing the scope for governmental interference. This specifically entailed that judges of the Supreme Court were appointed during good behaviour, with fixed salaries that could not be reduced to their disadvantage by the government, no retirement age and removal only by impeachment.[99] Permanence in office would ensure that an independent spirit pervaded the judiciary and possibilities of governmental interference reduced substantially. Non-reduction of compensation would be equally crucial to maintain this spirit, since pecuniary control over judges would render them answerable to the government and jeopardise their autonomous institutional nature. The procedure for impeachment too was multi-layered, such that the threat of removal could not be used as a stick by the government to ensure conformity by the judiciary.[100] Creating a separate judicial institution and providing safeguards for its independence were thus envisaged as important checks against the concentration of political power in either the legislative or executive organ of state.

A related linkage between judicial independence, separation of powers and the rule of law lies in the ability of the judiciary to uphold a government by

[98] Federalist Paper No. 47 in Federalist Papers, 316.

[99] Federalist Paper Nos. 78, 79 in Federalist Papers, 514, 520.

[100] The grounds for impeachment too were restricted to certain kinds of malpractice; inability was specifically excluded as a ground. Federalist Paper No. 79 in Federalist Papers, 519–20.

law through checking transgressions of the law by the political organs of state. The judiciary, an organ of state, set up by law is vested with the crucial task of ensuring that the government itself is bound by the laws it makes. This checking function is performed by the judiciary through the exercise of the judicial power vested in it, to quash illegal administrative decisions taken by the government, as well as striking down unconstitutional statutes, if it has the power of judicial review of primary legislation. Independence of the judicial institution from the political organs of government regarding decision-making and administration, as well as regarding judicial behaviour of individual judges, is a *sine qua non* for such a checking function to be performed. The lack of independence, as has been demonstrated earlier, leads to the grave improbability of impartial adjudication, thereby reducing the possibility of checking and balancing government. But given the institutional weakness of courts and their consequent dependence on the government to enforce its orders and decrees, can judicial independence itself lead to effective checks and balances thereby preventing transgressions by the government and ensuring the rule of law? This is enquired into in Chapter 7.

In the final analysis, judicial independence is necessary for impartial adjudication, as well as for securing separation of powers. While an analysis of the former demonstrates the distinct nature of the two concepts of independence and impartiality, a deeper scrutiny of the arguments underlying the separation of powers leads to the understanding that separation of powers concerns are at their core, part concern for impartial adjudication and part about ensuring that the judiciary is effective in checking and balancing government and upholding the rule of law. This idea of a judiciary adjudicating impartially and ensuring separation of powers, termed 'an effective judiciary' in shorthand henceforth in this book, *prima facie* has some parallels with the idea of responsible decision-making by the judiciary, considered in Chapter 5 as a rationale for judicial accountability. After all, decision-making by the judiciary is synonymous with adjudication and responsibility was considered to apply both to the substantive correctness of the decision reached and to the process that led to the decision. The latter encompasses the need for impartiality and, subject to the outcome of the arguments in the following chapter, factors relevant for ensuring checks and balances on other organs of government as well. The exact nature of this inter-relation will be the subject matter of Chapter 7.

## 6C Conclusion

This chapter began with a modest objective: to provide a better understanding of what judicial independence 'looks like'. To this end, the sections of this chapter deconstructed a monolithic conceptualisation of judicial independence using the fivefold model employed in relation to judicial accountability in Chapter 5. Each of these sections not only furthered our understanding of judicial independence in a number of ways but also threw up specific inter-connections with judicial accountability. The subjects of independence (individual judges and the institution of the judiciary) represent distinct sites for judicial independence protection, overlapping with the subjects of judicial accountability as well. A similar overlap can be seen in the analysis of the persons and institutions from whom independence is sought, and the aspects of judicial behaviour for which it is so sought. Specifically, individual judges and the judicial institution have to be independent from both the political organs of the state and the parties to the case, which is secured by a range of political and apolitical methods; they also have to be accountable to the same political organs and parties to the case, which is itself secured by a conspectus of distinct methods. Judicial independence and accountability thus operate in an identical plane insofar as its subjects, objects and subject matters are concerned, while the methods to secure them are contingent on the extent of independence and accountability deemed desirable. At the same time, judicial independence and accountability seem to be underpinned by a similar rationale—the judiciary adjudicating impartially and ensuring separation of powers, that is, 'an effective judiciary' in the case of the former and responsible decision-making in case of the latter. If these two objectives are analogous or one is subsumed in another, then a conceptual reconciliation between the two seems possible. Whether indeed such a speculative assertion is borne out by argument is the question we turn to next, in Chapter 7.

# 7 In Search of an Effective Judiciary

## *A Doctrinal Reconciliation of Judicial Independence and Accountability*

The quest for judicial independence has long obsessed public law academics, judges and political theorists. The historical struggles to establish independent judiciaries, its prominent espousal in constitutional arrangements and its centrality to judicial functioning have made such obsession inevitable. As a result, whether a particular judicial system in a country is independent or not is often the sole lens through which existing constitutional arrangements as they affect the judiciary are analysed.[1] This 'one-dimensional holism',[2] though understandable, is limiting. Especially when used to analyse or shape the structuring and functioning of courts, it is closed to the other factors that are responsible for 'an effective judiciary'.[3] We most certainly want the judiciary to be independent, but we also want the judiciary to be competent, impartial and sufficiently powerful to check government and possess a range of other virtues.

To briefly substantiate this argument—in Indian constitutional jurisprudence, the Supreme Court has focused solely on judicial independence amongst all normative values, when interpreting provisions relating to appointment of judges to the higher judiciary.[4] The justification for such an interpretive exercise is traced to the intention of the drafters of the Constitution. However, if the intention of the drafters is carefully scrutinised, an alternative touchstone for interpretation can be found—preserving the institutional dignity and high status of the judiciary. This is what, one might argue, guided members of the

1 *SCAORA*, para 8 (Justice Verma); Redish, 'Good Behavior, Judicial Independence.'

2 Saikrishna Prakash and Steven D. Smith, 'Reply: (Mis)Understanding Good Behavior Tenure,' *The Yale Law Journal* 116 (2006): 159, 163.

3 'An effective judiciary' is used as a term of art in this book. See Chapter 6, Section 6B.5; Effectiveness, as generally understood, may have other facets but that is not the concern of this book.

4 This can be seen in the majority opinion in *Gupta* and *SCAORA*.

Constituent Assembly to make the president the appointing authority and the chief justice of India a mandatory consultee for all appointments to the higher judiciary. At the same time, this is why, as a matter of fact, proposals for legislative ratification of proposed appointees were rejected, since it was felt that such voting would reduce the esteem in which the higher judiciary ought to be held.[5] *Prima facie*, this argument seems plausible. But like the argument that views provisions on appointments and transfers solely from the perspective of judicial independence, it would be incorrect. This is because as Prakash and Smith point out 'appealing to one among many competing commitments in a "holistic" way and then construing a provision to further *that* value is no way to respect the constitutional design'.[6] Likewise, a carefully crafted constitution more often than not envisages balance between factors, trade-offs and compromises—to not look at the conspectus of relevant factors in a constitutional scheme is myopic.

The one-dimensional holistic approach focusing on judicial independence will be challenged in this chapter at two levels: First, in demonstrating the factors apart from judicial independence which are required for an effective judiciary ('basic anti-holism'). Second, by arguing how judicial accountability is crucial to the presence of such factors. Through these twin arguments, it will be contended that judicial independence and accountability are both essential factors for achieving an effective judiciary ('meta-level anti-holism'). How these factors will be balanced in practice will then be addressed in Section 8A of Chapter 8.

In Chapter 6, we found that judicial independence when deconstructed is needed for judicial impartiality and checking and balancing other organs of government. These aims of judicial independence, described succinctly as necessities for 'an effective judiciary', I argue, are equally served by other factors. I advance three hypotheses in Section 7A. First, impartiality is closely linked with judicial integrity and not judicial independence alone—despite being independent, if a judge lacks integrity, impartiality will not be firmly secured. What integrity means and how it leads to an effective judiciary is described in Section 7A.1. Second, maintaining a distinct institutional status of the judiciary, which is part of a wider need to ensure effective checks and balances, is dependent on the ability of the judiciary to secure public confidence in its functioning. This is an obvious proposition and is thus briefly discussed in Section 7A.2. Third, to be able to check and balance other organs of government, it is imperative that the judiciary is part of a mutual checks and balances scheme.

5 See Chapter 2, Section 2A.

6 Prakash and Smith, '(Mis)Understanding Good Behavior Tenure,' 164.

It is when 'ambition counteracts ambition'[7] that judicial decisions are respected by more powerful coordinate organs of state. The mutual checks and balances scheme, which I term the 'web of integrated government', is analysed in Section 7A.3. Thus, sub-sections 7A.1–3 together comprise a consolidated argument supporting basic anti-holism.

It can unarguably be claimed that other factors may be equally relevant for a well-functioning judiciary. By limiting arguments to the aforesaid three hypotheses and the facets of an effective judiciary they relate to, I make no claims to the contrary. The rationale for such limitation, however, is twofold—first, integrity, public confidence and the ability to check and balance other organs of government are widely acknowledged as essential for any well-functioning judiciary; second, as I will demonstrate in Section 7B, they serve as a bridge between judicial independence and accountability. Constructing such a normative bridge between these two concepts is precisely the point of this chapter.

Having delineated the multiple prerequisites of an effective judiciary in Section 7A, Section 7B outlines how integrity, public confidence and the web of integrated government also require judicial accountability for their fulfilment. Chapters 5 and 6 demonstrated a structural similarity in the conceptual contours of judicial accountability and independence. But such structural similarity is hardly a guarantee for conceptual coherence. There is, on the contrary, a certain intuitive attractiveness to the popular arguments that independence and accountability are inherently contradictory. For example, the argument that judicial elections that promote judicial accountability, by making judges answerable to voters, affect their independent functioning is quite obviously correct.

Several reasons have been suggested as to why particular conflicts between judicial independence and accountability are resolved in the ways they are, based on a consideration of the balance between independence and accountability, keeping in mind the constitutional culture of the jurisdiction in question.[8] To assess the validity of these claims is beyond the remit of this book, especially as they are contingent on specific constitutional contexts. Instead, by arguing that judicial independence and accountability are both needed for an effective

7 Per Madison, Federalist Paper No. 51 in Federalist Papers, 341; For commentary, see David F. Epstein, *The Political Theory of the Federalist* (Chicago: University of Chicago Press, 1984).

8 Martin Redish, 'Judicial Discipline, Judicial Independence and the Constitution: A Textual and Structural Analysis,' *Southern California Law Review* 72 (1999): 673; Lord Hope of Craighead, 'Judicial Independence,' *Supreme Laws Today* 13 (2002): 105; *Krishna Swami*.

judiciary, Section 7B provides a normative resolution to such conflicts. Doing so, it advances an argument for meta-level anti-holism, seeing both judicial independence and accountability as significant for achieving the same aim—an effective judiciary.

## 7A Constituents of an Effective Judiciary

### 7A.1 *Integrity*

From an ethical perspective, integrity is a virtue that is widely considered essential for any decision-maker to possess. When the decision-maker is also a judge who is morally and legally required to decide impartially, intuitively it may seem that the requirement of integrity becomes even more crucial to the exercise of judicial functions.[9] But what does integrity as a core concept entail? Is there a separate conception of judicial integrity comprising virtues that are not covered by the core concept? Stated differently, are there distinct connotations of integrity depending on the role in question?

'Integrity' in the *Oxford English Dictionary* has two meanings: 'the quality of being honest and having strong moral principles' and 'the state of being whole and undivided'.[10] The etymology suggests a derivation from the Latin *integer* meaning 'intact'.[11] Both these senses of 'integrity' can be seen in common, non-legal usage. Let us consider a few examples. A recent statement from the British Foreign office on the international legal status of Gibraltar read:

> Self determination is far more significant than territorial integrity. The people of Gibraltar have repeatedly expressed and overwhelmingly their wish to remain under British sovereignty.[12]

Integrity in terms of territory directly makes use of the second meaning of integrity above, that is, that the territory must remain whole and undivided. This same meaning can be seen in Dworkin's understanding of integrity as an

9 Michael Kirby, 'Judicial Integrity: A Global Social Contract,' *Commonwealth Law Bulletin* 29 (2003): 976.

10 *OED*, available at www.oxfordreference.com/view/10.1093/acref/9780199571123.001.0001/m_en_gb0415130 (accessed 27 September 2013).

11 Ibid.

12 Press Association, 'Spain to Take Gibraltar Dispute to UN,' *The Guardian*, 11 August 2013, available at www.theguardian.com/world/2013/aug/11/spain-gibraltar-dispute-uk-un (accessed 21 August 2013).

adjudicative principle, which instructs judges to decide a case after taking into account the law as an undivided whole, that is, a coherent set of principles.[13]

On the other hand, writing about Abraham Lincoln, historian Daniel Howe says:

> Moral integrity occupied the core of the kind of person Lincoln made himself. Financial honesty represented one important aspect of this integrity. When his partner in a grocery business, William Berry, died in 1835, leaving behind serious debts, Lincoln worked long and hard to pay off not only his own share but Berry's as well...[14]

Here, Howe's understanding of Lincoln's integrity springs from his financial honesty. But it seems to go beyond such honesty to encompass a spirit of humanity and brotherhood that makes Lincoln repay his business partner Berry's business debts. Integrity here is value-laden, tied to certain substantive principles, which gives it meaning. A similar value-laden understanding, albeit with different values deemed essential to integrity, can be seen in the Bangalore Principles of Judicial Conduct. The commentary to the principles describes integrity as 'the attribute of rectitude and righteousness',[15] which for judges comprises 'honesty and judicial morality'.[16]

Third, there are usages of integrity when both the aforesaid meanings—being an undivided whole and connoting certain substantive values—are implied. Polonius, while advising his son Laertes who is at the onset of a major voyage to France, ends his sermon with the words:

> This above all: to thine own self be true,
>
> And it must follow, as the night the day,
>
> Thou canst not then be false to any man.[17]

[13] Dworkin, *Law's Empire*, 225.

[14] Daniel Walker Howe, 'Honest Abe: Abraham Lincoln and the Moral Character' (2008), 13 Footnotes (Foreign Policy Research Institute Newsletter), available at www.fpri.org/footnotes/1316.200806.howe.honestabemoralcharacter.html (accessed 21 August 2013).

[15] United Nations Office on Drugs and Crime, 'Commentary on the Bangalore Principles of Judicial Conduct,' September 2007, available at www.unodc.org/documents/corruption/publications_unodc_commentary-e.pdf (accessed 21 August 2013) (hereinafter 'Bangalore Principles Commentary').

[16] Ibid.

[17] William Shakespeare, *Hamlet*, Act 1 Scene 3, Lines 78–81, available at http://shakespeare.mit.edu/hamlet/full.html (accessed 21 August 2013).

Polonius' words suggest that if one is true to oneself, an idea that is shorn of substantive moral considerations, then one will not be false to anyone else. This has been widely seen as the cornerstone of integrity,[18] that is, a man who lives life based on a coherent set of principles. But in the context of Polonius' speech, there is a well-defined way for Laertes to remain true to himself and thereby have integrity. This involves not borrowing or lending money, not associating with women of dubious character, not dressing ostentatiously and a range of moral guidelines that must be adhered to.[19] This points to a value-laden conception of integrity, which is substantive and tied to certain specific moral values.

Comparing the substantive aspect of Polonius' idea of integrity with Howe's description of Lincoln's integrity, it is clear that the values deemed central to integrity in these conceptions are distinct. The understanding of relevant values is contingent on the nature of the person in question—as a businessman, the moral principles central to Lincoln's integrity are his honesty and humanity, whereas as a young man on the verge of travelling to live abroad, a more eclectic combination of values broadly underpinned by the need for moderation determines Laertes' integrity in his father's eyes. Thus, the values deemed relevant for integrity in each case are determined by the identity of the persons described.[20] It would suffice to say that integrity connotes certain substantive values ('identity-conferring commitments'[21]) that differ based on the person in question, on values deemed central to her existence as a moral being and the

[18] Terence Eagleton, *Shakespeare and Society: Critical Studies in Shakespearean Drama* (London: Chatto and Windus, 1976), 65; John Kekes, 'Constancy and Purity,' *Mind* XCII (1983): 499, 500.

[19] Preceding the extracted quote from Polonius above is a set of moral precepts that Polonius advises Laertes to follow. These include:

> Costly thy habit as thy purse can buy,
>
> But not express'd in fancy; rich, not gaudy (Lines 70–71)
>
> Neither a borrower nor a lender be;
>
> For loan oft loses both itself and friend,
>
> And borrowing dulls the edge of husbandry. (Lines 75–77).
>
> Shakespeare, Hamlet.

[20] These are to be seen in contradistinction to defeasible commitments that reflect particular social settings rather than aspects central to a person's identity. See Kekes, 'Constancy and Purity,' 514–16.

[21] Lynne McFall, 'Integrity,' *Ethics* 98, no. 1 (1987): 5, 13.

moral principles she is expected to adhere to given the nature of her position.[22] This is a theme we will revisit in the context of judicial integrity.

On the other hand, the conception of integrity of territory, adverted to in the statement by the British Foreign Office, connotes a sense of wholeness, an opposition to division. When transplanted to actions of individuals, as Dworkin or Polonius do, such an understanding corresponds to the need for acting according to principle. It is only when one espouses coherent principles and takes actions strictly in consonance with such principles that integrity is possible. For Polonius, being true to oneself is only possible when one adheres to principles—this ensures that one is not false to any other man. Similarly for Dworkin, a judge must view the entire body of a community's legal practice relevant to a case as a coherent whole. Deciding a case would thus require finding the best fit within this coherent body of principles. Both Polonius' and Dworkin's views embrace coherence in choosing the relevant principles (it would be incoherent to adhere to inconsistent principles) as well as coherence between principles and action (it would be incoherent to act contrary to the principles chosen).[23] This understanding of integrity as acting according to coherent principles thus provides a value-free, first-order understanding of integrity that is not contingent on other virtues for its existence.

However, as a standard for assessment, evaluating whether indeed a person acts according to principle is a difficult matter.[24] Shorn of any consideration of substantive values, it may often lead to counter-intuitive inferences of lack of integrity. Laertes may, on this meaning, have complete integrity, despite adhering to the principle of working solely for selfish gains including cheating people where necessary to uphold this principle, as long as it does not detract from a contrary principle he holds. This is squarely contrary to our intuitive inference in this regard. Again, as McFall points out, if one has a principle of friendship which one fails to honour by betraying one's friend in self-interest, to say that one's action lacked integrity because it was marked by incoherence between principle and action would be a curious charge.[25] On the contrary, such an allegation would be much more strongly founded on a charge of betrayal of friendship. Thus, the concept of integrity as acting according to coherent principles does not *per se* correspond with common usages of integrity. This suggests that

[22] Ibid.

[23] Gabriele Taylor, 'Integrity,' *Proceedings of the Aristotelian Society* (Supplementary Volumes) 55 (1981): 143.

[24] Ibid.

[25] McFall, 'Integrity,' 11.

the idea of integrity needs to necessarily factor in identity-conferring values described above. It is this combination of principle and identity-conferring values in conceptualising integrity that is useful in understanding the integrity that is expected of judges.

For judges, the first-order notion of the aforesaid integrity applies as it would to any other decision-maker for whom integrity is ethically a prerequisite.[26] Canon 4.2 of the Guide to Judicial Conduct in the United Kingdom (2009), which deals with integrity, provides that judges must avoid behaviour that might 'expose them to charges of hypocrisy'.[27] Hypocritical judges, like other hypocritical persons, would by definition act contrary to held principles and would thereby lack integrity. At the same time, the Commentary to the Bangalore Principles of Judicial Conduct mandates that in order to have integrity, judges must avoid 'conduct that is indicative of bias, prejudice or improper influence'.[28] Any decision-maker who allows her decision to be affected by improper and extraneous considerations can be said to lack integrity *qua* her role as a decision-maker. This is specifically so since the action is contrary to the principle of impartiality that a decision-maker ought to espouse. For a judge, such impartiality, as discussed earlier, is the keystone for judicial functioning and a lack thereof represents an erosion of integrity. Other first-order manifestations of a lack of integrity are provided by Taylor—the insincere, weak-willed and self-deceiving, all of whom demonstrate a stark lack of principle in their actions for various reasons.[29]

Ensuring the selection of judges of high integrity as understood above, and safeguarding such integrity while in office, makes the achievement of identity-conferring values, the substantive aspect of integrity, more likely. Having a judicial officer who possesses first-order integrity implies necessarily that she is a thinking individual who has carefully considered her position on issues and actions in light of the evidence that is available. It also means that the person is necessarily free of certain undesirable traits—hypocrisy, deception, cowardice, insincerity and weak will, all of which are contrary to such a notion of integrity.[30] It must though be admitted that neither of these reasons guarantees that such a person will possess the substantive values deemed desirable for a

[26] For the role of integrity in decisions generally, see John Teehan, 'Character, Integrity and Dewey's Virtue Ethics,' *Transactions of the Charles S Peirce Society* 31, no. 4 (1995): 841.

[27] UK Judicial Guide.

[28] Bangalore Principles Commentary, 81.

[29] Taylor, 'Integrity,' 144–47.

[30] Ibid.

judge, but only makes such possession more likely. To the contrary, it is quite possible that a thinking individual may have reprehensible moral qualities. At the same time, the undesirable traits that a judge is free of (that allows her to have first-order integrity) may not be the sum total of undesirable traits that judges ought not to possess. This caveat of the lack of a seamless transition from first-order non-substantive integrity to its second-order value-laden counterpart ought to be kept in mind.

So what are these substantive values that a judge with integrity ought to possess? Space precludes an exhaustive enumeration of such values—in fact, it is doubtful whether such an exhaustive enumeration is possible *per se*. Perhaps, this is why most understandings of integrity are general—viewing integrity as that conduct which befits proper discharge of judicial office.[31] While this is eminently sensible since integrity is incapable of easy definition, it gives us little idea of the substantive values entailed by it. A useful way to arrive at such an understanding, albeit in an illustrative manner, might be by analysing the values implicated in prominent cases of judicial impeachments where the lack of integrity was alleged and widely accepted. Through factors that constitute lack of integrity, a better understanding of the values needed in order to have integrity can emerge.

In the impeachment motion against Justice Dinakaran, the grounds for which are discussed in Chapter 2, the memorandum submitted by the Supreme Court Bar Association to the chief justice of India repeatedly stated that Justice Dinakaran's actions made him a person of 'doubtful integrity'.[32] The Bar Association of India, in a similar plea to the chief justice asserted that the key issue was not whether the charges against Justice Dinakaran were correct or not; instead it was a question of whether 'the appointment of such a person whose integrity is widely perceived to be doubtful would affect the faith of the common man in this glorious institution'.[33] Even the impeachment motion moved against him in parliament alleged that the judge through his actions demonstrated an utter lack of probity and integrity, 'basic qualities of being a judge'.[34]

31 For an illustrative example, see Bangalore Principles, Value 3.

32 J. Venkatesan, 'Plea Not to Elevate Justice Dinakaran,' *The Hindu*, New Delhi, 3 December 2009, available at http://www.thehindu.com/news/national/plea-not-to-elevate-justice-dinakaran/article59077.ece (accessed 11 September 2013).

33 *The Hindu*, 'Do Not Elevate Dinakaran.'

34 'Notice of Motion for Presenting an Address to the President of India for the Removal of Mr. Justice Paul Daniel Dinakaran, chief justice of the Karnataka High Court, also

The charges against him which formed the basis of the aforesaid allegations of lack of integrity were twofold. He was accused of dishonestly passing certain judicial orders by deciding cases where he himself or an acquaintance was an interested party. At the same time, he was alleged to have violated the law by acquiring property illegally. Thus, two qualities that were deemed lacking in Justice Dinakaran, making him unfit for judicial office, were honesty and law-abiding behaviour. Dishonesty was a causal factor for corrupt practices, that is, actions by a judge contrary to conduct befitting judicial office owing to extraneous reasons, often monetary. The lack of law-abiding behaviour was both a causal factor and indicative of such corruption since the properties owned were entirely disproportionate to known sources of income. Taken together, it simply exhibited behaviour that was unbecoming of a judge.[35]

During the impeachment of Justice Samuel Chase, discussed in Chapter 5, the main allegations against him were regarding his integrity as a judge of the Supreme Court.[36] Specifically, it was alleged that his integrity was compromised since he was acting as a mouthpiece of the Federalists from the Supreme Court Bench. He was accused of not only spewing political propaganda from the bench but also allowing his political views to determine the outcome of trials. Thus, his lack of integrity was a consequence of his political partisanship. This affected his ability to adjudicate impartially and led to political grandstanding, which was contrary to the rectitude expected of a judge. Though the impeachment motion itself failed, its failure was not a repudiation of the view that Justice Chase lacked integrity—on the contrary, it espoused the principle that substantive decisions rendered, including questions of integrity raised in connection therein, would not form the basis of impeachment.[37]

Through these two examples of a lack of integrity, we have some idea of the values it entails—honesty, law-abiding behaviour, impartiality and rectitude. It is by no means claimed that these values constitute the sum total of values that integrity entails. Other examples of lack of integrity in common usage will lead to other values being implicated. But it does provide some substantiation to the meaning of integrity, moving beyond its rhetorical appeal as a portmanteau term consolidating all the values that a judge ought to reasonably possess.

---

known as Mr. Justice Paul Daniel Dinakaran Premkumar under Article 217 read with 124(4) of the Constitution of India' (Rajya Sabha), 2009, available at www.outlookindia.com/article/Impeachment-Motion/263269 (accessed 13 September 2012).

35 For details of charges, see Chapter 2, Section 2C.3.

36 See Chapter 5, Section 5B.1.

37 For more, see Rehnquist, *Grand Inquests*, 1–134.

Like individual integrity of a judge, the idea of institutional integrity entails the conditions necessary for the exercise of the judicial function by courts of law. Unlike individual integrity, however, which has primarily been discussed in codes of conduct and academic debate, institutional integrity is a doctrine that has been used in several jurisdictions in order to invalidate legislation. The most prolific and continuing use of 'institutional integrity' has been in Australia, an understanding which explains the rationale for the doctrinal use of such a concept. In *Kable* v. *Director of Public Prosecutions*,[38] the High Court of Australia invalidated section 5(1) of the Community Protection Act, 1994, which vested the power to order continued detention of a specified prisoner in the Supreme Court of New South Wales, for the reason that such vesting was incompatible with the institutional integrity of the judiciary. In *Kable* and subsequent cases that have used this doctrine to invalidate legislation,[39] the underlying justification for its use has been cited as the need to protect the institutional competence of the court. This entails maintaining the sanctity of the judicial process, safeguarding it from threats, especially those affecting the independence and impartiality of judges. It is only such safeguarding which secures public confidence in the judiciary, expressed as the meta-norm necessitating the doctrine of institutional integrity.[40]

In India too, reference to this principle was made in the recent case of *Centre for Public Interest Litigation* v. *Union of India*.[41] In this case, the Supreme Court invalidated the appointment of the central vigilance commissioner, not chiefly because his personal integrity was in question, but because appointment of a person who had pending criminal charges would compromise the institutional integrity of the Central Vigilance Commission. Integrity of such an institution would require that it can function competently with its independence and impartiality secured.[42] Thus institutional integrity, from both these doctrinal uses in Australia and India, implies the overall character of an institution that allows it to function competently—in the context of courts, such functioning must be independent and impartial at the very least to secure public confidence. It is hence tied to the substantive values that are deemed essential for courts to do their task.

38 (1996) HCA 24 (High Court of Australia).

39 For analyses of subsequent cases, see Chris Steytler and Iain Field, 'The "Institutional Integrity" Principle: Where Are We Now, and Where Are We headed?' *The University of Western Australia Law Review* 35 (2011): 227.

40 Ibid., 244–46, 262–64.

41 (2011) 4 SCC 1 (Supreme Court of India).

42 Ibid., 39, para 33.

The aim of this sub-section was to construct a general understanding of judicial integrity, using which its relation with judicial impartiality could be examined. On the basis of such a general understanding, the first hypothesis—impartiality has a close link with judicial integrity distinct from its linkage with judicial independence—appears justified. This is because integrity has a two-way connection with judicial impartiality. On the one hand, the lack of judicial impartiality leads to an inference of lack of integrity given that impartiality is an identity-conferring value for an individual judge or the judicial institution. In this sense, impartiality is constitutive of integrity. On the other hand, the lack of judicial integrity is likely to have a deleterious impact on judicial impartiality. Since impartial functioning is key to the judicial function, the effects of a judge failing to act according to principle or demonstrating a lack of other identity-conferring values are likely to affect her impartial functioning. This is widely seen in instances of judicial corruption. This symbiotic relationship between impartiality and integrity—impartiality is a constituent factor for judicial integrity and integrity in turn making impartiality in adjudication more likely—is a complex, multi-layered inter-relation. Given that it is incidental to the point of this chapter (and the book) it must be explored further elsewhere.[43] The relevant lesson for our purpose is that integrity, apart from judicial independence, is relevant for understanding the preconditions for impartial functioning of a judge, and consequently an effective judiciary.

### *7A.2 Public Confidence*

> The Court's authority—possessed of neither the purse nor the sword—ultimately rests on sustained public confidence in its moral sanction.[44]

That judiciaries must enjoy public confidence in order to function authoritatively is a platitude. Public confidence in the judiciary was identified as a cornerstone of judicial functioning in the Federalist Papers.[45] In the Constituent Assembly of India, Jawaharlal Nehru, in a similar vein, underlined the need for judges to be persons capable of commanding absolute respect from the people and other organs of government.[46] Creating public confidence in the judiciary (or revitalising it) has been the underlying rationale for several judicial reforms

[43] See generally Jonathan Soeharno, *The Integrity of a Judge: A Philosophical Inquiry* (Farnham: Ashgate, 2009).

[44] *Baker* v. *Carr*, 369 US 186 (1962) (US Supreme Court) (Justice Frankfurter).

[45] Federalist Paper No. 78 in Federalist Papers, 508.

[46] CAD, vol. VIII (May–June 1949), 246–47.

undertaken in recent times.[47] Thus, Justice Frankfurter's belief that public confidence is the bedrock for the court's authority is part of a long-standing and well-established view.

The requirement of public confidence, being self-evident, need not be laboured here. It can simply be said that as a public institution that enjoys sovereign power, courts ultimately rely on public confidence and support to function.[48] In this respect, it is similar to other public institutions—coordinate organs of government or state agencies.

But there is a distinct instrumental sense in which such public confidence is generally essential that is, to secure the autonomous institutional status of the judiciary, which in turn is necessary for the judiciary to effectively check and balance other organs of government.[49] Judicial independence, as shown in Chapter 6, is central to structurally insulating the judiciary from governmental interference, as well as in securing such confidence. But as several studies demonstrate,[50] neither is judicial independence the sole basis for public confidence nor (as Chapter 6 suggests) is it sufficient to secure such institutional status. In order to achieve the latter, the judiciary needs to enjoy wide public confidence and support based on its structure and performance. The factors that ensure such support and confidence depend to a large extent on the jurisdiction in question and cannot be enquired into here.[51] However,

[47] As an illustrative example, see Statement of Objects and Reasons accompanying the Judicial Appointments Commission Bill, 2013 (India). Justifying the Bill, the Minister of Law and Justice writes: 'The proposed Bill would enable equal participation of Judiciary and Executive, make the system of appointments more accountable, and thereby increase the confidence of the public in the institutions.'

[48] This is a widely accepted proposition. See Federalist Paper No. 78 in Federalist Papers, 508.

[49] In countries such as the United Kingdom which had an independent judiciary without a distinct institutional status, such need for public confidence still exists because of the continuing need to check and balance other organs of government, thereby ensuring the rule of law.

[50] Sara Benesh, 'Understanding Public Confidence in American Courts,' *The Journal of Politics* 68, no. 3 (2006): 697; Gregory Caldeira and James Gibson, 'The Etiology of Public Support for the Supreme Court,' *American Journal of Political Science* 36 (1992): 635; James L. Gibson, Gregory A. Caldeira, and Vanessa A. Baird, 'On the Legitimacy of National High Courts,' *The American Political Science Review* 92, no. 2 (1998): 343.

[51] For an illustrative example, see Gregory A. Caldeira, 'Neither the Purse nor the Sword: Dynamics of Public Confidence in the Supreme Court,' *The American Political Science Review* 80, no. 4 (1986): 1209.

the fact of such confidence ensures that coordinate organs of government, which crucially depend on public support for continuance in office, would show a greater likelihood of respecting judicial decisions, thereby making the judiciary an effective organ.[52] It thus feeds into the mutual checks and balances scheme that is constitutionally envisaged, thereby acting as a deterrent for the government trampling over the judiciary and upsetting the separation of powers scheme. This will become evident after the discussion of the role of mutual checks and balances scheme in creating an effective judiciary below.

## *7A.3 The Web of Integrated Government*

This book argued in Chapter 6 that judicial independence is necessary for preventing transgressions of the law by government, thereby serving as a check and balance upon untrammelled legislative and executive power. This checking function is performed through the exercise of judicial review by courts. While judicial independence is significant to ensure impartial adjudication in such judicial review cases where the government is a litigating party before the judiciary, ensuring that the government respects the results of such adjudication is a crucially connected, albeit wider, enquiry.[53] History is replete with instances of independent judiciaries failing to check government—Frederick the Great's courts in Prussia provide a telling example. Frederick had taken a number of steps to secure the independence of the courts from the monarchy, refusing on several occasions to interfere in the impartial administration of justice as his predecessors had, a system known as *Kabinettsjustiz*.[54] Nonetheless, the idea of *Rechstaat* or the king himself being subject to the decisions of the courts was never given any credence. Thus, though the judiciary was independent, its decisions did not bind the monarch himself. On the other hand, there are several other instances when even decisions seemingly to the dissatisfaction of the ruling government, handed down by an independent judiciary, have

[52] This is a reasonable presumption of which space precludes further enquiry. For more, see Eckhoff, 'Impartiality, Separation of Powers,' 31–32.

[53] The need for government to respect judicial decisions as a distinct and equally significant requirement apart from judicial independence has been succinctly underlined by Justice Stephen Breyer of the United States Supreme Court. See Stephen G. Breyer, 'Judicial Independence in the United States,' *Saint Louis University Law Journal* 40 (1996): 989, 994.

[54] Herman Weill, *Frederick the Great and Samuel von Cocceji: A Study in the Reform of the Prussian Judicial Administration 1740–1755* (Madison: The State Historical Society of Wisconsin, 1961), 61.

been respected—President Eisenhower sending federal troops to Arkansas to implement court-mandated plans of allowing nine African-American pupils to be admitted to Central High School, despite his widely publicised opposition to the judicial orders in the preceding litigation, provides a case in point.[55] What are the crucial factors distinguishing these two types of examples? And what, apart from independent judicial review, is necessary for courts to effectively check and balance other organs of government?

Of course, some differences are patently visible. Frederick was an all-powerful king in a monarchy whereas Eisenhower was the president of a republic. Crucially, however, the republic was governed by a Constitution that strictly separated powers between various organs of government. The effectiveness of the judiciary was thus not contingent on the benevolence of the monarch, but rather a product of carefully crafted constitutional design.

Such an example of careful construction of constitution design can be traced to the Federalist Papers. So perceptive were their insights into checks and balances on organs of government and the role of the judiciary that this section bases its arguments primarily on these writings. While the practical manifestation of separation of powers might have limited generalisability beyond the United States of America, its theoretical bases, the need to weave a constitutional scheme of checks and balances and the mechanisms to ensure judicial independence and accountability in such a scheme, are crucial to the argument being made in this section, that is, that judicial independence and accountability both lead to an effective judiciary.

Madison, writing in Federalist No. 47, stressed the need to keep organs of government, including the judiciary, separate and distinct from each other. In fact, he agreed with critics who had commented that his proposed scheme of separation was insufficient by agreeing with the basis of their objection, that no 'political truth' other than the separation of powers was 'of greater intrinsic value'.[56] At the same time he defended his proposed scheme by arguing that nothing in the concept of separation of powers required absolute separation between the legislature, executive and judiciary. Instead, he believed that

> [u]nless these departments be so far connected and blended with each other as to give to each a constitutional control over the others, the degree

[55] Anthony Lewis, 'President Warns of Anarchy Peril,' *New York Times*, 25 September 1957, available at http://www.nytimes.com/learning/general/onthisday/big/0925.html (accessed 14 September 2013).

[56] Federalist Paper No. 47 in Federalist Papers, 316.

of separation which the maxim requires, as essential to a free government, can never in practice be duly maintained.[57]

The logical flow of this argument is not obvious—in order to maintain an optimal degree of separation between organs of government, Madison believed that the organs must be connected in particular ways. Part of the rationale for such a counter-intuitive proposition lies in Madison's belief, justified by experience, of the ineffectiveness and impracticality of complete separation of powers.[58] But *per se* this rationale only suggests that there must be *some* blending of powers. However, Madison makes a much stronger claim when he writes that such blending is not merely necessary because complete separation is ineffective and impractical but rather because it performs a positive function—allowing organs to exercise mutual control, thereby maintaining an optimal degree of separation essential for free government. To test this claim, two of its premises need further scrutiny: How does blending lead to mutual control? And how does such mutual control lead to an optimal degree of separation of powers?

In the separation of powers scheme envisaged by the authors of the Federalist Papers, blending of powers of various organs is part of a larger enterprise of maintaining a balance of political power.[59] Maintaining such balance was a key aim for Montesquieu, from whom Madison was greatly inspired. Montesquieu, on several occasions, writes of the need to maintain a nuanced degree of separation in order to maintain equilibrium of political power.[60] In fact, his high praise for the British system of balanced government as the epitome of a state that adheres to separation of powers demonstrates the centrality of the need for balance in his separation of powers scheme.[61]

Similarly for Madison, maintaining a balance of political power is crucial. But constant clashes between the king and parliament in Britain, a by-product of the intensely blended Westminster model of government, made him, and other founding fathers of the Constitution, rightfully wary of interconnections between personnel in agencies of government.[62] Thus, such balance was sought to be achieved without any blending in terms of institutional personnel.

57 Federalist Paper No. 48 in Federalist Papers, 324.

58 Vile, *Constitutionalism and the Separation of Powers*, 14.

59 For an excellent analysis of this scheme, see Burin, 'Theory of the Rule of Law.'

60 Cohler, Miller and Stone, *Montesquieu's The Spirit of Law*, 164–66.

61 Ibid., 156–66.

62 William Seal Carpenter, 'The Separation of Powers in the Eighteenth Century,' *American Political Science Review* 22, no. 1 (1928): 32, 35–44.

Consequently, two key methods were devised—weakening or strengthening the power of each organ depending on their intrinsic nature and potential to adversely affect the balance of power (which I call 'modulated starting points'), and blending of powers between the three organs of government (which I call 'mutual checks and balances'). Since the biggest threat to the balance of power was perceived to emanate from the legislature, bicameralism was seen as the foremost method by which the legislature could be weakened.[63] Similarly, by sourcing the legitimacy of the executive directly from the people rather than the legislature, as was the case in England, and strengthening the judiciary by giving federal judges life tenure subject only to a cumbersome impeachment procedure, the executive and the judiciary were sought to be propped up. These meant that the starting points for each organ of government, in terms of the constitutional power they wielded and the protection they were provided, were sought to be modulated to prevent a skewing of the balance of power.

However, such 'parchment divisions' between organs of government were deemed insufficient.[64] It is because of this that I believe blending of powers, in terms of creating a scheme of mutual checks and balances between organs of government, was proposed. This operated in two ways—first, more than one organ would have to coordinate in order to constitutionally perform a particular function. For example, the power of appointing Supreme Court justices and executive officials whose specific form of appointment was not provided for in the Constitution would be by the president 'by and with the advice and consent of the Senate'.[65]

Second, an organ of government would provide an external check on the exercise of a function by another. For example, the power of judicial review was vested in the judiciary to ensure that the other organs were acting in consonance with the Constitution. Though such a power was not an essential corollary to

[63] The reasons for incorporating a bicameral legislature can be traced back to the colonies prior to the formation of the United States of America, specifically Massachusetts. See Benjamin F. Wright, 'The Origins of the Separation of Powers in America,' *Economica* 40 (1933): 169, 173–76.

[64] The reasons for such a conclusion were based both on principle and experience in the colonies. For details, see Federalist Paper No. 48 in Federalist Papers, 326–30.

[65] Art. II section 2 of the US Constitution in relevant part reads:

> [H]e [The President] shall nominate, and by and with the advice and consent of the Senate, shall appoint ambassadors, other public ministers and consuls, judges of the Supreme Court, and all other officers of the United States, whose appointments are not herein otherwise provided for, and which shall be established by law.

the exercise of legislative and executive power, it was posited as an inherent check on its arbitrary and unconstitutional exercise.

However, if Madison's words are scrutinised closely, he seems to understand constitutional control, in terms of having 'control over' an organ, that is, being able to make an organ do one's bidding.[66] This interpretation, commended by the text, is anomalous when considered in the context of the overall theme of maintaining the functional competence of each organ, espoused by the Federalist Papers. If organs of government were to control each other, their functional competence would be put in grave doubt since organs would not be autonomous in their actions and thus unable to exercise their functions as they might otherwise have done. It could, however, be plausibly claimed that if two organs were to jointly control the third, that might cancel out arbitrary extraneous influences of each and promote functional competence of the third organ, albeit in a circuitous manner. However, this is an option that the Federalist No. 49 expressly repudiates. A proposal for a mandatory constitutional convention for amendment when two-thirds of two organs of government were in its favour was rejected on the ground that multiple checks, including through recourse to the people, on the legislature, even though it was the key threat sought to be curbed, would weaken respect for the government.[67] This rejection bears testimony to the fact that control of an organ by the two remaining organs was not an option contemplated by the authors of the Federalist Papers.

The insertion of the article 'a' before 'constitutional control', however, might point to an alternative meaning. 'A constitutional control' suggests a question of degree, that is, each organ can control other organs to a certain extent. The meaning of 'control' adverted to earlier, that is, to be in a position to make an organ do one's bidding, is *prima facie* incongruous when seen as a question of degree. This points to an alternative meaning of 'control' that is harmonious with such an interpretation, that is, each organ limits the functioning of another in a delineated manner. 'Control' as 'limit' is an established meaning in the English language.[68] At the same time, the Madisonian blending of powers scheme, involving mutual checks and balances, does precisely that—the executive power of appointment is checked by the need for advice and consent of the Senate; the legislative power of law-making is subject to independent judicial review of constitutionality. Control as enforcing limits leading to balanced government

66 Federalist Paper No. 48 in Federalist Papers, 324.

67 Federalist Paper No. 49 in Federalist Papers.

68 OED, available at www.oxfordreference.com/view/10.1093/acref/9780199571123.001.0001/m_en_gb0176220 (accessed 22 September 2013).

thus best captures Madison's understanding of the purpose of blending of powers in the American constitutional scheme.

At the same time, this interpretation of 'control' is instrumental in answering the second question posed earlier, that is, how such control leads to separation of powers. If organs exercise mutual constraints on each other, what makes them mutually coordinate and stay within their demarcated spheres, thereby maintaining separation of powers rather than compete in a quest for one-upmanship? The theoretical premise on the basis of which the Federalists' proposals for ensuring separation of powers through an appropriately designed scheme of mutual checks and balances rested is succinctly stated in Federalist No. 51:

> But the great security against a gradual concentration of the several powers in the same department consists in giving to those who administer each department the necessary constitutional means and personal motives to resist encroachments of the others.[69]

This statement is made in the wider context of preventing legislative overreach. As is apparent, vesting each department with the 'necessary constitutional means' to resist encroachment, applicable mainly to the executive and the judiciary, harks back to the issue of modulated starting points. Making the judiciary independent and the executive directly accountable to the people provides them the means to remain immune from legislative control to a great degree. But this is not sufficient. In addition, 'personal motives' are also essential. If personal motives, like constitutional means, are seen as a defensive tactic to resist encroachments, the inference is anomalous. Surely no self-respecting authority requires personal motives to keep itself free from interference—it is commonsensical that it would do so anyway. There is instead a more meaningful understanding of personal motives that, I believe, is possible. In the very next sentence, Madison writes:

> The provision for defense in this, as in all other cases, be made commensurate to the danger of attack. Ambition must be made to counteract ambition.[70]

Personal motives, it seems from this quote, need not be defensive tactics—after all, incentives for attack are key to shaping such tactics in the first place.

69 Federalist Paper No. 51 in Federalist Papers, 340.

70 Ibid. For an analysis of this phrase in specific and the separation of powers scheme in the Federalist Papers generally, see Mark Tushnet, 'Principle, Politics and Constitutional Law,' *Michigan Law Review* 88, no. 1 (1989): 49, 66.

If, on the contrary, personal motives are seen as motives that disincentivise an organ from attacking another, its use is rather more appropriate in this context. They supply each organ with the modulated ambition to respect the ambition of its coordinate organ and act accordingly. They thus resist encroachment, not simply by motivating organs to protect their own turf. Instead, it is done far more subtly by integrating organs into a wider web, where the desire to encroach and consequently the resistance to be encroached upon are intrinsically connected to each other. Ambition of one organ thus counteracts, rather than overpowers, ambition of others—by being fused within what I call the 'web of integrated government'.

Illustrative of the conceptualisation of the web of integrated government is the structuring and functioning of the federal judiciary in the Constitution of the United States of America. The constitutional means to protect itself from attack are ensured by Art. III section 1 which mandates appointment of federal judges during good behaviour and ensures that their salary is not varied to their disadvantage while in office.[71] These are significant protections to ensure that an independent spirit pervades the judiciary. They are also crucial in ensuring that the judiciary is perceived to be an impartial arbiter in disputes where the government is a litigating party. However, these protections do not, in and of themselves, ensure that the judiciary is effective in enforcing a check and balance on other organs of government. In structuring the institution, the power of appointment is a two-stage process involving both coordinate organs of government. Whereas the Senate plays a key role in advising and consenting to the nomination of the president, the power of initially nominating a candidate vests with the president.[72] This creates a constitutional mandate for the legislature and executive to cooperate. The rationale for such a scheme is to seemingly provide 'some qualified connection between the weaker department [the Presidency] and the weaker branch of the stronger department [the Senate]'.[73] Crucially, this offsets the power of the House of Representatives, deemed, by extrapolation from the general principle that large membership and consequently diminished responsibility is the key reason for legislative

[71] US Constitution, Art. III section 1.

[72] US Constitution, Art. II section 2. For an analysis of the practical working of the checks and balances contained in this provision, see Rachel Brand, 'Judicial Appointments: Checks and Balances in Practice,' *Harvard Journal of Law and Public Policy* 33, no. 1 (2010): 47.

[73] Federalist Paper No. 51 in Federalist Papers, 342.

encroachment,[74] to be the strongest threat to separation of powers. At the same time, it forces the Senate, despite being a part of Congress, to act in concert with the presidency, organs whose interests in several other instances are orthogonal to each other.[75] Thus, the web of integrated government strengthens the judiciary on the one hand by making it independent, while making it vulnerable to its coordinate organs acting collectively on the other. It then makes provision to protect against the practical manifestation of such vulnerability by requiring organs, set up as antithetical to each other, to coordinate. This in turn affects the dynamic between these two organs, which again in turn has numerous, diverse effects on other facets of the web. The web is thus all-encompassing—a tug in one strand sets off a multitude of pulls in others.[76]

This understanding of the web of integrated government also explains why it is necessary for an effective judiciary. Whereas judicial independence provides the constitutional means insulating the judiciary from extraneous pressures, mostly from other organs of government, the personal motives to resist encroachment of the judiciary are provided by the mutual checks and balances scheme envisaged in the web of integrated government. This fosters an acknowledgement of the respective roles played by each organ in the constitutional framework. Such acknowledgement, specifically for the judiciary, translates into a respect for decisions rendered by it, in particular those which are adverse to the government. When such acknowledgement of the judicial role is supplemented by the knowledge of the high degree of public confidence enjoyed by the judiciary, its effectiveness as an institution is further bolstered.

Checks and balances through independent judicial review, on other organs of government, are thus made effective as a result of counter-checks and balances on the judiciary. These checks and balances on, rather than by, the judiciary primarily relate to methods of appointment and removal of judges. Both, especially in recent times, are instrumental measures in enforcing judicial accountability in India as demonstrated in Chapters 2 and 3. Thus, they are discussed in Section 7B in the context of how judicial accountability is key to securing the web of integrated government.

74 Federalist Paper No. 51 in Federalist Papers, 341–42; Today of course the dominant view is that such a mantle has transferred to the executive. See Martin S. Flaherty, 'The Most Dangerous Branch,' *The Yale Law Journal* 105, no. 7 (1996): 1725.

75 For an analysis of the instances where the Senate is used to check the House, see Epstein, *Political Theory of the Federalist*, 176–78.

76 This is analogous to the 'spider's web' metaphor used by Lon Fuller to explain his concept of polycentricity. See Fuller and Winston, 'Forms and Limits of Adjudication,' 395.

Sub-sections 7A.1–3 together exemplify the constituent factors of an effective judiciary. Since 'an effective judiciary' is used in this book as a term of art, criticisms that there are other factors that can lead to an effective judiciary, as generally understood, are beside the point. This does not, however, imply that I claim other values for the judiciary as unimportant. It is obvious that judiciaries need to be diverse, efficient, financially prudent, and so on. But such values have little to do with the central purpose of this chapter—to construct a doctrinal reconciliation for judicial independence and accountability. To this end, this section has explained what integrity, public confidence and the web of integrated government mean and how they lead to an effective judiciary. Doing so has encapsulated the idea of basic anti-holism, underlining the need to look beyond judicial independence when attempting to understand and analyse the structure and functions of the judiciary. Section 7B argues how, like judicial independence, judicial accountability is needed for an effective judiciary. Doing so not only continues the pattern of anti-holistic argumentation but also provides a clear normative reconciliation for judicial independence and accountability.

## 7B Judicial Accountability and an Effective Judiciary

### *7B.1 Strengthening the Web of Integrated Government*

> [T]he judiciary is beyond comparison the weakest of the three departments of power; that it can never attack with success either of the other two; and that all possible care is requisite to enable it to defend itself against their attacks.[77]

The authors of the Federalist Papers had a nuanced conceptualisation of the judiciary in their separation of powers scheme. On the one hand, as we have seen in Chapter 6, the judiciary was, for the first time, accorded a distinct constitutional status.[78] On the other hand, as the quote above demonstrates, they did not envisage judicial power as posing any threat to the checks and balances scheme itself. Thus no real checks and balances on the judiciary were considered necessary to constrain judicial power, in the way they were crucial to constraining legislative and executive power.[79]

As a result, the discourse surrounding the judiciary, both in the Federalist Papers and in subsequent academic literature, has primarily centred on

[77] Federalist Paper No. 78 in Federalist Papers, 508.

[78] See Chapter 6, Section 6B.5.

[79] Federalist Paper No. 78 in Federalist Papers, 508.

judicial independence to enable the judiciary to defend itself from attacks, if any. Rendering the judiciary independent through 'good behaviour' tenure and non-diminishing salaries provided the fortification necessary to impede legislative or executive control of the judicial power. Since union of either of these powers with judicial power would be destructive of separation of powers, independence of the judiciary was a *sine qua non*. However, it is instructive to note that though independence entailed a degree of separation from the coordinate organs of government, it did not mean insulation of the judiciary. Since separation of powers was not absolute, and the judiciary had a key role in enforcing checks and balances, it would have to be made a part of the web of integrated government in a manner not affecting its independence.[80] This would ensure that institutional reasons would prevail to prevent attacks on the judiciary by its two coordinate organs. Two methods of integration were proposed—the power to appoint and impeach federal judges. Both the power of appointment and impeachment are seen as key measures to hold judiciaries accountable in several parts of the world today.[81]

According to the Constitution of the United States of America, federal judges, like the president, vice-president and other civil officers, could be impeached on account of treason, bribery or 'other high Crimes and Misdemeanors'.[82] All impeachments would have to take place in the House of Representatives[83]

80 According to M. J. C. Vile, absolute separation of powers and consequently a complete insulation of the judiciary, which he terms 'pure separation', is only an ideal type and has 'rarely been held in this extreme form.' Vile, *Constitutionalism and the Separation of Powers*, 14.

81 For example, the recent impeachment motion against Justice Soumitra Sen of the Calcutta High Court for alleged financial improprieties underlined the hard accountability nature of the impeachment power. For more, see RS Secretariat Motion; the importance of a carefully designed appointments process in order for the judiciary to be accountable can be seen in judicial reforms in several jurisdictions. See Malleson and Russell, *Appointing Judges in an Age of Judicial Power.*

82 Art. II section 4 of the US Constitution reads:

> The President, Vice President and all civil officers of the United States, shall be removed from office on impeachment for, and conviction of, treason, bribery, or other high crimes and misdemeanors.
>
> It is important to note that the provision applies to both federal executive and judicial officers and not to judges alone.

83 Art. I section 2 clause 5 of the US Constitution reads: 'The House of Representatives shall choose their speaker and other officers; and shall have the sole power of impeachment.'

and tried in the Senate.[84] The effect of such impeachment would be removal from office and certain attendant disqualifications.[85] For federal judges, it was specifically provided that they would hold office during 'good behaviour'.[86] This was widely interpreted as securing life tenure, subject only to impeachment on the basis of the specific grounds and following the procedure outlined above.[87] Hamilton specifically underlined the limited nature of the impeachment power when he rejected a proposal for incorporating 'inability' as a ground for impeachment for being vague and thereby vesting too much discretion in the legislature. He commended the existing constitutional provision for being 'the only provision on the point which is consistent with the necessary independence of the judicial character'.[88]

*Prima facie*, such a view is anomalous. Would impeachment not hang like Damocles' sword above judges' heads ensuring favourable decisions especially in cases involving judicial review of legislation? Hamilton offers two plausible defences—the complex procedure and the limited grounds for impeachment. Procedurally, a judge would have to be impeached by the House of Representatives. Following a successful motion there, he would have to be tried in the Senate by a

[84] Art. I section 3 clause 6 of the US Constitution reads: 'The Senate shall have the sole power to try all impeachments…'

[85] Art. I section 3 clause 7 of the US Constitution reads:

> Judgment in cases of impeachment shall not extend further than to removal from office, and disqualification to hold and enjoy any office of honor, trust or profit under the United States: but the party convicted shall nevertheless be liable and subject to indictment, trial, judgment and punishment, according to law.

[86] Art. III section 1 of the US Constitution reads:

> The judicial power of the United States, shall be vested in one Supreme Court, and in such inferior courts as the Congress may from time to time ordain and establish. The judges, both of the supreme and inferior courts, shall hold their offices during good behavior, and shall, at stated times, receive for their services, a compensation, which shall not be diminished during their continuance in office.

For an explanation of the term, see Raoul Berger, 'Impeachment of Judges and "Good Behavior" Tenure,' *The Yale Law Journal* 79, no. 8 (1970): 1475.

[87] Berger, 'Impeachment of Judges.' *Per contra*, Prakash and Smith have argued that 'good behavior' is a tenure-limiting term, that is a judge holds tenure till misbehaviour is judicial proven. See Prakash and Smith, '(Mis)Understanding Good Behavior Tenure.'

[88] Federalist Paper No. 79 in Federalist Papers, 519.

two-thirds majority. Both the numerical requirement in the Senate and the necessity of having an impeachment confirmed by both wings of Congress independently are suitably onerous. Similarly with regard to grounds for impeachment, a careful delineation of the grounds in the Constitution itself left little scope for expansive interpretation. Although 'high Crimes and Misdemeanors' were not expressly specified, they did have a specific, limited meaning at the time.[89]

Over time, the limited use of the impeachment power has affirmed Hamilton's belief in this regard. Such confidence might have been premature at the time and grossly misplaced had Justice Chase's impeachment motion on grounds of lack of impartiality in decision-making been successful. But it failed and subsequently impeachment became used as a 'last resort' measure to hold judges accountable for unbecoming behaviour. This ensured that it did not act as a threat to judicial independence.[90] At the same time, it was clear that impeachment was not designed as a measure *in order to secure judicial independence*. It was certainly conceptualised in a manner that did not overly affect judicial independence, but independence could hardly be said to be its *raison d'etre*. On the contrary, the positive justification for vesting the power of impeachment in the House of Representatives and the Senate lay, in my opinion, in the need to foster judicial accountability.

This is the overriding impression from Hamilton's reasons for justifying the vesting of the power of impeachment in the legislature. As representatives of the people, the house would be ideally placed to enquire into breaches of public trust, that is, conduct a 'national inquest into the conduct of public men'.[91] This is a key accountability function—making judges accountable for their behaviour to the people. Its mode of enforcement is political—through the political representatives of the people; its consequence is removal from office.

The preference of the Senate over the Supreme Court as the forum for trial for all impeachments also evinces a similar accountability rationale.[92] Impeachment, following the practice in England, was seen as a 'bridle' in the hands of the

89 Michael J. Gerhardt, 'The Lessons of Impeachment History,' *The George Washington Law Review* 67 (1999): 603, 609–10.

90 This is demonstrable from the few instances of the use of impeachment power by Congress subsequent to the Chase impeachment for federal judges and the even fewer number of times the Senate elected to convict such judges. See Jason J. Vicente, 'Impeachment: A Constitutional Primer,' *Texas Review of Law and Politics* 3 (1998): 117, 133–41.

91 Federalist Paper No. 65 in Federalist Papers, 429.

92 Ibid.

legislature over officers of the Union including its judges.[93] Given the nature of the trial—between a distinguished public officer accused of impropriety and the representatives of the people, who accused him—the forum for conducting such a trial, it was felt, ought to be public, presided over by a large number of members and of sufficient stature and independence. The Senate, with its more numerous composition, in comparison to the Supreme Court, high status as an elected wing of the legislature and with the independence necessary to reach an impartial verdict that would be widely respected, would thus commend itself.

When analysed, it is clear that there are two key reasons as to why the Senate is vested with the power to try impeachment. First, if impeachment is a 'bridle' held by the legislature, the Senate, set up as the less faction-ridden and more objective organ of the legislature, has an obvious role in putting its imprimatur on the impeachment motion. This underlines the public accountability function of impeachment while at the same time ensuring it is exercised in a fairly independent manner. Second, while the Supreme Court would ordinarily be equally if not more independent, neither would it have the fortitude nor would its decision have the public respect that such a decision regarding impeachment ought to command. Regarding the former, the view of the authors of the Federalist Papers is consistent with its overall impression of the Supreme Court as 'the weakest branch'. Neither were its members seen to have any special qualities nor was it foreseen that they would be repositories of public trust and respect. Needless to say, the history and development of the Supreme Court has belied such bleak portents. As far as the latter is concerned, the authors of the Federalist Papers viewed public respect as concomitant with a large number of presiding officers at trial. Public faith in the superior wisdom of a collectivity is a long established view.[94] However, it is not merely the numerical strength of the Senate that justifies its role but also the nature of the proceeding. Given that impeachment does not resemble a judicial proceeding, the Supreme Court would not be ideally suited to render a verdict that

[93] Ibid. For the practice of impeachment in England, see Berger, *Impeachment*, 1–73.

[94] This is reflected in the practice in several jurisdictions, where a court can overrule itself when the matter is heard by a bench larger in size than the bench of the same court which initially gave the decision. Nick Robinson et al., 'Interpreting the Constitution: Supreme Court Constitution Benches since Independence,' *Economic and Political Weekly* 46, no. 9 (2011): 27. Alternatively, *en banc* review by federal circuit courts is designed to place 'a maximum of judicial authority behind decisions of exceptionally important questions.' 'En Banc Review in Federal Circuit Courts: A Reassessment,' *Michigan Law Review* 72, no. 8 (1974): 1637, 1648, 1649.

would command public confidence.[95] On the contrary, the Senate, comprising a large number of public representatives who, it was expected, would exercise such power responsibly, would. Given that an impeachable offence is one deemed to be committed against the public, a Senate impeachment trial would thus be an authentic verdict delivered on behalf of the people.

Whether vesting such power in the Senate was wise or not is a determination that must be made elsewhere. What is relevant for the purpose of this section is the inference that with respect to judges, impeachment was a method to foster judicial accountability. Such accountability was owed politically to the legislature and enforced through an impeachment motion in the house followed by a public trial in the Senate. Fostering such inter-branch accountability through the impeachment provision was an important facet of stringing together the web of integrated government, one that has become increasingly significant over time. Its effect was to provide 'personal motives'[96] for the legislature, the key threat to an independent judiciary, to respect judicial decisions rather than attack them. Impeachment would be a constitutionally mandated channel by which legislative dissatisfaction with the judiciary would be expressed. Given the limited grounds and complex procedure for impeachment, such an accountability measure would thus not operate at the cost of judicial independence.[97] Judicial accountability would strengthen the web of integrated government in two ways—by giving a constitutional stake in the judiciary to the legislature, its perceived bête noire, while doing so in a manner that did not derogate from judicial independence, crucial to the sustainability of such a web.[98]

Likewise, the power to appoint federal judges was seen, as demonstrated earlier, as a fundamental component of the web of integrated government. Reiterating briefly, it was invested in the president who could act with the 'advice and consent'

95 Federalist Paper No. 65 in Federalist Papers, 430.

96 Federalist Paper No. 51 in Federalist Papers, 340.

97 In practice, this meant that impeachment was rarely used. See Vicente, 'Impeachment: A Constitutional Primer.'

98 It is not apparent that the theoretical understanding of judicial accountability indeed resulted in respect for judicial decisions by the legislature immediately. On the contrary, the use of a jurisdiction-stripping legislation following the Civil War and several instances of non-compliance suggested otherwise. Barry Friedman, 'History, Politics and Judicial Independence,' in *Judicial Integrity*, ed. András Sajò (Leiden; Boston: Martinus Nijhoff Publishers, 2004), 99, 110–12. However, the acceptance of judicial decisions over time for a number of reasons suggests these were teething troubles in the setting up of an effectively designed web of integrated government.

of the Senate.[99] It was designed to ensure that neither the legislature nor the executive could single-handedly influence the composition of the judiciary. In this counter-intuitive way, by which both the executive and the legislature were given a constitutional role in appointment, the 'truly distinct'[100] nature of the judiciary, independent of either of these organs, was sought to be protected. As a result, the organs of government were integrated with the legislature and executive checking and balancing each other, while appointing members of the judiciary.

The appointment power, however, was not seen at the time as a check and balance on the actual exercise of judicial power. The judiciary was considered to pose little threat to liberty of citizens given the highly circumscribed nature of judicial power. Such a check was thus presumably considered superfluous. This was why despite vesting the power of appointment in political organs of state, such power was not seen, at the time, as wielding any judicial accountability function. The potential for it to serve such a function, however, was apparent: if the judiciary exceeded its constitutional remit, a clear signal of the displeasure of its coordinate organs could be sent out in exercise of the power of appointment. Though they could not make the judges directly accountable for the questionable decisions rendered, as that would be inconsistent with the need for judicial independence, an appropriate use of the appointment power nonetheless had considerable potential to check judicial power.

This was explained theoretically in Chapter 5 as an example of an institutional accountability measure. While appointments could not make individual judges accountable (since they had already been appointed), they could make the judicial institution accountable for its decisions, behaviour and administration.[101] To do so legitimately, they would have to take into account the need for respecting the independence of the judiciary. Certain appointments, designed to foster accountability, fail this test. The appointment of judges with social philosophies that matched the government's own by Indira Gandhi's government in India, not appointing others, provides such an example.[102] But in principle, the enforcement of institutional accountability through a careful use of the appointment power need not *per se* affect judicial independence. Increasing diversity through the exercise of appointment power makes the

[99] US Constitution, Art. II section 2.

[100] Federalist Paper No. 78 in Federalist Papers, 508.

[101] See Chapter 5, Section 5B.1.

[102] See text accompanying notes 38–42 in Chapter 2.

judiciary accountable for its composition, a key aspect of its administration; appointing a judge with a record of efficiency likewise makes the existing judiciary accountable for its performance. The power to appoint thus plays an important soft accountability function—though not enforcing hard punitive consequences for actions or decisions for which the judiciary ought to provide account, it provides a less intrusive method of sending key performance-related messages to the judiciary.[103]

This suggests that like several other provisions in the Constitution, the provision for appointment of judges neither was designed nor operates to solely serve one value. Securing judicial accountability through appointments is key, but as is respecting judicial independence, promoting diversity and a range of other desiderata necessary for having competent judges in a well-functioning judicial institution. Much like impeachment, the appointment power must be understood in the context of the 'personal motives' of each organ that are key to this process of integration. Institutional accountability of the judiciary owed to the appointing authority, usually the executive, provides personal motive to such authority to desist from encroachment of the judicial function. At the same time, it provides personal motives to the judiciary to not overstep its jurisdictional remit and remain administratively efficient. Failure to do so would result in a strong political signal being delivered to the judiciary through an appropriate use of the appointment provision.[104] As judicial power has grown in the overall scheme of government, such rationale has developed considerable significance in integrating organs rather than allowing them to function in disparate ways. In this way, the web of integrated government is strengthened—by making the judiciary institutionally accountable and thereby a stakeholder in the maintenance of the overall constitutional scheme of checks and balances.

Over time, the relationship between judicial accountability measures and the web of integrated government has become dynamic on account of two key developments. First, the growing power of the judiciary in several jurisdictions, briefly adverted to aforesaid, has increased demands for judicial accountability.[105] For a diverse range of reasons, the judiciary, especially the

[103] For the distinction between soft and hard accountability, see Chapter 5, Section 5B.3.c.

[104] President Franklin Delano Roosevelt's 'court-packing' plan can be seen as an extreme instance of using the power of appointment to signal the government's displeasure with an activist judiciary. William Leuchtenberg, *Franklin D. Roosevelt and the New Deal* (New York: Harper and Row, 1963), 236.

[105] Cappeletti conducting a review of judicial systems in several jurisdictions writes: '[I]t is generally recognized that one feature common to many modern societies

apex court in several countries, has assumed a central role in governance.[106] As a result, several new forms of holding the judiciary accountable have developed. Amongst institutional accountability measures, the setting up of the Judicial Appointments Commission for England and Wales provides an example of a growing demand for greater public accountability of the judiciary. Comprising fifteen members, a majority of whom are non-judicial, the commission is vested with the power to appoint judges at most levels in England and Wales and for certain tribunals whose jurisdiction extends to Scotland and Northern Ireland.[107] Both the establishment of such a commission and the transparent processes of application and interview that it follows for appointment have significantly bolstered institutional accountability of the judiciary.[108] For augmenting individual accountability of judges, several other jurisdictions have instituted judicial performance evaluation programmes.[109] Originally conceptualised as feeders for well-informed voting of state judges in certain states in the United States of America, today several American states have adopted a carefully delineated judicial performance evaluation programme.[110] Its acceptability has also spread beyond the United States (albeit with significant variations) as countries seek diverse measures to evaluate the legal ability, administrative

has been a tremendous growth of judicial power.' Cappelletti, 'Who Watches the Watchmen?' 5.

[106] This is particularly conspicuous in courts in South Asia and Latin America. See Nick Robinson, 'Expanding Judiciaries: India and the Rise of the Good Governance Court,' *Washington University Global Studies Law Review* 8 (2009): 1; Cesar Rodriguez-Garavito, 'Beyond the Courtroom: The Impact of Judicial Activism on Socioeconomic Rights in Latin America,' *Texas Law Review* 89, no. 7 (2011): 1669.

[107] Part 4 of the Constitutional Reform Act establishes the Commission and sets out its powers, duties and other necessary provisions. Schedule 12 to the Act provides the composition and processes to be followed by the Commission. It will be useful to note that appointments to the Supreme Court for the United Kingdom are, however, excluded from its remit, as it is by a special Selection Commission of which the Chairperson of the Commission is a member. This is as per relevant provisions in Part 3 of the Act read with Schedule 8.

[108] This is reflected in a set of high-quality essays analysing the impact of the setting up and working of the Judicial Appointments Commission. See Jeffrey Jowell et al., *Judicial Appointments: Balancing Independence, Accountability and Legitimacy* (London: Judicial Appointments Commission, 2010), available at http://jac.judiciary.gov.uk/static/documents/JA_web.pdf (accessed 10 September 2013) (hereinafter 'JAC UK').

[109] Kourlis and Singer, 'Performance Evaluation Program.'

[110] David C. Brody, 'The Use of Judicial Performance Evaluation to Enhance Judicial Accountability, Judicial Independence and Public Trust,' *Denver University Law Review* 86 (2008): 115.

performance and efficiency of judges.[111] The underlying rationale is thus to make judges accountable to the public for their performance, albeit in a manner that does not affect their independence.[112]

At the same time, the web of integrated government itself has evolved considerably. As Bruce Ackerman has argued after drawing from developments in several jurisdictions, the key transformation has been the dilution of the strict conception of a trinitarian model comprising the legislature, executive and judiciary. The underlying principle of Ackerman's point, that is, the web of integrated government is more intricate than a strict threefold division of power suggests, is reaffirmed by the developments in the enforcement of judicial accountability. A pervasive aspect of such measures has been their enforcement by an inter-branch or an independent commission. A key function in appointment of judges,[113] their disciplining,[114] performance evaluations[115] and even a role in their removal [116] has been entrusted to, or envisaged for, such a commission. This has necessarily made the web of integrated government and consequently inter-branch relations between the legislature, executive and judiciary more complex. While the exact implications of such complexity will be a key area for research going forward, for the purpose of this book, it is clear that judicial accountability measures are central to the evolving web of integrated government, whether conceptualised in its Madisonian form or its modern avatar. Irrespective of the shape the web of integrated government takes—modern or

[111] Richard Mohr and Francesco Contini, 'Judicial Evaluation in Context: Principles, Practices and Promise in Nine European Countries,' *European Journal of Legal Studies* 1, no. 2 (2007): 1.

[112] For more, see Kourlis and Singer, 'Performance Evaluation Program'; Brody, 'Use of Judicial Performance Evaluation.'

[113] For an illustrative example, see JAC UK.

[114] For an illustrative example, see the working of the Judicial Conduct Committee, part of the Judicial Service Commission in South Africa. See International Bar Association, 'Beyond Polokwane: Safeguarding South Africa's Judicial Independence,' July 2008, available at www.ibanet.org/Document/Default.aspx?DocumentUid=4c7e8c0f-652d-44bd-a459-d9ac85d6872e (accessed 10 September 2013).

[115] Kourlis and Singer, 'Performance Evaluation Program.'

[116] An independent statutory committee comprising judges and jurists under the Judges' Inquiry Act, 1968 (India), plays a key role in recommending impeachment of sitting judges to Parliament. See V. K. Agnihotri, *Impeachment of a Judge in the Indian Parliament* (Kampala: Communication to Association of Secretary Generals of Parliament, 2012), available at www.asgp.info/Resources/Data/Documents/WJPUTLJMWGFXUZDYEQLPKUDKVXTAPQ.doc (accessed 10 September 2013).

Madisonian—measures enforcing judicial accountability are key facets of such a web. In Chapter 6, we found measures securing judicial independence as equally key in sustaining the mutual checks and balances scheme that are entailed by such a web. In this lies a fundamental normative congruence between judicial independence and accountability that is spelt out presently.

## *7B.2 Bolstering Public Confidence*

Academic writing, extra-judicial comment, and qualitative and quantitative analyses concerning the judiciary have widely conceived of judicial accountability as central to public confidence in courts and democracy. This relationship is often deemed axiomatic, requiring little explanation. Take former Chief Justice of Canada Beverly Mclachlin's statement:

> The underlying principle of democracy that power should not go uncontrolled is furthered by an accountable, independent judiciary.[117]

Charles Geyh, explaining the relationship a bit further, writes:

> [J]udicial accountability promotes public confidence in judges and the judiciary. Regardless of whether independent judges follow the law, if the public's perception is otherwise, reforms calculated to render judicial decision-making subject to popular or political branch control are sure to follow ...[118]

If the logic underlying such statements is scrutinised, it would go something like this: Judicial accountability means that the courts are answerable to the people for their actions; such answerability is required for all state organs in a democracy; as long as they are answerable, they enjoy public confidence; if people lose public confidence in courts for any reason whatsoever, they can enforce such accountability; this can either lead to removal from office or an analogous remedy for the defect which caused such lack of confidence in the first place. This is an elegant logical proposition, which is *per se* unproblematic. The difficulties lie either in the foundational political principle—should the implication of democracy as leading to public control apply to the judiciary as well or be limited to the elected organs of government; or whether methods of enforcement of such accountability, designed to lead to public confidence, are adequately respectful of judicial independence and other values necessary

[117] Beverly McLachlin, 'Courts and Judges in the Framework of Accountability,' *Journal of Parliamentary and Political Law* 1 (2008): 293, 298.

[118] Geyh, 'Rescuing Judicial Accountability,' 916.

for the judiciary. The former is beyond the remit of this book for reasons explained in Chapter 5;[119] the latter is normatively dealt with presently. Subject to a satisfactory resolution of both issues, concerns with the enforcement of accountability do not in principle affect the axiomatic relationship it has with public confidence.

Subject to the issue above, it is unnecessary to belabour the significance of judicial accountability to public confidence in the judiciary excessively. Such a view is commonsensical—after all, managing expectations from the judiciary by holding it to account is a device to ensure that it is functioning in a manner that promotes stakeholder confidence. Though the methods of enforcement may be diverse, the implication is clear—commonly understood facets of judicial accountability provide the foundation for the public to enjoy confidence in the judiciary.

## *7B.3 Promoting Substantive Virtues*

The analysis of judicial integrity in Section 7A suggested the conceptualisation of integrity as a portmanteau virtue. While at its core it entailed acting on the basis of coherent principle, this core understanding was supplemented by several virtues that are widely considered essential for a judiciary to have. Both individual integrity of judges and institutional integrity of the judiciary as a whole have a two-way relationship with such virtues, which are both constitutive of integrity and follow as a consequence from the presence of integrity. However, neither in the said discussion nor in general discussions of judicial integrity was judicial accountability seen as such a virtue.[120] But at the same time the significance of judicial accountability in shaping an effective judicial institution is widely accepted. If it is not constitutive of integrity as other values are and does not follow as a consequence, what is the nature of the relationship between judicial accountability and integrity? Or on the contrary, are they not related in any significant way?

To assess this, it is necessary to revisit the concept of 'responsible decision-making' viewed as the rationale for judicial accountability in Chapter 5. Judicial accountability, I argued, was needed to ensure that judicial decisions were made responsibly. This applied to both decisional and behavioural accountability measures for individual judges and institutional accountability measures.

[119] See Chapter 5, section 5B.3.

[120] While this is true of most accounts, an exception is the conceptualisation of 'external accountability' as constitutive of judicial integrity by Jonathan Soeharno. Soeharno, *Integrity of a Judge*, 69–75. Such conceptualisation seems to wrongly conflate factors constitutive of integrity with those demonstrative of it.

Responsibility itself was seen in terms of 'responsibility-as-virtue', that is, whether in the course of decision-making, the virtues considered necessary for the judiciary were upheld. Now we have an indicative idea of what these virtues are—we want judiciaries to have integrity, to be independent and impartial, and to possess all the second-order values these concepts entail. Once 'responsibility' is fleshed out in this manner, it follows as a necessary consequence that judicial accountability is needed for such values to be seen to be upheld. We can thus safely exclude the second possibility noted here that accountability is not related to such values in a significant way.

To understand how judicial accountability positively upholds such values is also entailed in such an account. The methods of enforcement of judicial accountability, classified on the basis of addressee into legal, political, public and internal and on the basis of consequence into hard and soft, provide a comprehensive account of how judicial accountability is sought to be incorporated into the functioning of the judiciary. These methods thus must, in certain specific ways, lead to the upholding of one or the other of the substantive virtues deemed necessary for the judiciary. This is achieved, as the subsequent examples demonstrate, by rendering the substantive virtues that the judiciary ought to possess more likely or serving as a condition precedent to their realisation or demonstrating the possession of such virtues. Some measures may do so effectively, others less so. However, in principle, all methods for enforcement of judicial accountability are significant in furthering the instrumental rationale of an effective judiciary. Thus, while it is neither constitutive of integrity *per se* nor does it follow as a consequence of integrity, mechanisms of judicial accountability nonetheless provide a crucial foundation for substantive virtues of a judiciary to thrive.

To understand the specific inter-connections, let us take the argument made by Soeharno who posits that 'external accountability' is necessary in order to demonstrate integrity of the judicial institution to the public.[121] Since the purpose of integrity, in his explanation, is to create public trust, the mere possession of virtuous character is necessary but not sufficient. It needs to be supplemented by methods of accountability that demonstrate such virtuous character. Demonstrating such integrity to the public is distinct from having integrity in the first place.[122] For example, the disclosure of financial assets by all judges of the higher judiciary in India is a transparency measure that

[121] Soehamo, *Integrity of a Judge*, 69.

[122] Ibid.

facilitates direct accountability of individual judges for their behaviour.[123] At the same time, it promotes institutional accountability of the judiciary to the public by allowing for public questioning of finances of judges should there be suspicion of disproportionate assets or wilful misstatement by judges or other cause for concern.[124] The incorporation of such an accountability mechanism is not constitutive of the integrity of judges—judges, individually, as well as the judiciary institutionally may have integrity notwithstanding. But such a measure demonstrates the possession of such integrity by providing the public a direct method of holding the judge to account should there be a suspicion of such integrity being lacking.

Similar examples can be used to demonstrate analogous relationships between judicial accountability and other virtues deemed essential for the judiciary. The underlying principle that emerges is that accountability measures are necessary appendages to the substantive virtues that judiciaries ought to possess. As an appendage, it either demonstrates the possession of such virtues, as seen earlier in the case of integrity, or makes such possession more likely. In this manner, it either points out the shortcomings of the judiciary, thereby deterring their incidence in the future or reaffirms its virtues. So widely prevalent and useful are these functions that despite being appendages to other substantive virtues, judicial accountability *per se* becomes a necessary virtue for the effective functioning of the judiciary. Without it, either the substantive virtues would be less manifested (or not at all), there being little incentive for their possession, or they would be futile, given that the public would have little knowledge of their existence. The use and limits of this conceptual relation are revisited in the opening pages of Chapter 8.

123 Though such disclosure is not mandated by law, judges of the Supreme Court by an administrative resolution decided to declare their assets and liabilities on the official website of the court. They could, however, not be questioned on the basis of such declaration. Dhananjay Mahapatra, 'Supreme Court Judges to Disclose Assets,' *Times of India*, 27 August 2009, available at http://articles.timesofindia.indiatimes.com/2009-08-27/india/28160981_1_full-court-meeting-assets-and-liabilities-judges (accessed 10 September 2013).

124 Such asset declarations have given rise to forms of direct public accountability. Justice Gyan Sudha Mishra (Judge of the Supreme Court) describing her unmarried daughters as liabilities led to a spirited public discussion on her ideological views. The declaration is available at 'Disclosure of Assets: Hon'ble Mrs. Justice Gyan Sudha Misra,' http://supremecourtofindia.nic.in/assets/gsmisra.pdf (accessed 10 September 2013); for a discussion, see Anita Nair, 'Daughter a Liability for SC Woman Judge,' *One India*, 29 December 2010, available at http://news.oneindia.in/2010/12/29/sc-judge-gyan-sudha-mishra-daughters-liability.html (accessed 10 September 2013).

## 7C Conclusion

This chapter, building on the rationales for judicial independence and accountability discussed in Chapters 5 and 6, has demonstrated that judicial independence is needed for impartial adjudication as well as checking and balancing other organs of government (together termed 'an effective judiciary'). For impartial adjudication, judicial integrity is a significant factor; for checking and balancing other organs of government, the judiciary needs to enjoy public confidence and be part of a web of integrated government. Judicial accountability measures are a necessary component of the web of integrated government while at the same time bolstering public confidence and demonstrating or rendering the possession of substantive virtues such as integrity and impartiality more likely. On this basis, it can thus be argued that judicial independence and accountability are both constituent factors of 'an effective judiciary'. This meta-level non-holistic argument suggests that *normatively* judicial independence and accountability are needed for an effective judiciary, an end which is served by other constituent factors as well. The extent to which the former is present is conditioned not only by the impact on the latter directly but also by the impact such a measure has on the effectiveness of the judiciary as a whole.

This conceptual understanding of both judicial independence and accountability leading to an effective judiciary has three significant merits. First, it provides a distinct normative basis to assess the justifiability of independence and accountability-promoting measures. Second, it is capacious enough to accommodate other factors, closely connected with independence and accountability, though distinct from them, which such measures may promote or affect. For example, judicial elections do not just affect judicial independence but plausibly affect public confidence in the judiciary, which provides additional reason to argue against their use as a method of selecting judges. Third, the normative idea that judicial independence and accountability are needed for an effective judiciary can provide a doctrinal device to assess the validity of measures taken to promote either judicial independence or accountability. Such a doctrine can provide a positive basis for how real-life conflicts between judicial independence and accountability will be resolved. The development of 'an effective judiciary' as a doctrinal idea and its application to systems of appointment, transfers, impeachment and post-retirement employment in the Indian higher judiciary are taken up in the next part which concludes the book.

# PART III

# TYING THE STRANDS

# Harmonising Judicial Independence and Judicial Accountability in India

# 8

We are now in a position to tie the strands from Parts I and II of the book together. In Part I, a close analysis of systems of appointments, transfers, impeachment and post-retirement employment of judges of the higher judiciary in India revealed grave doubts about the legal basis for the operation of appointments and transfers. It pointed out the ineffectiveness of impeachment as a disciplinary mechanism and the pervasive practice of post-retirement employment of judges in government-appointed positions, often very shortly after retirement. It also documented the widespread concerns regarding the independence of the judiciary and its tension with judicial accountability, while at the same time highlighting that these concepts were being used in a number of diverse ways, often with divergent meanings.

This necessitated a closer conceptual enquiry of judicial accountability and independence in Part II. This was done through a fivefold enquiry into both concepts through which their diverse elements were captured. Fleshing out the rationales for judicial independence and accountability, it was argued that both are necessary for creating 'an effective judiciary'. The various components of an effective judiciary were delineated together with how judicial independence and accountability impacted them.

On the basis of this normative assessment, in Section 8A a putative doctrinal device—whether the measure in question leads to an effective judiciary—can now be advanced. The purpose of such a device is purely analytical—to provide researchers and observers of judiciaries with a useful tool with which to analyse the justifiability of measures that affect or promote judicial independence or accountability.

Section 8B applies this doctrine to the working of appointments, transfers, impeachment and post-retirement employment of judges in India. It examines the impact each of these mechanisms has on judicial independence and accountability as understood in Part II. On this basis, it infers whether the said measure is justifiable on independence–accountability grounds. No implication ought to be drawn regarding the justifiability of such a measure in terms of other virtues deemed desirable for the judiciary—that is a distinct analytical exercise.

For measures found unjustifiable, Chapter 9 advocates necessary reforms. The proposals advanced do not seek to reinvent the wheel as far as reforms are concerned. Much work has been done on reform and several reform proposals are pending consideration of the government and widely discussed publicly. Accordingly, it either modifies existing reform proposals to incorporate the findings from this chapter or, where no law or proposal exists, suggests the broad framework for reform.

## 8A The Doctrine: Does the Measure Lead to an Effective Judiciary?

We are now in a position to distil our conceptual findings in Part II to a five-step doctrine. The doctrine consists of a set of logically sequential questions, the answers to which determine the justifiability or otherwise of the measures under scrutiny. The doctrine, in full, is described below followed by an explanatory note on each of its steps.

1. Does the measure in question (hereinafter 'the measure'/'it') 'promote/safeguard' judicial independence pertaining to a relevant aspect of judicial functioning or 'adversely affect' it?
2. Does it 'promote/safeguard' judicial accountability pertaining to a relevant aspect of judicial functioning or 'adversely affect' it?
3. (a) If *the answer to 1 above is 'promote/safeguard' and 2 above is also 'promote/safeguard'*, then the measure is justifiable in terms of judicial independence and judicial accountability (no inference is drawn regarding its impact on other substantive virtues a judiciary is expected to possess);

   (b) If *the answer to 1 above is 'adversely affect' and 2 above is 'adversely affect'*, then the measure is not justifiable in terms of judicial independence and judicial accountability (no inference is drawn regarding its impact on other substantive virtues a judiciary is expected to possess);

   (c) If *the answer to 1 above is 'promote/safeguard' and 2 above is 'adversely affect' or vice versa*, then does the measure:

i. Enjoy public confidence?

ii. Promote another substantive virtue deemed desirable for the judiciary?

iii Strengthen the web of integrated government thereby promoting mutual checks and balances?

Explanation: *Per contra*, if the answer to 1 or 2 above *is 'no impact'*, then the determination of justifiability is purely on the basis of its impact on the other (that is, if 'no impact' on judicial independence, then justifiability is determined on the basis of impact on judicial accountability and vice versa). If the answer to both 1 and 2 above is 'no impact', then determining the justifiability of the measure is outside the remit of this doctrine.

4. (a) If the answer to 3(c)(i), (ii) and (iii) is *YES*, then it is a justifiable measure in terms of judicial independence and judicial accountability;

   (b) If the answer to 3(c)(i), (ii) and (iii) is *NO*, then it is not a justifiable measure in terms of judicial independence and judicial accountability;

   (c) If the answer to 3(c)(i), (ii) and (iii) is *YES to one or more and NO to the remaining or vice versa*, is the measure indispensable to, or does it emasculate one of the following desiderata: public confidence in the judiciary, a substantive virtue considered desirable for the judiciary or the web of integrated government?

5. (a) If the answer to 4(c) is *YES to emasculation of any of the desiderata*, then the measure in not justifiable;

   (b) If the answer to 4(c) is *YES to indispensability of any of the desiderata*, then it is justifiable;

   (c) If the answer to 4(c) is *NO to emasculation or indispensability of any of the desiderata, the extent* to which the measure promotes/safeguards or adversely affects the three factors must be assessed for its suitability in the constitutional culture of the jurisdiction in question.

The doctrinal device has been pictorially represented through the following flowcharts (Figure 8.1 showing when a measure is justifiable or non-justifiable and Figure 8.2 showing when a measure has no impact):

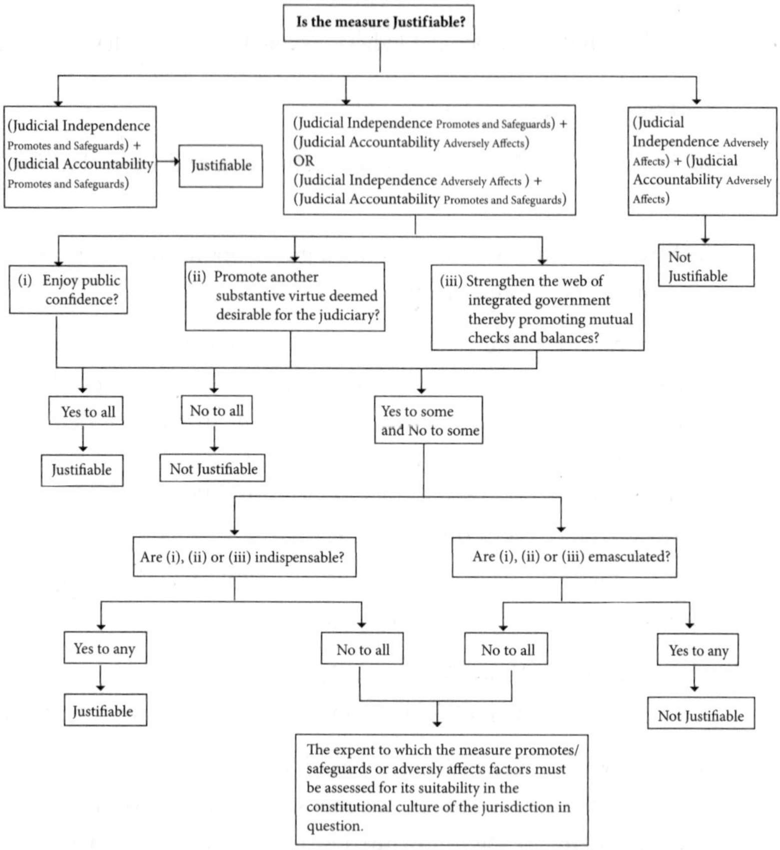


**Figure 8.1** Impact of a measure on judicial independence and accountability

*Source*: Author.

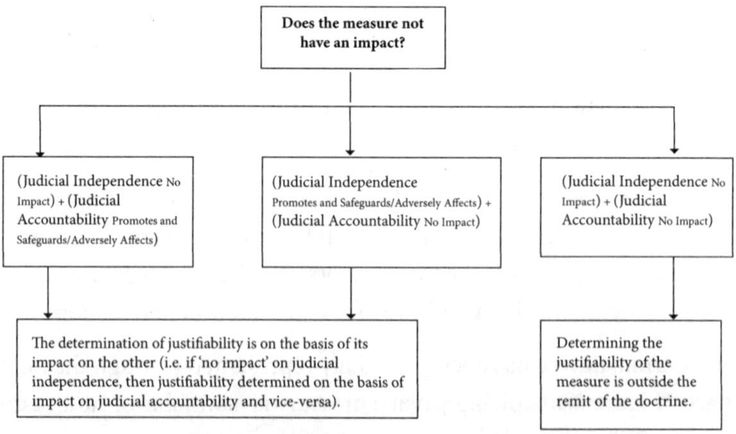


**Figure 8.2** When a measure has no impact on either judicial independence or judicial accountability or both

*Source*: Author.

A brief elaboration of each of the steps with examples will be useful in explaining the doctrine. At steps 1 and 2, the doctrine refers back to a finding in Chapters 5 and 6—judicial independence and accountability must each be seen in a disaggregated manner. There are certain kinds of independence and accountability that we want judges and the judicial institution to have, that is, with regard to their decisions, behaviour and administration. Steps 1 and 2 assess whether the measure in question indeed promotes independence and accountability in such relevant ways or adversely affects them. The purpose is to thus establish whether the measure in question raises a conflict between judicial independence and accountability at all in the first place. For example, reason-giving, adverted to above, pursuant to step 2 promotes individual decisional accountability of judges since judges can be held accountable for the decisions they hand down on the basis of the reasons they provide. Such a measure does not affect judicial independence, pursuant to the analysis in step 1, in any relevant way. This is because while the requirement to provide reasons impedes judges from deciding as they wish, it does not specifically dictate how they must decide the case. Thus, it is a justifiable measure *per se*, not resulting in any notable independence–accountability conflict.

Step 3, consequent to steps 1 and 2, filters out the measures that require further analysis from others that are either beyond the remit of this doctrinal device or can be resolved without further enquiry. Thus, if a measure does not promote or adversely affect either independence or accountability in any relevant way, then the measure, quite naturally, is extraneous to this doctrinal device (explanation to step [3]). If on the other hand it promotes both (step 3[a]), it is justifiable *per se* in terms of judicial independence and accountability. Alternatively, if it adversely affects both (step 3[b]), then it is unjustifiable. It is, however, instructive to note that steps 3(a) and (b) are silent on the overall justifiability of any of those measures since that is a wider determination that may have to take into account factors beyond the remit of what is being considered here. This will be demonstrated in the context of post-retirement employment of judges of the Indian higher judiciary in Chapter 9.

Step 3(c) subjects those measures that raise genuine independence–accountability conflicts to further scrutiny. Three sub-questions are used as the starting point for resolving such conflicts. The criteria alluded to in these sub-questions—of whether the measure bolsters public confidence, promotes substantive virtues considered desirable for the judiciary (such as impartiality and integrity) and strengthens the web of integrated government thereby promoting mutual checks and balances—are derived from the requirements of an effective judiciary delineated in Chapter 7. Such criteria are entirely jurisdiction-specific—certain measures may bolster public confidence in the judiciary in one jurisdiction and not others;[1] certain substantive virtues may be prized more in certain jurisdictions than others,[2] and the web of integrated government is wholly contingent on the constitutional structure in question.

Step 4 distils the results of the enquiry in step 3(c). If the measure in question returns an affirmative answer to all three sub-questions, then it is justifiable in the concerned jurisdiction. Likewise, if the answer is negative to all three, then it is unjustifiable. However, it is possible that a measure may lead to an effective judiciary in some ways and derogate from it in others. To account for such situations, step 4(c) provides a supplementary test, that is, whether it is indispensable to or emasculates any of the measures in question. The rationale behind such a test is that if a measure both promotes and derogates from the need for an effective judiciary, the extent to which it does each becomes relevant. Thus at the extremes, as steps 5(a) and (b) posit,if the measure emasculates any of the three specified desiderata, then it is unjustifiable; on the contrary, if it is indispensable to any of the three desiderata, it is justifiable.[3]

However, if this supplementary test also fails to return an affirmative answer, step 5(c) provides a residuary test as a closure principle, that is, a subjective determination of the extent to which the measure promotes or affects each of the desiderata in the constitutional context of the jurisdiction in question. Such a subjective residuary principle is unavoidable—however, by making its application a last-resort measure, consequent to several stringent preceding stages, its remit is sought to be expressly circumscribed.

1 Senate confirmation of candidates for the Supreme Court was considered key to preventing favouritism by the president in choosing candidates. See Federalist Paper No. 77 in Federalist Papers; in India, a similar proposal for parliamentary ratification was rejected for fear that it would reduce the high status of the judiciary. See Rohini Kumar Chaudhari, CAD, vol. VIII (May–June 1949), 251; B. R. Ambedkar, CAD, vol. VIII (May–June 1949), 258.

2 Continuing with the USA–India comparison, the perception of impartiality does not encompass absolute issue impartiality in the USA where the ideological views of judges are sought to be made public during the appointments process; in India, the perception of impartiality extends to incorporating a higher degree of issue impartiality with ideological views of judges not being readily apparent in public at the time of appointment.

3 The possibility of a measure emasculating one of the desiderata while being indispensable to another is a theoretical possibility that has not been considered because of its unlikelihood. In such an eventuality, the residuary test in step 5(c) can be used.

This doctrinal device is the logical consequence of the need to translate the normative understanding of judicial independence and accountability being necessary for an effective judiciary into a practical analytical tool, a key purpose of this book. Using this doctrine, the next section evaluates systems of judicial appointments, transfers, impeachment and post-retirement of judges of the higher judiciary in India from the perspective of their impact on judicial independence and accountability. Not only does this provide a practical example of the working of the doctrine but it also brings the book full circle, isolating specific independence–accountability conflicts in India and suggesting appropriate avenues for reform.

## 8B Doctrinal Assessment of Systems in India

Part I analysed the theoretical conceptualisation and working of the systems of judicial appointments, transfers, impeachment and post-retirement employment of judges in India. Through such analysis both the interpretive issues surrounding the constitutional provisions governing these aspects and the practical difficulties faced in their operation were highlighted. Outstanding, however, was the effect that the working of these systems had on judicial independence and accountability. Though all four facets of judicial functioning were widely seen as affecting judicial independence and accountability in specific ways, a determinative assessment of such impact could not be carried out without a deeper analysis of the two concepts. This problem became particularly acute in situations, such as collegium-led appointments, that were justified on the basis of preserving judicial independence and criticised for riding roughshod over calls for judicial accountability. Having undertaken this conceptual exercise and distilled the interface between judicial independence and accountability to the five-step doctrine described in Section 8A earlier, we are now in a position to assess the impact that the working of each of these four systems has had on the need for an effective judiciary. The analysis in this section thus provides a way out of the conundrum of whether measures ostensibly promoting independence and diminishing accountability or vice versa are, all things considered, justifiable or not.

Two caveats are necessary at this stage: First, the results of the doctrinal analysis will be different depending on the point of time the analysis is being undertaken. For example, an analysis of the working of executive appointments in the early 1970s would look starkly different from a similar analysis in the late 1970s. To obviate this difficulty, all analyses are undertaken with the time of writing the book (2012–2018) as the reference point, that is, an analysis of systems as they have developed over time. Second, methodologically, this analysis is based on primary material, that is, judicial opinions and Constituent Assembly debates, and secondary material, that is, books, newspaper pieces and scholarly works. The research, while being representative of the perceived merits and demerits of various mechanisms, makes no claims to comprehensiveness. Nor does it make any claim to objectivity since the results of the doctrinal analysis are a subjective assessment of the working of these mechanisms in India. Different views are of course possible, though every effort has been made to formulate the results of the doctrinal enquiry on the basis of objective facts and, where unavailable, widely held public opinion.

## *8B.1 Appointments*

The working of mechanisms for judicial appointments in India evidence two distinct phases. Between 1950 and 1993, the process was led by the executive with the chief justice of India playing a significant consultative role. The perceived deficiency of this process—a failure to safeguard judicial independence—led to the decision of the Supreme Court in *SCAORA*, marking the commencement of the second phase of judicial appointments, when it was led by the judicial collegium. These mechanisms are distinct and are thus analysed separately.

### ***8B.1.a. Executive-Led Appointments***

**Does it promote/safeguard judicial independence pertaining to a relevant aspect of judicial functioning or adversely affect it?**

The mechanism of executive-led appointments in the scheme of the Constitution was specifically designed to preserve judicial independence. The history of a dependent colonial judiciary was fresh in the minds of the drafters and thus a strong-willed counter-majoritarian institution was the key desideratum underlying judicial appointments. Specifically, the intention was to keep individual judges decisionally independent of the government such that no extraneous threats could be brought to bear on their judgment. At the same time, a credible appointments mechanism would also lead to the high status of the judiciary being entrenched in the public mind.[4]

While the intention underlying executive-led appointments may have been lofty, in practice judicial independence was adversely affected by the operation of this mechanism. In its early years, the 14th Law Commission Report pointed

[4] See Chapter 2, Section 2A.

to the pervasive nature of politicised appointments based on caste and religion.[5] Such politicised appointments, according to the commission, affected the independence of the judiciary leading the commission to recommend making concurrence of the chief justice of India mandatory for all appointments. If scrutinised further, the commission's view of independence would include both individual and institutional independence from any extraneous threats to impartial adjudication. Thus, appointments on the basis of caste and religion would put impartial adjudication in doubt for particular judges who were purportedly appointed for extraneous reasons. It would likewise affect the institutional independence of the judiciary itself owing to its politicised nature stemming from the predominant role of government in appointments.

This was exacerbated during the early 1970s when Mohan Kumaramangalam's philosophy of a 'committed judiciary' held sway. The appointment of Justice Ray as chief justice of India, superseding Justices Shelat, Hegde and Grover, and again the appointment of Justice Beg, superseding Justice Khanna, sent out a clear signal to judges that their career progression was contingent on a compromise of their decisional independence.[6] At the same time, there was a concerted effort to appoint persons as judges who would share the government's social and political goals. A widely held perception was that many of the judges appointed during this period, while being fine judges of exceptional quality, bore an ideological affinity to the government's socialistic agenda.[7] So deeply entrenched was this perception that it persisted through the 1980s after the judgment in *Gupta*, which had certified executive-led appointments as constitutional and not *per se* inimical to judicial independence.

Executive-led appointments were thus a grave threat to the decisional independence of judges, of both the Supreme Court and the High Court, from governmental interference and other extraneous threats to decision-making. If Supreme Court judges were fearless in their decision-making, it would affect their chances of becoming chief justice of India; if High Court judges had political views that did not align with the government's, they would not be elevated to the Supreme Court. It can be fairly said that a graver threat to decisional independence of judges has scarcely existed in India.

5 Law Comm., 14th Report.

6 Nayar, *Supersession of Judges*.

7 T. R. Andhyarujina, *The Kesavananda Bharati Case* (Gurgaon: Universal Law Publishing, 2011), 81–87.

**Does it promote/safeguard judicial accountability pertaining to a relevant aspect of judicial functioning or adversely affect it?**

Politicised appointments of judges, on religion, caste or other ascriptive criteria or ideological views, promoted both individual and institutional decisional accountability. Individual decisional accountability for High Court judges was enforced politically by the executive in the nominations made to the Supreme Court. Given the hitherto prevalent view of the importance of a candidate's social and political views to his/her appointment, such views would be primarily discernible though judgments delivered in the High Court. Since the substance of High Court judgments was considered significant, it thus follows that individual judges were held accountable by the executive for the substantive decisions handed down. This was enforced through the exercise of appointment power, which was a political act. Likewise individual decisional accountability for Supreme Court judges was enforced through the power of appointing the chief justice of India. Since the seniority convention had been dispensed with, judges whose decisions were aligned with the ideological mooring of the government were made chief justice on two occasions overlooking their more senior colleagues.[8]

The political nature of the appointment act also meant that appointments became a tool for enforcing institutional decisional accountability. By appointing judges on the basis of their political and constitutional views, rewarding aligned judges and punishing those whose views on important constitutional issues differed with that of the government, the effect was to create a judiciary that was *de facto* held to account by the government for the collective decisions of the judges. It was a judiciary 'made to measure',[9] one that would be an ideological prop for the reform efforts of the government rather than a strong, counter-majoritarian organ that it was intended to be.

Since executive-led appointments, promote decisional accountability at the cost of decisional independence, according to step 3(c) of the doctrine, the relevant questions are:

**(3)(c) Does the measure:**

- **i. Enjoy public confidence?**
- **ii Promote another substantive virtue deemed desirable for the judiciary?**
- **iii Strengthen the web of integrated government thereby promoting mutual checks and balances?**

[8] Nayar, *Supersession of Judges.*

[9] Palkhivala, *Our Constitution: Defaced and Defiled.*

Concerns surrounding the politicisation of executive-led appointments were concomitant with their introduction in the constitutional scheme. The government's proclivity towards caste, region and religion-based appointments in the first two decades was pointed out in detail by the Law Commission based on exhaustive nationwide surveys and analysis. However, this remained a concern largely internal to the judiciary, rarely having any discernible effect on public confidence. With the onset of the committed judges theory, together with the substantive nature of several decisions handed down at this time and the two supersessions adverted to aforesaid, governmental takeover of the appointments process became a matter of public concern. Journalists provided careful accounts of the government's covert attempts to create a pliant judiciary through the tool of supersession.[10] Lawyers were outraged by this attempt by the government to browbeat the judiciary into dependence.[11] Despite such active interference ceasing with the electoral defeat of the Congress Party in 1977, its entrenchment, adverted to aforesaid, meant that on the Congress' return to power in 1980, the same fears resurfaced. This was not merely myth-making—in *Gupta,* the non-confirmation of an additional judge, despite the continuing existence of arrears, was attributed to certain judicial orders passed by him in his tenure as district judge.[12] Executive interference in judicial composition and consequently decision-making was all-pervasive leading the chief justice of India to say:

> As the head of the judiciary does not interfere with the functioning of the Cabinet or Ministry, so the head of the executive should not interfere with the functioning of the judiciary.[13]

The widespread nature of such claims, the erudition of their advocates and the history of executive interference meant that executive-led appointments suffered from a severe shortage of public confidence. The Law Commission thus suggested an alternative;[14] however, executive appointments continued

[10] Nayar, *Supersession of Judges*; 'No Landmark, This,' *Economic and Political Weekly* 8, no. 18 (1973): 813–14; for a collection of journalistic pieces, see Bhagwan D. Dua, 'A Study of Executive-Judicial Conflict: The Indian Case,' *Asian Survey* 23, no. 4 (1983): 463.

[11] Nani A. Palkhivala, 'A Judiciary Made to Measure' in *Supersession of Judges,* ed. Nayar (New Delhi: Indian Book Company), 120–29.

[12] *Gupta*, para 95 (Justice Bhagwati).

[13] Per CJI Chandrachud, *Illustrated Weekly of India*, 12–18 July 1981, in Dua, 'Study of Executive-Judicial Conflict,' 474.

[14] Law Commission of India, *A New Forum for Judicial Appointments*, 121st Report, Ministry of Law and Justice, Government of India, 1987.

as a discredited mechanism. The most telling testimony of the fact that public confidence in executive-led appointments was shattered came from the Statement of Objects and Reasons of a bill introduced by the law minister in 1990 (67th Constitution Amendment Bill) to amend the provisions of the Constitution pertaining to appointment. It read:

> The Government of India have in the recent past announced their intention to set up a high level judicial commission, to be called the National Judicial Commission for the appointment of Judges of the Supreme Court and of the High Courts and the transfer of Judges of the High Courts so as to obviate the criticisms of arbitrariness on the part of the Executive in such appointments and transfers and also to make such appointments without any delay.[15]

This was quoted with approval by the Supreme Court and used as the basis for overhauling the system entirely through judicial interpretation.[16] The merits of such exercise notwithstanding, it demonstrated that the government, the Supreme Court and civil society were united in condemning executive-led appointments as a mechanism that had lost public confidence.

One of the key reasons underlying this loss of public confidence in the appointments mechanism was the widespread perception that institutional integrity was affected as a consequence of decisional independence of individual judges being compromised. A perverse consequence of the assertion of executive dominance over appointments was case-specific impartiality of judges being affected. While there is no sustained evidence to justify this perception, it has been widely acknowledged by lawyers, judges and public commentators that the decision of the Supreme Court in *ADM Jabalpur* v. *Shivkant Shukla*[17] exemplified a court whose impartiality in matters involving the state and consequently its institutional integrity was compromised. In *ADM Jabalpur,* the question was whether the right to move court by a *habeas corpus* petition for the enforcement of the right to life under Art. 21 by detenus undergoing preventive detention was available when such right was suspended by a proclamation of Emergency by the president under Art. 359(1). Nine High Courts had held that while the right to life and liberty could be suspended, a detenu could still approach court to test the legality of the detention order and allege that it was *mala fide*. The Supreme Court reversed the opinion of the High Courts and held that as long

[15] Constitution (67th Amendment) Bill, 1990 (India).

[16] *Subhash Sharma.*

[17] *ADM Jabalpur.*

as the appropriate detaining authority was subjectively satisfied of the need for detention there was no scope for judicially reviewing its validity in *habeas corpus* proceedings.

The legal reasoning employed to reach this conclusion is severely suspect, and has been dealt with elsewhere.[18] However, it was the excessive deference shown to the executive by the majority judges, bordering on an unsubstantiated belief in its innate goodness, that raised deep misgivings about the impartiality of the judges and the integrity of the judiciary. Chief Justice Ray said:

> Liberty itself is the gift of the law and may by the law be forfeited or abridged...People who have faith in themselves and their country will not paint pictures of diabolic distortion and mendacious malignment of the governance of the country.[19]

Again Justice Chandrachud reversing the judgments of the various High Courts and questioning their motivation held:

> The mind then weaves cobwebs of suspicion and the Judge, without the means to knowledge of full facts, covertly weighs the pros and cons of the political situation and substitutes his personal opinion for the assessment of the Executive, which, by proximity and study, is better placed to decide whether the security of the country is threatened by an imminent danger of internal disturbance.[20]

The unsubstantiated hope of Chief Justice Ray and the excessive deference shown by Justice Chandrachud, questioning the motivation of the High Court judges who did not adopt a similar approach, was 'more executive-minded than the executive'.[21] Coming as it did after the supersession of three independent-minded judges, it was representative of an attitude that was widely viewed as a direct consequence of an executive takeover of the appointments process. In fact, Seervai goes so far as to say that the judgment 'is the most glaring instance in which the Supreme Court of India has suffered most severely from a self-inflicted wound'.[22]

Finally, an effect of executive-led appointments was also to attempt to appoint chief justices sympathetic to the government. Through this process, the

[18] Seervai, *Constitutional Law of India*, vol. 2, Appendix, 2208–29.

[19] *ADM Jabalpur*, 572 (Chief Justice A.N. Ray).

[20] *ADM Jabalpur*, 651 (Justice Chandrachud).

[21] *Liversidge* v. *Sir John Anderson and another* (1942) AC 206 (House of Lords, UK), para 11 (Lord Justice Atkin).

[22] Seervai, *Constitutional Law of India*, vol. 2, 2229.

significance of the role of the chief justice of India in securing the independence of the judiciary in the appointments process was sought to be whittled down. This affected the web of integrated government since the inter-institutional equilibrium that was envisaged by the drafters and necessary for maintaining both judicial independence and accountability was upset. As Justice Bhagwati remarked, 'the so-called safeguard of consultation with the Chief Justice of India has proved to be of no avail'.[23]

However, executive assertion in appointments led to the development of a new check and balance—public opinion. Appointments, which had hitherto been an issue internal to the legal fraternity, now became a matter of public debate. Criticisms were vociferous in newspapers, journals and books.[24] Though this was not enough to strengthen the web of integrated government, it re-adjusted somewhat, with some new checks and balances replacing old ones.

Thus for adversely affecting public confidence and institutional integrity and not strengthening the web of integrated government, step 4(a) of the doctrine applies and executive appointments are consequently not doctrinally justifiable.

### *8B.1.b Collegium-Led Appointments*

**Does it promote/safeguard judicial independence pertaining to a relevant aspect of judicial functioning or adversely affect it?**

The *raison d'etre* for the Supreme Court's judgment in *SCAORA* establishing the collegium mode of appointment was to preserve judicial independence. Executive-led appointments suffered from excessive discretionary authority of the government and tainted the apolitical image of the judiciary. This, in turn, affected the rule of law to which unguided discretion is anathema. It also compromised the independence of the judiciary because 'the constitutional purpose of selecting the best available for composition of the Supreme Court and the High Courts',[25] the underlying goal of the appointments process, remained unfulfilled. Judicial independence, which was viewed as an essential prerequisite for the rule of law, would thus provide the conceptual framework to reshape the appointments process. This is captured in the opening substantive sentence in the opinion of Justice Verma in *SCAORA*:

[23] *Sankalchand*, 250 (Justice Bhagwati).

[24] For a set of sources, see Dua, 'Study of Executive-Judicial Conflict.'

[25] *SCAORA*, para 19 (Justice Verma).

> These questions [primacy of the CJI in judicial appointments and fixation of judge strength in courts] have to be considered in the context of the independence of the judiciary, as a part of the basic structure of the Constitution, to secure the 'rule of law' ...[26]

An analysis of the working of the collegium method of appointment over the last two decades in the fivefold framework of judicial independence demonstrates an effective safeguarding of individual decisional independence of judges from executive interference in public perception. In contradistinction with executive appointments, where such independence was squarely affected, the crystallisation of power in the collegium meant that the role of the executive and consequently its ability to affect judicial independence was severely circumscribed. Thus, even in cases where the government was dissatisfied with the choice of the collegium and returned the file, it had little option if the collegium decided to stick to its recommendation.[27] This represented a method of safeguarding judicial independence that found its warrant in the Constitution itself, given that the *SCAORA* case read the requirement of the collegium and judicial primacy in appointments to Art. 124 and Art. 217 in the Constitution. The key question is thus the extent to which such a method affected judicial accountability and, consequently, whether on balance, it is justified.

**Does it promote/safeguard judicial accountability pertaining to a relevant aspect of judicial functioning or adversely affect it?**

Concerns with judicial accountability were scarcely countenanced by the majority judges in *SCAORA*. The operation of the collegium has thus shown a discernible adverse effect on judicial accountability, specifically its institutional accountability. Given that the appointment power is now a core administrative function of the judiciary, it is apposite that requisite norms of accountability develop over time. However, practice over the last two decades has shown that not only has such accountability failed to develop but also that the judiciary

26 *SCAORA*, para 8 (Justice Verma).

27 It was reported that the collegium nominations of Justices Ganguly, Lodha and Dattu were questioned by the government on the grounds that the seniority criteria had been overlooked. This was rejected by the collegium and the aforesaid were appointed judges of the Supreme Court of India. See Sudhanshu Ranjan, 'Judges Need Critical Juries,' *The Asian Age*, 14 May 2014, available at http://www.asianage.com/columnists/judges-need-critical-juries-831 (accessed 13 June 2014). At the time of writing, the collegium recommendation of Justice K. M. Joseph has been reiterated by the collegium. It remains to be seen whether the government will accept such reiteration.

has been hostile to any such development. Collegium recommendations are not public, the candidates who were considered are not disclosed, reasons for selection and non-selection not divulged and criteria for selection remain unknown.[28] Further, despite a High Court order holding the chief justice of India to be a 'public authority' thereby subject to the Right to Information Act,[29] the office of the chief justice of India has refused to divulge information in response to Right to Information (RTI) applications. In fact, it has appealed against the order to the Supreme Court.[30]

Since collegium appointments promote/safeguard judicial independence and adversely affect judicial accountability, specifically institutional administrative accountability, according to 3(c) of the doctrine, the relevant questions are:

**(3)(c) Does the measure:**

i. **Enjoy public confidence?**

ii. **Promote another substantive virtue deemed desirable for the judiciary?**

iii. **Strengthen the web of integrated government thereby promoting mutual checks and balances?**

The operation of the collegium method of appointments was welcomed at the time of the *SCAORA* decision. As evidenced in the discussion of government appointments, there was widespread disaffection with the role of the executive in the appointments process. The collegium presented a viable alternative with the promise of a mechanism that enjoyed public confidence. Two decades of practice have belied that promise. Apart from a few voices from within the judiciary, former judges and scattered members of the Bar,[31] the bulk of public

[28] It is only from October 2017 that an element of transparency has been brought in, insofar as collegium resolutions with brief reasons are made available publicly together with the names of candidates with whom the collegium has interacted in relation to considering them for judgeship. See Chapter 2, Section 2E.2.

[29] *Secretary-General Supreme Court of India* v. *Subhash Chandra Agarwal*, AIR 2010 Del 159 (High Court of Delhi, India).

[30] Ibid. The matter came up in appeal before a two-judge Bench of the Court in *Central Public Information Officer, Supreme Court of India* v. *Subhash Chandra Agarwal*, (2011) 1 SCC 496 (Supreme Court of India) (hereinafter '*Agarwal*'). Owing to the case raising fundamental questions of constitutional importance it was referred to the chief justice of India for 'constitution of a Bench of appropriate strength.' This bench has not been constituted till date.

[31] Dhananjay Mahapatra, 'Collegium System for Judges' Appointment, Best Option: Chief Justice P. Sathasivam,' *Times of India*, 25 April 2014, available at http://

opinion unarguably underlines that the collegium method today is discredited and enjoys very little public confidence. This view has been espoused across party lines in parliament,[32] and the Bar.[33] The saga surrounding the proposed appointment of Justice Dinakaran, the brazenness of the collegium in refusing to retract its recommendation despite evidence to the contrary and the culture of opacity that it revealed, strongly affected public confidence in the mechanism. The recent controversies over the NJAC and the fierce resistance of the judiciary to such changes, evidenced by their order in the matter, as well as subsequent sparring with the government, have bolstered this view.

Though other appointments have taken place subsequently, given the complete lack of transparency in the process and opportunity to hold judges accountable, several appointments are tainted by aspersions of extraneous factors at play.[34] In the absence of detailed records (which are not publicly available), this point can neither be proved nor disproved.[35] However, it is widely accepted that the possibility of extraneous factors at work in collegium appointments is no longer a far-fetched possibility but a probability that lurks uncomfortably close to many appointments.

The constant harbouring of this possibility in the public mind has also meant that the institutional integrity of the collegium, and consequently the judiciary, has been put under severe strain. Though in most instances these are unsubstantiated rumours and hearsay, because of the lack of transparency in the

---

timesofindia.indiatimes.com/india/Collegium-system-for-judges-appointment-best-option-Chief-Justice-P-Sathasivam/articleshow/34169844.cms (accessed 14 June 2014).

32 See Speech of Mr Kapil Sibal, Hon'ble Minister for Law and Justice, Government of India, Rajya Sabha, Parliament of India, 5 September 2013, available at http://164.100.47.5/newdebate/229/05092013/12.00NoonTo13.00pm.pdf (accessed 21 January 2014); Speech of Mr. Arun Jaitley, Leader of the Opposition, Rajya Sabha, Parliament of India, 5 September 2013, available at http://164.100.47.5/newdebate/229/05092013/13.00pmTo14.00pm.pdf (accessed 21 January 2014).

33 Raju Ramachandran, 'Judicial Supremacy and the Collegium,' *Seminar* No. 642 (2013), available at http://india-seminar.com/2013/642/642_raju_ramachandran.htm (accessed 15 June 2014); Fali S. Nariman, 'Weighed in the Balance,' *Hindustan Times*, 9 May 2013, available at www.hindustantimes.com/comment/columns/weighed-in-the-balance/article1-1057629.aspx (accessed 14 June 2014).

34 This is not to cast doubt about the qualifications of the judges who were appointed but merely the process of their appointment.

35 Whether file notings and correspondence between the collegium and the executive on judicial appointments is to be made public is sub judice in *Agarwal*.

collegium mechanism, there has been no official method to dispel the doubts about institutional integrity that such persistent rumours give rise to. For example, the continuous non-appointment of Justice Patnaik, a judge originally belonging to the Odisha High Court, to the Supreme Court, while his senior colleague from the High Court, Justice Pasayat, was a member of the collegium, and his appointment soon after the latter retired led to concerns about the reasons for his non-selection.[36] Again, the non-appointment of Justices Bhattacharya, Ghosh and Shah, the chief justices of Gujarat, Uttarakhand and Bombay High Courts respectively to the Supreme Court and the Chief Justice of India Altamas Kabir's consequent defence saying that such appointment would be 'counter-productive'[37] for the judiciary raised several questions. What are the reasons for such an appointment to be counter-productive? How could such appointment to the Supreme Court be counter-productive whereas his continuing to function as the chief justice of a High Court would not? Specifically, given Justice Bhattacharya's strongly worded letter against the recommendation of judgeship to the sister of the chief justice of India (a judge herself),[38] should the chief justice of India have recused himself from the selection process? The opacity of the collegium process, specifically the lack of channels to verify or disprove such allegations, and their significant number has meant that the institutional integrity of the collegium process is questionable in the public mind.

Its impact on institutional integrity and public confidence notwithstanding, collegium appointments have emasculated the web of integrated government that the constitutionally mandated participatory nature of judicial appointments reinforced. As Chapter 7 demonstrated, a key rationale for both judicial independence and accountability was to create a system of government where the judiciary played an instrumental role checking other organs of government, which in turn had a role in appointment and removal of judges. This inter-institutional equilibrium in processes relating to judicial personnel was a conscious endeavour of the drafters of the Constitution. Specifically in appointments, participatory decision-making was envisaged as a means to creating a stake for the executive in

36 Ranjan, 'Judges Need Critical Juries.'

37 Nagendar Sharma, 'Panel Finds 3 Top Judges Unfit for SC,' *Hindustan Times*, 17 March 2013, available at www.hindustantimes.com/india-news/newdelhi/panel-finds-3-top-judges-unfit-for-sc/article1-1027632.aspx (accessed 14 June 2014).

38 Appu Esthose Suresh and Maneesh Chibber, 'Lost SC Berth for Opposing HC Judgeship for CJI Kabir's Sister: Guj CJ,' *Indian Express*, 24 July 2013, available at http://archive.indianexpress.com/news/lost-sc-berth-for-opposing-hc-judgeship-for-cji-kabirs-sister-guj-cj/1140897/0 (accessed 14 June 2014).

the working of the judiciary. Such stake would ensure that organs of government, while separate in terms of personnel and function, collaborated with each other in key tasks without encroaching excessively in the core functions of another organ. The supremacy of the judiciary in the appointments process established by the collegium and the consequent practice that evolved undid this inter-institutional equilibrium decisively.

In *SCAORA*, the appointment of judges was made, for all practical purposes, a prerogative of the judiciary with the role of the executive severely circumscribed. In *Presidential Reference*, it was underlined that the determinative view in appointments would henceforth be that of the collegium. It was only in cases where the opinion of the chief justice of India was formed without adherence to the consultation process would the recommendation not be binding on the government. The clear implication was that in all other cases, it would. Subsequent practice has demonstrated this.[39] That the executive role has been reduced in public perception to being that of a rubber stamp of the choice made by the collegium would be a fair representation of the power dynamic in the process. Unfortunately, the executive has chosen to correct this image by adopting delaying tactics, thereby increasing the number of vacancies in the Supreme Court and High Courts.[40]

As a result of the emasculation of the web of integrated government, the lowering of public confidence and a diminution of institutional integrity, according to step 4(a), the method of collegium appointments does not lead to an effective judiciary and is not justifiable.

## *8B.2 Transfers*

Analogous to appointments, transfers can be classified into two phases—executive-led and collegium-led. The analysis follows the same structure.

### ***8B.2.a Executive-Led Transfers***

**Does it promote/safeguard judicial independence pertaining to a relevant aspect of judicial functioning or adversely affect it?**

Transfer of judges was seen at the time of drafting of the Constitution as an internal administrative measure. Its ramifications on independence were neither

39 Ranjan, 'Judges Need Critical Juries.'

40 Currently, there are 8 vacancies at the Supreme Court which has a sanctioned strength of 31. Judicial Vacancies (2018).

debated nor envisaged. The context of its inclusion was the need to provide compensatory allowance for judges who might be required in other High Courts apart from the ones to which they were appointed. This was analogous to other government employees who could be transferred.[41] In the first 25 years, only 25 judges were transferred with their consent.[42] Given the consensual nature of the transfer, no allegation of the independence of the judges being affected is tenable. At the same time, evidence of non-consensual transfers[43] could also not be said to affect the independence of judges transferred. Both known instances were cases of transfers being used to discipline judges for questionable administrative orders and creating an atmosphere non-conducive to the effective functioning of the High Court. The mere fact of consent not having been obtained was not an indication that the decisional, behaviour or administrative independence of judges was affected in any meaningful way.

Non-consensual transfers took a far more egregious form when a mass transfer of 16 judges was ordered during the Emergency. The threat of transfers at the instance of the executive affected decisional independence of judges. This is especially so since this transfer order was seen in the backdrop of the government's attempts at creating a pliant judiciary whose independence was severely circumscribed. Notwithstanding the fact that all 16 judges were given the option of being re-transferred to their original High Courts, the impact on decisional independence was more lasting. The very fact that both in *Sankalchand* and *Gupta* the judges of the Supreme Court unanimously felt the need for fortifying the protections for judicial independence inherent in the provision on transfers bears testimony to the adverse impact executive transfers had on it. This has been the widely held view in public commentary as well.[44]

**Does it promote/safeguard judicial accountability pertaining to a relevant aspect of judicial functioning or adversely affect it?**

Logic might demand that analogous to executive appointments wherein an adverse effect on judicial independence would be compensated by augmenting of judicial accountability, the same might be true of executive transfers, which, as seen above, adversely affected judicial independence. However, this is not the case for three reasons. First, for appointments in the first 25 years since the enactment of the Constitution, caste, religion and region played an important

[41] See Chapter 3.

[42] Ibid.

[43] Ibid.

[44] Baxi, *Indian Supreme Court and Politics*, 198.

role. The same is not true for transfers that were used primarily as an internal administrative measure. The two known instances of clearly non-consensual transfers, however, demonstrate the possibility of transfers functioning as behavioural accountability devices for individual judges, owed to the chief justice of India. These, however, were clearly relatively minor exceptions, unlike appointments on ascriptive criteria, which were more widespread. Second, the mass transfer order of 16 High Court judges did not entrench transfers as a mechanism for enforcing decisional accountability. The order was one-off; subsequently, all judges were re-transferred and in any event transfers did not have any impact, favourable or adverse, on Supreme Court judges. Third, for transfers post-*Sankalchand* in which the court had laid down safeguards for consultation, they were pursuant to a transfer policy by the government to promote national integration. While it was seen by several as a ruse to harm the independence of the judiciary, neither was it contended nor could it be so that such a policy engendered any form of judicial accountability to the executive. This is because the policy was limited to transferring additional judges and new appointees rather than existing ones. Contending that this is a method to enforce decisional accountability would be far-fetched.

Thus for adversely affecting judicial independence and having no clear impact on promoting or safeguarding judicial accountability, executive-led transfers are doctrinally indefensible under step 3(b) read with the explanation to step 3.

### *8B.2.b Collegium-Led Transfers*

**Does it promote/safeguard judicial independence pertaining to a relevant aspect of judicial functioning or adversely affect it?**

The *SCAORA* judgment vested the power to transfer judges between High Courts in the judicial collegium. Unlike in the case of appointments where securing judicial independence was the primary consideration, the broader purpose articulated for transfers was the promotion of 'public interest'. Public interest would have several facets of which protecting judicial independence, specifically decisional independence of individual judges from threats from the executive, was key.[45] The mass transfer order of judges during the Emergency and the executive-mandated transfer policy to promote national integration were evidence of the potential that transfers had to adversely affect the decisional independence of judges. To obviate such potential, the collegium, comprising

[45] See Chapter 3.

the chief justice of India and two senior most puisne judges,[46] would henceforth be the focal body for deciding on appointments in the higher judiciary.

The working of the collegium over the last two decades, despite its faults, has reaffirmed the salutary effect its creation was envisaged to have had, in terms of protecting decisional independence of judges. In public discourse, it has scarcely been claimed that collegium-led transfers have been occasioned as responses to judgments rendered by particular judges. In addition, it has bolstered institutional administrative independence of the judiciary. Unlike appointments, transfer of High Court judges is a matter of internal administration of the judiciary with limited consequences on separation of powers. Vesting the collegium with the focal power of transfer facilitated this objective. Further, making the view of the chief justice of India determinative in the matter of transfers meant that institutional administrative independence in the matter of transfer of judges was effectively secured.

**Does it promote/safeguard judicial accountability pertaining to a relevant aspect of judicial functioning or adversely affect it?**

Collegium-led transfers affected institutional administrative accountability for the same reasons that collegium-led appointments did. Given the power to transfer becoming a key administrative function of the judiciary, there was no accountability for the decision taken, either to the executive whose role was circumscribed or publicly, since no alternative was prescribed, or to the judiciary itself, since judicial review was emasculated. Further it failed to adequately promote individual behavioural accountability. Though several instances of transfers described in Chapter 3 were owing to indiscipline, transfers as a whole failed to serve this purpose owing to the lack of reasons being publicly provided in transfer orders. The lack of reasons meant that it was not public knowledge whether the transfer was indeed owing to indiscipline, thereby seeking to hold the judge behaviourally accountable, or for other reasons. This meant that in cases where a judge ought to be held behaviourally accountable for misbehaviour, the enforcement of such accountability was unclear and in some cases where no question of behavioural accountability arose, such an impression persisted.[47]

[46] *Presidential Reference.*

[47] This does not imply that I am advocating that reasons for transfer orders are provided in all cases. That is neither desirable in principle nor workable in practice. My reform proposal can be found in Chapter 9.

Since collegium transfers promoted/safeguarded judicial independence and failed to adequately promote judicial accountability, according to 3(c) of the doctrine, the relevant questions are:

**(3)(c) Does the measure:**

i. **Enjoy public confidence?**

ii. **Promote another substantive virtue deemed desirable for the judiciary?**

iii. **Strengthen the web of integrated government thereby promoting mutual checks and balances?**

It is unsurprising that in public perception collegium transfers are tainted by similar concerns as those related to collegium appointments. The opacity of the process, the lack of inter-institutional participation and widespread speculation have led to doubts about its integrity. However, unlike appointments, the scale of public disaffection with collegium transfers has not been as pronounced. Two plausible reasons can be discerned for this: First, transfer of judges between High Courts is not a matter of as much public concern as are appointments. Like other institutions where transfers are internal administrative measures, transfers in the judiciary too are widely viewed as internal. This is unlike appointing judges, which involves selecting candidates from the Bar and the district judiciary, thereby having a wider public interface, besides greater public interest. Second, the role of the executive is more crucial in appointments in establishing an inter-institutional equilibrium than in transfers in the constitutional scheme. It was the intention of the drafters that appointment be primarily an executive function with the chief justice of India having a crucial consultative role to preserve judicial independence. However, despite adopting a similar structure for Art. 222 governing transfers, no real threat to judicial independence from executive appointments was envisaged. The power of transfer being vested in the president was primarily keeping in view the high status of judicial office and finding an appropriate authority to perform the function of appointment.

Disaffection has been expressed by several judges who have been transferred, alleging bias against the collegium.[48] In third-party commentary, public outcry has been primarily against the practice of purportedly punitive transfers to the High Courts of Gauhati and Sikkim.[49] While this is a pernicious practice *per se*, it has little to do with judicial independence or accountability. It has

[48] For an illustrative example, see A. Singh, ‘MP HC Judge Says SC Judge Got Him Moved out of Delhi.’

[49] Kamaroopi, ‘Punishment Postings’; *The Sentinel*, ‘Junkyard for Judges’.

resulted in several questions being raised about the grounds and process followed while transferring judges, but has not destroyed public confidence in the system. This is unfortunate testimony to the general lack of significance attached to the northeastern parts of India in national-level public discourse. At the same time while the doubts have not extended to questioning the institutional integrity of the collegium process, the constant nature of transfers seemingly for punitive purposes, contrary to the Supreme Court's own order in *SCAORA*, has questioned the institutional wisdom of the collegium. It is clearly not in public interest to transfer an indisciplined judge to another High Court. At the same time, it does not behove the Supreme Court to be in violation of the spirit of its own order, inasmuch as *SCAORA* was based on the premise that a transfer recommended by the chief justice of India could never be punitive and hence not reviewable. It is unfortunate, but true, that the collegium has often recommended transfer on the grounds of indiscipline, most notably in the recent case of Justice Karnan of the Madras High Court. Having taken the liberty of walking into a courtroom as an advocate and openly defying the chief justice, Justice Karnan's reprimand was a transfer to the Calcutta High Court.[50] So unacceptable in law and common sense is such a transfer order that engaging with it further is unnecessary.

As far as the web of integrated government is concerned, vesting the power of transfer in the president is part of the overall schema of blending of powers between organs of government. To the extent that the institution of collegium appointments takes away a substantive role for the executive, the web of integrated government is disturbed. However, unlike collegium appointments, which were viewed to have emasculated the web because of their seminal importance to the web itself, collegium transfers do not have an analogous impact. This is because transfers were viewed by the drafters and seen publicly, subject to an aberration, as a measure that ought to be purely administrative. Given this, while the web of integrated government was affected leading to relative insulation of the judiciary, the institution of the collegium for transfers cannot be said to have emasculated it.

[50] In an extraordinary step, he stayed his own transfer order, without any authority of law. This action had to be quashed by the Supreme Court and he was subsequently transferred. Utkarsh Anand, 'SC Steps in after Madras HC Judge Stays Own Transfer,' *Indian Express*, 16 February 2016, available at http://indianexpress.com/article/india/india-news-india/justice-c-s-karnan-supreme-court-to-madras-high-court/ (accessed 5 September 2016). See text accompanying note 56 in Chapter 3.

On the basis that collegium transfers have not bolstered public confidence, promoted any substantive virtue deemed desirable for the judiciary or strengthened the web of integrated government, according to 4(b) it is unjustifiable.

## *8B.3 Impeachment*

**Does it promote/safeguard judicial independence pertaining to a relevant aspect of judicial functioning or adversely affect it?**

At the time of drafting of the provision pertaining to impeachment of judges of the higher judiciary, safeguarding judicial independence was a prime consideration. As discussed in Chapter 3, a strict delineation of grounds of impeachment together with a numerically onerous and multi-phase process consisting of a judicial enquiry followed by parliamentary ratification was designed to ensure that the provision could not be used wantonly. The fact that impeachment proceedings have reached parliament only on two occasions in six decades demonstrates that the provision has not been overused and consequently misused. Further, even in the two instances that proceedings have reached parliament, there has been no criticism of impeachment being used to affect decisional, behavioural or administrative independence of the judges.[51] Institutionally, independence has not been adversely affected by the use of the impeachment provision given its negligible use. Further there have been no demands from the judiciary to be focally responsible for removing its own personnel, like its determinative role in appointments. Even conceptually, impeachment does not affect the independence of judges in any meaningful way that affects their ability to adjudicate impartially. Hence, no question of affecting administrative independence of the judicial institution arises.

This conclusion has, however, been recently put in doubt with the attempted impeachment of Chief Justice Misra. As described in Chapter 3, the impeachment motion, despite making several grave allegations, was mired in partisan politics, making the clear, though unstated, imputation that the CJI was biased towards the government. Whether indeed the assertion is true or not would depend on a detailed enquiry into the matter. But the first use of impeachment in a clearly politicised fact situation is a possible sign of things to come. It is particularly suggestive of the fact that the threat of impeachment is likely to affect decisional

[51] The defences taken by both judges subject to impeachment proceedings were procedural, together with allegations of bias. See Chapter 3.

independence of judges in the near future, particularly in sensitive, political matters, though the same may not be true today.

**Does it promote judicial accountability pertaining to a relevant aspect of judicial functioning or adversely affect it?**

The fundamental rationale of an impeachment provision is to enforce judicial accountability. Specifically, the operation of impeachment in India has shown that it primarily serves to hold judges behaviourally accountable. In the case of Justice Ramaswami, the enquiry under the JIA as well as the impeachment proceedings in parliament brought several financial transactions carried out by Justice Ramaswami during his tenure as chief justice of Punjab and Haryana High Court under close scrutiny. Again in the case of Justice Soumitra Sen, his role as a High Court–appointed Receiver and financial transactions in that capacity were questioned. Through the course of both impeachment proceedings, aspects of individual behaviour of judges *prima facie* deemed unbecoming of a judge were closely examined by the enquiry committee and parliament. Even in instances when there were no proceedings in parliament, such as the enquiry against Justice Dinakaran, the statutory enquiry proceedings were vital in bringing to public notice several purported instances of abuse of power. The fact that Justice Dinakaran had to reply to the charges levelled against him having earlier refused to pay heed to the directions of the judicial collegium itself demonstrates the soft political accountability function that impeachment plays.

Given its promotion of judicial accountability and no adverse effect on judicial independence, doctrinally impeachment is justifiable according to step 3(a). This neither speaks to the effectiveness of impeachment as an accountability measure nor suggests that the requirement of accountability is met by the operation of the impeachment provision. In fact, the failure of the Ramaswami impeachment meant that its efficacy as a hard accountability mechanism was severely questioned. This is an impression that has persisted given that Justices Sen and Dinakaran resigned before they could be impeached. Further, its non-acceptance in the case of CJI Misra also demonstrated its limitations in functioning as an effective accountability mechanism in a heavily politicised environment.

At the same time, the fact that impeachment has onerous procedural requirements has meant that in several cases[52] impeachment proceedings could

52 A list of allegations against several judges can be found on the website of a civil society organisation Campaign for Judicial Accountability and Judicial Reforms. See Campaign for Judicial Accountability and Judicial Reforms, 'Judge Watch,' available at www.judicialreforms.org/what-we-do/judge-watch.html (accessed 14 June 2014). Citing this website is not an endorsement of the allegations it contains.

not be brought. It is appropriate, given the heavy penalty that impeachment carries, that the procedural threshold is high—at the same time, this cannot preclude the development of other forms of accountability, less severe, for judicial misbehaviour that requires sanction. Both methods for improving the extant impeachment provision and suggestions for supplementary disciplining mechanisms are advocated in Chapter 9.

### *8B.4 Post-Retirement Employment*

**Does it promote/safeguard judicial independence pertaining to a relevant aspect of judicial functioning or adversely affect it?**

In Chapter 4, we found that the practice of post-retirement employment of judges in government-appointed positions was potentially a grave threat to judicial independence and impartial adjudication. Specifically, the high proportion of judges who held such positions (37 out of 50), the short time gap between their retirement and post-retirement employment (19 out of 37 within the first year of retirement) and the large number of appointments made primarily at the instance of the government (25 out of 46) buttress such an inference. Besides, the perception of judicial independence being affected by such appointments has been widely expressed in mainstream media and academic writing.

Having deconstructed judicial independence, it is clear that such post-retirement employment affects decisional independence of judges from government. This inference is based on the short time gap between retirement of judges and their post-retirement employment. As seen in Chapter 4, 19 judges were appointed within one year of their retirement, 13 of whom were appointed in the first three months. It is a fair assumption that in all these instances, the process of appointment would have been initiated when the person still held judicial office. This, read with the fact that the government is the largest litigant, leads to the perception of decisional independence of judges in matters involving the government being affected. While this has been sought to be offset by consultation with the chief justice of India before appointments to several statutory positions, this is insufficient in protecting decisional independence for two reasons. First, it is only in 20 out of 46 surveyed posts that consultation with the chief justice of India is mandated or a requirement placed that the chief justice nominates the office holder. Thus, in a large majority of cases, appointments continue to remain purely political. Second, consultation with the chief justice of India has, according to the judiciary itself, become a discredited mechanism for countering the political elements in the process of appointment of judges. There is no reason to believe why, having failed to secure judicial independence in appointment of judges, it can secure such independence in the process of post-retirement employment of judges by government.

**Does it promote/safeguard judicial accountability pertaining to a relevant aspect of judicial functioning or adversely affect it?**

Post-retirement employment of judges in government-appointed positions is justified on the basis that the expertise of judges is necessary in a range of quasi-judicial institutions at a time when they are still mentally and physically active to use their knowledge and skills. *Per se*, this has no connection with judicial accountability, individual or institutional. It simply represents an *ad hoc* method for meeting a manpower shortage that currently plagues tribunals, commissions and other quasi-judicial and executive bodies that require persons with judicial expertise.

In light of the fact that post-retirement appointments affect judicial independence without a consequent beneficial impact on judicial accountability, according to 3(b) of the doctrine read with the explanation to step 3, the measure is not justifiable in independence–accountability terms. However, as adverted to earlier, the need for such post-retirement appointments is distinct—using the expertise of judges in a range of positions where such expertise will be beneficial. How that need of expertise can be managed without simultaneously impacting judicial independence detrimentally will be enquired into in Chapter 9 which concludes this book.

# Conclusion

## *A Reform Proposal for the Indian Higher Judiciary*

# 9

A book critiquing systems of appointments, transfers, impeachment and post-retirement employment provisions and practices in the Indian higher judiciary through the lens of judicial independence and accountability would be incomplete without offering viable alternatives. Limiting oneself solely to criticisms of such provisions might have considerable intrinsic value; however, absent specific proposals for reform, such criticisms will always be vulnerable to the charge of being unconstructive. This is not meant to belittle description, analysis and critique *per se*—in fact, without these, reforms can scarcely be successful. But a proposal for law reform is the next logical step, and on the basis of the materials analysed and the practices surveyed, this book is in a position to take this step, offering an overview of what reform in these areas might look like.

The suggested reforms in this section are more in the nature of a detailed overview rather than a comprehensive account. This is deliberate, for two reasons. First, to offer a detailed solution requires a close look at comparative systems in other common law jurisdictions as well as countries in South Asia which share similar legal histories and societal contexts. This is a different project, one that cannot be undertaken here. Second, judicial independence and accountability provide one set of parameters amongst many, which ought to be kept in mind while reforming systems pertaining to the judiciary. Appointment reform needs to factor in diversity, subject matter competence; transfers have to account for administrative convenience; impeachment must take into account the high status of the judiciary; and post-retirement employment must be sensitive to a socio-political context where apolitical judges are seen as ideal candidates for significant quasi-judicial positions. Such a multi-dimensional reform proposal is beyond the remit of this book. Thus the reform proposal advanced herein must necessarily be viewed as limited and focused on two issues—first, devising systems that lead to an effective judiciary, drawing an optimal balance between judicial independence and accountability; second, doing so in a manner that is constitutional, as a matter of positive law. Accordingly, this chapter approaches each of the four topics—appointments, transfers, impeachment and post-retirement employment—from the perspective of the two aforementioned issues. It gleans both why the position of law is unsatisfactory from the substantive Chapters 2, 3 and 4 and the results of the doctrinal enquiry in Chapter 8.

This task is made easier by the fact that several reform proposals are already being considered by parliament or the subject of widespread public debate. Appointments and transfers were the subject of wholesale reform through the 99th Amendment and the NJAC Act. Both were struck down by the Supreme Court as unconstitutional. Subsequent to the judgment, appointments reverted to the collegium system, albeit with the government and the collegium engaged in a constant tussle over proposed appointees. Regarding disciplining of judges, several measures short of impeachment were put forward by the Judicial Standards and Accountability Bill, 2010, passed by the Lok Sabha in 2012.

As a result, this chapter focuses on such existing reform proposals wherever they have been advanced. It assesses their merits *per se* and recommends changes that make such reforms better accord with the twin considerations of judicial independence and accountability. Where measures are found unworkable or no reforms have been suggested (such as in post-retirement employment of judges), it offers some thoughts for reforms, which are likely to be more efficacious in practice.

## 9A Appointments: The *NJAC Case* and Institutional Reform

The NJAC attempted to provide a role to all three organs of government. The judiciary with three members, the chief justice and two seniormost puisne judges, played the predominant role; the executive with the Union minister for law and justice being a member of the commission had equally crucial, though numerically inferior, representation. The legislature too had a role in the commission, with the prime minister, as the leader of the house, and the leader of the opposition in the Lok Sabha being members of the committee (apart from the chief justice of India) to select two eminent persons to the commission. At the same time, the inclusion of two 'eminent persons', as opposed to 'distinguished jurist(s)', which is an eligibility condition for being a judge of the Supreme Court[1] or to serve on the enquiry committee constituted under

[1] Constitution of India, Art. 124(3)(c).

the JIA,[2] is instructive. It suggested a direct role to be played by two members of the civil society in appointing judges to the higher judiciary, thereby making the system more publicly accountable.

Such a system created a web of integrated government, both by modulating the starting point for the judiciary and by introducing a system of appointments that requires different organs to coordinate with each other. First, by making all three organs as well as representatives of the public direct stakeholders in the process of judicial appointments, it replaced the insulation that currently characterises the appointments process, dominated in practice by the judicial collegium. Modulation of the starting point for thinking of the composition of the higher judiciary was unarguably a political response to the growing power of the judiciary in the country's constitutional scheme. Post-*SCAORA*, the judicial collegium has had a determinative influence over the appointment of candidates without an effective check and balance.[3] The NJAC sought to make the process of appointments more participatory in a manner that integrated the judiciary in the constitutional scheme, without affecting its independence.

This integration also leads to greater blending of powers, which is key to a well-functioning institution based on a separation of powers. Its blended mechanism envisaged a more equal role for representatives of the judiciary, executive, legislature and members of the public in the appointments process. By doing so, it not only modulated the starting point for the judiciary, as mentioned earlier, but equally made the representatives of the judiciary in an administrative capacity coordinate with the Union minister of law and justice and representatives of the public to find the most suitable candidates for judicial office. In the overall scheme, such blending countered both the insulated nature of judicial functioning while at the same time requiring coordination between the government and the judiciary in the exercise of the appointment function. Contrary to the fears of loss of independence as narrowly understood by the majority judges, such a blended mechanism promotes the checks and balances scheme in the Constitution, thereby creating an effective judiciary.

Six decades of intervening experience must make us alive to the fact that any future appointment mechanism must additionally incorporate two key process-based checks. First, there is a need for a well-regulated procedure along with criteria for shortlisting candidates for judicial office. This was absent in the

2 Section 3(2)(c), JIA.

3 This was recognised by the Justice Kurian Joseph part of the majority in the *NJAC Case*. See *NJAC Case*, 911–12.

NJAC Act. It is necessary for any commission model to set up high-powered search committees in each High Court, for High Court appointments and the Supreme Court for appointments to it. These may be constituted by the chief justice of the High Court and comprise both members of the Bar and bench as the chief justice may find suitable. The purpose of search committees is to draw up a shortlist of candidates from which the commission can select appointees to the Supreme Court and the High Courts. The number in the shortlist must be commensurately wider than the number of vacancies, leaving the commission with a real choice to be made. This vests the task of shortlisting in representatives of the legal profession, thereby optimising chances of candidates being chosen primarily on the basis of merit alone.

Second, to take forward the recommendations of the search committees, the commission must establish a proper secretariat.[4] The task of the secretariat must be to provide thorough background checks on all shortlisted candidates. This involves two elements—a positive ascertainment of performance and a negative determination of doubts regarding the candidate's personal and financial integrity. Currently, this task is achieved through consultation with the relevant government. As several questionable appointments have shown, greater scrutiny than what the *status quo* provides is necessary. Thus, establishing a proper secretariat that will have both the manpower and the skills to gather data on candidates for judicial office is necessary for presenting a full picture of the candidate to the commission in order to make an informed decision.

Third, once the matter reaches the commission, in principle it must be entitled to take a subjective decision on who in its opinion best fulfils the attributes of a judge in the Indian higher judiciary without further criteria being provided. Being a high-powered, bipartisan body following a transparent process, with diverse representation comprising members of the judiciary, executive and

4 This has been recommended by the 64th Report of the Department-Related Parliamentary Standing Committee on Personnel, Public Grievances, Law and Justice on the Judicial Appointments Commission Bill, 2013, Rajya Sabha Secretariat, Parliament of India, 2013, available at http://164.100.47.5/newcommittee/reports/EnglishCommittees/Committee%20on%20Personnel,%20PublicGrievances,%20Law%20and%20Justice/64.pdf (accessed 14 May 2014). It has also been recognised as a key necessity in a supplementary order in the *NJAC Case* leading to consultations between government and judiciary on incorporating it suitably in the memorandum of procedure. The Supreme Court said, 'In the interest of better management of the system of appointment of Judges, the Memorandum of Procedure may provide for the establishment of a Secretariat for each High Court and the Supreme Court and prescribe its functions, duties and responsibilities', *NJAC Consequence Order*.

eminent public persons, there is considerable divergence in backgrounds, interests and worldviews to ensure that wise choices are made without further legal provisions in this regard. Learning from the experience in executive and collegium appointments, however, it is important for the commission, when recommending a name for appointment, to detail the procedure that was followed in making the appointment, similar to what is currently done by the collegium. While it must not disclose identities of the candidates (except for the person recommended for appointment), being respectful of their privacy, it must closely detail the search committee process and the number of shortlisted candidates, the secretariat process and a further shortlist, if necessary, and finally the selection of the candidate(s) for office and whether the decision was unanimous and if not, the split in the commission vote. This must be accompanied by a list of dates, specifying the time taken for each of these processes.

## 9A.1 *Transfers*

The analysis of the doctrine and practice relating to transfer of judges from one High Court to another in Chapter 3 demonstrated four key defects.[5] First, the arrogation of the power to transfer judges by the judiciary, vesting it in a judicial collegium, proceeds on an indefensible interpretation of Art. 222 of the Constitution; second, the power of transfer has been widely used as a punitive device holding judges accountable for misbehaviour, a pattern which treats similarly placed High Courts unequally; third, the connotation of 'public interest', the ground under which transfers are justified, has remained ill-defined, thereby allowing the collegium unguided discretion to transfer; fourth, as a result of the second and third defects, there is a widely prevalent notion that transfers, even when arguably ordered for valid reasons, are punitive, a conflation that lowers both the status of the concerned judge and the collegium that orders the transfers.

The 99th Amendment responded to the first concern. The power to transfer chief justices and judges of High Courts was vested in the president acting on the recommendation of the NJAC by amending Art. 222 of the Constitution. Curiously however, neither the 99th Amendment nor the NJAC Act contains any further details on the grounds on which transfers may be effectuated, indicates whether

5 The reform proposal deals only with transfer of judges from one High Court to another, not the policy of having a transferee chief justice in each High Court. The reasons for this exclusion may be found earlier in the book: See Chapter 3.

it is allowed for punitive purposes or lays down the procedure to be followed. As a result, both fail in addressing the remaining defects outlined above.

It is imperative that the grounds on which transfers are permissible be expressly spelt out. This entails an explication of the concept of 'public interest', which is the sole ground on which transfers are permitted.[6] Given that the term itself is of vague import and no judicial interpretation is available since transfers made by the collegium are deemed to be non-punitive and non-justiciable,[7] it is necessary to lay down its meaning clearly. From a survey of transfers in Chapter 3, it is proposed that four types of transfers are defined to constitute 'transfers in public interest'.

First, a large number of transfers are ordered when relations of the concerned judge are practising in the same High Court. In fact, one of the most important rationales of the transfer policy introduced by Justice Venkatachaliah, during his tenure as the chief justice of India, was to reduce instances of kith and kin of a judge practising in the same High Court.[8] Derisively called the 'uncle judges' syndrome',[9] it had led to several questions being asked of the integrity of judges.[10] Since having relations at the Bar quite obviously leads to doubts concerning the perception of independence of judges, it is necessary that this is laid down as a ground of transfer in public interest.

Second, the creation of new High Courts or the need for subject matter specialists in certain High Courts provides another legitimate reason for transfer of judges. Recently, three new High Courts were set up in Manipur, Meghalaya and Tripura. All the judges in these High Courts were transferred from the Gauhati High Court where they were serving earlier and from whose jurisdiction the jurisdictions of the three new High Courts were carved out.[11] Again, judges specialising in certain subject matters may be lacking in particular High Courts.

6 *SCAORA*, para 62 (Justice Verma).

7 *SCAORA*, para 80 (Justice Verma).

8 Text accompanying note 52 in Chapter 3.

9 Text accompanying note 53 in Chapter 3; Law Comm., 230th Report, 9–10.

10 Text accompanying note 53 in Chapter 3.

11 The details of the judges who were appointed to the High Courts of Manipur, Meghalaya and Tripura at their inception and the duration of their previous tenures in the Gauhati High Court may be found respectively at: website of the High Court of Manipur, available at http://hcmimphal.nic.in/ (accessed 14 May 2014); website of the High Court of Meghalaya, available at http://meghalayahighcourt.nic.in/Home.html (accessed 14 May 2014); website of the High Court of Tripura, available at http://thc.nic.in/ (accessed 14 May 2014).

This need was pointed out by the 1st Law Commission in its 14th Report and is eminently sensible given the unitary nature of India's higher judiciary.[12]

Third, it is important to retain the power of transfer in order to maintain amicable relations between the Bar and the bench and amongst judges *inter se*. There have been several situations when relations between the Bar and a single judge have deteriorated significantly. The agitations by lawyers pursuant to Justice Subhashan Reddy, chief justice of the Madras High Court, introducing a code of conduct for advocates provide a telling example. Matters had come to such a head that it was impossible for the court to function normally. Chief Justice Reddy was subsequently transferred to the Kerala High Court.[13] Neither does having such a ground for transfers validate such protests nor does it entail using transfers as a disciplinary measure. On the contrary, it underlines the importance of transfers as a method of ensuring the smooth administration of the judiciary.

Finally, transfers should be permitted when a judge in a High Court voluntarily requests for a transfer for valid personal reasons. It is a matter of courtesy that such request be heeded by the president. However, this provision should not be used as a device to pressurise people into accepting transfers that they would not otherwise consent to. Thus, the law must provide that the request be voluntary and at the same time it must be founded on personal reasons that satisfy the test of validity. The requirement of voluntariness in the request and the second-order justification for the reasons underlying such request thus provide sufficient protection against misuse of this provision.

In all these four grounds of transfer, the procedure must be initiated by the chief justice of the concerned High Court who must indicate the need to transfer a particular judge, communicate a request by a particular judge to be transferred, or request for judges specialising in certain subject matters. In case of establishment of a new High Court, this procedure ought to be initiated by the chief justice of the High Court from whose territorial jurisdiction the jurisdiction of the new High Court is sought to be carved out. However, the power of the appointing body to initiate a transfer *suo motu* must also exist. This is not only to take into account situations of transfer of chief justices, an issue that this book does not deal with, but also situations when the chief justice of

12 Law Comm., 14th Report, 100.

13 T. S. Subramanian, 'Lawyers on the Warpath,' *Frontline* 21, no. 18 (August–September 2004), available at www.frontline.in/static/html/fl2118/stories/20040910007813000.htm (accessed 14 May 2014).

the High Court may be unwilling to act despite good reason. Basing the entire mechanism of transfer on the chief justice of the High Court is an institutional design that suffers from a lack of checks and balances. To introduce such a check, it is thus necessary that the appointing body has the *suo motu* power to initiate transfers in public interest.

It is imperative that when such transfers are ordered, two principles are strictly followed. First, the reasons for a transfer of a judge must be disclosed. Currently the transfer order merely contains the fact of the transfer and no reasons.[14] To ensure transparency, it is necessary that the ground of transfer is provided in the transfer order. This will have the salutary effect of curbing wanton rumour-mongering about the reasons for transfer.[15] In turn, it should lead to dispelling the myth that all transfers are punitive, which affects the respect in which the judiciary is held. Equally significant for this purpose is a principled decision not to use transfers as disciplinary measures. As the next section demonstrates, the measure of impeachment is sought to be supplemented by several other disciplinary measures short of impeachment. Given the armoury of measures that will be available for disciplining judges for various levels of misconduct, transfers should cease to be used for disciplining judges. As pointed out earlier, it is strictly unconstitutional for being punitive, and in any event, unprincipled since it is not in the public interest of the transferee High Court to have a tainted judge being transferred to it. These reforms must be carried out concomitantly with reforms to appointment systems with the fundamental facets of who can effect a transfer and the grounds for doing so being specified in the Constitution. Specific details can then follow in implementing legislation.

## 9B *Impeachment*

The description and analysis of the working of the provision for impeachment of judges in the Constitution in Chapter 3 and Section 8B of Chapter 8 demonstrate

[14] A record of recent transfer orders may be found at: Department of Justice, Ministry of Law and Justice, Government of India, 'Appointment of Judges: Latest Orders of Appointment, Transfer etc.,' available at http://doj.gov.in/appointment-of-judges/latest-orders-appointment-transfer-etc. (accessed 20 July 2018).

[15] For an illustrative example, see the controversy generated by the transfer of a high-performing judge Justice Rajiv Shakhder from the Delhi High Court to the Madras High Court. See Maneesh Chibber, 'Jurists Protest Transfer of Delhi High Court Judge Who Gave Greenpeace Case Order,' *Indian Express*, 1 March 2016, https://indianexpress.com/article/india/india-news-india/jurists-protest-transfer-of-delhi-hc-judge-who-gave-greenpeace-case-order/ (accessed 20 February 2017).

three key inferences: first, impeachment is directed at promoting and does promote judicial accountability though not as effectively as it might have been envisaged; second, the ineffectiveness is owing to extraneous political factors determining voting choices of parliamentarians as well as excessive delays in the process from initiation of the enquiry to its culmination, in part due to constant judicial interventions; third, impeachment is unsuitable as a one-size-fits-all remedy for any instance of judicial misconduct—other supplementary methods are necessary. Making the process of impeachment more effective, thereby augmenting extant levels of judicial accountability while exploring alternative accountability methods for misconduct not warranting impeachment, is thus the focus of this section.[16]

The legacy of the Ramaswami impeachment episode has been to hold parliament responsible for the ineffectiveness of the impeachment procedure as a judicial accountability mechanism. For a judge who was found guilty of wrongdoing amounting to impeachable misconduct by a statutory committee to be absolved on the basis of extraneous considerations instead of being held accountable for his actions understandably de-legitimised impeachment as a method of enforcement of accountability.[17] Since that has been the only instance when both houses of parliament have been called upon to vote on an impeachment motion, this legacy persists today.

Regulating the use of the parliamentary power to impeach is thus essential. If, as is the case today, a quasi-judicial expert committee under the JIA finds a judge guilty and reports its findings to parliament, does a *de novo* hearing before parliament serve any useful purpose? Here, a distinction must be drawn between the vesting of such power in parliament and the basis for its use. Regarding the former, there are well-established principled and practical reasons for the exercise of impeachment power by the legislature.[18] But how such power is to be used might, in principle, be usefully circumscribed to prevent the influence of factors not directly connected to a determination of whether indeed the behaviour of the judge concerned warrants impeachment. However, this is a difficult proposition to implement for two reasons. First, it is intrinsic to vesting such power with holders of elected public office that political considerations will greatly determine voting choices. The attempt to

16 The discussion is limited to impeachment on account of misbehaviour. While impeachment is also possible on grounds of incapacity, this has rarely been controversial and is thus not discussed.

17 See Chapter 3.

18 See Chapter 3.

circumscribe such considerations by law will thus be cutting against the grain of a method of holding judges publicly accountable. If there are good reasons for vesting such power in parliament in the first place (as there are), then the possibility of extraneous considerations is the price one has to pay for it.

Second, regulating the use of such power is tantamount to regulating how parliament votes in a particular matter. This is the sole prerogative of each member as well as the rules of the house.[19] The rules of each house, which provide for the procedure to be adopted in passage and voting of motions, do not specify any special restriction for a particular type of motion other than the majority that is expressly required by law. To do so for an impeachment motion would be anomalous. On the contrary, if it is indeed felt that extraneous considerations should not affect voting on an impeachment motion, appropriate parliamentary conventions to this effect ought to develop. One key convention that might usefully develop is conscience voting, that is, voting by members without a party whip being issued. This can have a significant effect on preventing impeachment motions being subject entirely to political considerations in voting.[20] At the same time, a presumption should be established that if a statutory enquiry committee has found a judge guilty of proved misbehaviour then, unless such decision can be shown to be perverse, *mala fide*, bad for lack of natural justice or suffers from an error on the face of the record, parliament should accept such decision. A decision made by a statutory committee comprising judges and jurists who apply their mind to the facts of the case, hear both parties and come to a reasoned conclusion as to whether a case of 'proved misbehaviour' is made out or not should be entitled to the greatest weight. If parliament can merely dismiss such a report out of hand without any justifiable reason, that would amount to making a mockery out of the process of enquiry. Both these conventions circumscribing the power of parliament and the manner in which such power is to be exercised are purely in the domain of parliamentary procedure and cannot be introduced by law. It is thus recommended that appropriate parliamentary conventions to this effect develop over a period of time.

More immediate reform of the impeachment process ought to focus on the stage anterior to parliamentary voting, that is, the enquiry process. As is clear from Chapter 3, there were two severe shortcomings at this stage: first,

[19] This is provided for by Art. 118 of the Constitution of India.

[20] This was strongly recommended by the Chairman of the Rajya Sabha, the Vice-President of India, in 2009 who argued that whips should be limited to bills that 'threaten the survival of a government'. See Hamid Ansari, 'Inauguration Speech' (Seminar on 'Evaluating Committees and Committee System: Changing Contours of Governance and Policy', New Delhi, 18 November 2009), available at http://pib.nic.in/newsite/erelease.aspx?relid=54190 (accessed 13 April 2014).

delay caused by the protracted nature of proceedings and, second, the ability of the concerned judge to continue without established legal sanction, thereby severely damaging the need for judicial accountability. If the problem of delay is deconstructed, there are two significant reasons that are responsible: the onerous process of initiating an impeachment process and the continuing availability of judicial review. From the Ramaswami impeachment discussed in Section 3B of Chapter 3, it is clear that from the time the allegations against the concerned judge came to light until the time the process of impeachment under the JIA commenced, eight months had already elapsed. Further time was taken up since the JIA does not envisage a permanent enquiry body but rather requires such a body to be set up every time the process of impeachment is initiated. Similar delays were seen in the impeachment processes concerning Justice Soumitra Sen and Justice P. D. Dinakaran as well. In the meantime, the judges continued functioning without any established legal sanction.

Four reforms are necessary to offset the problem of delay and ensure more effective judicial accountability during the process of impeachment. First, institute alternate mechanisms of initiating an impeachment; second, set up a permanent institution to conduct judicial enquiries in impeachment cases; third, limit the availability of judicial review during the pendency of the process; fourth, institute norms of judicial accountability during the pendency of the process applicable to the judge in question.

The first two reforms are the subject of the Judicial Standards and Accountability Bill, 2012 (hereinafter 'JSA Bill'). It repeals the JIA and establishes two mechanisms for impeachment—first, it retains the *status quo* provided under the JIA, that is, a motion to be presented by a requisite number of members of parliament leading to an independent enquiry; second, it allows for complaints to be filed alleging misbehaviour by judges. To hear such complaints as well as enquire into misbehaviour referred to it by a motion by members of parliament, the Act sets up a three-tier mechanism consisting of the National Judicial Oversight Committee (hereinafter 'Oversight Committee'), the supervisory body, a Complaints Scrutiny Panel (hereinafter 'Scrutiny Panel') for *prima facie* vetting of complaints and an Investigation Committee for investigation. The first two are envisaged as permanent institutions (though the latter might change depending on the tenure of the judges on the Scrutiny Panel on the Supreme Court or the particular High Court in question),[21] whereas the

[21] The average tenure of a Supreme Court judge is 5.26 years. See Abhinav Chandrachud, 'The Age Factor,' *Frontline* 28, no. 21 (October 2011), available at

third is constituted *ad hoc* when investigation is deemed necessary. While the JSA Bill covers several other aspects pertaining to judicial behaviour, it is this architecture for conducting enquiries on complaints leading to impeachment that will be the main focus of this section.[22]

The establishment of the Oversight Committee and Scrutiny Panel as permanent nodal institutions administering the process of impeachment is a significant improvement on the JIA. First, by virtue of being permanent there will be no delay in constituting the body as is the case under the JIA every time an enquiry has to be conducted. Second, it reduces scope for seeking judicial review on the ground of bias in constitution of the enquiry committee as happened in the impeachment proceedings involving Justice Ramaswami as well as Justice Dinakaran.[23] This is, however, not to suggest that these institutions have no problems of their own. Three key issues threaten the effectiveness of this architecture.

First, the JSA Bill sets up an unnecessarily complex procedure for dealing with complaints. Specifically, the multiplicity of institutions and the statutory requirement of involving all such institutions mandatorily in case a complaint is filed will perpetuate delay and inefficiency. Clause 10 provides for the constitution of a Scrutiny Panel in the Supreme Court and every High Court to scrutinise the complaints against a judge. Under Clause 19, the Oversight Committee, upon the receipt of a complaint relating to misbehaviour of a judge except the chief justice of India, is mandated to refer the complaint to the Scrutiny Panel of the Supreme Court or concerned High Court to scrutinise and report thereon within three months of receiving the complaint. In the case of a complaint against the chief justice of India, under Clause 21, the complaint shall not be referred to the Scrutiny Panel but be scrutinised by the Oversight Committee itself.

Except the case of complaints against the chief justice of India, the scrutiny and oversight mechanism is superfluous and time-consuming. When seen

---

www.frontline.in/static/html/fl2821/stories/20111021282104900.htm (accessed 13 April 2014). No similar data is available for tenure of High Court judges and chief justices though one can assume that the former will be significantly longer than the latter.

22 For a detailed analysis and critique of the JSA Bill, see PLBS, 'The Judicial Standards and Accountability Bill, 2010'. Though the JSA Bill has lapsed, its template is relevant for future reforms pertaining to judicial accountability.

23 See Chapter 3.

alongside a distinct machinery for investigation into such complaints it is also excessively unwieldy. The three-body mechanism makes the Oversight Committee, which ought to be a high-powered decision-making body, a clearing house for complaints filed. This inference is clear from Clause 19, which mandates that all complaints will be forwarded by the Oversight Committee within three months of its receipt to the Scrutiny Panel. This provision is pointless—if all matters are to be sent for scrutiny, the complaints might as well be filed with the respective Scrutiny Panel. Alternatively, if centralisation and uniformity demand the filing of all complaints before the Oversight Committee, then the time period available to the committee to forward complaints to the Scrutiny Panel ought to be shortened significantly.

On the other hand, if it is intended that the Oversight Committee takes a *prima facie* view of the matter in these three months, then the very rationale for a separate scrutiny process becomes superfluous. Two levels of scrutiny by one's peers prior to investigation is excessive and it is unclear what different purpose each of these scrutiny processes will serve. Even accounting for the fact that the Scrutiny Panel consists of judges from the particular court in which the judge who is the subject of the complaint serves whereas the Oversight Committee is national, there is nothing in the type of members it is composed of (a majority of retired and sitting judges) or in its processes that justify such duplication. It is, thus, recommended that complaints received by the Oversight Committee are forwarded to the Scrutiny Panel without delay for speedy scrutiny.

This process of initial scrutiny and oversight is followed by the actual investigation to be conducted by an Investigation Committee. The Investigation Committee is constituted *ad hoc* when such need arises. It frames definite charges against the concerned judge, hears her and presents a report to the Oversight Committee for a final decision on whether to recommend impeachment to the president. It is thus clear that the stage of investigation is the key judicial phase of the enquiry where charges of wrongdoing are established or negated. Given this, it is anomalous that investigation is conducted by an *ad hoc* body. The Oversight Committee, while it possesses the ultimate power on deciding whether to recommend impeachment or not to the president, has been placed in a curious position as a consequence. Neither is it vested with the power to investigate matters itself nor are the bases for which it acts on the recommendation of the Investigation Committee provided in law. This is indicative of an unclear institutional vision for the Oversight Committee. At the same time, the Oversight Committee is vested with unfettered discretion to decide whether the charges, if proved, amount to misbehaviour that warrants impeachment. While this power is a key discretionary power vested in the Oversight Committee justifying its status as the nodal body under the Act, the said power being unrestricted, and being exercised without hearing, leads to doubts about its validity. It is a well-established principle of natural justice that the body that conducts hearings is also the one which takes a final decision on the matter.[24] Allowing the Oversight Committee to take the ultimate decision of impeachment on the basis of hearings focusing on the distinct question of whether the charges have been proved before the Investigation Committee falls foul of this principle. Either the procedure and bases for the decision of the Oversight Committee ought to have been statutorily provided or hearings should be mandated before it and not the Investigation Committee.

The failure to do so leads to the distinct possibility of the filing of several applications for judicial review of the process of investigation by the Investigation Committee and recommendation of impeachment by the Oversight Committee on the basis of its report. As was evident from the protracted impeachment episode of Justice Ramaswami and subsequently of Justices Dinakaran and Sen, seeking judicial review to clarify the legal position regarding impeachment procedure is a common occurrence, which has the effect of delaying proceedings substantially. While the bill takes a few key steps to avert this by clearly spelling out powers of respective bodies, the bases for their use and the procedures to be followed, the same cannot be said of the process of investigation. The *ad hoc* nature of the selection of members of the Investigation Committee, the procedure adopted by it and the lack of clarity regarding the basis on which the Oversight Committee accepts the recommendations made by it are all possible causes for judicial review applications to be filed. Such applications have significant potential to derail the process of impeachment under the bill, thereby replicating the same problems the bill is expected to address.

While providing statutory clarity on the aforesaid matters is essential, there is no constitutional bar to filing constitutional writ petitions, no matter how frivolous. Thus, preventing excessive filing of judicial review applications is primarily contingent on the attitude that the court takes to such petitions being filed. In the *Ramaswami* impeachment, the court was accommodating, passing considered judgments in the several petitions, some seemingly filed with the primary intention of delaying the process. Appropriate judicial norms thus need to develop by which the court is prepared to stamp out applications filed for extraneous purposes which have the effect of delaying the trial significantly. It

[24] *Maneka Gandhi* v. *Union of India*, (1978) 1 SCC 248 (Supreme Court of India).

is only when such deterrence is created will judicial review applications become manageable and consequently the process of impeachment more efficient.

Finally the JSA Bill, despite some overtures in this regard, does not question the principle of impeachment being a one-size-fits-all consequence for judicial misbehaviour. Neither are accountability measures short of impeachment seriously considered nor are interim accountability measures pending impeachment given adequate thought. Clause 34(1)(b) provides for the possibility of issuing advisories and warnings by the Oversight Committee when although charges have been proved, they do not warrant impeachment. However, the punitive weight of such advisories and warnings is unclear. The bill fails to state whether such advisories and warnings will be public or private in nature or what the consequences of breach of these will be. Unlike the bill, the Law Commission recommended that the nodal body under the Act (the National Judicial Council in the Judges Inquiry Bill, 2005, that the Law Commission was considering, analogous to the Oversight Committee in the present bill) be empowered not only to issue advisories and warnings but also censure or admonition, public or private. Not only does this empower the nodal body with a range of remedies for different kinds of judicial misbehaviour, crucially such remedies include public accountability measures short of impeachment.

The possibility of a public censure is key as a measure enforcing judicial accountability, short of impeachment. This is because the independent statutory body set up under the Act is not an institution that fosters internal accountability but rather is designed to foster external public accountability. Systems of internal accountability are already in place in the form of the Restatement of the Values of Judicial Life (1999) and the in-house procedure for investigation into indiscipline that it sets up.[25] It is a recognition of the inadequacy of the procedure, specifically its opaque and private functioning, that is a *raison d'etre* of the JSA Bill. Thus, the Oversight Committee as a high-powered, bipartisan

[25] Restatement. The inadequacy of the in-house procedure became clear when an errant judge Justice C. S. Karnan (of the Madras High Court, later transferred to Calcutta High Court) who had frequently made sensational allegations against fellow judges clearly in violation of the Restatement of Values of Judicial Life could not be reined in by using such procedure. Instead, in a remarkable turn of events, he was issued notice by the Supreme Court for contempt of Court under Art. 129 of the Constitution. Using contempt power to discipline a sitting judge evidences the lack of disciplinary measures short of impeachment. See In re: CS Karnan, Suo motu, Contempt Petition No. 1 of 2017 (Supreme Court of India), available at https://www.sci.gov.in/pdf/jud/4408_2017_Judgement_09-May-2017.pdf (accessed 25 July 2018).

statutory body is the means through which public accountability for judicial indiscipline is enforced without compromising on judicial independence. If such a process is stripped of its public element with only private advisories, warnings and censures, then the rationale for setting up an independent statutory forum for judicial accountability would be significantly jeopardised. Further, no adverse impact on judicial independence or on the institutional integrity of the judiciary is envisaged given the eminence of the composition of the Oversight Committee and its transparent processes.

Pending the investigation being completed, clause 35 allows the Oversight Committee to recommend stoppage of judicial work to facilitate a free and fair enquiry. It is recommended that the provision for stoppage of judicial work be made mandatory once the Scrutiny Panel certifies that there are sufficient grounds for proceedings against the judge. This concretises the *ad hoc* procedure adopted by Chief Justice Mukharji when confronted with the question of whether Justice Ramaswami would continue on the bench when he was the subject of an enquiry under the JIA[26] and the order of the Supreme Court against Justice Karnan in exercise of contempt power.[27] There are three reasons for such concretisation: First, as a matter of principle, a judge who is the subject matter of investigation for misbehaviour ought to recuse herself from functioning as an adjudicator. Since the hallmark of judicial office is integrity, which is in question during the investigation process, to uphold respect for the office, such stoppage of judicial work is necessary. Second, this provides a credible deterrent for judicial misbehaviour. Since the process of investigation, despite strict time limits, is protracted and parliamentary procedures pertaining to impeachment more protracted still, the lack of imminent sanctions makes the enforcement of judicial accountability remote. Stoppage of judicial work is a transparent, public and immediate form of interim sanction that attaches to purported judicial misbehaviour certified by the Scrutiny Panel as requiring further enquiry. Third, making such stoppage mandatory obviates a spate of judicial review applications being filed. Were it permissive, there would be a high chance of such a decision by the Oversight Committee being challenged. Justice Ramaswami's case itself provides a precedent in this regard when the order of Chief Justice Mukharji sending him on long leave was challenged successfully on the administrative side. Making such a remedy mandatory on the Scrutiny Panel recommending further investigation nullifies the scope for

[26] See Chapter 3.
[27] See text accompanying note 25.

discretion and consequently judicial or other review proceedings that could significantly hold up the process.

Such a recommendation must, however, be harmonised with the need for confidentiality of proceedings, as envisaged by clauses 39 and 43 of the bill. Confidentiality is necessary for ensuring that the complaints procedure does not become a tool to tarnish the reputation of judges. An order of stoppage of judicial work by the Oversight Committee in relation to a particular judge once the Scrutiny Panel recommends investigation runs contrary to this principle. This is especially so since at that stage no investigation has been carried out and the judge has not been found guilty of misbehaviour. Thus, an argument might plausibly be made that stopping judicial work and consequently making the identity of the judge public affects his reputation without a fair hearing and consequently might shake public confidence in the institution.

There is a twofold response to this argument. First, at the level of principle, it possesses little merit. Disclosing the fact that a judge is being investigated for potential misbehaviour ought not to tarnish her reputation. It is a well-established principle that a person is innocent till proven otherwise and there is no reason as to why a judge of a superior court should not benefit from the operation of this principle. As far as public confidence in the institution is concerned, such confidence should be strengthened by the establishment of a transparent mechanism to promptly investigate and stamp out any instances of misbehaviour.

In practice, however, it must be frankly admitted that persons are often publicly deemed guilty when accused of a wrongdoing. Much of this has to do with declining standards of reporting and its propensity towards sensationalisation, matters which cannot be gone into here. However, given the reality of public perception being divorced from principle it is essential to insulate judges under investigation and the judiciary from such taint to the extent feasible.

The JSA Bill contains one key safeguard in this regard: the stoppage of judicial work will only be pursuant to two stages of the complaints process—forwarding of the complaint from the Oversight Committee to the Scrutiny Panel and scrutiny by the panel. Since both are high-powered bodies, the latter especially consisting solely of judges of the High Court to which the complaint pertains or the Supreme Court of India and thereby vigilant of the need to protect the public confidence in the institution, the judge who is the subject of complaint is statutorily assured of a fair consideration of this case. However, since the reform that is suggested seeks to make stoppage mandatory pursuant to the Scrutiny Panel report (and not at the discretion of the Oversight Committee as the bill currently does), it is essential to provide a further safeguard to guarantee fair hearing. To this end, the bill must provide that the judge who has been complained against must have an opportunity to file a written response to the complaint before the Scrutiny Panel. Such an opportunity must be provided in order to ensure fair hearing at the stage of scrutiny. This will ensure that if subsequently the complaint is investigated and judicial work stopped then such step will have been taken after providing the judge concerned an opportunity to be heard proportionate to the stage of proceedings. Currently, clause 13 vests the Scrutiny Panel with the power to regulate its own procedure. Either an express incorporation of the right of the judge to file a written response to the complaint must be made a mandatory part of this procedure or an appropriate statutory amendment introduced to this effect.

In conclusion, reform of the impeachment procedure ought to be viewed in two stages. First, the procedure in parliament pertaining to impeachment cannot be mandated statutorily. It is the rightful domain of parliamentary procedure and certain conventions—namely conscience voting and a default acceptance of recommendations by the investigating expert/ enquiry body—have to develop if parliament is to remain true to the faith vested in it by the drafters of the Constitution. Second, the focus of impeachment reform should thus be at the stage anterior to parliamentary proceedings for impeachment. Four specific reforms need to be introduced at this stage: simplifying extant procedures in the JSA Bill, reducing multiplicity of institutions, disincentivising delay and introducing supplementary disciplinary measures short of impeachment. A conspectus of such measures, it is believed, has significant potential to expedite a currently ineffective process of impeachment, while making it an effective tool of public accountability for judges. At the same time, it facilitates development of other disciplinary measures, equally relevant to achieving this end. They ensure a clear and coherent regime governing impeachment and other forms of disciplining for judges, thereby bolstering respect for the judiciary in India.

## *9B.1 Post-Retirement Employment*

From the analysis of post-retirement employment of judges in government-appointed positions in Chapters 4 and 8, three inferences are discernible: First, post-retirement employment adversely affects the perception of independence of the judiciary, specifically decisional independence of individual judges on the verge of their retirement; second, its non-regulation serves no judicial accountability function; on the contrary and third, it is justified by the low retirement age of judges and consequently their capability of being engaged in post-retirement employment as well as the need for high-quality judicially trained personnel for a range of quasi-judicial offices who are otherwise seemingly unavailable. From these inferences, two conclusions follow: first, post-retirement employment requires regulation because of its adverse impact on judicial independence; second, such regulation must proceed both on the assumption of the law as it currently stands and in an ideal scenario where ancillary aspects pertaining to retirement age of judges and staffing of quasi-judicial offices are also reformed. On this basis, this section offers a two-pronged proposal for reform; first, on the basis of the *status quo* and, second, after advocating appropriate reform of retirement age of judges and proposing alternative suggestions for staffing quasi-judicial offices. Such a proposal is principled as well as pragmatic, offering both an ideal and an intermediate solution, in both instances ensuring that the perception of decisional independence of judges being adversely affected is effectively nullified.

### *9B.2 Ceteris Paribus Reform*

As demonstrated by the data collected in Chapter 4, 65 per cent of all post-retirement appointments in the period under study were to statutory tribunals or commissions. Of these appointments, 92 per cent were made within three years of the appointed judge's retirement from judicial office. If other appointments to post-retirement positions are also considered (other than tribunals or commissions), the number of appointments made within three years of a judge's retirement drops, but is still a significant 68 per cent. As far as appointing authorities for appointments to statutory tribunals and commissions are concerned, a majority, that is, 66 per cent, were made by the government after consultation with an appropriate authority. If other appointments to post-retirement positions are also considered, this number drops, albeit to a statistically significant 57 per cent. In 77 per cent of these cases, such authority was the chief justice of India or a relevant judicial office holder who was either consulted or responsible for the nomination of the candidate; in the remaining instances, it was the representative of the opposition as laid down in statute.

Thus, it is clear that a majority of appointments in the period under study were to statutory tribunals or commissions, made within three years of the judge's retirement by the executive government in consultation with an appropriate authority, which in a majority of cases was the chief justice of India or a relevant judicial officer. To undo the effect that such practice has had on the independence of the judiciary, many reforms pertaining to authorities involved in the process, the nature of available post-retirement positions and the eligibility of retired judges for such positions are plausible. One key change is imperative as an immediate remedy—a three-year moratorium on post-retirement appointment of judges to government-appointed positions. This is advocated based on the assumption that the *status quo* pertaining to retirement age of judges remains. The effect of a change in the law relating to retirement age requires an alternative reform proposal that will be advanced presently.

A moratorium or 'cooling off period' before judges are appointed to a post-retirement position has been widely advocated.[28] In principle, the operation of such a period is designed to ensure that the decisional independence of judges while in office, and consequently the high status in which the judiciary is held, is not affected by post-retirement prospects. As Justice Krishna Iyer's trenchant observation quoted in the introduction to Chapter 4 combined with former Law Minister Arun Jaitley's view that some judgments are handed down with a view to curry favour with the government alluded to thereafter suggest, the temptation for a post-retirement government-appointed position is significant for judges on the verge of retirement.[29] To prevent this from occurring, a cooling-off period seeks to debar a judge from accepting any post-retirement appointment from the government for a specified period of time after retirement. Such a view is based on two assumptions: first, that in the fluid nature of Indian politics, whether indeed the same government will be in power at the end of a particular judge's cooling-off period as at her retirement is a matter of doubt;[30] second, even if it is, an appointment decision after a passage of time will more likely be based on merit without any obvious possibility of a *quid pro quo*. Both assumptions

[28] J. Venkatesan, 'Experts Call for Amendments to Prevent Judges Taking Up Jobs after Retirement,' *The Hindu*, 3 October 2012, available at www.thehindu.com/news/national/experts-call-for-amendments-to-prevent-judges-taking-up-jobs-after-retirement/article3958819.ece (accessed 10 February 2014).

[29] Krishna Iyer, *Justice at Crossroads*; Arun Jaitley, 'Quit or Be Sacked,' *Outlook*, 17 February 2013, available at www.outlookindia.com/article.aspx?283944 (accessed 10 February 2014).

[30] Since 1990, changes in government in India have been frequent. The Ninth, Eleventh and Twelfth Lok Sabhas were in session for 15 months, 18 months and 13 months respectively instead of the expected 5 years. For more information, see 'Duration and Sittings of Lok Sabha' (Parliament of India), available at http://164.100.47.132/estudy/duration.pdf (accessed 10 February 2014).

are *prima facie* valid and space precludes any further scrutiny.

The key question which then arises, not satisfactorily answered in the extant literature, is the duration of such period. Two factors must be kept in mind while deciding what such period should be: it must be long enough to offset any perception of judicial independence being affected while the judge holds judicial office; at the same time, it must be short enough so that the retired judge is at an age when she can meaningfully fulfil her post-retirement role. The latter can be determined relatively simply—in several existing proposals for higher judicial reform, it is recommended that the retirement age of judges be increased to 70.[31] Though several proposals recommend 68 instead,[32] it is instructive for our purposes that it is never beyond 70. This proceeds on the assumption that till the age of 70, a holder of judicial office is fit for her task. Since the post-retirement offices of judges are similar in relevant ways to the task of a judge herself, the same assumption can be made here. If the upper limit for holding post-retirement office is fixed at 70, and retirement age of Supreme Court judges continues (as assumed) at 65, and High Court judges at 62, the range of the cooling-off period in order to provide a post-retirement tenure of reasonable duration is fairly circumscribed.

These two factors, that is, a cooling-off period long enough to offset perceptions of judicial independence being affected, while short enough to lead to a meaningful post-retirement tenure, are questions of institutional design. The data indicate that 68 per cent of all post-retirement appointments surveyed were within three years of the judge's retirement. If it is reduced to two years, then the number drops significantly to 48 per cent. If it is increased to four years, though the number increases to 76 per cent, the post-retirement tenure of a Supreme Court judge (assuming 70 as the outer age for judicial or quasi-judicial work) is reduced to one year. Thus, the second factor, that is, a cooling-off period short enough so that there is a meaningful post-retirement tenure, is not satisfied in this case.

[31] T. R. Andhyarujina, 'The Age of Judicial Reform,' *The Hindu*, 1 September 2012, available at www.thehindu.com/opinion/lead/the-age-of-judicial-reform/article3845041.ece (accessed 10 February 2014); per Raju Ramachandran in Venkatesan, 'Experts Call for Amendments.'

[32] National Commission to Review the Working of the Constitution, *Report of the National Commission to Review the Working of the Constitution: Vol. I*, Ministry of Law and Justice, Government of India, 2002) [7.3.10] available at http://lawmin.nic.in/ncrwc/finalreport/v1ch7.htm (accessed 1 March 2017); A. R. Lakshmanan, 'Age of Retirement of High Court and Apex Court Judges,' *Lawyers' Update*, November 2010, www.lawyersupdate.co.in/LU/1/226.asp (accessed 10 February 2014).

On the basis of the aforesaid evidence, a clear reform proposal can be advocated. The cooling-off period post-retirement ought to be fixed at three years.[33] This will sufficiently ensure that the perception of judicial independence being affected by post-retirement employment will be offset significantly, while at the same time providing judges a reasonable post-retirement tenure of two years for Supreme Court retirees and five years for High Court retirees. If two years of post-retirement office is deemed inadequate, then further research is needed to establish the suitability for office of such retired judges beyond the age of 70. For the moment, such a proposal is sufficient to thwart adverse perceptions regarding decisional independence of judges being compromised by temptations of post-retirement office, while at the same time ensuring a reasonable post-retirement tenure.

Two practical steps are necessary to implement this proposal. First, a new provision, Art. 124(8) of the Constitution, must be inserted, which provides that no retired judge of the Supreme Court shall be eligible for a government position up to three years from the date of her retirement. An analogous insertion of Art. 220A is necessary for High Court judges. Second, it is imperative that the Ministry of Law and Justice, Government of India, maintains a chronological list of retirees of the Supreme Court and all High Courts along with the date for their re-eligibility for appointment in a post-retirement position. Such a list is necessary in order to ensure strict conformity with this provision. It is also an important step towards making the Ministry of Law and Justice a nodal body for all post-retirement appointments, a matter that is dealt with briefly in the following section.

In order to ensure the same spirit of judicial independence once judges are appointed to a judicial or quasi-judicial post-retirement position, several other reforms might be necessary. This particularly concerns the nature of the appointing authority for post-retirement employments. Given the disparate appointing authorities for similar post-retirement offices, a uniform process of appointment by a single nodal, representative authority might be apposite. Given that most appointments are made by the government in consultation with the chief justice of India, it is tangential insofar as judicial independence is concerned and not dealt with here. Its importance, however, should not be underestimated.

[33] The proposal assumes the same cooling-off period for both Supreme Court and High Court judges despite the difference in retirement ages and no survey of the latter being conducted. This is because the perception of judicial independence being affected is identical in both instances.

### 9B.2.a Widening the Reform Lens

Notwithstanding the proposal of a cooling-off period, reform of post-retirement employment of judges, if sought holistically, needs to focus on two related areas—rethinking the retirement age for judges of the Supreme Court and High Courts and exploring alternative staffing mechanisms for tribunals, statutory commissions, *ad hoc* commissions and commissions of enquiry where a majority of judges are currently employed post-retirement. Whereas the former has been the subject of considerable discussion both within government and outside,[34] the latter, despite the proliferation of such institutions putting considerable attendant pressure on retired judges and bureaucrats, has not been seriously proposed. The attempt in this section is thus to advance a considered proposal regarding the revised age of retirement of Supreme Court and High Court judges, while exploring a plausible alternative to retired-judge staffed commissions and tribunals.

There are two key questions regarding the retirement age for judges: first, whether it should be increased from the *status quo*, that is, 62 years for High Court judges[35] and 65 years for Supreme Court judges;[36] second, whether there should be parity in retirement ages of Supreme Court and High Court judges. The latter question has limited relevance to questions of judicial independence and accountability. In any event, the Constitution (114th Amendment) Bill, 2010, seems to explicitly accept the rationale for providing parity and there are good reasons, already widely articulated, for supporting such a view.[37] This section will not revisit this issue.

Regarding the former, it is instructive to note that the Constituent Assembly, which originally fixed the retirement age for High Court judges at 60 and Supreme Court judges at 65, looked upon this issue as one that required a clear,

[34] Within government, it has led to the formulation of the Constitution (114th Amendment) Bill, 2010 (India), that seeks to increase retirement age of High Court judges to 65; outside government, this has led to a public interest litigation being filed praying for an increase in retirement age of Supreme Court judges. See Dhananjay Mahapatra, 'Increase Retirement Age of Supreme Court Judges to 68 yrs: PIL,' *Times of India*, 6 October 2013, available at http://articles.timesofindia.indiatimes.com/2013-10-06/india/42762666_1_hc-judges-60-to-62-years-retirement-age (accessed 11 February 2014).

[35] As provided for by Constitution of India, Art. 217(1).

[36] Ibid., Art. 124(2).

[37] Abhinav Chandrachud, 'The Need to Have a Uniform Retirement Age for Judges,' *Economic and Political Weekly* 47, no. (2012): 24.

dispositive rule, as opposed to one which had a right answer.[38] Three principled considerations were determinative—first, the retirement age should be such that the experience and wisdom of erudite judges should not be lost at an age when they were still capable of rendering their services; second, whether there was a need to provide an additional tenure to Supreme Court judges, given the importance of their role and the necessity to incentivise judges to take up a position in the Supreme Court of India in New Delhi, thereby moving from their respective cities at an advanced age; third, ensuring that the retirement age is not so low such that judges, who are drawn from the Bar and are constitutionally barred from returning to practice, consider it an unattractive proposition. On this basis, three views were widely prevalent—keep the age for judicial retirement at 60, thereby making a concession of five years over and above the retirement age of ICS officials, which was 55, in view of the less onerous nature of judicial work;[39] increase it to 68 for Supreme Court judges[40] and fix it at 62 or 63 for High Court Judges as per the suggestion of the Chief Justices' Conference[41] drawing from international best practices and the need to incentivise judges coming to the Supreme Court;[42] or fix it at 60 for High Court judges and 65 for Supreme Court judges, with a provision for *ad hoc* appointment past the retirement age by the president, the provision that was finally adopted.[43] Other views were also advocated, though not considered by the assembly with much seriousness.[44]

Ambedkar was cognizant that 'sixty five cannot always be regarded as the zero hour in a man's intellectual ability'.[45] However, the matter had to be fixed in the Constitution in order to provide security to proposed holders of judicial office and could not be left to parliament to decide. The age of 65 recommended itself for best satisfying the aforesaid three principled considerations in the views of the majority of the Constituent Assembly. Nothing, however, precluded future parliaments from revising such age (or the High Court retirement age) if such revision would better satisfy the three considerations at a given time.

38 Nehru, CAD, vol. VIII (May–June 1949), 246.

39 Jaspat Roy Kapoor, CAD, vol. VIII (May–June 1949), 236–37.

40 Naziruddin Ahmed, CAD, vol. VIII (May–June 1949), 256.

41 Shiva Rao et al., *Framing of India's Constitution*, vol. IV, 195, 197–99.

42 M. Ananthasayanam Ayyangar, CAD, vol. VIII (May–June 1949), 254.

43 Ambedkar, CAD, vol. VIII (May–June 1949), 259.

44 K. T. Shah proposed appointment during good behaviour as in the USA, CAD, vol. VIII (May–June 1949), 235.

45 Ambedkar, CAD, vol. VIII (May–June 1949), 259.

This indeed was done when parliament introduced the 15th Amendment Act increasing the retirement age of High Court judges to 62, which it felt better balanced the three principled considerations. Subsequent reports viewed these three considerations in the context of achieving parity between retirement ages of Supreme Court and High Court judges. This culminated in the tabling of the 114th Constitution Amendment Bill, 2010, which sought to equalise retirement ages at 65.[46] The factors cited for such increase can be found in the 39th Report of the Standing Committee on Personnel, Public Grievances, Law and Justice. Though the report is silent on the underlying reasons for such recommendation, the 44th Report of the same committee used the reasons for the 5th Pay Commission recommendation of increase of retirement age of central government employees to support such a proposal. This includes 'global practices, increased life expectancy, improved health standards, need for utilisation of experience and wisdom of senior employees'.[47] In addition, the committee recommended such increase to check vacancies from arising in the High courts, thereby preventing a further backlog in the court.[48] It is curious, however, that these reasons are not seen as sufficient for increasing the retirement ages *per se* but rather for the limited purpose of introducing parity.

If the reasons for the 5th Pay Commission recommending an increase in the age of superannuation for central government employees from 58 to 60 are scrutinised, it is clear that three reasons have analogous applicability to the absolute increase of retirement age of judges *per se* rather than for merely seeking parity between High Court and Supreme Court retirement ages—global practices, increasing life expectancy and the need to prevent extension-seeking by office holders which might affect their impartiality. Global practices for retirement of judges are not uniform and space precludes a full analysis. However, it would suffice to say that there is a discernible trend of using 70 or higher as the age of retirement in several countries. As far as life expectancy in India is concerned, in 1962 (when the last revision to retirement age of judges

[46] For more see *V. Vasanthkumar* v. *Secretary to Government, Union of India*, W/P No. 24907 of 2013 (Madras High Court, India). This was a public interest litigation filed in the Madras High Court praying for an issue of *mandamus* to direct the government to pass and implement the Constitution (114th Amendment) Bill.

[47] Department-Related Parliamentary Standing Committee on Personnel, Public Grievances, Law and Justice, The Constitution (114th Amendment) Bill, 2010 (44th Report, Rajya Sabha Secretariat, Parliament of India 2010), 13.

[48] For details of vacancies and backlogs, see ibid.

was made), average life expectancy was 42.85 whereas in 2011 it was 65.48.[49] This is a significant increase and provides adequate justification for an increase in retirement age across the board. Curbing extension-seeking, a widespread and pernicious practice noted by the Pay Commission with regard to bureaucrats, was sought by a carrot-and-stick approach. Having recommended an increase in retirement age to 60, the commission sought to prohibit post-retirement employment thereafter with the exception of a few specialist areas.[50] For judges too, as the data suggest, 19 judges were appointed within one year of their retirement, with one judge being appointed prior to his retirement. Though this does not confirm the prevalence of soliciting for post-retirement jobs while in office, a fact that has been confirmed elsewhere,[51] it does create a very strong presumption. Coupling any proposed increase in the retirement age for judges with a prohibition on post-retirement employment provides a solution that is both principled and pragmatic.

These three factors provide considerable justification for an increase in retirement age of judges, both of the Supreme Court and of the High Court. However, none of these prescribe what the quantum of such age increase should be. That determination will depend on the age that best balances the three principled considerations taken into account by the Constituent Assembly, in contemporary times. Given the increase in life expectancy and global practices pertaining to retirement ages today, it is only apposite that the retirement age be increased to 70. An increase in life expectancy by 22.63 years supports this conclusion, as does the fact that 70 is a widely accepted retirement age globally. Further, 70 is an age to which all of the last 50 retirees surveyed have been gainfully engaged in their post-retirement capacity, whether in government employment or elsewhere, and thus ensures that the wisdom and training of judges is used optimally. At the same time, it will act as an incentive for worthy members of the Bar to take up judgeship, many of whom are deterred by the early retirement age existing currently. Thus for both principled and pragmatic reasons, it is recommended that the retirement age of both Supreme Court and High Court judges in India is increased to 70.

There are two reasons why such age increase must be combined with a general bar on post-retirement employment of judges. In principle, a bar on

49 'India—Life Expectancy at Birth,' available at http://countryeconomy.com/demography/life-expectancy/india (accessed 12 February 2014).

50 Fifth Central Pay Commission (Part VI), 'Report on Civilian Employees Pensions and other Retirement Benefits,' All India Railwaymen's Federation, 1995), 1752.

51 Jaitley, 'Quit or Be Sacked.'

post-retirement employment is the most optimal method to maintain judicial independence, public perceptions regarding which have been strained by the increasing regularity of such appointments. It would also ensure the independence of the office to which an appointment is made since such appointment would not be attributable to any possibility of influence. In practice, such a bar can be most plausibly enforced when combined with the benefit of a minimum of five additional years of judicial tenure. In any event, the previous proposal of a cooling-off period of three years might be viewed as unworkable when read with the proposal for increased retirement age since judges will only be eligible for post-retirement appointment only at 73, by all accounts a fairly advanced age.

Second, such a bar on post-retirement employment is the trigger that is necessary for an overhaul of the functioning of tribunals and commissions in India. It is a widely held view that tribunals are largely slow and ineffective institutions that are not independent of the executive and function as post-retirement sinecures for retired bureaucrats and judges.[52] At the same time, commissions are often ineffectual, lacking teeth and routinely ignored by governments.[53] Much has been recommended in terms of reform; however, such reform has not been (and cannot be) seriously considered until the identification of such offices as post-retirement benefits for judges and bureaucrats is not decisively rejected. Barring post-retirement employment of judges would thus bell the cat, thereby setting the foundation for wider tribunal reform.

However, two caveats to this position are necessary. First, in commissions of enquiry, executive-appointed commissions of an exceptional nature or committees that are *ad hoc* enquiries set up by governments to investigate matters of public importance,[54] a retired judge may be essential because of

52 S. P. Sathe, *The Tribunal System in India* (Mumbai: NM Tripathi, 1996); Law Commission of India, *Review of Functioning of Central Administrative Tribunal, Customs, Excise and Gold Control Appellate Tribunal and Income Tax Appellate Tribunal*, 162nd Report, Ministry of Law and Justice, Government of India, 1998).

53 This is not the case across the board but a widely held view in respect of many commissions. For illustrative examples, see G. P. Joshi, 'National Human Rights Commission—Need for Review' (Commonwealth Human Rights Initiative), available at www.humanrightsinitiative.org/programs/aj/police/papers/gpj/national_human_rights_commission.pdf (accessed 24 February 2014); Swagata Raha, 'Multiplicity of Human Rights Institutions,' *Infochange India*, March 2013, available at http://www.infochangeindia.org/agenda/access-to-justice/multiplicity-of-human-rights-institutions.html (accessed 24 February 2014).

54 These are set up by either the central or state governments under the power vested in them by section 3 of the Commissions of Inquiry Act, 1952 (India).

her impartiality and the widespread respect she commands. At the same time, such appointments being *ad hoc* and thereby rarely the subject of parleying for position, there is no systemic concern about the erosion of judicial independence. A provision exempting commissions of enquiry and *ad hoc* enquiry committee appointments from the general bar on post-retirement employment would thus be warranted.

Second, such a general bar would put in jeopardy the continued functioning of the tribunals and commissions listed in the Appendix. As adverted to in Chapter 4, out of the 46 post-retirement government positions to which judges have been appointed, 28 have required a judge by law. Any general bar to post-retirement employment would thus require a change in each of the statutes where such an eligibility condition is mandated. The alternative system to be instituted ought to be a professional cadre of tribunal judges and commissioners, selected and administered by the Ministry of Law and Justice as the nodal ministry (for all Government of India tribunals and commissions; for state government bodies, this nodal body could be the Ministry of Law in the concerned state). This can be achieved through a single statute, repealing contrary provisions in other laws, such as the Tribunals, Courts and Enforcement Act, 2007, in the United Kingdom.[55] This cadre, of rank equivalent to a High Court judge or district court judge (as appropriate) for tribunal members, and to a suitably equivalent rank for commissioners, would be drawn both from the Bar and from specialist and technical backgrounds. Appropriate eligibility criteria and selection processes would have to be devised keeping in view the nature of the tribunal and the extent of experience required. Judgeship in a tribunal would be during good behaviour subject to retirement, with the possibility of elevation to higher appellate courts; for commissioners, analogous promotion benefits outside the judiciary would have to be explored. Given this reform is likely to be time-consuming, the *ceteris paribus* reform proposal should continue till the mechanics of the alternative proposal are fully worked out.

[55] Andrew Leggatt, 'Tribunals for Users: One System, One Service,' March 2011, available at http://webarchive.nationalarchives.gov.uk/+/http://www.tribunals-review.org.uk/leggatthtm/leg-00.htm (accessed 14 February 2014); Robert Carnwath, 'Tribunal Justice: A New Start,' *Public Law* (2009): 48. The Ministry of Law and Justice, Government of India, has introduced a bill titled The Tribunals, Appellate Tribunals and Other Authorities (Conditions of Service) Bill, 2014, in the Rajya Sabha which seeks to bring some uniformity to tribunal appointments, available at http://164.100.47.4/BillsTexts/RSBillTexts/asintroduced/Tribnul-E.pdf (accessed 12 May 2014).

In terms of law, this reform proposal will require three amendments. First, an amendment to Art. 124(2) and Art. 217(1) replacing the existing retirement age of 65 (for Supreme Court judges) and 62 (for High Court judges) with a uniform retirement age of 70. Second, amending Art. 124(7) and Art. 220, which currently provide some restrictions on post-retirement employment, to bar post-retirement employment in all statutory positions by the Union or state governments except commissions of enquiry. Other purely executive appointments would also be excluded by implication since they are not statutory positions in the first place. Third, necessary amendments will have to made in the relevant statutes setting up various tribunals and commissions regarding the eligibility norms for its chairpersons and members. The contents of such amendments can only be determined after a detailed study of how best a professional cadre of tribunal judges and independent commissioners can be created. This, as stated earlier, is beyond the remit of this book.

This section has outlined the shape that reforms in post-retirement employment of judges must take. It has pointed to the need for wider systemic reform within whose framework the question of the desirability of judges holding quasi-judicial and executive offices post-retirement needs to be situated. Such reform must combine a complete bar on post-retirement employment of judges along with increasing their tenure to the age of 70. This strikes an ideal compromise—judges are given additional years of service at a time when they are more than capable of doing so; at the same time, an impetus is provided for an overhaul of the functioning of tribunals and commissions, professionalising them rather than viewing them as post-retirement benefits for judges and bureaucrats. However, such reform is complex and time-consuming. Hence, in the short run, since independence of judges while in office is the key value that needs to be preserved, a cooling-off period of three years is proposed before a retired judge is eligible for post-retirement government employment. Such a proposal is based on concrete data and will ensure that the perception of lobbying for positions while in office, a charge that sullies the high status of the judiciary, is effectively nullified.

# Epilogue

## *The Moment the Judiciary Came Out*

This book is being written in the aftermath of a press conference by Justices Chelameswar, Gogoi, Lokur and Joseph convened 'to communicate to the nation to take care of the institution (of the judiciary)'.[1] In the annals of India's judicial history, this was an unprecedented event. Judges by tradition and training, speak only through their judgments. Communicating with members of the press, let alone calling a press conference in the middle of a working day in the Supreme Court, is anathema. Yet the four seniormost justices of the Supreme Court chose to openly share their grievances about the functioning of the judiciary, the lack of independence and courage shown by the chief justice of India, and thinly veiled suggestions of governmental interference in the judiciary. It is a 'discharge of a debt to the nation,' said Justice Gogoi; '[we] don't want someone to say 20 years later that the four judges sold their souls and did not take care of this institution so we place it before the people of this country,' remarked Justice Chelameswar.

What they placed before the people of India was a letter written by them to the chief justice of India alleging a breach of well-established judicial conventions regarding allocation of cases. The letter, while revealing in part, appeared to say much more by implication. It underlined the fact that the chief justice of India was the first among equals, with no superior authority over other judges of the Supreme Court. He functions as the master of the roster to allocate cases because such allocation is necessary in a court that convenes in multiple benches. In this allocation, he is guided by time-tested conventions regarding strength of the bench and its composition. The letter goes on to allege that such conventions were breached in the case of *RP Luthra* v. *Union of India* (hereinafter '*Luthra*').[2]

1 Judges' Press Conference.

2 Order dated 27 October 2017 in *R. P. Luthra* v. *Union of India*, Diary No. 22906/2017 (Supreme Court of India), available at https://www.supremecourtofindia.nic.in/supremecourt/2017/22906/22906_2017_Order_27-Oct-2017.pdf (accessed 25 July 2018).

In this case, a two-judge bench ordered that there should be no further delay in finalising the memorandum of procedure in public interest and listed the matter for further hearing.

That the case was assigned to a two-judge bench, the letter implies, was wrong, since the order to the government to finalise the memorandum of procedure taking into account public suggestions had earlier been given by the five-judge bench that heard the *NJAC Case* in a consequential hearing.[3] Thus, any further order in this matter, according to convention, should be passed by the same bench or a constitution bench of coordinate strength. The two-judge bench, by taking unto itself this power, exacerbated this wrongness. Judicial discipline demanded that this matter be sent back by them, even if wrongly listed in the first instance, to the chief justice for setting up a constitution bench. The letter concludes by asking for remedial measures in this case, as a prelude to remedying other instances where similar breaches have occurred. It is made clear, again by implication, that this was not a one-off instance.

This implication was made explicit at the press conference itself. When asked whether the issues being raised included the assignment of a case asking for an independent probe into the death of Judge Loya, who died while presiding over a trial where the president of the Bharatiya Janata Party, the single largest party in the Lok Sabha and the central government, Amit Shah, was an accused, Justice Gogoi appeared to reply in the affirmative. This suggestion made it clear that the allegation of improper assignment of cases by the chief justice was not a benign break with convention; it was perhaps done with governmental interests in mind. If true, this signalled a body blow to the administrative independence of the judiciary in deciding which judge would hear which case.

The press conference also highlighted the unsatisfactory manner in which the improper allocation of the *Luthra* case was remedied. Instead of the matter being sent to a constitution bench, as the letter requested, the chief justice constituted a three-judge bench of which he was a part, and recalled the earlier order. This was done in view of the constitution bench judgments in *SCAORA* and the *NJAC Case*, which rendered a new order in this case unnecessary. While the recall order was unarguably sound in result, as Justice Chelameswar admitted at the press conference, the fact of a three-judge bench comprising the chief justice correcting his own error in wrongly allocating a case in the first instance only heightened concerns about listing of cases in the Supreme Court.

3 *NJAC Consequential Order.*

These concerns multiplied in the handling of the *Prasad Education Trust* case.[4] The genesis of this case lies in the filing of petitions by Prasad Education Trust before the Supreme Court and Allahabad High Court. The trust operated a medical college whose permission to run certain courses had been declined.[5] Against this order, several petitions were filed in multiple jurisdictions. Justices Misra, Roy, Pant, Khanwilkar and Chandrachud heard the parties and passed several orders in the Supreme Court; Justices Shukla and Kumar passed an interim order in Allahabad High Court.[6]

A simultaneous investigation by the CBI indicated a possible criminal conspiracy to ensure a favourable judicial order in this matter. According to its first information report (FIR), two persons managing the affairs of the trust approached a retired judge of Allahabad and Odisha High Courts, Justice I. M. Quddusi, through Sudhir Giri of the Venkateshwara Medical College (part of Venkateshwara University, in whose case another judgment had been passed by Justice Misra in the Supreme Court).[7] Quddusi recommended the filing of a petition before the Allahabad High Court, in which partial relief was granted.

Subsequently, when the matter again reached the Supreme Court, the FIR reveals that Quddusi and his associates assured the trust of getting the matter 'settled' in the Supreme Court through 'their contacts' and engaged Biswanath Agrawala, a resident of Bhubaneswar. Agrawala claimed 'very close contact with senior relevant public functionaries' and demanded significant gratification for settling the case.[8] Quddusi, Agrawala and four associates were arrested for offences under the Prevention of Corruption Act and the Indian Penal Code.

Since the FIR indicated an attempt to fix a judicial proceeding, the Campaign for Judicial Accountability and Judicial Reforms filed a writ petition in the Supreme Court requesting that a special investigation team under a retired chief justice

4 *Prasad Education Trust.*

5 Order dated 25 August 2017 in *Prasad Education Trust* v. *Union of India*, Miscellaneous Bench No. 19870 of 2017, MANU/UP/3326/2017 (High Court of Allahabad).

6 Ibid.

7 *Shri Venkateshwara University* v. *Union of India*, (2017) 15 SCC 735 (Supreme Court of India).

8 Rajesh Ahuja, 'Medical Admission Scam: Retired HC Judge, Five Others Arrested by CBI,' *Hindustan Times*, 21 September 2017, available at https://www.hindustantimes.com/india-news/medical-admission-scam-retired-hc-judge-four-others-arrested-by-cbi/story-dFki96jREbRALyISgkEOlI.html (accessed 31 December 2018).

of India be set up. This request was made since it was apprehended that leaving the investigation to the CBI might mean allowing the government to influence judges who would be brought under investigation.

The merits of such a request are a distinct matter. However, propriety plausibly demanded that since the FIR pertained to a case where Justice Misra had been the presiding judge, as chief justice of India, he would not perform his default role of allocating benches for determination of this case or exercise his prerogative of hearing the case himself. Doing so would mean that the chief justice would not be 'like Caesar's wife', the puritanical standard of propriety the judiciary expects of public servants.[9] The same principle would apply to any judge in the Supreme Court and Allahabad High Court who had earlier participated in the proceedings. Recusal would not be an admission of complicity; instead it would be an affirmation of the principle that justice not only be done but also be seen to be done.

Unfortunately, by allocating the matter to a division bench himself, the chief justice gave this principle a go-by. It is moot whether the bench entrusted by the chief justice would ensure justice or not—the critical point is that such a bench, chosen by the chief justice, was congenitally defective. This impropriety set off a chain of improper actions—filing of a second petition in the same matter, hearing of the second petition by Justice Chelameswar, the second-most senior judge of the Supreme Court, and an order by his bench that the matter should be heard by five senior-most judges of the court.

What followed this order marked a remarkable departure from the fundamental tenet of justice delivery that no person shall be a judge in her own cause. Instead of the seniormost five judges hearing the case, as had been ordered by Justice Chelameswar, the chief justice constituted a distinct five-judge bench on the same matter, presided over it himself, overturned the earlier order passed by Justice Chelameswar's bench and resoundingly reiterated the powers of the chief justice alone to allocate cases as the master of the roster.[10]

Again, the question of correctness of this order is moot—more crucially, the order displayed either an astonishing lack of self-awareness or an alarming

9 'The standard of conduct expected of a Judge is much higher than an ordinary man…. Judge, like Caesar's wife, must be above suspicion,' para 29, *R. C. Chandel* v. *High Court of Madhya Pradesh*, (2012) 8 SCC 58 (Supreme Court of India). 'For the persons who hold the public office the normal benchmark of his character and behavior in the common man's language is Caesar's wife must be above suspicion,' para 23, *Sureshkumar* v. *State of Maharashtra*, (2001) 1 Mah LJ 901 (High Court of Bombay).

10 *CJAR (November 2017).*

design to stop further enquiry. This resulted in turning the focus away from the substantive concern of judicial corruption to the arcane conventions of bench allocation. Even in relation to bench allocation, while efficient listing of cases by the chief justice is a practical necessity in a multi-member court such as the Supreme Court of India, to place it above the principle that no person shall be a judge in her own cause, as the order does, is a prioritisation that even the most hard-nosed pragmatist will be at pains to defend. This explains why much of the press conference was concerned with the manner of allocation of cases by the chief justice—allocation was simply a polite proxy for seemingly murkier allegations of judicial corruption and government interference in the administrative independence of the judiciary.

Despite the press conference being characterised by the use of proxy and implication, it marked a watershed in India's judicial history as the moment when the Supreme Court of India came out to the people of the country. By tradition and design, the Supreme Court has been a cautious institution, chary of expressing itself except through its judgment, maintaining a respectable distance from government, aloof from the hurly-burly of politics. Much credit for this institutional design goes to the drafters of the Constitution and the judges who interpreted it in its early years. The drafters ensured that the Supreme Court was sufficiently empowered and independent of government, yet functioning as a coordinate organ of the state towards achieving its constitutional objectives. The judges were individuals of integrity, refusing to be drawn into the political thicket, yet going about their task of laying down the law independently and fearlessly.

Over time, however, as described in detail in this book, the assaults on judicial independence meant that a perverse conception of independence as insulation took hold. This was exacerbated by the perception of diminishing integrity of judges, as cases of corruption and misbehaviour appeared in the judiciary. In response, the judiciary became even more inward-looking, suspicious of the government and resistant to public demands for transparency and reform. In this they were aided by a peculiar institutional vision, shared widely at the Bar and echoed unthinkingly by some commentators—that the judiciary alone could protect its independence, any parliamentary intervention is to be resisted as being suspect by default and efforts at transparency are to be eschewed lest the judiciary's darkest secrets leak into the public domain.[11]

[11] Fali S. Nariman, doyen of the Bar, asked commentators to 'lump it' instead of commenting on possible irregularities in judicial functioning. Fali S. Nariman, *God Save the Hon'ble Supreme Court* (New Delhi: Hay House Publishers, 2018), 59;

The press conference decisively rejected this ill-conceived vision. Though the judges said very little and their letter to the chief justice too left considerable details open to interpretation, the import of their actions was unmistakable—that the Supreme Court was in disarray and only the people of the country could save it. In one stroke, the perils of an insular institution were brought sharply into focus—intrigue, which has characterised much of the functioning of the judicial collegium, inaction, in taking proactive measures to curb judicial corruption, and an unprincipled reliance on convention when it came to allocating benches to hear cases. In the darkness that pervaded the inner sanctum of the Supreme Court, these debilitating forces roamed freely. A self-serving and indefensible conception of judicial independence as insulation had firmly shut out the sunlight.

In contrast, the sight of four seniormost justices of the court on a lawn in central Delhi, harassed by reporters, presented an alternate vision for the court. In this vision, which might strike old-timers in the Supreme Court as heretical, the court is a transparent institution, functioning in a democratic polity, asking the people to whom it is accountable to set right the wrongs in its inner working. It is a vision where the independence of the judges does not derive its strength from a system of appointment closed to stakeholder participation, but instead from the integrity of the holders of the office and the public confidence that emanates from their transparent functioning. Equally, the people, whose representatives, the 'two eminent persons' on the NJAC, the Supreme Court had earlier struck down as unconstitutional, were not to be feared as hostile to judicial independence. Instead, in crisis, they were to be supplicated to, as the 'demos' who formed the lifeblood of democracy. The judiciary itself, which hitherto had wrested exclusive control over its own institutional future, could no longer function above the people. Calling on the nation to save the judiciary was a clarion call to parliamentarians to fulfil their duties as statesmen to bring in legislation in the name of the people, to reform a broken institution.

This alternate vision of a transparent and participatory judiciary will undoubtedly make it a more political institution. It might lead to jockeying for positions, headline-grabbing antics, and candid criticism of judges and their orders in the media. These are part and parcel of any institution that derives its legitimacy primarily from public confidence in its transparent functioning

---

see also Arun K. Thiruvengadam, who equates proposal for parliamentary intervention as naivete or dangerous design, 'The Crisis in Context,' *Frontline*, 16 February 2018, available at https://www.frontline.in/cover-story/the-crisis-in-context/article10055190.ece?homepage=true (accessed 25 July 2018).

rather than the unquestioned wisdom of its judges. For the Supreme Court of India, and the higher judiciary on the whole, such a day was bound to come. A combination of immense constitutional power to strike down legislation and speak truth to government was always unsustainable with incommensurate accountability facilitated by an opaque appointments system and relative anonymity of individual justices. The press conference represents the unravelling of this unsustainability. It marks the moment when the court begins a slow transformation from a post-colonial institution that is feared to an independent institution that is widely respected and at ease in India's noisy democracy.

The critical reset in such a transformation, as this book has pointed out, is in the court's own understanding of judicial independence and accountability. By holding the press conference, the four judges held themselves publicly accountable in a manner in which the Supreme Court had never done before. This was in stark contrast to the judgments in *SCAORA*, *Presidential Reference* and the *NJAC Case*, which upheld a puritanical form of judicial independence at the cost of accountability. Neither untrammelled accountability nor closeted independence is sustainable for any well-functioning judicial institution. As this book has shown, a balance between the two concepts is both possible and necessary for the Indian higher judiciary. It is now time for those who care about the Indian higher judiciary, whether they are in the court, the government, the parliament, the university or on the streets, to come together and give the common man and woman in India the higher judiciary they deserve.

# Appendix

## *Post-Retirement Employment of Judges in Government-Appointed Positions*

| Judge | Date of retirement | Post-retirement appointment (with dates when available) | When appointed after retirement | Type of body | Appointing authority | Whether judge required by law (Y/N) |
|---|---|---|---|---|---|---|
| 1. Justice K. T. Thomas | 29 January 2002 | Mullaperiyar Panel—Kerala Appointment | > 5 years (exact date unavailable) | SC panel | State executive | N |
| 2. Justice S. P. Bharucha | 05 May 2002 | Chairman, National Committee for Promotion of Social and Economic Welfare (1.2.11) | 9 years | Constituted by a notification by the central government (Department of Revenue) | Union executive | N |
| 3. Justice D. P. Mohapatra | 02 August 2002 | Chairperson, Odisha Human Rights Commission, (24.6.2003) | 10–11 months | Statutory body (Protection of Human Rights Act, 1993) | Governor on recommendations of committee consisting of government and opposition (CJI to be consulted only if sitting judge is to be appointed) | Y |

| Judge | Date of retirement | Post-retirement appointment (with dates when available) | When appointed after retirement | Type of body | Appointing authority | Whether judge required by law (Y/N) |
|---|---|---|---|---|---|---|
| 4. Justice S. N. Phukan | 31 March 2002 | Chairman of the Tehelka Commission (January 2004) | 2 years | Commission ofenquiry set up by the government by notification under the Commission of Inquiry Act | By central or state government with approval of parliament/SL | N |
| 5. Justice R. P. Sethi | 06 July 2002 | Chairman, Jammu and Kashmir State Accountability Commission (27 August 2005) | 3 years | Statutory body; (Jammu and Kashmir Accountability Commission Act) | Governor on recommendations of committee comprising government, opposition and CJ HC | Y |
| 6. Justice B. N. Kirpal | 07 November 2002 | Chairman, National Forest Commission, (February 2003) | 3 months | Executive authority constituted by notification by Ministry of Environment and Forests | Union executive | N |
| 7. Justice U. C. Banerjee | 17 November 2002 | Commission to enquire into Godhra violence | 4 years (exact date unavailable) | Commission of enquiry | By central or state government with approval of Parliament/ SL | N |

| | | | | | | |
|---|---|---|---|---|---|---|
| 8. Justice G. B. Pattanaik | 18 December 2002 | – | – | – | – | – |
| 9. Justice S. S. M. Quadri | 04 April 2003 | Chairman, Authority on Advance Rulings | Date not available | Statutory body (Income Tax Act, 1961) | Central Government | Y |
| 10. Justice V. N. Khare | 01 May 2004 | – | – | – | – | – |
| 11. Justice M. B. Shah | 24 September 2003 | Commission on Enquiry on Illegal Mining; State Government commissions in Gujarat regarding corruption and encounter killings | Dates not available | Commission of enquiry | By central or state government with approval of Parliament/SL | N |
| 12. Justice S. Rajendra Babu | 31 May 2004 | Chairman, NHRC (2 April 2007), Pay Revision Commission (Kerala), (20.2.2010) | 3 years | Statutory body (Protection of Human Rights Act, 1993); other executive body (Pay Revision Commission) | Political Committee with government and opposition after consultation with CJI for sitting judges | Y and N |

| Judge | Date of retirement | Post-retirement appointment (with dates when available) | When appointed after retirement | Type of body | Appointing authority | Whether judge required by law (Y/N) |
|---|---|---|---|---|---|---|
| 13. Justice Doraiswamy Raju | 01 July 2004 | Chairman, National Railway Rates Tribunal (28.8.2004) | 2 months | Statutory body (Railways Act, 1989) | Not mentioned specifically; presumably Railway Ministry | Y |
| 14. Justice Brijesh Kumar | 09 June 2004 | Chairman, Krishna Water Dispute tribunal (Tribunal constituted in April 2004; effective date 1.2.2006) | 20 months | Statutory body (Interstate River Water Disputes Act, 1956) | Central government (nominated by the CJI amongst sitting or retired judges) | Y |
| 15. Justice N. Santosh Hegde | 15 June 2005 | Chairman TDSAT, 27.6.2005; Karnataka Lok Ayukta | 1 month | Statutory body (TRAI Act, 1997); Statutory body—Lokayukta, Karnataka (Karnataka Lokayukta Act, 1984) | Central government (in consultation with the CJI); Governor on advice of CM in consultation with committee of government, opposition and CJ | Y and Y |

| | | | | | | |
|---|---|---|---|---|---|---|
| 16. Justice R. C. Lahoti | 31 October 2005 | – | – | – | – | – |
| 17. Justice S. N. Variava | 07 November 2005 | Arunachal/Assam Local Commission (25.9.2006) | 11 months | Commission appointed by the SC | Supreme Court | – |
| 18. Justice D. M. Dharmadhikari | 13 August 2005 | Chairperson, MP Human Rights Commission, Civil Aviation Ministry Committee on Air India | Date not available | Statutory body—MP Human Rights Commission (Protection of Human Rights Act, 1993); other executive body (Civil Aviation Ministry Committee) | Governor on recommendations of committee consisting of government and opposition; Civil Aviation Ministry | Y and N |
| 19. Justice P. Venkatarama Reddi | 09 August 2005 | Chairman, Authority on Advance Rulings (March 2007); Chairman Law Commission of India (1.9.2009) | 14 months | Statutory body—Authority on Advance Rulings (Income Tax Act, 1961); non-statutory post appointed by the Government of India (Law Commission of India) | Central government; Law Ministry for Law Commission | Y and Y (by convention) |

| Judge | Date of retirement | Post-retirement appointment (with dates when available) | When appointed after retirement | Type of body | Appointing authority | Whether judge required by law (Y/N) |
|---|---|---|---|---|---|---|
| 20. Justice Shivaraj V. Patil | 11 January 2005 | Karnataka Lokayukta (July 2011); Telecom Commission (pricing of 2G auction) | 6 years | Statutory body—Lokayukta, Karnataka (Karnataka Lokayukta Act, 1984); executive body (Telecom Commission)—set up by Office Memorandum of the Ministry of Communica-tions & Information Technology | Governor on advice of CM in consultation with committee of government, opposition and CJ | Y and N |
| 21. Justice Ruma Pal | 02 June 2006 | – | – | – | – | – |
| 22. Justice B. N. Srikrishna | 20 May 2006 | Chairman, Financial Sector Legislative Reforms Commission (24.3.2011); Telengana Commission | 5 years | Executive body; set up by government notification; commissions of enquiry | Finance Ministry; Standard COI appointment | N and N |

| | | | | | | | |
|---|---|---|---|---|---|---|---|
| 23. | Justice Arun Kumar | 11 April 2006 | Chairman, TDSAT (6.9.2006) | 5 months | Statutory body (TRAI Act, 1997) | Central government (in consultation with the CJI) | Y |
| 24. | Justice Y. K. Sabharwal | 13 January 2007 | – | – | – | – | – |
| 25. | Justice A. R. Lakshmanan | 21 March 2007 | Chairman, Law Commission of India (May 2007); Mullaperiyar Panel (exact date not available) | 2 months | Non-statutory post appointed by the Government of India (Law Commission of India): state representative on SC-appointed panel (Mullaperiyar Panel) | Law Ministry; state executive | Y (by convention) and N |
| 26. | Justice B. P. Singh | 08 July /2007 | – | – | – | – | – |
| 27. | Jutice P. K. Balasubramanyan | 27 August 2007 | Chairman, Authority on Advance Rulings (IT Act) | Date not available | Statutory body (Income Tax Act, 1961) | Central government | Y |
| 28. | Justice H. K. Sema | 01 June 2008 | Chairman, UP Human Rights Commission, 2008 (exact date unavailable) | Within 1 year | Statutory body (Protection of Human Rights Act, 1993) | Governor on recommendations of committee consisting of government and opposition (CJI if sitting) | Y |

| Judge | Date of retirement | Post-retirement appointment (with dates when available) | When appointed after retirement | Type of body | Appointing authority | Whether judge required by law (Y/N) |
|---|---|---|---|---|---|---|
| 29. Justice G. P. Mathur | 19 January 2008 | Member, NHRC, (15.04.2008) | 3 months | Statutory body (Protection of Human Rights Act, 1993) | Political Committee with government and opposition after consultation with CJI for sitting judges | Y |
| 30. Justice Ashok Bhan | 02 October 2008 | Chairperson, National Consumer Disputes Redressal Commission (October 2008) | Within 1 month | Statutory body (Consumer Protection Act, 1986) | Central government on recommendation by a selection committee of a SC judge, Secretary DLA, Secretary, Consumer Affairs | Y |
| 31. Justice P. P. Naolekar | 29 June 2008 | Lokayukta in MP (November 2011) | 3 years 5 months | Statutory body (Madhya Pradesh Lokayukt evam Up-Lokayukt Adhiniyam, 1981) | Government after consultation with CJ HC and LO | Y |

| | | | | | | |
|---|---|---|---|---|---|---|
| 32. Justice A. K. Mathur | 07 August 2008 | Chairperson, Armed Forces Tribunal (August 2008) | Within 1 month | Statutory body (Armed Forces Tribunals Act, 2007) | Sec. 6 and 7: President after consultation with CJI | Y |
| 33. Justice C. K. Thakker | 10 November 2008 | – | – | – | – | – |
| 34. Justice Tarun Chatterjee | 14 January 2009 | Arunachal Commission | Prior to retirement, by SC order | Commission appointed by SC | Supreme Court | – |
| 35. Justice Lokeshwar Singh Panta | 23 April 2009 | Chairman, National Green Tribunal: HP Lok Ayukta | Less than 2 years (exact dates unavailable) | Statutory body (National Green Tribunal Act, 2010; Himachal Pradesh Lokayukta Act, 1983) | Section 6(2)—Chairperson by central government in consultation with CJI; HP Lokayukta—Government after consultation with CJ HC and LO | Y and Y |
| 36. Justice S. B. Sinha | 08 August 2009 | Chairman, TDSAT: (3.11.2009) | 3 months | Statutory body (TRAI Act, 1997) | Central government (in consultation with the CJI) | Y |

| Judge | Date of retirement | Post-retirement appointment (with dates when available) | When appointed after retirement | Type of body | Appointing authority | Whether judge required by law (Y/N) |
|---|---|---|---|---|---|---|
| 37. Justice Arijit Pasayat | 10 May 2009 | Chairman, Competition Appellate Tribunal: (20.5.2009); Chairman, AAR (CBEC) | 10 days | Statutory body (Competition Act, 2002) | Central government after recommendations of committee of judge of SC and two secretaries (like consumer commission) | Y and Y |
| 38. Justice B. N. Agrawal | 15 October 2009 | Chairman, Vansadhara Water Dispute Tribunal (24.1.2010) | Less than 1 year (resigned) | Statutory body (Interstate River Water Disputes Act, 1956) | Central government (nomination of CJI) | Y |
| 39. Justice K. G. Balakrishnan | 11 May 2010 | Chairman, National Human Rights Commission (7.6.2010) | 1 month | Statutory body (Protection of Human Rights Act, 1993) | Political Committee with government and opposition after consultation with CJI for sitting judges | Y |

| | | | | | | | |
|---|---|---|---|---|---|---|---|
| 40. | Justice H. S. Bedi | 04 September 2011 | Jammu and Kashmir Commission of Enquiry (November 2011); SC monitoring committee on encounter killings in Gujarat (March 2012) | 2 months | Commission of enquiry; SC committee | Commission of Enquiry; Supreme Court Committee | N |
| 41. | Justice J. M. Panchal | 05 October 2011 | Chairman, Mahadayi Water Disputes Tribunal (January 2012) | 4 months | Statutory body (Interstate River Water Disputes Act, 1956) | Central government (nomination of CJI) | Y |
| 42. | Justice B. Sudershan Reddy | 07 July 2011 | Lok Ayukta, Goa (March 2013) | 18 months | Statutory body (Goa Lokayukta Act, 2011) | Government after consultation with CJ HC and LO | Y |

| Judge | Date of retirement | Post-retirement appointment (with dates when available) | When appointed after retirement | Type of body | Appointing authority | Whether judge required by law (Y/N) |
|---|---|---|---|---|---|---|
| 43. Justice V. S. Sirpurkar | 21 August 2011 | Chairman, Competition Appellate Tribunal (July 2012) | 1 year | Statutory body (Competition Act, 2002) | Central government after recommendations of committee of Judge of SC and two secretaries (like consumer commission) | Y |
| 44. Justice Mukundakam Sharma | 17 September 2011 | Chairman, Vansadhara Water Dispute Tribunal | Nominated/ Apointed before retirement on 30.3.2011 | Statutory body (Interstate River Water Disputes Act, 1956) | Central government (nomination by CJI) | Y |

| | | | | | | |
|---|---|---|---|---|---|---|
| 45. Justice Markandey Katju | 19 September 2011 | Chairman, Press Council of India (5.10.12) | 1 month | Statutory body (Press Council Act, 1978) | Committee comprising Chairman RS, Speaker LS and a member of the Press Council to nominate chairperson | N |
| 46. Justice R. V. Raveendran | 15 October 2011 | – | – | – | – | – |
| 47. Justice Cyriac Joseph* | 27 January 2012 | – | – | – | – | – |
| 48. Justice A. K. Ganguly | 03 February 2012 | Chairman, West Bengal Human Rights Commission (March 2012) | Within 2 months | Statutory body (Protection of Human Rights Act, 1993) | Governor on recommendations of committee consisting of government and opposition (and CJI if sitting judge) | Y |

* Was appointed as Member, NHRC, after cut-off date of research and hence not considered for the analysis.

| Judge | Date of retirement | Post-retirement appointment (with dates when available) | When appointed after retirement | Type of body | Appointing authority | Whether judge required by law (Y/N) |
|---|---|---|---|---|---|---|
| 49. Justice Deepak Verma | 28 August 2012 | – | – | – | – | – |
| 50. Justice S. H. Kapadia | 28 September 2012 | – | – | – | – | – |

*Notes*: Abbreviation key:

CJ = Chief Justice

CM = Chief Minister

HC = High Court

SL = State Legislature(s)

CJI = Chief Justice of India

LO = Leader of Opposition in Parliament

SC = Supreme Court

The cut-off date of retirement of judges from the Supreme Court for this study is 1 October 2012 and post-retirement appointments updated till 1 April 2013.

*Source*: Author.

# Bibliography

## Journal Articles

Andrews, Penelope. 'The South African Judicial Appointments Process.' *Osgoode Hall Law Journal* 44 (2006): 565–72.

Barber, Nick. 'Prelude to the Separation of Powers.' *The Cambridge Law Journal* 60 (2001): 59–88.

Barberis, Peter. 'The New Public Management and a New Accountability.' *Public Administration* 76 (1998): 451–70.

Benesh, Sara. 'Understanding Public Confidence in American Courts.' *The Journal of Politics* 68, no. 3 (2006): 697–707.

Berger, Raoul 'Impeachment of Judges and "Good Behavior" Tenure.' *The Yale Law Journal* 79, no. 8 (1970): 1475–531.

Bermant, Gordon, and Russell R. Wheeler. 'Federal Judges and the Judicial Branch: Their Independence and Accountability.' *The Mercer Law Review* 46 (1995): 835.

Bhushan, Prashant. 'The Dinakaran Imbroglio: Appointments and Complaints against Judges.' *Economic and Political Weekly* 44, nos 41–42 (2009): 10–12.

Bopp, James, Jr., and Josiah Neeley. 'How Not to Reform Judicial Elections: Davis, White, and the Future of Judicial Campaign Financing.' *Denver University Law Review* 86 (2008): 195.

Bovens, Mark. 'Analysing and Assessing Public Accountability: A Conceptual Framework.' *European Law Journal* 13, no. 4 (2007): 447–68.

Brand, Rachel. 'Judicial Appointments: Checks and Balances in Practice.' *Harvard Journal of Law and Public Policy* 33, no. 1 (2010): 47–52.

Breyer, Stephen G. 'Judicial Independence in the United States.' *Saint Louis University Law Journal* 40 (1996): 989.

Brody, David C. 'The Use of Judicial Performance Evaluation to Enhance Judicial Accountability, Judicial Independence and Public Trust.' *Denver University Law Review* 86 (2008): 115–56.

Burin, Frederic S. 'The Theory of the Rule of Law and the Structure of the Constitutional State.' *The American University Law Review* 5, no. 3 (1966): 313.

Calabresi, S. G., and G. Lawson. 'The Unitary Executive, Jurisdiction Stripping, and the Hamdan Opinions: A Textualist Response to Justice Scalia.' *Columbia Law Review* 107 (2007): 1002–48.

Caldeira, Gregory A. 'Neither the Purse Nor the Sword: Dynamics of Public Confidence in the Supreme Court.' *The American Political Science Review* 80, no. 4 (1986): 1209–26.

Caldeira, Gregory A., and James Gibson. 'The Etiology of Public Support for the Supreme Court.' *American Journal of Political Science* 36 (1992): 635–64.

Cameron, Edwin. 'Judicial Accountability in South Africa.' *South African Journal on Human Rights* 6 (1990): 251–65.

Cappelletti, Mauro. 'Who Watches the Watchmen? A Comparative Study on Judicial Responsibility.' *The American Journal of Comparative Law* 31, no. 1 (1983): 1–62.

Carnwath, Robert. 'Tribunal Justice: A New Start.' *Public Law* (2009): 48–69.

Carpenter, William Seal. 'The Separation of Powers in the Eighteenth Century.' *American Political Science Review* 22, no. 1 (1928): 32–44.

Chakravartty, Nikhil. 'Reflections on Impeachment Debate.' *Mainstream* 31, no. 28 (1993): 5.

Chandrachud, Abhinav. 'The Need to Have a Uniform Retirement Age for Judges.' *Economic and Political Weekly* 47, no. 46 (2012): 24–27.

Chayes, Abram. 'The Role of the Judge in Public Law Litigation.' *Harvard Law Review* 89 (1976): 1281–316.

Contini, Francesco, and Richard Mohr. 'Reconciling Independence and Accountability in Judicial Systems.' *Utrecht Law Review* 3, no. 2 (2007): 26–43.

Corder, Hugh. 'Judicial Authority in a Changing South Africa.' *Legal Studies* 24 (2004): 253–74.

Corson, James C. 'Judges and Statutory Tenure in England in the Seventeenth Century.' *Juridical Review* 42 (1930): 136.

Cottrell, Jill. 'The Indian Judges' Transfer Case.' *International and Comparative Law Quarterly* 33 (1984): 1032–45.

Dhavan, Rajeev. 'Removing Judges: The Quest for Fair Solutions.' *The Indian Advocate* XXIII (1991): 42–57.

Dua, Bhagwan D. 'A Study of Executive-Judicial Conflict: The Indian Case.' *Asian Survey* 23, no. 4 (1983): 463–83.

Eckhoff, Torstein. 'Impartiality, Separation of Powers and Judicial Independence.' *Scandinavian Studies* 9 (1965): 9–48.

'En Banc Review in Federal Circuit Courts: A Reassessment.' *Michigan Law Review* 72, no. 8 (1974): 1637–55.

Ferejohn, John. 'Independent Judges, Dependent Judiciary: Explaining Judicial Independence.' *Southern California Law Review* 72 (1998–99): 353–84.

Ferejohn, John, and Larry Kramer. 'Independent Judges, Dependent Judiciary: Institutionalizing Judicial Restraint.' *New York University Law Review* 77 (2002): 962–1039.

Fite, Warner. 'The Theory of Independence—Once More.' *Journal of Philosophy, Psychology and Scientific Methods* 10, no. 20 (1913): 546.

Flaherty, Martin S. 'The Most Dangerous Branch.' *The Yale Law Journal* 105, no. 7 (1996): 1725–839.

Fuller, Lon L., and Kenneth I. Winston. 'The Forms and Limits of Adjudication.' *Harvard Law Review* 92, no. 2 (1978): 353–409.

Gerhardt, Michael J. 'The Lessons of Impeachment History.' *The George Washington Law Review* 67 (1999): 603–25.

Geyh, Charles Gardner. 'Rescuing Judicial Accountability from the Realm of Political Rhetoric.' *Case Western Reserve Law Review* 56 (2006): 911–35.

Gibson, James L., Gregory A. Caldeira, and Vanessa A. Baird, 'On the Legitimacy of National High Courts,' *The American Political Science Review* 92, no. 2 (1998): 343–58.

Greene, Ian. 'The Doctrine of Judicial Independence Developed by the Supreme Court of Canada.' *Osgoode Hall Law Journal* 26 (1988): 177–206.

Grove, Tara Leigh. 'The Structural Safeguards of Federal Jurisdiction.' *Harvard Law Review* 124 (2011): 869–940.

Haines, Nicolas. 'Responsibility and Accountability.' *Philosophy* 30 (1955): 141–63.

Hope of Craighead, Lord. 'Judicial Independence.' *Supreme Laws Today* 13 (2002): 105.

Howe, Daniel Walker. 'Honest Abe: Abraham Lincoln and the Moral Character' (2008), 13 Footnotes (Foreign Policy Research Institute

Newsletter). Available at www.fpri.org/footnotes/1316.200806.howe.honestabemoralcharacter.html (accessed 21 August 2013).

Jayawickrama, Nihal. 'Developing a Concept of Judicial Accountability: The Judicial Integrity Group and the Bangalore Principles of Judicial Conduct.' *Commonwealth Law Bulletin* 28, no. 2 (2002): 1091–108.

Kamaroopi. 'Punishment Postings: Centres and Peripheries.' *Economic and Political Weekly* 37, no. 49 (2002): 4877.

Karlan, Pamela S. 'Two Concepts of Judicial Independence.' *Southern California Law Review* 72 (1998–99): 535–58.

Kaufman, Irving R. 'The Essence of Judicial Independence.' *Columbia Law Review* 80 (1980): 671–701.

Kekes, John. 'Constancy and Purity.' *Mind* XCII (1983): 499–518.

Kirby, Michael. 'Judicial Accountability in Australia.' *Legal Ethics* 6, no. 1 (2003): 41.

———. 'Judicial Integrity: A Global Social Contract.' *Commonwealth Law Bulletin* 29 (2003): 976.

Knight, C. J. S. 'Bipolar Sovereignty Restated.' *The Cambridge Law Journal* 68 (2009): 361–87.

Kourlis, Rebecca Love, and Jordan M. Singer. 'A Performance Evaluation Program for the Federal Judiciary.' *Denver University Law Review* 86 (2008): 7–51.

Laycock, D. 'Constitutional Theory Matters.' *Texas Law Review* 56 (1987): 767.

Le Sueur, A. 'Developing Mechanisms for Judicial Accountability in the UK.' *Legal Studies* 24, no. 1 (2004): 73–98.

Little, Laura E. 'Loyalty, Gratitude and the Federal Judiciary.' *American University Law Review* 44 (1995): 699.

Malleson, Kate 'Parliamentary Scrutiny of Supreme Court Nominees: A View from the United Kingdom.' *Osgoode Hall Law Journal* 44 (2006): 557–63.

Mason, Anthony. 'Judicial Independence and Separation of Powers, Some Problems Old and New.' *University of British Columbia Law Review* 24 (1990): 345–46.

McFall, Lynne. 'Integrity.' *Ethics* 98, no. 1 (1987): 5–20.

McLachlin, Beverly. 'Courts and Judges in the Framework of Accountability.' *Journal of Parliamentary and Political Law* 1 (2008): 293.

Mohr, Richard, and Francesco Contini. 'Judicial Evaluation in Context: Principles, Practices and Promise in Nine European Countries.' *European Journal of Legal Studies* 1 no. 2 (2007): 1.

Mtshaulana, Patrick, and Melanie Thomas. 'The Constitutional Court of South Africa: An Introduction.' *Review of Constitutional Studies* 3 (1996): 98–140.

Mulgan, Richard. 'Accountability: An Ever-Expanding Concept.' *Public Administration* 78, no. 3 (2000): 555–73.

Nagel, Thomas. 'Moral Conflict and Political Legitimacy.' *Philosophy & Public Affairs* 16, no. 3 (1987): 215–40.

'No Landmark, This.' *Economic and Political Weekly* 8, no. 18 (1973): 813–14.

Noorani, A. G. 'Transfer of High Court Judges.' *Economic and Political Weekly* 15, no. 38 (1980): 1578.

O'Connor, Sandra Day. 'Keynote Address: Symposium on State Judicial Independence—A National Concern.' *Seattle University Law Review* 33 (2010): 559–67.

Prakash, Saikrishna, and Smith, Steven D. 'How to Remove a Federal Judge.' *The Yale Law Journal* 116 (2006): 72–137.

———. 'Reply: (Mis)Understanding Good Behavior Tenure.' *The Yale Law Journal* 116 (2006): 159–69.

Reddy, V. R. 'Judges and Medals.' *The Indian Advocate* 31 (2000): 27

Redish, Martin. 'Good Behavior, Judicial Independence and the Foundations of American Constitutionalism.' *The Yale Law Journal* 116 (2006): 139–58.

———. 'Judicial Discipline, Judicial Independence and the Constitution: A Textual and Structural Analysis.' *Southern California Law Review* 72 (1999): 673.

Rehnquist, William H. 'Judicial Independence: Symposium Remarks.' *The University of Richmond Law Review* 38 (2004): 579–96.

Robinson, Nick. 'Expanding Judiciaries: India and the Rise of the Good Governance Court.' *Washington University Global Studies Law Review* 8 (2009): 1–69.

———. 'Structure Matters: The Impact of Court Structure on the Indian and US Supreme Courts.' *The American Journal of Comparative Law* 61, no. 1 (2013): 173–208.

Robinson, Nick, et al. 'Interpreting the Constitution: Supreme Court Constitution Benches since Independence.' *Economic and Political Weekly* 46, no. 9 (2011): 27–31.

Rodriguez-Garavito, Cesar. 'Beyond the Courtroom: The Impact of Judicial Activism on Socioeconomic Rights in Latin America.' *Texas Law Review* 89, no. 7 (2011): 1669–98.

Romzek, Barbara, and Melvin Dubnick. 'Accountability in the Public Sector: Lessons from the Challenger Tragedy.' *Public Administration Review* 47, no. 3 (1987): 227–38.

Rosenberg, Gerald N. 'Judicial Independence and the Reality of Political Power.' *The Review of Politics* 55, no. 3 (1992): 369–88.

Sathe, S. P. 'Accountability of the Supreme Court.' *Economic and Political Weekly* 37, no. 15 (2002): 1383–84.

Schotland, Roy A. 'Six Fatal Flaws: A Comment on Bopp and Neeley.' *Denver University Law Review* 86 (2008): 233–49.

Sengupta, Arghya. 'Appointment of Judges and the Basic Structure Doctrine in India.' *Law Quarterly Review* 132 (2016): 201.

Shapiro, Scott. 'Judicial Independence: The English Experience.' *North Carolina Law Review* 55 (1977): 577–652.

Singh, M. P. 'Merit in the Appointment of Judges.' *SCC Journal* 8 (1998): 1.

Smith, Christopher E. 'Federal Judicial Salaries: A Critical Appraisal.' *Temple Law Review* 62 (1989): 849–73.

Smith, Joseph H. 'An Independent Judiciary: The Colonial Background.' *University Of Pennsylvania Law Review* 124 (1976): 1104–56.

Spigelman, J. J. 'Judicial Accountability and Performance Indicators.' *Civil Justice Quarterly* 21 (2002): 18.

Stevens, Robert. 'The Act of Settlement and the Questionable History of Judicial Independence.' *Oxford University Commonwealth Law Journal* 1 (2001): 253–67.

Steyn, Johan. 'The Case for a Supreme Court.' *Law Quarterly Review* 118 (2002): 382–96.

Steytler, Chris, and Iain Field. 'The "Institutional Integrity" Principle: Where Are We Now, and Where Are We headed?' *The University of Western Australia Law Review* 35 (2011): 227–64.

Stone, Bruce. 'Administrative Accountability in the "Westminster" Democracies: Towards A New Conceptual Framework.' *Governance* 8, no. 4 (1995): 505–26.

Taylor, Gabriele. 'Integrity.' *Proceedings of the Aristotelian Society* (Supplementary Volumes) 55 (1981): 143–59.

Teehan, John. 'Character, Integrity and Dewey's Virtue Ethics.' *Transactions of the Charles S Peirce Society* 31, no. 4 (1995): 841–63.

Tushnet, Mark. 'Principle, Politics and Constitutional Law.' *Michigan Law Review* 88, no. 1 (1989): 49–81.

Vanberg, George. 'Establishing Judicial Independence in West Germany: The Impact of Opinion Leadership and the Separation of Powers.' *Comparative Politics* 32, no. 3 (2000): 333–53.

Vicente, Jason J. 'Impeachment: A Constitutional Primer.' *Texas Review of Law and Politics* 3 (1998): 117.

Vijaywargiya, M. 'No Allocation of Judicial Work to a Judge under Impeachment: Need for Constitutional Amendment.' *Indian Bar Review* 27, no. 1 (2000): 163.

Waldron, Jeremy. 'Separation of Powers in Thought and Practice.' *Boston College Law Review* 54, no. 2 (2013): 433–68.

Woodhouse, Diana. 'United Kingdom: The Constitutional Reform Act 2005—Defending Judicial Independence the English Way.' ' *International Journal of Constitutional Law* 5 (2007): 153–65.

Wright, Benjamin F. 'The Origins of the Separation of Powers in America.' *Economica* 40 (1933): 169–85.

## Monographs

Agnihotri, V. K. *Impeachment of a Judge in the Indian Parliament*. Kampala: Communication to Association of Secretary Generals of Parliament, 2012. Available at www.asgp.info/Resources/Data/Documents/WJPUTLJMWGFXUZDYEQLPKUDKVXTAPQ.doc (accessed 10 September 2013).

Andhyarujina, T. R. *The Kesavananda Bharati Case*. Gurgaon: Universal Law Publishing, 2011.

Austin, Granville. *Working a Democratic Constitution: The Indian Experience*. Oxford: Oxford University Press, 1999.

Aylmer, G. E. *The King's Servants*. London: Routledge and Kegan Paul, 1974.

Barak, Aharon. *Purposive Interpretation in Law*. Princeton: Princeton University Press, 2005.

Barber, Sotirios. A. *The Constitution of Judicial Power*. London: Johns Hopkins University Press, 1993.

Baxi, Upendra. *The Indian Supreme Court and Politics*. Lucknow: Eastern Book Co., 1980.

Becker, Carl L. *The Declaration of Independence: A Study in the History of Political Ideas*. New York: Vintage Books, 1958.

Berger, Raoul. *Impeachment: The Constitutional Problems*. Cambridge: Harvard University Press, 1974.

Bhushan, Shanti. *Courting Destiny: A Memoir*. New Delhi: Penguin, 2008.

Bhuwania, Anuj. *Courting the People: Public Interest Litigation in Post-Emergency India*. Cambridge: Cambridge University Press, 2016.

Chandrachud, Abhinav. *The Informal Constitution*. New Delhi: Oxford University Press, 2014.

Das, Gobind. *The Supreme Court in Quest of Identity*. 2nd ed. Lucknow: Eastern Book Co., 2000.

Day, Patricia, and Rudolf Klein. *Accountabilities: Five Public Services*. London: Tavistock Publishers, 1987.

Dworkin, Ronald. *Law's Empire*. Cambridge: Belknap Press, 1986.

Dyzenhaus, David. *Judging the Judges, Judging Ourselves: Truth, Reconciliation and the Apartheid Legal Order*. Oxford: Hart Publishing, 2003.

Eagleton, Terence. *Shakespeare and Society: Critical Studies in Shakespearean Drama*. London: Chatto and Windus, 1976.

Eaton, Dorman Bridgeman. *Should Judges Be Elected? Or the Experiment of an Elective Judiciary in New York*. New York: JW Amerman, 1873.

Epstein, David F. *The Political Theory of the Federalist*. Chicago: University of Chicago Press, 1984.

Gadbois, G. H., Jr. *Judges of the Supreme Court of India: 1950–1989*. New Delhi: Oxford University Press, 2011.

Gajendragadkar, P. B. *To the Best of My Memory*. Mumbai: Bharatiya Vidya Bhavan, 1983.

Godbole, Madhav. *The Judiciary and Governance in India*. New Delhi: Rupa & Co., 2009.

Gray, John Chipman. *The Nature and Sources of Law*. New York: Columbia University Press, 1909.

Gupta, Vijay K., *Decision Making in the Supreme Court of India*. New Delhi: Kaveri Books, 1995.

Hamilton, Alexander, James Madison and John Jay. *The Federalist*. Cambridge: Belknap Press, 2009.

Hammond, Grant. *Judicial Recusal: Principles, Process and Problems*. Oxford: Hart Publishing, 2009.

Hart, H. L. A. *The Concept of Law*. Oxford: Clarendon Press, 1963.

Hausegger, Lori, Matthew Henniger and Troy Riddell. *Canadian Courts: Law, Politics and Process*. Don Mills: Oxford University Press, 2009.

Krishna Iyer, V. R. *Justice at Crossroads*. New Delhi: Deep and Deep, 1992.

Kumaramangalam, Mohan. *Judicial Appointments: An Analysis of the Recent Controversy over the Appointment of the Chief Justice of India*. New Delhi: Oxford & IBH Pub. Co., 1973.

Leuchtenburg, William. *Franklin D. Roosevelt and the New Deal*. New York: Harper and Row, 1963.

Malleson, Kate. *The New Judiciary: The Effects of Expansion and Activism*. Ashgate/Dartmouth, 1999.

Marshall, T. David. *Judicial Conduct and Accountability*. Scarborough: Carswell, 1995.

Masterman, Roger. *Separation of Powers in the Contemporary Constitution: Judicial Competence and Independence in the United Kingdom*. Cambridge: Cambridge University Press, 2011.

McIlwain, C. H. *Constitutionalism and the Changing World: Collected Papers*. Cambridge: Cambridge University Press, 1939.

Mulgan, Richard. *Holding Power to Account: Accountability in Modern Democracies*. London/Basingstoke: Palgrave Macmillan, 2003.

Nariman, Fali. *God Save the Hon'ble Supreme Court*. New Delhi: Hay House Publishers, 2018.

Noorani, A. G. *Constitutional Questions and Citizens' Rights*. Oxford: Oxford University Press, 2006.

Organisation for Democratic Institutions and Human Rights. '*Strengthening Judicial Independence and Public Access to Justice*.' (OSCE Human Dimension Seminar Consolidated Summary, Warsaw 17–19 May 2010).

Palkhivala, N. A. *Our Constitution: Defaced and Defiled*. New Delhi: MacMillan, 1974.

Paul, Santosh. *Appointing Our Judges: Forging Independence and Accountability*. Gurugram: LexisNexis, 2015.

Pocock, J. G. A. *The Machiavellian Moment: Florentine Political Thought and the Atlantic Republican Tradition*. Princeton: Princeton University Press, 1975.

Rehnquist, William H. *Grand Inquests: The Historic Impeachments of Justice Samuel Chase and President Andrew Johnson*. New York: William Morrow, 1992.

Roberts, Jennifer T. *Accountability in Athenian Government*. Madison: University of Wisconsin Press, 1982.

Sahay, S. *Gone at Last? The Story of V Ramaswami's Impeachment*. New Delhi: Har Anand Publications, 1993.

Sathe, S. P. *The Tribunal System in India*. Mumbai: NM Tripathi, 1996.

Seervai, H. M. *Constitutional Law of India*. 4th ed. New Delhi: Universal Law Publishing 2008 rep.

———. *The Emergency, Future Safeguards and the Habeas Corpus Case: A Criticism*. Mumbai: NM Tripathi Pvt Ltd., 1978.

Shiva Rao, B., et al. *The Framing of India's Constitution, Select Documents*. New Delhi: The Indian Institute of Public Administration, 1966.

Shourie, Arun. *Mrs. Gandhi's Second Reign*. New Delhi: Vikas Publishing House, 1983.

Sinha, B. P. *Reminiscences and Reflections of a Chief Justice*. New Delhi: BK Publishing, 1985.

Sodhi, S. S. Justice. *The Other Side of Justice*. New Delhi: Hay House India, 2007.

Soeharno, Jonathan. *The Integrity of a Judge: A Philosophical Inquiry*. Farnham: Ashgate, 2009.

Stevens, Robert. *The English Judges: Their Role in the Changing Constitution*. Oxford: Hart Publishing, 2002.

Veeraswami, K. *The Perils to Justice: A Judge Thinks Aloud*. Kolkata: Eastern Law House, 1996.

Vile, M. J. C. *Constitutionalism and the Separation of Powers*. 2nd ed. Indianapolis: Liberty Fund, 1998.

Weill, Herman. *Frederick the Great and Samuel von Cocceji: A Study in the Reform of the Prussian Judicial Administration 1740-1755*. Madison: The State Historical Society of Wisconsin, 1961.

Woodhouse, Diana. *The Office of the Lord Chancellor*. Oxford: Hart Publishing, 2001.

## Edited Books

Broom, Herbert, and Edward Hadley, eds. *Blackstone's Commentaries on the Laws of England*. London: Maxwell, 1869.

Brown, Lesley, ed. *The New Shorter Oxford English Dictionary*. 4th ed. Oxford: Clarendon Press, 1993.

Canivet, Guy, Mads Andenas and Duncan Fairgrieve, eds. *Independence, Accountability and the Judiciary*. London: British Institute of International and Comparative Law, 2006.

Cohler, Anne, Basia Miller and Harold Stone, eds. *Montesquieu's The Spirit of Laws*. Cambridge: Cambridge University Press, 1989.

Jai, Janak Raj, ed. *Assault on Judiciary and the Role of Parliament*. New Delhi: Associated Legal Advisers, 1995.

Malleson, Kate, and Peter H. Russell, eds. *Appointing Judges in an Age of Judicial Power: Critical Perspectives from Around the World*. Toronto; Buffalo: University of Toronto Press, 2007.

Nayar, Kuldip, ed. *Supersession of Judges*. New Delhi: Indian Book Co., 1973.

Onions, C. T., ed. *The Oxford Dictionary of English Etymology*. Oxford: Clarendon Press, 1966.

Paul, Santosh, ed. *Choosing Hammurabi: Debates on Judicial Appointments*. Gurugram: LexisNexis, 2013.

Sengupta, Arghya, and Ritwika Sharma, eds. *Appointment of Judges to the Supreme Court of India: Transparency, Accountability and Independence*. New Delhi: Oxford University Press, 2018.

Stevenson, Angus, ed. *The Oxford Dictionary of English*. 3rd ed. Oxford: Oxford University Press, 2010. Available at http://www.oxfordreference.com/view/10.1093/acref/9780199571123.001.0001/m_en_gb0661030 (accessed 27 September 2013).

Tate, C. Neal, and T. Vallinder, eds. *The Global Expansion of Judicial Power*. New York; London: New York University Press, 1995.

## Chapters in Edited Books

Andhyarujina, T. R. 'A Committed Judiciary: Indira Gandhi and Judicial Appointments'. In *Appointment of Judges to the Supreme Court of India:*

*Transparency, Accountability and Independence*, edited by Arghya Sengupta and Ritwika Sharma. New Delhi: Oxford University Press, 2018.

Baxi, Upendra. 'The Avatars of Indian Judicial Activism: Explorations in the Geography of (In)justice.' In *Fifty Years of the Supreme Court of India: Its Grasp and Reach*, edited by S. K. Verma and K. Kusum. New Delhi: Oxford University Press, 2000.

——. 'The Myth and Reality of Judicial Independence: The Judges Case and All That.' In *Courage, Craft and Contention: The Indian Supreme Court in the Eighties*, edited by Upendra Baxi. Mumbai: NM Tripathi Pvt. Ltd., 1985.

Cooke of Thorndon, Lord. 'Where Angels Fear to Tread.' In *Supreme but Not Infallible: Essays in Honour of the Supreme Court of India*, edited by B. N. Kirpal, et al. New Delhi: Oxford University Press, 2000.

Epstein, Lee, Jack Knight and Olga Shvetsova. 'Selecting Selection Systems.' In *Judicial Independence at the Crossroads: An Interdisciplinary Approach*, edited by Stephen B. Burbank and Barry Friedman. Thousand Oaks: Sage Publications, 2002.

Friedman, Barry. 'History, Politics and Judicial Independence.' In *Judicial Integrity*, edited by András Sajò. Leiden; Boston: Martinus Nijhoff Publishers, 2004.

Ginsburg, Tom. 'Judicial Independence in East Asia: Lessons for China.' In *Judicial Independence in China: Lessons for Global Rule of Law Promotion*, edited by Randall Peerenboom. Cambridge: Cambridge University Press, 2010.

Locke, John. 'An Essay Concerning the True Original, Extent, and End of Civil Government.' In *Two Treatises of Government*, edited by Peter Laslett. Cambridge: Cambridge University Press, 1988.

Nariman, Fali. 'A Case I Won—But Which I Would Prefer to Have Lost.' In *Before Memory Fades: An Autobiography*, edited by Fali S. Nariman. Carlsbad: Hay House, 2010.

——. 'Judicial Independence in India.' In *Democracy, Human Rights and the Rule of Law: Essays in Honour of Nani Palkhivala*, edited by Venkat Iyer. New Delhi: Butterworths, 2000.

Rajamani, Lavanya, and Arghya Sengupta. 'The Supreme Court.' In *The Oxford Companion to Politics in India*, edited by Niraja Gopal Jayal and Pratap Bhanu Mehta. New Delhi: Oxford University Press, 2010.

Schepple, Kim Lane. 'Declarations of Independence: Judicial Reactions to Political Pressure.' In *Judicial Independence at the Crossroads: An Interdisciplinary Approach*, edited by Stephen B. Burbank and Barry Friedman. Thousand Oaks: Sage Publications, 2002.

Sengupta, Arghya. 'Justice Chelameswar's Dissent: Reforming to Preserve'. In *Appointment of Judges to the Supreme Court of India: Transparency, Accountability and Independence*, edited by Arghya Sengupta and Ritwika Sharma. New Delhi: Oxford University Press, 2018.

Tulzapurkar, V. D. 'Our Judicial System.' In *Selection and Appointment of Supreme Court Judges: A Case Study*, edited by Rajeev Dhavan and Alice Jacob. Mumbai: NM Tripathi Pvt Ltd., 1978.

## Newspaper and Magazine Articles

Anand, Utkarsh. 'How Judges Appoint Judges, the Debate around It.' *Indian Express*, New Delhi, 15 November 2016. Available at http://indianexpress.com/article/explained/collegium-system-supreme-court-how-judges-are-appointed-and-transferred-the-debate-around-it-4375719/ (accessed 1 March 2017).

———. 'SC Steps in after Madras HC Judge Stays Own Transfer,' *The Indian Express*, 16 February 2016, available at http://indianexpress.com/article/india/india-news-india/justice-c-s-karnan-supreme-court-to-madras-high-court/ (accessed 5 September 2016).

Ananthakrishnan, G., and S. Singh. 'Govt. Snubs Supreme Court.' *Indian Express*, 27 April 2018. Available at https://indianexpress.com/article/india/govt-rejects-joseph-supreme-court-judge-all-eyes-on-chief-dipak-misra-5153173/ (accessed 23 July 2018).

Andhyarujina, T. R. 'Disciplining the Judges.' *The Hindu*, 19 February 2010. Available at www.thehindu.com/opinion/lead/disciplining-the-judges/article109167.ece (accessed 19 December 2012).

———. 'Appointment of Judges by Collegium of Judges.' *The Hindu*, 18 December 2009. Available at http://beta.thehindu.com/opinion/op-ed/article66672.ece (accessed 13 May 2010).

———. 'The Age of Judicial Reform.' *The Hindu*, 1 September 2012. Available at www.thehindu.com/opinion/lead/the-age-of-judicial-reform/article3845041.ece (accessed 10 February 2014).

Bhatia, Gautam. 'Upsetting a Very Fine Balance.' *The Hindu*, New Delhi, 20 February 2017. Available at http://www.thehindu.com/todays-paper/tp-opinion/upsetting-a-very-fine-balance/article17331540.ece (accessed 1 March 2017).

Bhatt, Sheela. 'Memorandum of Procedure: Behind the Scenes, Govt and SC in Tug of War over Appointments and Turf.' *Indian Express*, 15 July 2016. Available at https://indianexpress.com/article/india/india-news-india/supreme-court-high-court-judge-appointment-procedure-criteria-collegium-government-judiciary-2914823/ (accessed 24 July 2018).

Bhushan, Ranjit, and Purabi Patnaik. 'Whose Right Is It Anyway?' *Outlook*, 3 August 1998. Available at www.outlookindia.com/article.aspx?205943 (accessed 13 May 2010).

Chandrachud, Abhinav. 'The Age Factor.' *Frontline* 28, no. 21 (October 2011). Available at www.frontline.in/static/html/fl2821/stories/20111021282104900.htm (accessed 13 April 2014).

Chatterjee, Avijit. 'You Were Wrong, My Lords.' *The Telegraph* (Kolkata), 2 August 2015. Available at https://www.telegraphindia.com/1150802/jsp/7days/story_34917.jsp (accessed 1 March 2017).

Chhibber, Maneesh. 'MoP on Appointments: SC Puts Its Foot Down, Rejects Govt Plan to Veto Postings on National Security Grounds.' *Indian Express*, 24 March 2017. Available at https://indianexpress.com/article/india/mop-on-appointments-sc-puts-its-foot-down-rejects-govt-plan-to-veto-postings-on-national-security-grounds-collegium-4582978/ (accessed 24 July 2018).

———. 'CJI Wants Future Judges to Clarify If Kin Practising in Court.' *Indian Express*, New Delhi, 11 November 2008. Available at www.indianexpress.com/news/cji-wants-future-judges-to-clarify-if-kin-practising-in-court/383993/0 (accessed 8 January 2013).

———. 'Jurists Protest Transfer of Delhi High Court Judge Who Gave Greenpeace Case Order.' *Indian Express*, 1 March 2016. Available at https://indianexpress.com/article/india/india-news-india/jurists-protest-transfer-of-delhi-hc-judge-who-gave-greenpeace-case-order/ (accessed 21 February 2017).

*Daily News and Analysis*. 'Mayawati Writes to PM on Dinakaran Issue.' 19 December 2009. Available at www.dnaindia.com/india/1325456/report-mayawati-writes-to-pm-on-dinakaran-issue (accessed 17 June 2013).

Divan, Anil. 'Judging the Judges.' *Indian Express*, 5 December 2002. Available at www.indianexpress.com/storyOld.php?storyId=14190 (accessed 19 December 2012).

*Economic Times*. 'Ex-Solicitor General, Former CBI Chiefs Accused of Targeting Amit Shah.' 27 June 2014. Available at http://articles.economictimes.indiatimes.com/2014-06-27/news/50912371_1_amit-shah-sohrabuddin-case-sohrabuddin-sheikh (accessed 1 July 2014).

Forum for Judicial Accountability. 'Issues of Deep Concern.' *Outlook*, 16 September 2009. Available at www.outlookindia.com/article.aspx?261852 (accessed 17 June 2013).

Gandhi, Jatin. 'Cloak and Stagger.' *Open*, 12 December 2009. Available at www.openthemagazine.com/article/nation/cloak-and-stagger (accessed 17 June 2013).

Hegde, Sanjay. 'Borking Gopal Subramanium.' *The Hindu*, 26 June 2014. Available at www.thehindu.com/opinion/op-ed/borking-gopal-subramanium/article6148766.ece (accessed 1 July 2014).

*Indian Express*. 'President Refers Judges Appointment Law to SC.' New Delhi, 18 July 1998. Available at www.indianexpress.com/res/web/pIe/ie/daily/19980728/20950754.html (accessed 13 May 2010).

Jaitley, Arun. 'Quit or Be Sacked.' *Outlook*, 17 February 2013. Available at www.outlookindia.com/article.aspx?283944 (accessed 10 February 2014).

Khare, Harish. 'Rule of Law versus Rule of Judges.' *The Hindu*, 26 October 2006. Available at www.thehindu.com/2006/10/26/stories/2006102603841000.htm (accessed 20 May 2010).

Kolappan, B. 'Survey Work Begins in Kaverirajapuram.' *The Hindu*, 8 January 2010. Available at www.hindu.com/2010/01/08/stories/2010010854680400.htm (accessed 17 June 2013).

Krishna Iyer, V. R. 'For a National Judicial Commission—I.' *The Hindu*, 30 October 2002. Available at www.hinduonnet.com/2002/10/30/stories/2002103000121000.htm (accessed 20 May 2010).

———. 'Issues Raised by L'affaire Dinakaran.' *The Hindu*, 17 September 2009. Available at www.thehindu.com/opinion/op-ed/issues-raised-by-laffaire-dinakaran/article21767.ece (accessed 17 June 2013).

Krishnaprasad. 'In Elevation to SC, Two HC Judges 'Supersede' Seniors.' *The Hindu*, 16 February 2017. Available at https://www.thehindu.com/news/national/karnataka/In-elevation-to-SC-two-HC-judges-%E2%80%98supersede%E2%80%99-seniors/article17314177.ece (accessed 25 July 2017).

Kumar, Hemant. 'Retirement or Re-employment of Judges?' *Lawyers' Update*, November 2012. Available at http://lawyersupdate.co.in/LU/8/1031.asp (accessed 24 May 2014).

Lakshmanan, A. R. 'Age of Retirement of High Court and Apex Court Judges.' *Lawyers' Update*, November 2010. Available at www.lawyersupdate.co.in/LU/1/226.asp (accessed 10 February 2014).

Lewis, Anthony. 'President Warns of Anarchy Peril.' *New York Times*, 25 September 1957. Available at http://www.nytimes.com/learning/general/onthisday/big/0925.html (accessed 14 September 2013).

Mahapatra, Dhananjay. 'CJI Initiates "Discreet" Probe Against Dinakaran.' *Times of India*, 3 October 2009. Available at http://articles.timesofindia.indiatimes.com/2009-10-03/india/28094901_1_justice-dinakaran-collegium-recommendation-supreme-court-collegium (accessed 17 June 2013).

———. 'CJI SH Kapadia Recommends Justice Swatanter Kumar as Green Tribunal Chief.' *Times of India*, 18 September 2012. Available at http://articles.timesofindia.indiatimes.com/2012-09-18/india/33925050_1_sc-judge-cji-kapadia-justice-kapadia (accessed 7 May 2013).

———. 'Collegium Meetings Follow No Principles of Law, Says SC Judge.' *Times of India*, 28 August 2017. Available at https://timesofindia.indiatimes.com/india/collegium-meetings-follow-no-principles-of-law-says-sc-judge/articleshow/60250720.cms (accessed 24 July 2018).

———. 'Collegium System for Judges' Appointment, Best Option: Chief Justice P Sathasivam.' *Times of India*, 25 April 2014. Available at http://timesofindia.indiatimes.com/india/Collegium-system-for-judges-appointment-best-option-Chief-Justice-P-Sathasivam/articleshow/34169844.cms (accessed 14 June 2014).

———. 'Dinakaran Out of SC List.' *Times of India*, 3 October 2009. Available at http://articles.timesofindia.indiatimes.com/2009-10-03/india/28094901_1_justice-dinakaran-collegium-recommendation-supreme-court-collegium (accessed 17 June 2013).

———. 'Finally Justice Dinakaran Resigns.' *Times of India*, 30 July 2011. Available at http://articles.timesofindia.indiatimes.com/2011-07-30/india/29832583_1_justice-dinakaran-sikkim-high-court-thiruvallur-collector (accessed 18 June 2013).

———. 'Increase Retirement Age of Supreme Court Judges to 68 Yrs: PIL.' *Times of India*, 6 October 2013. Available at http://articles.timesofindia.indiatimes.com/2013-10-06/india/42762666_1_hc-judges-60-to-62-years-retirement-age (accessed 11 February 2014).

———. 'Justice Chelameswar Lit the Fire and Burnt His Fingers.' *Times of India*, 23 June 2018. Available at https://timesofindia.indiatimes.com/india/justice-chelameswar-lit-the-fire-and-burnt-his-fingers/articleshow/64705278.cms (accessed 24 July 2018).

———. 'Supreme Court Judges to Disclose Assets.' *Times of India*, 27 August 2009. Available at http://articles.timesofindia.indiatimes.com/2009-08-27/india/28160981_1_full-court-meeting-assets-and-liabilities-judges (accessed 10 September 2013).

*Mint*. 'Govt "Silent" on Campaign Against SC in Judiciary: NCSC.' 24 September 2009. Available at www.livemint.com/Politics/T0mozhi9F7rZ1OfiuntpHL/Govt-silent-on-campaign-against-SC-in-judiciary-NCSC.html (accessed 17 June 2013).

Mitta, Manoj, 'M.N. Venakatachaliah Takes Important Step to Restore Judicial Credibility.' *India Today*, 15 October 1993. Available at https://www.indiatoday.in/magazine/nation/story/19931015-m-n-venkatachaliah-takes-important-step-to-restore-judicial-credibility-811668-1993-10-15 (accessed 25 July 2018).

Nair, Anita. 'Daughter a Liability for SC Woman Judge.' *One India*, 29 December 2010. Available at http://news.oneindia.in/2010/12/29/sc-judge-gyan-sudha-mishra-daughters-liability.html (accessed 10 September 2013).

Nariman, Fali. 'My Unsolicited Suggestion.' *Indian Express*, 7 September 2016. Available at https://indianexpress.com/article/opinion/columns/supreme-court-judges-appointment-transparency-collegium-working-system-3017291/ (accessed 23 July 2018).

———. 'Unfair, a Slur on Sikkim if Judge Unfit for Gujarat Is Sent There.' *Indian Express*, 9 February 2007. Available at www.indianexpress.com/news/unfair-a-slur-on-sikkim-if-judge-unfit-for-gujarat-is-sent-there-says-nariman/22856/0 (accessed 8 January 2013).

———. 'Weighed in the Balance.' *Hindustan Times*, 9 May 2013. Available at www.hindustantimes.com/comment/columns/weighed-in-the-balance/article1-1057629.aspx (accessed 14 June 2014).

Nayar, Kuldip. 'Consultation Is the Key.' *Indian Express*, 4 August 1998. Available at www.indianexpress.com/ie/daily/19980804/21650954.html (accessed 13 May 2010).

*Outlook*. 'Congress Withdraws Petition on CJI's Impeachment.' 8 May 2018. Available at https://www.outlookindia.com/website/story/five-judge-sc-bench-to-hear-cong-mps-plea-on-cjis-impeachment-today/311775 (accessed 25 July 2018).

Prakash, Satya. 'A Matter of Transparency.' *Hindustan Times*, 31 August 2013. Available at http://www.hindustantimes.com/delhi/a-matter-of-transparency/story-YHfexnKKNqah7YODZcFSmI.html (accessed 1 March 2017).

Press Association. 'Spain to Take Gibraltar Dispute to UN.' *The Guardian*, 11 August 2013. Available at www.theguardian.com/world/2013/aug/11/spain-gibraltar-dispute-uk-un (accessed 21 August 2013).

Press Trust of India. 'CJI Lodha Favours Collegium System.' *The Hindu*, New Delhi, 27 April 2014. Available at www.thehindu.com/news/national/cji-lodha-favours-collegium-system/article5953295.ece (accessed 12 May 2014).

———. 'Defiant Karnataka CJ Refuses to Go on Leave.' *Times of India*, 6 April 2010. Available at http://articles.timesofindia.indiatimes.com/2010-04-06/india/28135084_1_justice-dinakaran-chief-justice-abuse-of-judicial-office (accessed 18 June 2013).

Raha, Swagata. 'Multiplicity of Human Rights Institutions.' *Infochange India*, March 2013. Available at http://www.infochangeindia.org/agenda/access-to-justice/multiplicity-of-human-rights-institutions.html (accessed 24 February 2014).

Rajagopal, Krishnadas. 'Justice Chelameswar Opts Out of Collegium.' New Delhi, 22 September 2016. Available at http://www.thehindu.com/news/national/Justice-Chelameswar-opts-out-of-collegium/article14621813.ece (accessed 1 March 2017).

———. 'Now, SC Collegium to Make Judge's Appointments Transparent.' *The Hindu*, 6 October 2017. Available at https://www.thehindu.com/news/national/sc-collegium-to-make-its-recommendations-public/article19807802.ece (accessed 24 July 2018).

Ranjan, Sudhanshu. 'For Judges, Life Begins after Retirement.' *Navhind Times*, 25 October 2012. Available at www.navhindtimes.in/opinion/judges-life-begins-after-retirement (accessed 7 May 2013).

———. 'Judges Need Critical Juries.' *The Asian Age*, 14 May 2014. Available at http://www.asianage.com/columnists/judges-need-critical-juries-831 (accessed 13 June 2014).

Rautray, Samanwaya. 'SC Collegium Agrees to Reiterate Justice KM Joseph's Name for Elevation to Top Court.' *Economic Times*, 11 May 2018. Available at https://economictimes.indiatimes.com/news/politics-and-nation/sc-collegium-agrees-to-reiterate-justice-k-m-josephs-name/articleshow/64125077.cms (accessed 23 July 2018).

Sachar, Rajindar. 'A Half-Baked Measure: Judicial Appointments Bill Needs a Calm Discussion.' *India Resists*, 3 October 2013. Available at www.indiaresists.com/a-half-baked-measure-judicial-appointments-bill-needs-a-calm-discussion/ (accessed 14 May 2014).

Sachdev, Vakasha. 'SC Judges Appointed on Basis of "Impressions": Justice Chelameswar.' *The Quint*, 10 April 2018. Available at https://www.thequint.com/news/india/justice-chelameswar-supreme-court-appointments-impressions-reform (accessed 23 July 2018).

Sengupta, Arghya. 'An Unsolicited Response.' *Indian Express*, 12 September 2016. Available at https://indianexpress.com/article/opinion/columns/fali-s-nariman-article-my-unsolicited-suggestion-justice-chelameswar-lack-of-transparency-collegium-judge-appointments-3026362/ (accessed 23 July 2018).

———. 'Court Is Now a Plaything of Politicians for Political Gains.' *Hindustan Times*, 21 April 2018. Available at https://www.hindustantimes.com/opinion/court-is-now-a-plaything-of-politicians-for-electoral-gains/story-xP1vjHQ9GNFPsSrCPyRF9O.html (accessed 25 July 2018).

Shah, Ajit Prakash. 'Judicial Standards and Accountability Bill.' *The Hindu*, 29 March 2011. Available at www.thehindu.com/opinion/lead/article1582573.ece?homepage=true (accessed 13 December 2011).

Sharma, Nagendar. 'Collegium Is a Failure, Say Top Jurists.' *Hindustan Times*, New Delhi, 29 November 2009. Available at www.hindustantimes.com/Collegium-is-a-failure-say-top-jurists/H1-Article1-481205.aspx (accessed 13 May 2010).

———. 'Panel Finds 3 Top Judges Unfit for SC.' *Hindustan Times*, 17 March 2013. Available at www.hindustantimes.com/india-news/newdelhi/panel-finds-3-top-judges-unfit-for-sc/article1-1027632.aspx (accessed 14 June 2014).

Singh, Ajmer. 'MP HC Judge Says SC Judge Got Him Moved out of Delhi,' *The Indian Express*, 25 August 2012, available at www.indianexpress.com/news/mp-hc-judge-says-sc-judge-got-him-moved-out-of-delhi/992931 (accessed 8 January 2013).

———. 'Gopal Subramaniam's Credibility and Integrity Is Beyond Doubt: SC Judge.' *Economic Times*, 25 June 2014. Available at http://articles.economictimes.indiatimes.com/2014-06-25/news/50856109_1_cji-sc-judge-nira-radia (accessed 1 July 2014).

Singh, V. J. 'Confidential Letter Justice Cries for Justice Denied.' *Tehelka*, 2 April 2005. Available at http://archive.tehelka.com/story_main11.asp?filename=ts040205confidential.asp (accessed 8 January 2013).

Sinha, Bhadra. 'Revolt in SC Collegium: Senior Judge Boycotts Meet Over Lack of Transparency.' *Hindustan Times*, 3 September 2016. Available at https://www.hindustantimes.com/india-news/revolt-in-sc-collegium-senior-judge-boycotts-meet-over-lack-of-transparency/story-g9MofXzIxCuHeRv1Q72VHI.html (accessed 24 July 2018).

Sorabjee, S. 'Clear Collegium Mess to Maintain Public Image of the Judiciary.' *The New Indian Express*, 25 September 2016. Available at http:// www.newindianexpress.com/opinions/columns/soli-j-sorabjee/2016/ sep/25/Clear-collegium-mess-to-maintain-public-image-of-the-judiciary-1522741.html (accessed 24 July 2018).

———. 'It's Time Judges Stopped Appointing Themselves and Shed Nepotism.' *New Indian Express*, 26 May 2013. Available at http://newindianexpress.com/opinion/Its-time-judges-stopped-appointing-themselves-and-shed-nepotism/2013/05/26/article1605918.ece (accessed 18 January 2013).

———. 'Judicial Accountability.' *Indian Express*, 8 May 2005. Available at http://expressindia.indianexpress.com/news/columnists/print. php?content_id=69957 (accessed 25 September 2012).

Srinivas, A. 'Leave the Judges Alone.' *The Hindu*, 30 June 2014. Available at www.thehindubusinessline.com/opinion/leave-the-judges-alone/article6163706.ece (accessed 1 July 2014).

Srinivasaraju, Sugata, and Chandrani Banerjee. 'His Feudal Lordship.' *Outlook*, 5 October 2009. Available at www.outlookindia.com/article.aspx?262025 (accessed 17 June 2013).

Subramanian, T. S. 'Lawyers on the Warpath.' *Frontline* 21, no. 18 (August–September 2004). Available at www.frontline.in/static/html/fl2118/stories/20040910007813000.htm (accessed 14 May 2014).

Suresh, Appu Esthose, and Maneesh Chibber. 'Lost SC Berth for Opposing HC Judgeship for CJI Kabir's Sister: Guj CJ.' *Indian Express*, 24 July 2013. Available at http://archive.indianexpress.com/news/lost-sc-berth-for-opposing-hc-judgeship-for-cji-kabirs-sister-guj-cj/1140897/0 (accessed 14 June 2014).

Tare, Kiran. 'Matter of Honour.' *India Today*, 12 November 2011. Available at indiatoday.intoday.in/story/bombay-hc-nishita-mhatre-dileep-bhosale-transfer-of-judges/1/159602.html (accessed 8 January 2013).

Thiruvengadam, Arun K. 'The Crisis in Context.' *Frontline*, 16 February 2018. Available at https://www.frontline.in/cover-story/the-crisis-in-context/article10055190.ece?homepage=true (accessed 25 July 2018).

*The Hindu*. 'Dinakaran Sworn in as Chief Justice.' 9 August 2010. Available at www.thehindu.com/news/national/other-states/dinakaran-sworn-in-sikkim-chief-justice/article560720.ece (accessed 18 June 2013).

———. 'Do Not Elevate Dinakaran.' 28 November 2009. Available at www.thehindu.com/news/national/do-not-elevate-dinakaran/article56522.ece (accessed 17 June 2013).

*The Sentinel*. 'Junkyard for Judges.' Editorial, 3 December 2002. Available at http://www.mail-archive.com/assam@pikespeak.uccs.edu/msg02480.html (accessed 8 January 2013).

*Times of India*. '70 Cong. MPs Were in Favour of Motion.' 13 May 1993.

———. 'Chelameswar Laments Non-Elevations of Justice Joseph as SC Judge.' 22 June 2018. Available at https://timesofindia.indiatimes.com/india/chelameswar-laments-non-elevation-of-justice-joseph-as-sc-judge/articleshow/64701991.cms (accessed 25 July 2018).

———. 'CJI Hopes to "Sort Out" Issues Raised by SC Judge on Collegium's Functioning.' 3 September 2016. Available at https://timesofindia.indiatimes.com/india/CJI-hopes-to-sort-out-issues-raised-by-SC-judge-on-collegiums-functioning/articleshow/53995340.cms (accessed 24 July 2018).

———. 'Controversial Chief Justice Dinakaran Shifted to Sikkim High Court.' 30 July 2010. Available at http://articles.timesofindia.indiatimes.com/2010-07-30/india/28290732_1_sikkim-hc-karnataka-high-court-uttarakhand (accessed 18 June 2013).

———. 'Interview with Justice Ruma Pal, Former Judge, Supreme Court of India.' New Delhi, 26 September 2016. Available at http://timesofindia.indiatimes.com/india/Truth-and-openness-no-matter-how-uncomfortable-are-better-than-gossip/articleshow/54515814.cms?from=mdr (accessed 1 March 2017).

———. 'On a Suicidal Path.' 13 May 1993.

Tripathi, Ashish. 'Has Collegium System of Judges' Appointment Outlived Its Utility.' *Deccan Herald*, 20 April 2011. Available at http://www.deccanherald.com/content/155018/has-collegium-system-judges-appointment.html (accessed 1 March 2017).

UNI. 'SC: Collegium Recommends Transfer of Judges Involved in GPF Scam.' *Indlaw*, 22 December 2008. Available at www.indlaw.com/guest/DisplayNews.aspx?10A6D9D5-DEDA-4932-A5D6-8687E44E2AC1 (accessed 8 January 2013).

Venkatesan, J. '3 New High Courts for NE.' *The Hindu*, 26 January 2013. Available at www.thehindu.com/news/national/3-new-high-courts-for-ne/article4345372.ece (accessed 23 September 2013).

———. 'Bar Council Wants Judges Appointment Bill Withdrawn.' *The Hindu*, 17 October 2013. Available at www.thehindu.com/todays-paper/tp-national/tp-newdelhi/bar-council-wants-judges-appointment-bill-withdrawn/article5242203.ece (accessed 14 June 2013).

———. 'BK Roy Is Gauhati High Court Chief Justice.' *The Hindu*, 5 February 2005. Available at www.hindu.com/2005/02/05/stories/2005020505881100.htm (accessed 8 January 2013).

———. 'Collegium Defers Decision on Dinakaran.' *The Hindu*, 18 September 2009. Available at www.thehindu.com/news/national/collegium-defers-decision-on-justice-dinakaran/article22096.ece (accessed 17 June 2013).

———. 'Collegium System Not Working Properly: Jurists.' *The Hindu*, 13 December 2009. Available at www.thehindu.com/2009/12/13/stories/2009121360091000.htm (accessed 20 May 2010).

———. 'Dinakaran Will Continue in His Post, Says CJI.' *The Hindu*, 18 December 2009. Available at www.thehindu.com/news/dinakaran-will-continue-in-his-post-says-cji/article66979.ece (accessed 17 June 2013).

———. 'Dinakaran's Elevation Put On Hold.' *The Hindu*, 10 October 2009. Available at www.thehindu.com/news/national/dinakarans-elevation-put-on-hold/article32105.ece (accessed 17 June 2013).

———. 'Experts Call for Amendments to Prevent Judges Taking Up Jobs after Retirement.' *The Hindu*, 3 October 2012. Available at www.thehindu.com/news/national/experts-call-for-amendments-to-prevent-judges-taking-up-jobs-after-retirement/article3958819.ece (accessed 10 February 2014).

———. 'Justice Dinakaran Asked to Go on Leave.' *The Hindu*, 3 April 2010. Available at www.hindu.com/2010/04/03/stories/2010040363460100.htm (accessed 18 June 2013).

———. 'Law Ministry Turns Down Gopal Subramanium's Elevation as SC Judge.' *The Hindu*, 19 June 2014. Available at www.thehindu.com/news/national/law-ministry-turns-down-gopal-subramaniums-elevation-as-sc-judge/article6127460.ece (accessed 1 July 2014).

———. 'Plea Not to Elevate Justice Dinakaran.' *The Hindu*, New Delhi, 3 December 2009. Available at http://www.thehindu.com/news/national/plea-not-to-elevate-justice-dinakaran/article59077.ece (accessed 11 September 2013).

———. 'Supreme Court Collegium Sticks to Shifting Justice Dinakaran to Sikkim.' *The Hindu*, 30 April 2010. Available at www.thehindu.com/news/national/supreme-court-collegium-sticks-to-shifting-justice-dinakaran-to-sikkim/article418119.ece (accessed 18 June 2013).

———. 'Supreme Court to Get Five New Judges.' *The Hindu*, 27 August 2009. Available at www.thehindu.com/news/supreme-court-to-get-five-new-judges/article10301.ece (accessed 17 June 2013).

———. 'Withdraw Judicial Appointments Commission Bill.' *The Hindu*, 16 October 2013. Available at www.thehindu.com/news/national/withdraw-judicialappointmentscommissionbill/article5237968.ece (accessed 14 May 2014).

Venkatesan, V. 'Controversial Choice.' *Frontline* 26, no. 22 (October–November 2009). Available at www.frontline.in/static/html/fl2622/stories/20091106262212200.htm (accessed 17 June 2013).

———. 'Judging the Judges.' *Frontline* 14, no. 20 (October 1997). Available at www.frontlineonnet.com/fl1420/14200180.htm (accessed 19 December 2012).

———. 'Question of Propriety.' *Frontline* 27, no. 9 (April–May 2010). Available at www.frontline.in/static/html/fl2709/stories/20100507270903300.htm (accessed 18 June 2013).

———. 'Honesty Matters: Interview with Justice J. S. Verma, Former Chief Justice of India.' *Frontline*, 10 October 2008. Available at https://www.frontline.in/static/html/fl2520/stories/20081010252003500.htm (accessed 24 July 2018).

Verma, J. S., Justice. 'Judicial Accountability Includes All.' *Deccan Herald*. Available at http://www.deccanherald.com/content/22337/judicial-accountability-includes-all.html (accessed 25 September 2012).

## News Services

ABP News. 'Judge's Press Conference.' 12 January 2018. Available at https://www.youtube.com/watch?v=BcZAsRxPnJA (accessed 23 July 2018).

Bagriya, Ashok. 'Justice Sen Defends Himself in Parliament.' *IBN Live*, 17 August 2011. Available at http://ibnlive.in.com/news/justice-sen-defends-himself-in-parliament/176427-37.html (accessed 4 June 2014).

*Bar & Bench*. 'Explanatory Note on the Motion for Impeachment of Mr. Justice Dipak Misra, Chief Justice of India.' Available at https://barandbench.com/read-impeachmentmotion-chief-justice-india-dipak-misra/ (accessed 25 July 2018).

———. 'Full Transcript of Justice Jasti Chelameswar's Interview.' 8 April 2018. Available at https://barandbench.com/devils-advocate-v-judge-fulltranscript-karan-thapar-interview-justice-jasti-chelameswar/ (accessed 23 July 2018).

## Internet or Electronic Documents

Aney, Madhav, Shubhankar Dam and Giovanni Ko. 'Jobs for Justice(s): Corruption in the Supreme Court of India.' *Research Collection School of Economics*, 2017. Available at https://ink.library.smu.edu.sg/cgi/viewcontent. cgi?article=2927&context=soe_research (accessed 23 July 2018).

Ansari, Hamid. 'Inauguration Speech' (Seminar on 'Evaluating Committees and Committee System: Changing Contours of Governance and Policy,' New Delhi), 18 November 2009. Available at http://pib.nic.in/newsite/erelease.aspx?relid=54190 (accessed 13 April 2014).

Campaign for Judicial Accountability and Judicial Reforms. 'Judge Watch.' Available at www.judicialreforms.org/what-we-do/judge-watch.html (accessed 14 June 2014).

———. 'Judge Watch: Justice Dinakaran.' Available at www.judicialreforms.org/judge-watch/609-justice-dinakaran.html (accessed 17 June 2013).

'Chief Justice of India's Statement to the Bar of the Supreme Court.' 20 July 1990. Available at www.indiancorruptjudges.com/Plot4Plot/008_00.htm#sawant (accessed 19 December 2012).

Dallison, Charles. *The Royalists Defence* (1648). Available at http://gateway.proquest.com/openurl?ctx_ver=Z39.88-2003&res_id=xri:eebo&rft_id=xri:eebo:image:54815:2 (accessed 14 July 2012).

Henderson, Keith. E. 'Asset and Income Disclosure for Judges: A Summary Overview and Checklist.' Available at http://siteresources.worldbank.org/INTLAWJUSTINST/Resources/IncomeAssetDisclosure.pdf (accessed 31 July 2012).

'India—Life Expectancy at Birth.' Available at http://countryeconomy.com/demography/life-expectancy/india (accessed 12 February 2014).

International Bar Association. 'Beyond Polokwane: Safeguarding South Africa's Judicial Independence,' July 2008. Available at www.ibanet.org/Document/Default.aspx?DocumentUid=4c7e8c0f-652d-44bd-a459-d9ac85d6872e (accessed 10 September 2013).

Joshi, G. P. 'National Human Rights Commission—Need for Review' (Commonwealth Human Rights Initiative). Available at www.humanrightsinitiative.org/programs/aj/police/papers/gpj/national_human_rights_commission.pdf (accessed 24 February 2014).

Jowell, Jeffrey, et al. *Judicial Appointments: Balancing Independence, Accountability and Legitimacy* (Judicial Appointments Commission 2010). Available at http://jac.judiciary.gov.uk/static/documents/JA_web.pdf (accessed 10 September 2013).

Leggatt, Andrew. 'Tribunals for Users: One System, One Service.' March 2011. Available at http://webarchive.nationalarchives.gov.uk/+/http://www.tribunals-review.org.uk/leggatthtm/leg-00.htm (accessed 14 February 2014).

Pal, Ruma, Justice. '5th V.M. Tarkunde Memorial Lecture: An Independent Judiciary' (New Delhi), 2011. Available at https://docslide.us/documents/5th-vm-tarkunde-memorial-lecture-2011.html (accessed 24 July 2018).

Palshikar, V. G. 'Transfer of Judges' (All India Seminar on Judicial Reforms, New Delhi), 5 December 1998.

Pre-Legislative Briefing Service. 'The Judicial Standards and Accountability Bill, 2010: A Briefing Document.' Available at www.vidhilegalpolicy.in/pdf/PLBS_Briefing_Document_JSA_Bill.pdf (accessed 13 April 2014).

Ramachandran, Raju. 'Judicial Supremacy and the Collegium.' Seminar No. 642 (2013). Available at http://india-seminar.com/2013/642/642_raju_ramachandran.htm (accessed 15 June 2014).

Shakespeare, William. *Hamlet*. Available at http://shakespeare.mit.edu/hamlet/full. html (accessed 21 August 2013).

Shylendra Kumar, D. V., Justice. 'Extraordinary Situations Call for Extraordinary Measures,' 17 December 2009. Available at http://sites.google.com/site/justdvskumar/extraordinary-measures (accessed 18 June 2013).

Subramanium, Gopal. 'Letter to the Chief Justice of India,' 25 June 2014. Available at http://www.scribd.com/doc/231242651/Gopal-Subramanium-letter-to-CJI (accessed 1 July 2014).

United Nations Office on Drugs and Crime. 'Commentary on the Bangalore Principles of Judicial Conduct,' September 2007. Available at www.unodc.org/documents/corruption/publications_unodc_commentary-e.pdf (accessed 21 August 2013).

Website of the High Court of Manipur. Available at http://hcmimphal.nic.in/ (accessed 14 May 2014).

Website of the High Court of Meghalaya. Available at http://meghalayahighcourt.nic.in/Home.html (accessed 14 May 2014).

Website of the High Court of Tripura. Available at http://thc.nic.in/ (accessed 14 May 2014).

Website of the Supreme Court of India. Available at https://www.sci.gov.in/ (accessed 25 July 2018).

Website of the UK Judiciary. 'Other Forms of Accountability.' Available at www.judiciary.gov.uk/about-the-judiciary/the-judiciary-in-detail/jud-acc-ind/other-forms-of-accountability (accessed 12 December 2011).

# INDEX